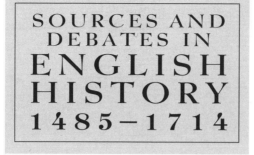

SOURCES AND
DEBATES IN
ENGLISH
HISTORY
1485–1714

To
Jenny Renn
Katie
Jeffrey
with love

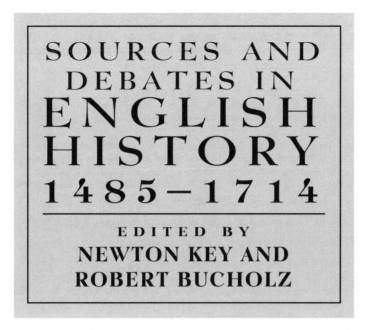

SOURCES AND DEBATES IN ENGLISH HISTORY 1485–1714

EDITED BY

NEWTON KEY AND ROBERT BUCHOLZ

Editorial matter and organization © 2004 by Newton Key and Robert Bucholz

350 Main Street, Malden, MA 02148–5020, USA
108 Cowley Road, Oxford OX4 1JF, UK
550 Swanston Street, Carlton, Victoria 3053, Australia

First published 2004 by Blackwell Publishing Ltd

Library of Congress Cataloging-in-Publication Data

Key, Newton.
Sources and debates in English history, 1485–1714 / Newton Key and Robert Bucholz.
p. cm.
Includes bibliographical references (p.) and index.
ISBN 0-631-21390-2 (alk. paper) – ISBN 0-631-21391-0 (pbk.: alk. paper)
1. Great Britain – History – Tudors, 1485–1603 – Sources. 2. Great Britain – History – Stuarts,
1603–1714 – Sources. 3. Great Britain – History – Tudors, 1485–1603.
4. Great Britain – History – Stuarts, 1603–1714. I. Bucholz, R. O., 1958– II. Title.

DA310.K49 2004
942.05–dc22   2003017984

A catalogue record for this title is available from the British Library.

Set in 10/12.5pt Sabon
by Kolam Information Services Pvt. Ltd, Pondicherry, India
Printed and bound in the United Kingdom
by TJ International Ltd, Padstow, Cornwall

Picture research: Jane Taylor

For further information on
Blackwell Publishing, visit our website:
http://www.blackwellpublishing.com

Contents

Plates

Preface and Acknowledgments

On the improvisation-based show "Whose Line Is It Anyway?" one game has participants act a scene speaking only in questions. Writing this sourcebook has felt a bit like participating in that game, as the authors have sought to provide context for the documents and questions for debate and further research in the "Discussion" sections of each chapter, without predetermining how you, the reader, interpret the words and actions of the sixteenth- and seventeenth-century people. Indeed, we have selected those documents best open to multiple interpretations, because we consider thinking and arguing about the past to be the center of doing history.

We have developed this sourcebook to accompany our *Early Modern England, 1485–1714: A Narrative History* (Oxford, 2004). Thus, chapter 1 of *Sources and Debates* can be read in conjunction with the introduction of *Early Modern England*, and so on, as in the following table:

Sources and Debates	*Early Modern England: A Narrative History*
Chapter 1	Introduction
Chapter 2	Chapter 1
Chapter 3	Chapters 2–3
Chapter 4	Chapters 4–5
Chapter 5	Chapter 6
Chapter 6	Chapter 7
Chapter 7	Chapter 8
Chapter 8	Chapter 9
Chapter 9	Chapter 10 and Conclusion

We refer to appropriate chapters of that narrative when we think additional detail might help you understand the context of a particular set of documents. As one argument of the textbook is that one can best understand the motivations and actions of the early Tudors if one examines the preceding period, we have here included a few documents from pre-1485, and added some explanation. If you wish to avoid the thickets of civil war and genealogical confusion, 1453–85, you might skip the "Tackling Noble Disorder" section of chapter 2. But we think that very confusion weighed heavily on the Tudor ruling elite, so we include the section (and documents 2.1–2.2).

For the sources in each chapter, you, the history student and reader, must use your own knowledge, consideration of author, audience, format, purpose (the basic tools of historical source criticism), and, above all, comparison with other sources and documents to tease out meaning, to decide which (or whose) reality you are reading, and to construct a more complete sense of what the past was really like. One way to maximize your use of this collection is to combine the questions and brief sources in the "Discussion" with the longer sources or "Documents" and some of the historians' views in the "Historiography." We have tried to point the reader to journal articles, chapters in collections, and shorter works where possible so that the student of early modern England might more easily read two or more historians on a certain subject to be able to compare and contrast their views and, perhaps, use some of the sources provided below to help the student develop her or his own point of view on the question at hand. General questions at the outset of each chapter provide a context unifying each set of documents. If you are reading this collection for a college course, we encourage you to use some of the questions as a springboard for debate (where each side can marshal proofs from the documents within the chapter to make a reasonable case for their point of view) and brief essays. Finally, we trust that encountering the "voices" of early modern English women and men (and some Irish, Scots, and Welsh voices too) will enliven and enrich your understanding of this crucial past.

We have made every effort to make this sourcebook reflect both the many types of sources and viewpoints from the period as well as the types of approaches used by different historians. But history, including sourcebooks, is a matter of selection and argument, and we encourage the students of early modern England to follow up the sources that interest them to see if parts of documents *not* selected affect their understanding of the documents, issues, and period. If you *are* familiar with early modern England, or some part of its history, we believe you will discover that we have selected both "standard" sources, which have intrigued (or baffled) generations of students of the period, and sources that have never or not recently been published. Even for standard sources, however, we have gone back to the source, or the fullest copy of the source available, and, in many cases, included lines of speeches, letters, etc., that we feel best capture the issues and the period.

Spelling and punctuation have been modernized and Americanized in most selections (except poems and published titles). Thus, "majestie" becomes "majesty," and "Honoure" becomes "honor." The exceptions are words like "durst," "appeareth," etc., where the meaning is quite clear (obscure meanings are explained in brackets). The rationale for this decision is easy enough in manuscripts, where, for example, "y" was used as a shorthand for "th," and, thus, writers meant "the" when they wrote "y^e." But in print too, we decided it more useful for someone approaching the history of this age for the first time to spare them the delights of Martin Marprelate's original orthography (1588; see chapter 4): "Nowe may it please your grace with yᵉ rest of your worships / to procure that the puritans may one day have a free disputatiõ with you about yᵉ cõtraversies of the Church /" in favor of "Now may it please your grace, with the rest of your worships, to procure that the Puritans may one day have a free disputation with you about the controversies of the Church." Where possible we have compared the original or the original printed source with a later edition (which, for modern professional editions, is often to be preferred) and cited both because modern editions are more accessible to the reader. (Place of publication is London, unless noted.)

We wish to thank our many students over the years, especially Kristan Crawford, Alex Dove, and the assistance of Andreas Dür, Jill Lauerman, and Jennifer Lancaster. We would especially like to thank the following historians for terms, dating, sources, and interpretations: Nicholas Canny, Dagni Bredesen, Gary de Krey, Bill Gibson, Michael Graham, Martin Ingram, Erin R. Kidwell, Michael Landon, Christina Lindeman, Linda Levy Peck, Stephen Roberts, N. A. M. Rodger, Claire Schen, Anita Shelton, Angus Stroud, Susan Wabuda, Joe Ward, Bailey Young, and Mike Young. Moreover, Mike Young and Jim Sack read a draft of the manuscript, and we are indebted to their perceptive comments. This book could not have been completed without the help of the librarians at Booth Library at Eastern Illinois, the Cudahy Library of Loyola University, the University of Illinois Library and Rare Book Room, and the Newberry Library, Chicago, for whose assistance we are quite grateful.

The author and publishers gratefully acknowledge the following for permission to reproduce copyright material: Cambridge University Press for T. Smith, *De Republica Anglorum*, ed. M. Dewar (1982), 64–7, 70–2, 74, 76–7; and F. Bacon, *The History of the Reign of King Henry VII and Selected Works*, ed. B. Vickers (1998), 202–4; Oxford University Press for M. Ingram, "Ridings, Rough Music and the 'Reform of Popular Culture' in Early Modern England," *P & P* 105 (1984): 105; Royal Historical Society for T. Starkey, *A Dialogue between Pole and Lupset*, ed. T. F. Mayer (Camden Society, 4th ser., 37, 1989), 52–4; and *The Anglica Historia of Polydore Vergil, A.D. 1485–1537*, ed. Denys Hay (Camden Society, 74, 1950), 4, 5, 143, 145, 147; Yale University Press for T. More, *Utopia*, ed. E. Surtz (1964), 24–8. They gratefully acknowledge the following for assistance with permissions: Helm Information Ltd., Pearson Education Limited, Penguin Books, University of Chicago Press.

The publishers apologize for any errors or omissions in the above list and would be grateful to be notified of any corrections that should be incorporated in the next edition or reprint of this book.

Abbreviations

£, s., d.	One pound (£) = 20 shillings (s.) = 240 pence (d.)
BL	British Library
Bart.	Baronet
Bucholz and Key	Robert Bucholz and Newton Key, *Early Modern England, 1485–1714: A Narrative History* (Oxford, 2004)
CJ	*Journals of the House of Commons*
CSP(D)	*Calendar of State Papers (Domestic)*
EcHR	*Economic History Review*
EHR	*English Historical Review*
Esq.	Esquire
HJ	*Historical Journal*
HMC	Historical Manuscripts Commission
HR	*Historical Research*
HT	*History Today*
JBS	*Journal of British Studies*
JEcclH	*Journal of Ecclesiastical History*
JMH	*Journal of Modern History*
JP	Justice of the Peace
Kt.	Knight
LJ	*Journals of the House of Lords*
MP	Member of Parliament
PH	*Parliamentary History*
P & P	*Past and Present*

PRO	Public Record Office, Kew
RO	Record Office
SPD	State Papers, Domestic
SR	*Statutes of the Realm*, 11 vols. (1810–28)
TRHS	*Transactions of the Royal Historical Society*

CHAPTER ONE

Order and Disorder in Tudor England

Great Chain of Being

Family, Household, Village, Town, Metropolis

State and Society

DISCUSSION

What were English society and economy like ca. 1500? How were families, villages, towns, the London metropolis, and the State ordered and how did they function? The first few documents reproduced in this chapter portray contemporary social ideals – of order, hierarchy, stability, the Great Chain of Being – while the later entries portray a messier world of disorder, tension, and change. But even portraits of Tudor disorder are sometimes idealized views, drawn by contemporaries to show how the ideal is unattainable for sinful man in an inherently corrupt world. As you read the documents in this chapter, you might ask:

- Which images or models of society used by sixteenth-century contemporaries are most effective (convincing) and which least?
- How did the authors of these early modern sources think about continuity or stasis, and how did they think about change?

Great Chain of Being

Early modern people embraced a socially conservative doctrine that every individual should know and keep his or her place in the divinely ordained social hierarchy. The Protestant reformer and first translator of the Scriptures into English, William Tyndale (ca. 1494?–1536), expressed the view succinctly in *The Parable of the Wicked Mammon* (1528):

Let every man therefore wait on the office wherein Christ hath put him, and therein serve his brethren. If he be of low degree, let him patiently therein abide, till God promote him, and exalt him higher. Let kings and head officers seek Christ in their offices, and minister peace and quietness unto the brethren, punish sin, and that with mercy, even with the same sorrow and grief of mind as they would cut off a finger or joint, a leg, or arm of their own body, if there were such disease in them, that either they must be cut off, or else all the body must perish.[1]

This ideal divided the English people by rank, age, and gender (see Bucholz and Key, introduction). It could be expressed metaphorically, as the Great Chain of Being (see the visual representation in plate 1), or as a Body Politic (see the verbal representation from 1536 in document 1.2), but perhaps the most famous description of Tudor social structure is found in *De Republica Anglorum* (1565, pub. 1583, document 1.1), by Sir Thomas Smith (1513–77), the first regius professor of civil law at Cambridge. Note how Smith defines the different levels of society. Are his definitions and distinctions precise? Do they help to distinguish among, say, knights, esquires, and gentlemen? Are his distinctions closer to caste divisions (based on birth) or class divisions (based on income)? Why might an agricultural laborer or cottager subscribe to such a hierarchical view?

Sumptuary laws attempted to prevent people from one social rank wearing "sumptuous" or extravagant clothing reserved for a higher social rank. Several English examples of such laws from the fourteenth and fifteenth centuries reveal both the ideal of the Great Chain of Being and fears that this ideal was being honored only in the breach. Such laws attempted to regulate dress quite rigidly and, although they might be used to encourage English manufacture, they mainly sought to preserve an ordered society of ranks. Can the 1510 Act Against Wearing Costly Apparel (document 1.3) be used to construct a status hierarchy in Tudor England? Is this an economic hierarchy? What might be the difficulties in enforcing such legislation? Further Acts – 6 Hen. VIII, c. 1; 7 Hen. VIII, c. 6; 24 Hen. VIII, c. 13; 1–2 Philip and Mary, c. 2 – followed. What does their proliferation suggest about their efficacy?

Family, Household, Village, Town, Metropolis

The family was both a unit of and a metaphor for an ordered society. Individual members had to accept their allotted roles and work together harmoniously. In 1465, John Paston (1421–66) wrote from London to his wife, Margaret (d. 1484), living on their estate in Norfolk, and two men in her service, John Daubeney and Richard Calle, to give them, among other advice, some general guidance on running the "household":

---

[1]   Tyndale, *The Parable of the Wicked Mammon taken out of the XVI Ca. of Luke* (1548 ed.), f. 37, sig. Eii; compared with M. D. Palmer, *Henry VIII*, 2nd ed. (1983), 111.

Plate 1 *"The Great Chain of Being."* (*Source*: Diego Valadés, *Rhetorica Christiana*, 1579, © British Library)

Note the hierarchical levels of nature and society reaching to God at the top, while fallen angels plummet toward Hell on the right. What morals might one draw from this image? How might this image or model have difficulty incorporating all social hierarchies within it? What other images or models, possibly drawn from nature, might also represent such a chain of being?

Also remember you in any household, fellowship, or company that will be of good rule, purveyance [provision] must be had that every person of it be helping and furthering after his discretion and power, and he that will not do so, without he be kept of alms, should be put out of the household or fellowship.[2]

Personal correspondence sometimes hides as much as it reveals by taking day-to-day life for granted and leaving it unexplained (or even unmentioned). What, exactly, is a household? How does it relate to the family? In chapter 2, we will see the Pastons defending their lands and household by legal means in London and force of arms in Norfolk. John wrote again later that year to Margaret, Daubeney, and Calle the following advice:

As for your son . . . , I let you weet [understand] I would know him or he know mine intent, and how well he hath occupied his time now he hath had leisure. Every poor man that hath brought up his children to the age of twelve year waiteth then to be helped and profited by his children; and every gentleman that hath discretion waiteth that his kin and servants that liveth by him and at his cost should help him forthward [henceforward].[3]

What ideals of the family and of social structure are revealed in this statement? What anxieties?

Contemporaries might marvel at London (see document 1.8, discussed below), but most wealth came from the ground. As the Elizabethan writer William Harrison (1534–93) wrote in 1577,

The soil of Britain . . . is more inclined to feeding and grazing than profitable for tillage and bearing of corn [grain, e.g. wheat, barley, oats], by reason whereof the country is wonderfully replenished with neat [oxen] and all kind of cattle; and such store is there also of the same in every place that the fourth part of the land is scarcely manured for the provision and maintenance of grain.[4]

The proportion between grain and cattle (often sheep) production worried Tudor writers as well as farmers throughout the century. The State lived off of taxes, and taxes were overwhelmingly based on agricultural rent and produce which, in turn, depended on how the land was tilled. Because crop yields were so minimal, perhaps averaging a harvest yield of four to one of seed, until about 1600, perhaps ten-to-one by 1720, agricultural production depended in large part on the numbers of farmers and agricultural laborers actually out in the fields. Note the Act Against Pulling Down of Towns (1489, document 1.4). According to the preamble, why does the State fear depopulation? Are there other possible reasons for the State fearing depopulation which are not mentioned? Why might a

---

[2] January 15, 1465; N. Davis, ed., *Paston Letters and Papers of the Fifteenth Century* (Oxford, 1971), 1: 127–8.
[3] June 27, 1465; Davis, *Paston Letters and Papers*, 1: 132.
[4] Harrison, *Elizabethan England*, ed. F. Furnivall (1877), 130–1; compared with *A Description of Elizabethan England* (New York, 1910), 307, from *A Description of England*, in R. Holinshed, *Chronicles* (1577).

landlord want to destroy a town? *Cui bono* (who benefits)? (You might want to consider this question after reflecting on documents 1.5 and 1.6, discussed below.)

Laws also proliferated in response to felonies such as assault and theft. Humanists, in particular, found the laws of England harshly disproportionate to crimes. Thomas More's (1478–1535) analysis of why people stole, the danger of "men-eating sheep," and the irrational punishments for theft is justly famous. Document 1.5 is from his *Utopia* (a word he coined, meaning "no place"), which was published in Latin in 1516, and translated into English (many times) and other languages soon thereafter. *Utopia* describes an imaginary, perfect state exactly opposite the globe (itself a concept only recently given weight by the voyages of Columbus and others, of course) from the flawed kingdom of England. According to the discussion, what major problems does Tudor England face? How does the narrator – at this point supposedly the fictional world-traveler, Raphael – propose to solve them? Would his solution work?

While early modern England was overwhelmingly agrarian, towns played a role disproportionate to their puny size. As you read the Complaint of the Norwich Shoemakers (1490, document 1.6), ask whether there is more order (or disorder) in towns or in the countryside? (Norwich was the second-largest city in England at the time; you might compare Norwich's problems with the situation in London, by examining document 1.8.) How does the Great Chain of Being help to explain the views expressed in the Complaint?

State and Society

Sixteenth-century authors disagreed as to why England was so disordered and what were the remedies. But all began with a fairly organic model of how society functioned. Richard Morison (d. 1556) was a Humanist (he may have introduced the work of Niccolò Machiavelli [1469–1527] to England), who had lived in the household of Reginald Pole (1500–58) at Padua, but returned to England to write for Thomas Cromwell (ca. 1485–1540). Morison's *A Remedy for Sedition* (1536, document 1.2) was published in the wake of the Pilgrimage of Grace of that year (see chapter 3). What metaphors (imagery) does Morison use to explain English society? Which are most effective? Which least? How does his view match up with Sir Thomas Smith's (document 1.1)? In *Dialogue between Pole and Lupset* (ca. 1529–32, document 1.7), Thomas Starkey (ca. 1500–38) blames England's ills on a different social group from documents 1.2 or even 1.5 (although both Morison and Starkey were influenced by Humanism and wrote in support of Cromwell). Compare and contrast these sources by asking what are their respective views on the ideal society. How might the Great Chain of Being be used to press for social change as well as the status quo?

Descriptions made by foreigners provide quite different problems and possibilities. Take document 1.8, the report on England from a noble of Venice (ca. 1500). Historians particularly value commentary by foreigners. Why? On what subjects might this report be most valuable? On what subjects might it be weakest or most unreliable? How are English family relations most different from those on the continent according to the Venetian? Is there an English national identity ca. 1500? Of what might it consist? Finally, note that we have presented these documents in this chapter by theme (roughly from the ideal to the actual). How might your vision of early Tudor society differ if you read them in chronological order (1.4, 1.6, 1.8, 1.3, 1.5, 1.7, 1.2, 1.1)?

HISTORIOGRAPHY

The hierarchical ideal of Tudor social order was refined in a time of crisis or perceived crisis. Historical debate on whether there was a crisis (relative or absolute) during the reigns of Edward VI and Mary has become known as the Mid-Tudor Crisis debate. The debate is summarized in D. M. Loades, *The Mid-Tudor Crisis, 1545–1565* (1992). But see also J. Loach and R. Tittler, eds., *The Mid-Tudor Polity, c.1540–1560* (1980).

Order was threatened by mobility – social as well as geographical. For the former, see L. Stone, "Social Mobility in England, 1500–1700," *P & P* 33 (1966); for the latter, see P. Clark and D. Souden, eds., *Migration and Society in Early Modern England* (1987). On the elite, in particular, a "storm" developed over whether the gentry were rising or falling, or whether they could be meaningfully distinguished at all. The debate began with a series of articles in *EcHR* by R. H. Tawney (1941), Stone (1948), and H. Trevor-Roper (1950–1, and Supplement, 1953), and is summarized and commented on in J. H. Hexter, "The Storm Over the Gentry," in his *Reappraisals in History*, 2nd ed. (1961, 1979), as well as Hexter's review of Stone's *The Crisis of the Aristocracy* (1965) in *JBS* 8 (1968). Stone himself summarized and extracted from the debate in *Social Change and Revolution in England, 1540–1640* (1965); though see now relevant chapters from F. Heal and C. Holmes, *The Gentry in England and Wales, 1500–1700* (Stanford, 1994); and S. Hindle, *The State and Social Change in Early Modern England, 1550–1640* (Basingstoke, 2000). For contemporary social structure terms, see K. Wrightson, "Estates, Degrees, and Sorts: Changing Perceptions of Society in Tudor and Stuart England," in *Language, History and Class*, ed. P. J. Corfield (Oxford, 1991); and chapter 5, below.

To compare with the Venetian's view of London, one might examine the eyewitness accounts in L. Manley, *London in the Age of Shakespeare: An Anthology* (1986) and the articles in A. L. Beier and R. Finlay, eds., *London 1500–1700: The Making of the Metropolis* (1986). While Smith's *De Republica Anglorum* has long been used as a factual, if ideal, portrait of English social hierarchy, A. McLaren, "Reading Sir Thomas Smith's *De Republica Anglorum* as Protestant Apologetic," *HJ* 42 (1999), questions that view. Other contemporary views are discussed in N. Wood, *Foundations of Political Economy: Some Early Tudor Views on State and Society* (Berkeley, 1994).

DOCUMENTS

1.1 Sir Thomas Smith, De Republica Anglorum (written 1565, pub. 1583)[5]

Chapter 16. The Divisions of the Parts and Persons of the Common Wealth.
We in England divide our men commonly into four sorts, gentlemen, citizens or burgesses, yeomen artificers, and laborers. Of gentlemen the first and chief are the king, the prince, dukes, marquises, earls, viscounts, and barons, and this is called ... the nobility, and all these are called lords and noblemen: next to these be knights, esquires, and simple gentlemen.

Chapter 17. Of the First Part of Gentlemen of England Called Nobilitas Major.
Dukes, marquises, earls, viscounts, and barons, either be created of the prince or come to that honor by being the eldest sons, or highest in succession to their parents. For the eldest of duke's sons during his father's life is called an earl ..., [etc.]

Chapter 18. Of the Second Sort of Gentlemen Which May Be Called Nobilitas Minor, and First of Knights.
No man is a knight by succession.... Knights therefore be not born but made.... Knights in England most commonly [are made] according to the yearly revenue of their lands being able to maintain that estate ... [but] not all [are] made knights in England that may spend a knight's lands but they only whom the prince will honor....

Chapter 19. Of Esquires.
Escuier or esquire ... be all those which bear arms (as we call them) ... which to bear is a testimony of the nobility or race from which they do come. These be taken for no distinct order of the commonwealth, but do go with the residue of the gentlemen....

Chapter 20. Of Gentlemen.
Gentlemen be those whom their blood and race doth make noble and known ..., for that their ancestor hath been notable in riches or for his virtues, or (in fewer

---

[5] Smith, *De Republica Anglorum*, ed. M. Dewar (1982), 64–7, 70–2, 74, 76–7; compared with B. Coward, *Social Change and Continuity: England, 1550–1750*, rev. ed. (1997), 104–5.

words) old riches or prowess remaining in one stock. Which if the successors do keep and follow, they be *vere nobiles....* If they do not, the fame and riches of their ancestors serve to cover them so long as it can, as a thing once gilted though it be copper within, till the gilt be worn away.... As other commonwealths were fain to do, so must all princes necessarily follow, where virtue is to honor it.... The prince and commonwealth have the same power that their predecessors had, and as the husbandman hath to plant a new tree when the old faileth, to honor virtue where he doth find it, to make gentlemen, esquires, knights, barons, earls, marquises, and dukes, where he seeth virtue able to bear that honor or merits, to deserve it, and so it hath always been used among us. But ordinarily the king doth only make knights and create the barons and higher degrees: for as for gentlemen, they be made good cheap in England. For whosoever studieth the laws of the realm, who studieth in the universities, who professeth liberal sciences, and to be short who can live idly and without manual labor, and will bear the port, charge, and countenance of a gentleman, he shall be called master, for that is the title which men give to esquires and other gentlemen, and shall be taken for a gentleman.... (And if need be) a king [officer] of Heralds shall also give him for money, arms newly made and invented, which the title shall bear that the said Herald hath perused and seen old registers where his ancestors in times past had born the same.... These men be called sometime in scorn gentlemen of the first head.

Chapter 21.   Whether the Manner of England in Making Gentlemen So Easily Is to Be Allowed.

A man may make all doubt and question whether this manner of making gentlemen is to be allowed or no, and for my part I am of that opinion that it is not amiss. For first the prince loseth nothing by it, as he should do if it were as in France: for the yeomen or husbandman is no more subject to *taile* or tax in England than the gentleman: no, in every payment to the king the gentleman is more charged, which he beareth the gladlier and dareth not gainesay for to save and keep his honor and reputation....

Chapter 22.   Of Citizens and Burgesses.

Next to a gentleman, be appointed citizens and burgesses, such as not only be free and received as officers within the cities, but also be of some substance to bear the charges.... Generally in the shire they be of no account, save only in ... Parliament....

Chapter 23.   Of Yeomen.

Those whom we call yeomen next unto the nobility, the knights, and squires, have the greatest charges and doings in the commonwealth.... I call him a yeoman whom our laws call *Legalem hominem* ..., which is a freeman born English, who may spend of his own free land in yearly revenue to the sum of 40s. sterling [£2] by the year.... This sort of people confess themselves to be no gentleman, but give honor to all which be or take upon them to be gentlemen, and yet they have a certain preeminence and more estimation than laborers and artificers, and commonly live wealthily, keep good houses, do their business, and travail [work] to get riches: they be (for the most part) farmers to gentlemen, and with grazing, frequenting of markets, and keeping servants, not idle servants as the gentlemen doth, but such as get their own living and part of their masters: by these means do come to such wealth, that they are able and daily do buy the lands of unthrifty gentlemen, and after setting their sons to the schools, to the universities, to the law of the realm, or otherwise leaving them sufficient lands whereon they may labor, do make their said sons by these means gentlemen....

Chapter 24.   Of the Fourth Sort of Men Which Do Not Rule.
The fourth sort or class amongst us is...day laborers, poor husbandmen, yea merchants or retailers which have no free land, copyholders, all artificers, as tailors, shoemakers, carpenters, brickmakers, bricklayers, masons, etc. These have no voice nor authorities in our commonwealth, and no account is made of these but only to be ruled, not to rule other, and yet they be not altogether neglected. For in cities and corporate towns for default of yeomen, they are fain to make their inquests of such manner of people. And in villages they be commonly made churchwardens, aleconners [local brewing inspectors], and many times constables.

1.2   *Richard Morison,* A Remedy for Sedition *(1536)*[6]

When every man will rule, who shall obey? Now can there be any commonwealth, where he that is wealthiest, is most like to come to woe? Who can there be rich, where he that is richest is in most danger of poverty? No, no, take wealth by the hand, and say farewell wealth, where lust is liked, and law refused, where up is set down, and down set up. An order, an order must be had, and a way found that they rule that best can, they be ruled, that most it becometh so to be....For as there must be some men of policy and prudence, to discern what is metest [best] to be done in the government of states, even so there must be others of strength and readiness, to do what the wiser shall think expedient, both for the maintenance of them that govern, and for the eschewing of the infinite jeopardies, that a multitude not governed falleth into: these must not go arm in arm, but the one before, the other behind....

A commonwealth is like a body, and so like, that it can be resembled to nothing so convenient, as unto that. Now, were it not by your faith, a mad herring, if the foot should say, I will wear a cap with an ouch [ornament], as the head doth? If the knees should say, we will carry the eyes, another while; if the shoulders should claim each of them an ear; if the heals would now go before, and the toes behind? This were undoubted a mad herring: every man would say, the feet, the knees, the shoulders, the heals make unlawful requests, and very mad petitions. But if it

---

[6]   Morison, *A Remedy for Sedition* (1536), sig. Aii–Aiiv, Biiv; compared with A. Fletcher and D. MacCulloch, *Tudor Rebellions*, 4th ed. (1997), 137–8.

were so indeed, if the foot had a cap, the knees eyes, the shoulders ears, what a monstrous body should this be? God send them such a one, that shall at any time go about to make as evil a commonwealth, as this is a body. It is not mete, every man to do, that he thinketh best.

1.3 An Act Against Wearing Costly Apparel (1 Hen. VIII, c. 14) (1510)[7]

Forasmuch as the great and costly array and apparel used within this realm contrary to good statutes thereof made hath been the occasion of great impoverishing of diverse of the king's subjects and provoked many of them to rob and to do extortion and other unlawful deeds to maintain thereby their costly array: in eschewing whereof, be it ordained by the authority of this present Parliament that no person, of what estate, condition, or degree that he be, use in his apparel any cloth of gold of purple color or silk of purple color but only the king, the queen, the king's mother, the king's children, the king's brothers and sisters upon pain to forfeit the said apparel wherewith soever it be mixed, and for using the same to forfeit 20 pound. And that no man under the estate of a duke use in any apparel of his body or upon his horses any cloth of gold of tissue upon pain to forfeit the same apparel wherewith soever it be mixed and for using the same to forfeit 20 mark [£13 6s. 8d.]. . . . And that no man under the degree of a baron use in his apparel of his body or of his horses any cloth of gold or cloth of silver or tinsel, satin, nor no other silk or cloth mixed or embroidered with gold or silver upon pain of forfeiture of the same apparel, albeit that it be mixed with any other silk or cloth, and for using of the same to forfeit 10 mark. And that no man under the degree of a lord or a knight of the Garter wear any woolen cloth made out of this realm of England, Ireland, Wales, Calais, or the Marches of the same, or Berwick, upon pain to forfeit the said cloth and for using of the same to forfeit 10 pound. And that no man under the degree of a knight of the Garter wear in his gown or coat or any other his apparel any velvet of the color of crimson or blue upon pain to forfeit the same gown or coat or other apparel and for using of the same to forfeit 40 shillings [£2]. . . . And that no man under the degree of a knight, except esquires for the king's body, his cupbearers, carvers, and sewers having the ordinary fee for the same, and all other esquires for the body having possession of lands and tenements or other hereditaments in their hands or other to their use to the yearly value of 300 mark [£200] and lords' sons and heirs, justices of the one Bench or of the other, the master of the Rolls, and barons of the king's Exchequer, and all other of the king's Council and mayors of the city of London for the time being, use or wear any velvet in their gowns or riding coats or furs of marten in their apparel upon pain to forfeit the same fur and apparel wherewith soever it be mixed and for using of the same to forfeit 40 shillings. Nor no person other than the above named wear velvet in their doublets nor satin nor damask in their gowns nor coats, except he be a lord's son or a gentleman having in his possession or other to his use lands or tenements or annuities at the least for term

[7] *SR*, 3: 8–9; compared with C. H. Williams, ed., *English Historical Documents, 1485–1558* (1967), 249–51.

of life to the yearly value of an hundred pound above all reprises, upon pain to forfeit the same apparel wherewith soever it be mixed and for using of the same to forfeit 40 shillings. Nor no person use or wear satin or damask in their doublets nor silk or camlet [silk and angora] in their gowns or coats not having lands or tenements in his possession or other to his use office or fee for term of life or lives to the yearly value of 20 pound, except he be a yeoman of the Crown or of the king's guard or grooms of the king's Chamber or the queen's having therefore the king's fee or the queen's upon pain to forfeit the same apparel wherewith so ever it be mixed and for using of the same to forfeit 40 shillings. And that no man under the degree of a gentleman except graduates of the universities and except yeomen, grooms, and pages of the king's Chamber and of our sovereign lady the queen's, and except such men as have ... an hundred pound in goods, use or wear any furs, whereof there is no like kind growing in this land of England, Ireland, Wales, or in any land under the king's obeisance, upon pain to forfeit the same furs and for using of the same to forfeit 40 shillings. The value of their goods to be tried by their own oaths. And that no man under the degree of a knight except spiritual men and sergeants at the law or graduates of universities use any more cloth in any long gown than four broad yards, and in a riding gown or coat above three yards upon pain of forfeiture of the same. And that no serving man under the degree of a gentleman use or wear any gown or coat or such like apparel of more cloth than two broad yards and an half in a short gown and three broad yards in a long gown, and that in the said gown or coat they wear no manner [of] fur upon pain of forfeiture of the said apparel. . . . And that no serving man waiting upon his master under the degree of a gentleman use or wear any guarded hose or any cloth above the price of 20d. the yard in his hose except it be of his master's wearing hose upon pain of forfeiture of 3s. 4d. And that no man under the degree of a knight wear any guarded or pinched shirt or pinched partlet [neckerchief or collar] of linen cloth upon pain of forfeiture of the same shirt or partlet and for using of the same to forfeit 10 shillings. And that no servant of husbandry nor shepherd nor common laborer nor servant unto any artificer out of city or borough nor husbandman having no goods of his own above the value of 10 pound use or wear any cloth whereof the broad yard passeth in price two shillings nor that any of the said servants of husbandry, shepherds, nor laborers wear any hose above the price of 10 d. the yard upon pain of imprisonment in the stocks by three days.

1.4 Act Against Pulling Down of Towns
(4 Hen. VII, c. 19) (1489)[8]

The king our sovereign lord, having a singular pleasure above all things to avoid such enormities and mischiefs as be hurtful and prejudicial to the common wealth of this his land and his subjects, remembering that among all other things great inconveniences daily do increase by desolation and pulling down and willful waste of houses and towns within this his realm, and laying to pasture lands

[8] *SR*, 2: 542; compared with R. H. Tawney and E. Power, eds., *Tudor Economic Documents* (1924), 1: 4–5.

which customarily have been tilled, whereby idleness ground and beginning of all mischiefs daily do increase, for where in some towns two hundred persons were occupied and lived by their lawful labors, now are there occupied two or three herdsmen and the residue fall in idleness, the husbandry which is one of the greatest commodities of this realm is greatly decayed, churches destroyed, the service of God withdrawn, the bodies there buried not prayed for, the patron and curates wronged, the defense of this land against our enemies outward feebled and impaired; to the great displeasure of God, to the subversion of the policy and good rule of this land, and remedy be not hastily therefore purveyed: Wherefore the king our sovereign lord by the assent and advice of the Lords spiritual and temporal and Commons in this present Parliament assembled and by authority of the same, ordains, enacts, and establishes that no person, what estate, degree, or condition that he be, that hath any house or houses, that any time within three years past has been or that now is or hereafter shall be let to farm with twenty acres of land at least or more lying in tillage or husbandry, that the owner or owners of every such house or houses and land be bound to keep, sustain, and maintain houses and buildings upon the said ground and land, convenient and necessary for maintaining and upholding of the said tillage and husbandry.

1.5 Thomas More, Utopia, Book I (Description of England) (1516)[9]

It happened one day that I was at his [the Cardinal John Morton's] table when a layman, learned in the laws of your country, was present. Availing himself of some opportunity or other, he began to speak punctiliously of the strict justice which was then dealt out to thieves. They were everywhere executed, he reported, as many as twenty at a time being hanged on one gallows, and added that he wondered all the more, though so few escaped execution, by what bad luck the whole country was still infested with them. I dared be free in expressing my opinions without reserve at the Cardinal's table, so I said to him:

"You need not wonder, for this manner of punishing thieves goes beyond justice and is not for the public good. It is too harsh a penalty for theft and yet is not a sufficient deterrent. Theft alone is not a grave offense that ought to be punished with death, and no penalty that can be devised is sufficient to restrain from acts of robbery those who have no other means of getting a livelihood. In this respect not your country alone but a great part of our world resembles bad schoolmasters, who would rather beat than teach their scholars. You ordain grievous and terrible punishments for a thief when it would have been much better to provide some means of getting a living, that no one should be under this terrible necessity first of stealing and then of dying for it. . . .

"Now there is the great number of noblemen who not only live idle themselves like drones on the labors of others, as for instance the tenants of their estates

---

[9]   More, *Utopia*, ed. E. Surtz (New Haven, 1964), 24–8; compared with B. L. Blakeley and J. Collins, *Documents in English History: Early Times to the Present* (New York, 1975), 1: 114–18, from *Utopia*, pub. in Latin, 1516.

whom they fleece to the utmost by increasing the returns (for that is the only economy they know of, being otherwise so extravagant as to bring themselves to beggary!) but who also carry about with them a huge crowd of idle attendants who have never learned a trade for a livelihood. As soon as their master dies or they themselves fall sick, these men are turned out at once, for the idle are maintained more readily than the sick, and often the heir is not able to support as large a household as his father did, at any rate at first. . . .

"Yet this is not the only situation that makes thieving necessary. There is another which, as I believe, is more special to you Englishmen."

"What is that?" asked the Cardinal.

"Your sheep," I answered, "which are usually so tame and so cheaply fed, begin now, according to report, to be so greedy and wild that they devour human beings themselves and devastate and depopulate fields, houses, and towns. In all those parts of the realm where the finest and therefore costliest wool is produced, there are noblemen, gentlemen, and even some abbots, though otherwise holy men, who are not satisfied with the annual revenues and profits which their predecessors used to derive from their estates. They are not content, by leading an idle and sumptuous life, to do no good to their country; they must also do it positive harm. They leave no ground to be tilled; they enclose every bit of land for pasture; they pull down houses and destroy towns, leaving only the church to pen the sheep in. And, as if enough English land were not wasted on ranges and preserves of game, those good fellows turn all human habitations and all cultivated lands into a wilderness.

"Consequently, in order that one insatiable glutton and accursed plague of his native land may join field to field and surround many thousand acres with one fence, tenants are evicted. Some of them, either circumvented by fraud or over-whelmed by violence, are stripped even of their own property, or else, wearied by unjust acts, are driven to sell. By hook or by crook the poor wretches are compelled to leave their homes – men and women, husbands and wives, orphans and widows, parents with little children and a household not rich but numerous, since farm work requires many hands. Away they must go, I say, from the only homes familiar and known to them, and they find no shelter to go to. All their household goods which would not fetch a great price if they could wait for a purchaser, since they must be thrust out, they sell for a trifle.

"After they have soon spent that trifle in wandering from place to place, what remains for them but to steal and be hanged – justly, you may say! – or to wander and beg. And yet even in the latter case they are cast into prison as vagrants for going about idle when, though they most eagerly offer their labor, there is no one to hire them. For there is no farm work, to which they have been trained, to be had, when there is no land for plowing left. A single shepherd or herdsman is sufficient grazing livestock on that land for whose cultivation many hands were once required to make it raise crops.

"A result of this situation is that the price of food has risen steeply in many localities. Indeed, the price of raw wools has climbed so high that the English poor who used to make cloth cannot possibly buy them, and so great numbers are driven from work into idleness. One reason is that, after the great increase in pasture land, a plague carried off a vast multitude of sheep as though God were punishing greed by sending upon the sheep a murrain [pestilence] – which should have fallen on the owners' heads more justly! But, however much the number of sheep increases, their price does not decrease a farthing [1/4 penny] because, though you cannot brand that a monopoly which is a sale by more than one person, yet their sale is certainly an oligopoly, for all sheep have come into the hands of a few men, and those already rich, who are not obliged to sell before they wish and who do not wish until they get the price they ask.....

"Thus, the unscrupulous greed of a few is ruining the very thing by virtue of which your island was once counted fortunate in the extreme. For the high price of food is causing everyone to get rid of as many of his household as possible, and what, I ask, have they to do but to beg, or – a course more readily embraced by men of mettle – to become robbers?

"In addition, alongside this wretched need and poverty you find ill-timed luxury. Not only the servants of noblemen but the craftsmen and almost the clodhoppers themselves, in fact all classes alike, are given to much ostentatious sumptuousness of dress and to excessive indulgence at table. Do not dives, brothels, and those other places as bad as brothels, to wit, wine shops and alehouses – do not all those crooked games of chance, dice, cards, backgammon, ball, bowling, and quoits, soon drain the purses of their votaries and send them off to rob someone?

"Cast out these ruinous plagues. Make laws that the destroyers of farmsteads and country villages should either restore them or hand them over to people who will restore them and who are ready to build. Restrict this right to rich individuals to buy up everything and this license to exercise a kind of monopoly for themselves. Let fewer be brought up in idleness. Let farming be resumed and let cloth-working be restored once more that there may be honest jobs to employ usefully that idle throng, whether those whom hitherto pauperism has made thieves or those who, now being vagrants or lazy servants, in either case are likely to turn out thieves. Assuredly, unless you remedy these evils, it is useless for you to boast of the justice you execute in the punishment of theft. Such justice is more showy than really just or beneficial. When you allow your youths to be badly brought up and their characters, even from early years, to become more and more corrupt, to be punished, of course, when, as grown-up men, they commit the crimes which from boyhood they have shown every prospect of committing, what else, I ask, do you do but first create thieves and then become the very agents of their punishment?"

1.6   Complaint of the Norwich Shoemakers against their Journeymen (September 21, 1490)[10]

To our right honorable masters, the mayor, and his brethren alderman and to our good masters and weelwillers [well-wishers] of the Common Council of the city: Showeth to your great discretions the poor artificers and craftsmen of shoemakers of the said city, that where diverse journeymen and servants of the said craft

[10]   Tawney and Power, *Tudor Economic Documents*, 1: 97–8, from *Records of the City of Norwich*, ed. W. Hudson and J. C. Tingey (1910), 2: 104.

greatly disposed to riot and idleness, whereby may succeed great poverty, so that diverse days weekly when them lust to leave their bodily labor till a great part of the week be almost so expended and wasted, against the advantage and profit werely [not only] of themselves and of their masters also. And also contrary to the law [of] God and good guiding temporal [temperance], they labor quickly toward the Sunday and festival days on the Saturdays and vigils [evening of festival days] from four of the clock at afternoon to the deepness and darkness of the night following. And not only that sinful disposition but much worse so offending in the mornings of such fests, and omitting the hearing of their divine service. Wherefore prayeth the said artificers heartily, that the rather for good cause and also that virtuous and true labor might help to the sustentation of the said craft, that by your general assent may be ordained and enacted for a laudable custom, that none such servant or journeyman from henceforth presume to occupy nor work after the said hour in vigils and Saturdays aforesaid, upon pain by your discretions to be set for punishment alsweel of [as much against] the said artificers for their favoring and supporting, as for the said journeymen so working and offending.

1.7   *Thomas Starkey,* Dialogue between Pole and Lupset *(ca. 1529–32)*[11]

Pole: There is also, in this politic body, another disease and sickness more grievous . . . , and that is this, shortly to say: A great part of these people which we have here in our country, is either idle or ill-occupied, and a small number of them exerciseth themself in doing their office and duty pertaining to the mainten-ance of the common weal, by the reason whereof this body is replenished and over-fulfilled with many ill-humors, which I call idle and unprofitable persons, of whom you shall find a great number, if you will a little consider all estates, orders, and degrees here in our country. First, look what an idle rout our noblemen keep and nourish in their houses, which do nothing else but carry dishes to the table and eat them when they have down [done]; and after, giving themselves to hunting, hawking, dicing, carding, and all other idle pastimes and vain [vanities], as though they were born to nothing else at all. Look to our bishops and prelates of the realm, whether they follow not the same trade in nourishing such an idle sort, spending their possessions and goods, which were to them given to be distributed among them which were oppressed with poverty and necessity. Look, furthermore to priests, monks, friars, and canons with all their adherents and idle train, and you shall find also among them no small number idle and unprofitable, which be nothing but burdens to the earth; insomuch that if you, after this manner, examine the multitude in every order and degree, you shall find, as I think, the third part of our people living in idleness, as persons to the common weal utterly unprofitable; and to all good civility, much like unto the drone bees

---

[11]   Starkey, *A Dialogue between Pole and Lupset*, ed. T. F. Mayer (Camden Society, 4th ser., 37, 1989), 52–4; compared with Williams, *English Historical Documents*, 297–9.

in a hive, which do nothing else but consume and devour all such thing as the busy and good bee, with diligence and labor, gathereth together.

Lupset: Master Pole, me seemeth you examine this matter somewhat too shortly, as though you would have all men to labor, to go to the plow, and exercise some craft, which is not necessary, for our mother the ground is so plenteous and bountiful, by the goodness of God and of nature given to her, that with little labor and tillage she will sufficiently nourish mankind none otherwise than she doth all beasts, fishes, and fowls which are bred and brought up upon her, to whom we see she ministereth food with little labor or none, but of her own fertile benignity. Wherefore if a few of our people busy themselves and labor therein, it is sufficient; the rest may live in triumph, at liberty and ease free from all bodily labor and pain.

Pole: This is spoken, Master Lupset, even as though you judged man to be born for to live in idleness and pleasure, all thing referring and applying thereto. But, Sir, it is nothing so; but, contrary, he is born to labor and travail (after the opinion of the wise and ancient antiquity) none otherwise than a bird to fly, and not to live (as Homer saith some do) as an unprofitable weight and burden of the earth. For man is born to be as a governor, ruler, and diligent tiller and inhabitant of this earth, as some, by labor of body, to procure things necessary for the maintenance of man's life; some by wisdom and policy to keep the rest of the multitude in good order and civility. So that none be born to this idleness and vanity, to the which the most part of our people is much given and bent, but all to exercise themselves in some fashion of life convenient to the dignity and nature of man. Wherefore, though it be so that it is nothing necessary all to be laborers and tillers of the ground, but some to be priests and ministers of God's Word, some to be gentlemen to the governance of the rest, and some [to be] servants to the same. Yet this is certain, that over-great number of them, without due proportion to the other parts of the body, is superfluous in any commonalty. It is not to be doubted but that here in our country of those sorts be over-many, and specially of them which we call servingmen, which live in service to gentlemen, lords, and others of the nobility. If you look throughout the world, as I think, you shall not find in any one country proportionable to ours like number of that sort.

Lupset: Marry, sir, that is truth. Wherein, me seemeth, you praise our country very much, for in them standeth the royalty of the realm. If the yeomanry of England were not, in time of war we should be in shrewd case; for in them standeth the chief defense of England.

Pole: O, Master Lupset, you take the matter amiss. In them standeth the beggary of England. By them is nourished the common theft therein, as hereafter at large I shall declare. Howbeit, if they were exercised in feats of arms, to the defense of the realm in time of war, they might yet be much better suffered. But you see how little they be exercised therein, insomuch that in time of war it is necessary for our plowmen and laborers of the country to take weapon in hand, or else we were not like long to enjoy England, so little trust is to be put in their feats and deeds.

Wherefore doubt you no more but of them, like as of other that I have spoken of before (as of priests, friars, monks, and others called religious), we have over-many, which altogether make our politic body unwieldy and heavy, and, as it were, to be grieved with gross humors, insomuch that this disease therein may well be compared to a dropsy in man's body.

1.8 *Venetian Nobleman's Report on England (ca. 1500)*[12]

The English are, for the most part, both men and women of all ages, handsome and well-proportioned; though not quite so much so, in my opinion, as it had been asserted to me, before your Magnificence went to that kingdom [perhaps 1496]; and I have understood from persons acquainted with these countries, that the Scotch are much handsomer; and that the English are great lovers of them-selves, and of everything belonging to them; they think that there are no other men than themselves, and no other world but England; and whenever they see a handsome foreigner, they say that "he looks like an Englishman," and that "it is a great pity that he should not be an Englishman"; and when they partake of any delicacy with a foreigner, they ask him, "whether such a thing is made in *their* country?" ... [T]hey think that no greater honor can be conferred, or received, than to invite others to eat with them, or to be invited themselves; and they would sooner give five or six ducats [Venetian ducats varied from 3s. 6d. to 4s.; thus, about £2] to provide an entertainment for a person, than a groat [4d.] to assist him in any distress. . . .

The want [lack] of affection in the English is strongly manifested towards their children; for after having kept them at home till they arrive at the age of 7 or 9 years at the utmost, they put them out, both males and females, to hard service in the houses of other people, binding them generally for another 7 or 9 years. And these are called apprentices, and during that time they perform all the most menial offices; and few are born who are exempted from this fate, for every one, however rich he may be, sends away his children into the houses of others, whilst he, in return receives those of strangers into his own. And on inquiring their reason for this severity, they answered that they did it in order that their children might learn better manners. But I, for my part, believe that they do it because they like to enjoy all their comforts themselves, and that they are better served by strangers than they would be by their own children. Besides which the English being great epicures, and very avaricious by nature, indulge in the most delicate fare themselves and give their household the coarsest bread, and beer, and cold meat baked on Sunday for the week, which, however, they allow them in great abundance. That if they had their own children at home, they would be obliged to give them the same food they make use of for themselves. That if the English sent their children away from home to learn virtue and good manners, and took them back again when their apprenticeship was over, they might, perhaps, be excused; but they never return, for the girls are settled by their

---

[12] *A Relation, or Rather a True Account, of the Island of England ..., about the Year 1500*, trans. C. A. Sneyd (Camden Society, 1847), 20–2, 24–9, 41–3; compared with A. F. Pollard, *The Reign of Henry VII from Contemporary Sources* (1914), 2: 216–18, 221–5; 3: 153–4, 194–5; and Williams, *English Historical Documents*, 197.

patrons, and the boys make the best marriages they can, and, assisted by their patrons, not by their fathers, they also open a house and strive diligently by this means to make some fortune for themselves; whence it proceeds that, having no hope of their paternal inheritance, they all become so greedy of gain that they feel no shame in asking, almost "for the love of God," for the smallest sums of money; and to this it may be attributed, that there is no injury that can be committed against the lower orders of the English, that may not be atoned for by money.

Nevertheless, the apprentices for the most part make good fortunes, some by one means and some by another; but above all, those who happen to be in the good graces of the mistress of the house in which they are domiciliated at the time of the death of the master; because, by the ancient custom of the country, every inheritance is divided into three parts; for the Church and funeral expenses, for the wife, and for the children. But the lady takes care to secure a good portion for herself in secret, first, and then the residue being divided into three parts as aforesaid, she, being in possession of what she has robbed, of her own third, and that of her children besides (and if she have no children, the two thirds belong to her by right), usually bestows herself in marriage upon the one of those apprentices living in the house who is most pleasing to her, and who was probably not *displeasing* to her in the lifetime of her husband; and in his power she places all her own fortune, as well as that of her children, who are sent away as apprentices into other houses.... No Englishman can complain of this corrupt practice, it being universal throughout the kingdom; nor does any one, arrived at years of discretion, find fault with his mother for marrying again during his childhood, because, from very ancient custom, this license has become so sanctioned, that it is not considered any discredit to a woman to marry again every time that she is left a widow, however unsuitable the match may be as to age, rank, and fortune.

I saw, one day, that I was with your Magnificence at court, a very handsome young man of about 18 years of age [Richard de la Pole], the brother of the duke of Suffolk, who, as I understood, had been left very poor, the whole of the paternal inheritance amongst the nobility descending to the eldest son; this youth, I say, was boarded out to a widow of fifty, with a fortune as I was informed, of 50,000 crowns [Venetian crowns, or, about £10,000]. And this old woman knew how to play her cards so well, that he was content to become her husband, and patiently to waste the flower of his beauty with her, hoping soon to enjoy her great wealth with some handsome young lady: because when there are no children, the husband succeeds to the whole of the wife's property, and the wife in like manner to her husband's, as I said before; the part, however, belonging to the Church always remaining untouched. Nor must your Magnificence imagine that these successions may be of small value, for the riches of England are greater than those of any other country in Europe, as I have been told by the oldest and most experienced merchants, and also as I myself can vouch....
This is owing, in the first place, to the great fertility of the soil, which is such, that, with the exception of wine, they import nothing from abroad for their subsistence. Next, the sale of their valuable tin brings in a large sum of money to the

kingdom; but still more do they derive from their extraordinary abundance of wool, which bears such a high price and reputation throughout Europe. And in order to keep the gold and silver in the country, when once it has entered, they have made a law, which has been in operation for a long time now, that no money, nor gold, nor silver plate should be carried out of England under a very heavy penalty. And everyone who makes a tour in the island will soon become aware of this great wealth . . . , for there is no small innkeeper, however poor and humble he may be, who does not serve his table with silver dishes and drinking cups; and no one, who has not in his house silver plate at least £100 . . . , is considered by the English to be a person of any consequence. . . .

[A]t present, all the beauty of this island is confined to London; which, although sixty miles distant from the sea, possesses all the advantages to be desired in a maritime town; being situated on the river Thames, which is very much affected by the tide, for many miles . . . above it; and London is so much benefited by this ebb and flow of the river, that vessels of 100 tons burden can come up to the city, and ships of any size to within five miles of it; yet the water in this river is fresh for twenty miles below London. Although this city has no buildings in the Italian style, but of timber or brick like the French, the Londoners live comfortably, and, it appears to me, that there are not fewer inhabitants than at Florence or Rome. It abounds with every article of luxury, as well as with the necessaries of life, but the most remarkable thing in London is the wonderful quantity of wrought silver. I do not allude to that in private houses, though the landlord of the house in which the Milanese ambassador lived, had plate to the amount of 100 crowns [£25], but to the shops of London. In one single street, named the Strand, leading to St. Paul's, there are fifty-two goldsmith's shops, so rich and full of silver vessels, great and small, that in all the shops in Milan, Rome, Venice, and Florence put together, I do not think there would be found so many of the magnificence that are to be seen in London. And these vessels are all either salt cellars, or drinking cups, or basins to hold water for the hands; for they eat off that fine tin, which is little inferior to silver [pewter]. These great riches of London are not occasioned by its inhabitants being noblemen or gentlemen; being all, on the contrary, persons of low degree, and artificers who have congregated there from all parts of the island, and from Flanders, and from every other place. No one can be mayor or alderman of London, who has not been an apprentice in his youth; that is, who has not passed the seven or nine years in that hard service described before. Still, the citizens of London are thought quite as highly of there, as the Venetian gentlemen are at Venice, as I think your Magnificence may have perceived.

CHAPTER TWO

A Yorkist or a Tudor Revolution in Government?

Tackling Noble Disorder
Claiming the Throne
Comparing Monarchs

DISCUSSION

What was the early Tudor achievement in government? The documents in this chapter examine the case for good (or innovative) government or lawlessness before and after 1485, as well as rival claims to legitimacy. The sources also weigh the strengths and weaknesses of early Tudor rule. Contemporaries paid close attention to the personal qualities of each monarch, and we should too. As you read the documents in this chapter, you might ask:

- Were the words and actions from the period dictated by the monarch's character, or by the monarch's situation?
- How did descriptions of monarchs' thoughts and actions at the beginning of the period (mid-fifteenth century) differ from those at the end (mid-sixteenth century)?

Tackling Noble Disorder

Were the first Tudors "new princes," in Machiavelli's terms, taming an anarchic nobility? Edward Hall (ca. 1496–1547) began his *Chronicle* (pub. 1548), one of the sources upon which William Shakespeare (1564–1616) based his history plays, by noting how the Tudors ended the "Wars" between Yorkist and Lancastrian noble affinities:

what misery, what murder, and what execrable plagues this famous region hath suffered by the division and dissension of the renowned houses of Lancaster and York.... But the old divided controversy between the fornamed families of Lancaster and York, by the union of matrimony celebrate[d] and consummate[d] between the high and mighty prince King Henry the Seventh and the Lady Elizabeth his most worthy queen, the one being indubitate [undoubted] heir of the house of Lancaster, and the other of York, was suspended and appalled [made faint] in the person of their most noble, puissant [powerful], and mighty heir king Henry the Eighth [1491–1547], and by him clearly buried and perpetually extinct.[1]

Hall, like Shakespeare, intended to praise the Tudor dynasty, and one way to make Henry VII (reigned 1485–1509) and Henry VIII (reigned 1509–47) look better was to make their immediate predecessors, the Yorkists, look worse (see also plate 2).

Tudor propagandists might date the onset of pre-Tudor instability from Henry Bolingbroke's overthrow of Richard II (1377–99) and his reign as Henry IV (1399–1413). But a better case might be made for 1453, when a disastrous defeat at the hands of the French in the Hundred Years' War led to the loss of all English lands on the continent outside the port of Calais, and of the mind of the Lancastrian King Henry VI (1422–61) (or, at least, the first of his increasingly frequent mental breakdowns). The resultant erosion of the authority and prestige of the monarchy encouraged widespread disorder. By 1453, there was a more or less private war in the West Country.

Monday the 17th ... of November, it was shown to the said lieutenant and all the Lords..., how the Commons had diverse times made requests to their good lordships, that they should be good means [intermediaries] to the king's highness, that there might be chosen and made a protector and defender of this land, of ... which requests as yet they have no answer. And ... forasmuch as this day they have knowledge and understanding by such persons which the Lords send to them that there be great and grievous riots done in the West Country at the city of Exeter, by the earl of Devonshire, accompanied with many riotous persons, as it is said with 800 horsemen and 4,000 footmen, and there have robbed the church of Exeter, and taken the canons [cathedral clergy] of the church and put them to finance [ransom], and also taken the gentlemen in that country, and done and committed many other great and heinous inconveniences [offenses], that in abridging of such riots..., such a protector and defender must be had..., and that he ... should ride and labor into that country, for unless the riots and inconveniences were resisted, it would cause the ruin of that land.[2]

In response, the king, or rather his advisers, appointed Richard, duke of York (1411–60), "Protector of the Realm." Who, normally, should be the realm's protector? To whom did the Commons appeal? Was a protector needed?

---

[1]   *Hall's Chronicle: containing the History of England, during the Reign of Henry the Fourth, and the Succeeding Monarchs, to the End of the Reign of Henry the Eighth* (1809), 1; compared with M. D. Palmer, *Henry VIII*, 2nd ed. (1983), 88, from Hall, *Union of the Two Noble and Illustre Famelies of Lancastre & Yorke* (1548).

[2]   *Rotuli Parliamentorum ut et Petitiones, et Placita in Parliamento* (1767), 5: 285–6; compared with A. R. Myers, ed., *English Historical Documents, 1327–1485* (1969), 1125–6.

Plate 2   Edward Hall, *The Union of the Two Noble and Illustre Famelies of Lancastre & Yorke*, title page (1550). (*Source*: © British Library)

The image here is branches of a bush or tree intertwined with descendants of Edward III from about 1399 to 1547. How does this relate to the subject of Hall's book? How does it relate to its argument (see discussion, below, and document 2.5)?

By 1461, the duke of York had died fighting against the Lancastrian monarchy he had sworn to protect. His son, Edward, claimed the throne for himself (reigned 1461–83), in Parliament in November 1461, by attacking the entire Lancastrian line:

Henry, late earl of Derby [Bolingbroke, Henry IV], son of... John of Gaunt, the fourth gotten son of the said King Edward III and younger brother of the said Lionel, temerously [rashly] against rightwiseness and justice, by force and arms, against his faith and allegiance, reared war at Flint in Wales against the said King Richard [II], him took and imprisoned in the Tower of London of great violence; and... usurped and intruded upon the royal power, estate, dignity, pre-eminence, possessions, and lordship aforesaid, taking upon him usurpingly the crown and name of king and lord of the same realm and lordship.[3]

The declaration discusses Edward IV's descent through his grandmother, herself a descendant of Lionel, duke of Clarence (1338–68, an older branch than that of the Lancastrians), and his claim to be the true heir of Richard II. How valid is this claim? How (using what reasons) does he make it?

While Yorkists and Lancastrians made rival claims based on descent and formal vows of allegiance, chaos sometimes reigned in the countryside. The Paston Letters (1465, document 2.1) are representative of this violence and disorder, in this case near Norwich. At the time, John Paston was in London attempting to make legal claim to lands willed to him, while his wife, Margaret, remained in Norfolk. Their letters are among the earliest surviving correspondence below the level of the nobility, or even royalty. Paston can be linked to the Yorkists through the duke of Norfolk, but so too can his rival for the lands, John de la Pole, duke of Suffolk (1443–91). Is this, then, the Wars of the Roses? What warlike actions are being taken? Is this a lawful or lawless society? During the 1470s, Edward IV worked to end disorder in the countryside. As document 2.2 (Star Chamber Decree, November 13, 1471) suggests, he tried to thwart local bullying by his nobles, something for which Henry VII is often given credit. Does document 2.2 suggest that Edward's approach was more bureaucratic or more personal?

Claiming the Throne

What royal line would, in the end, establish its legitimacy? Edward IV's Yorkist successor, Richard III (1483–5), had little time to reign before meeting an ignominious death at Bosworth Field on August 22, 1485 and then being "carried upon a horse behind a man, all naked, to Leicester, fast by the field, and there buried within the [Grey] Friars [Church]."[4] But some, particularly in Richard's northern strongholds, would mourn his death. Thus did York city council when they received word on August 23,

that King Richard, late mercifully reigning upon us, was, through [the rumored] great treason of the duke of Norfolk and many others that turned against him, with many other

[3] *Rotuli Parliamentorum*, 5: 436; compared with M. Levine, *Tudor Dynastic Problems, 1460–1571* (1973), 132–3.
[4] C. L. Kingsford, ed., *Chronicles of London* (Oxford, 1905), 193; compared with A. F. Pollard, *The Reign of Henry VII from Contemporary Sources* (1914), 1: 11.

lords and nobles of this North parts, piteously slain and murdered, to the great heaviness of this city.[5]

Documents 2.3 (June 23, 1485) and 2.4 (August 22?, 1485) are rival proclamations by Richard III against Henry Tudor and by Henry to his army on the eve of Bosworth. Compare and contrast Richard's proclamation with Henry's. Who is the intended audience for each? What are the charges against the opposing king? Why should the English support either claimant? For Henry's speech we have only Hall. Might Hall have tailored the speech to fit his overall argument (see chapter 1)? If so, how?

Once seated on the throne, Henry VII felt his rule to be threatened by both the legal power and the private armies (retainers) of his nobles in the localities. He feared that the cumbersome Common Law procedure in local courts remained too much under the sway of powerful lords. In 1487, the Act Giving the Court of Start Chamber Authority (3 Henry VII, c. 1) noted that "untrue demeanings of sheriffs in making of panels and other untrue returns [and the] taking of money by juries" had made "the laws of the land . . . take little effect." The Act decreed that Henry's chancellor or another chief minister be empowered to meet with two other justices in the Star Chamber – the same room in which Edward's council had met to investigate similar problems – and examine "misdoers" directly (much more directly, and immediately, than had been allowed under the Common Law).[6] How might this circumvent the problems noted in document 2.1? The Act Against Unlawful Retaining (1487, 3 Hen. VII, c. 15) ordered that anyone unlawfully retaining someone or being unlawfully retained was to have "all grants then made or had to him of any . . . offices, by the king or by any of the king's progenitors or predecessors, be then utterly void and of no effect," though it did not clearly define "unlawful" retainers.[7] Why not? How might this Act correct problems noted in document 2.1?

Henry also faced threats from pretenders to the throne, such as Perkin Warbeck (1474?–99), a young man who claimed to be Edward V's younger brother, escaped from the Tower of London to reclaim his usurped throne.

Whereas We ["Richard IV," that is Perkin] in our tender age, escaped by God's great might out of the Tower of London, and were secretly conveyed over the sea to divers other countries, there remaining certain years as unknown. The which season it happened one Henry son to Edmond Tydder [Tudor] – earl of Richmond created, son to Owen Tydder of low birth in the country of Wales – to come from France and entered into this our realm, and by subtle false means to obtain the crown of the same unto us of right appertaining: Which Henry is our extreme, and mortal enemy, as soon as he had knowledge of our being alive, imagined, compassed and wrought, all the subtle ways and means he could devise, to our final destruction, insomuch as he has not only falsely surmised us to be a feigned

---

[5] R. Davis, *Extracts from the Municipal Records of the City of York* (1843), 218; compared with Pollard, *Reign of Henry VII*, 1: 17–18.

[6] *SR*, 2: 509; compared with J. R. Tanner, ed., *Tudor Constitutional Documents, A.D. 1485–1603, with a Historical Commentary* (Cambridge, 1922), 258–9.

[7] *SR*, 2: 522–3; compared with Pollard, *Reign of Henry VII*, 2: 65–7.

person, giving us nicknames, so abusing your minds; but also to deter and put us from our entry into this our realm.[8]

Compare "Richard's" (Perkin's) argument for his legitimacy and the illegitimacy of Henry with similar arguments in Richard III's and Henry's declarations of 1485. What values prevail?

Henry's response to such pretenders – Lambert Simnel (ca. 1475–1525), Warbeck, and others – hardened. Document 2.5 (1499) describes the trial and execution of Warbeck and other alleged rebels. Read carefully and consider the various actions and statements about their trial and execution. Would this be effective theater? If you were in the audience, what might have the most effect on you and why? By 1500, "the execution which was done on Perkin and on the son of the duke of Clarence" suggested to contemporaries that Henry's throne was secure, as a Spanish diplomat wrote to his own king and queen, Ferdinand and Isabella: "Now it has pleased God that all should be thoroughly and duly purged and cleansed, so that not a doubtful drop of royal blood remains in this kingdom except the true blood of the king and queen and above all that of the lord Prince Arthur."[9] Was, then, the Tudor regime secure by 1500 and were the Wars of the Roses finally over? Within two years, Henry's eldest son, Arthur, was dead, leaving only Prince Henry in the male line. Once again, the succession was cast into doubt. A discussion on the succession, held ca. 1503 among "the king's true servants" at Calais, threw up various claimants:

some of them spake of my lord of Buckingham, saying that he was a noble man and would be a royal ruler. Others there were that spake, he said, in likewise of your traitor Edmund de la Pole, but none of them, he said, that spake of my lord prince [Prince Henry].[10]

Who should rule according to strict hereditary succession? Why didn't the discussants automatically follow that succession?

As for the overall nature of Henry VII's rule, we again turn to the comments of foreigners. A Milanese envoy in 1497 claimed that Henry

well knows how to temporize, as demonstrated by him before my arrival in this kingdom, when the French ambassadors wanted to go to Scotland under pretense of mediating for the peace, but he entertained them magnificently, made them presents, and sent them home without seeing Scotland; and now he sends one of his own gentlemen in waiting to France.[11]

What does "he well knows how to temporize" mean? Is this a sign of strength? Compare this analysis with that of another foreigner, whom Henry himself hired

---

[8] Pollard, *Reign of Henry VII*, 1: 150–5, from BL, Birch MS. 4160.

[9] Jan. 11, 1500, in J. Gairdner, ed., *Letters and Papers Illustrative of the Reigns of Richard III and Henry VII* (1861–3), 1: 113–14; compared with Levine, *Tudor Dynastic Problems*, 142, from BL, Egerton MS. 616.

[10] Gairdner, *Letters and Papers*, 1: 225; compared with Levine, *Tudor Dynastic Problems*, 144.

[11] *CSP...in the Archives and Collections of Venice* (1864), 1: 261; compared with S. Doran, *England and Europe, 1485–1603*, 2nd ed. (1996), 101.

as a professional historian, Polydore Vergil (1470?–1535). Vergil (ca. 1513, document 2.6) describes Henry's rule after his victory at Bosworth and later. What hopes and fears appear to be driving Henry's actions immediately after Bosworth? For which parts of this narrative does Polydore Vergil seem not well informed? Might any of Henry's avowed strengths be considered weaknesses? Any of his weaknesses strengths? By whom? These evaluations might be compared with that written a century later by the Jacobean scholar and politician Sir Francis Bacon (1561–1626) in document 2.7 (1622). Using Bacon, to what degree was the public persona of Henry VII shaped by his role and place in history? On the other hand, how might you suggest his own character shaped that role? Does your evaluation fit more contemporary (earlier) evidence?

Comparing Monarchs

How did Henry VIII's rule compare with that of his father? A Venetian report on Henry VII and Henry VIII from 1509 notes

sure news had been received . . . of the death of the king of England on the 20th of April, and his son [Henry VIII] had succeeded to the kingdom peaceably. . . . The new king is ___ years old, a worthy king and most hostile to France; it is thought he will indubitably invade France, and has perhaps had our galleys detained for the conveyance of troops. He is the son-in-law of the king of Spain. His name _____; and it seems that he was crowned there on the 26th. The king his father was called Henry, ___ years of age; was a very great miser, but a man of vast ability, and had accumulated so much gold that he is supposed to have more than well nigh all the other kings of Christendom. This king, his son, is liberal and handsome, the friend of Venice and the enemy of France.[12]

What do the Venetians want to know most about England? How is this intelligence useful to historians?

Henry VIII's chief minister in the early years was the archbishop of York and cardinal, Thomas Wolsey (ca. 1473–1530). About 1518, Wolsey wrote to his king on how he used the Court of Star Chamber to keep order.

Your realm . . . was never in such peace nor tranquility; for all this summer I have had neither of riot, felony, nor forcible entry, but that your laws be in every place indifferently ministered. . . . Albeit, there hath lately, as I am informed, been an affray between Piggot, your serjeant, and Sir Andrew Windsor's servants, for the seisin [freehold possession] of a ward whereto both they pretend titles; in the which fray one man was slain. I trust at the next term to learn them the law of the Star Chamber, that they shall ware [take heed] how from thenceforth they shall redress this matter with their hands. They be both learned in the temporal law, and I doubt not good example shall ensue to see them learn the new law

---

[12] May 8, 1509, in *CSP, Venice*, 1: 345–6; compared with Pollard, *Reign of Henry VII*, 1: 330–1, blanks in original MS.

of the Star Chamber, which, God willing, they shall have indifferently administered to them according to their deserts.[13]

Compare this to the absence of such authority in the Paston letters. Admittedly, the "new law of Star Chamber" was hardly new. But the new power, for a while, seemed to be Wolsey himself. Two descriptions of Wolsey's power are found in documents 2.8 (Venetian Ambassador's report on Wolsey, 1519) and 2.9 (John Skelton's satire on Wolsey, 1523). In what way was the cardinal's power religious? In what way was Wolsey a force for centralization or decentralization of governmental power? After circulating "Why come Ye not to Court?," Skelton (1460?–1529) was forced to take sanctuary in Westminster Abbey to avoid Wolsey's wrath. Was his analysis correct? Does no one like Wolsey's power? Is there any defense to be made of Star Chamber? *Cui bono* (who benefits)? The State? The country's inhabitants?

The fall of Wolsey and his death in 1530 did not end State centralization. Instead, many historians would argue that new ministers like Thomas Cromwell extended centralization – through the assimilation of Wales into England (1536), through bureaucratic reform of the central administration, through the Act of Uses (1536), and, ideologically, through a new assertion of kingship. As early as 1515, Henry had declared:

By the ordinance and sufferance of God we are king of England, and the kings of England in time past have never had any superior but God alone. Wherefore know you well that we shall maintain the right of our crown and of our temporal jurisdiction as well in this point as in all others.[14]

As we shall see in chapter 3, argument over the king's supremacy flourished in early sixteenth-century religious debates. Why might there be doubt about the king's supremacy in temporal matters? The Act in Restraint of Appeals (1533, document 2.10), ascribed to the influence of Thomas Cromwell, made the argument for the king's *imperium*, the idea that there is no claim to control over England above that of its monarch and government, more concretely. Who might object to this assertion most? On the other hand, what governmental institutions stand to benefit from such a revolutionary change?

Finally, any such revolution in government that occurred between the mid-fifteenth and mid-sixteenth centuries in England might be contrasted with the situation in Ireland, where the documents point to a change rather later, from the 1540s. A description of Ireland from 1515 noted

[t]here be more than 60 countries, called regions in Ireland, inhabited with the king's Irish enemies; some regions as big as a shire, some more, some less ... where reigneth more than

---

[13] Aug. 1517 or 1518, *Letters and Papers, Foreign and Domestic, of the Reign of Henry VIII* (1864), 2, part 2: 1539; compared with Palmer, *Henry VIII*, 91.

[14] Nov. 1515, J. Guy, "Henry VIII and the Praemunire Manoeuvres of 1530–1531," *EHR* 97 (1982): 497, from Huntington Library, Ellesmere MS. 6109, vol. 34/C/49.

60 chief captains...and every of the said captains maketh war and peace for himself, and holdeth by sword, and hath imperial jurisdiction within his room, and obeyeth to no other person, English or Irish except only to such persons as may subdue him by the sword.... Also, there is no folk daily subject to the king's laws, but half the county of Uriel (Louth), half the county of Meath, half the county of Dublin, half the county of Kildare.[15]

From the twelfth century, the kings of England had been lords of Ireland. But how is the sense of effective *imperium* limited in this report?

In fact, mere lordship implied subservience to the papacy, as Pope Adrian IV (1154–9) had bestowed the title on Henry II (1154–89). An Act for the King of England to be King of Ireland (1542, 33 Hen. VIII, c. 1) echoed the Act in Restraint of Appeals (1533):

Forasmuch as the king our most gracious dread sovereign lord, and his Grace's most noble progenitors, kings of England, have been lords of this land of Ireland, having all manner [of] kingly jurisdiction, power, pre-eminences, and authority royal, belonging or appertaining to the royal estate and majesty of a king, by the name of lords of Ireland.... [And whereas there] hath been great occasion, that the Irish men and inhabitants within this realm of Ireland have not been so obedient to the king's highness and his most noble progenitors, and to their laws, as they of right and according to their allegiance and bounden duties ought to have been: wherefore at the humble pursuit, petition, and request of the Lords spiritual and temporal, and other the king's loving, faithful, and obedient subjects of this his land of Ireland, and by their full assents, be it enacted, ordained, and established by authority of this present Parliament, that the king's highness, his heirs and successors, kings of England, be always kings of this land of Ireland.[16]

This did not, of course, mean that the Irish would automatically be more obedient. But, that same year, Henry's government began the program of surrender and regrant by which the heads of clans gave up their quasi-independent status as Irish chiefs and accepted new positions as Anglo-Irish nobles (1541, document 2.11). O'Donnell and O'Neill were the most powerful landlords in the northern part of Ireland. Conn O'Neill (1484–1559) was granted the title earl of Tyrone in October 1542. What were the grounds for independence and disobedience before 1541? How are the Irish lords to be integrated into the English nation? Could this be the basis of a Tudor Revolution in Ireland as has been argued for England?

Finally, as you read both these documents and those in chapter 3, you might ask whether Henry VIII's role in his government was central and manipulating or distant and manipulated by, say, Wolsey or Cromwell. You might also consider the relation between changes in government and changes in religion. Finally, you might contemplate which of these changes actually affected the lives of commoners.

[15]   C. Maxwell, *The Foundations of Modern Ireland: Select Extracts from Sources Illustrating English Rule and Social and Economic Conditions in Ireland in the Sixteenth and Early Seventeenth Century*, part 1, *The Civil Policy of Henry VIII and the Reformation* (1921), 16–17, from *State Papers Henry VIII* (1534), 2: 1–11.

[16]   *The Statutes at Large, Passed in the Parliaments Held in Ireland* (Dublin, 1786), 1: 176; compared with Maxwell, *Foundations of Modern Ireland*, 28–9.

HISTORIOGRAPHY

Twentieth-century historians have had to combat Tudor propaganda on their monarchs' achievements. Like much of the Tudor Revolution, effective royal propaganda was borrowed from the Yorkists. Whether the Wars of the Roses were "wars" at all has been debated by R. L. Storey and S. B. Chrimes, their argument transcribed (along with an evaluation of Henry VII) in W. Lamont, ed., *The Tudors and Stuarts* (London, 1976). For Edward IV's achievements, see an essay by C. Ross in *Fifteenth-Century England, 1399–1509: Studies in Politics and Society*, ed. S. B. Chrimes, C. D. Ross, and R. A. Griffiths (Manchester, 1972); and C. Carpenter, *The Wars of the Roses: Politics and the Constitution in England, c.1437–1509* (Cambridge, 1997), chs. 8–9. See also D. R. Starkey, "From Feud to Faction: English Politics c.1450–1550," *HT* 32 (November 1982); M. Bush, "Tax Reform and Rebellion in Early Tudor England," *HR* 76 (1999); J. P. Cooper, "Retainers in Tudor England," in *Land, Men and Beliefs: Studies in Early-Modern History*, ed. G. E. Aylmer and J. S. Morrill (Hambledon, 1983), ch. 4; G. L. Harriss, "Political Society and the Growth of Government in Late Medieval England," *P & P* 138 (1993); S. Anglo, "Ill of the Dead: The Post-humous Reputation of Henry VII," *Renaissance Studies* 1 (1987); and, for revived debate on the first Tudor, contributions by B. Thompson, C. Carpenter, and J. L. Watts to *The Reign of Henry VII: Proceedings of the 1993 Harlaxton Symposium*, ed. Thompson (Stamford, 1995).

The Tudor Revolution in Government debate is largely over the nature of Henry VIII's rule. Was Henry a despot, ruling by fiat? Was he a ham, play-acting his way through the reign, but leaving day-to-day decisions to his chief ministers? If the latter, did Cromwell, as Elton has argued, remodel the relationship between king, bureaucrats, and Parliament so as to begin a shift from medieval to modern government? A. F. Pollard once suggested that Henry was in full control after the fall of Wolsey and directed the Reformation government. But Elton argued that (a) Wolsey was never fully in charge before 1529; and (b) Cromwell had a much greater role in creating and implementing policy after 1529; see, for example, Elton, "King or Minister?: The Man behind the Henrician Reformation," *History* 39 (1954). Elton sees the king actively working with Cromwell, who best realized the advantages of working with and using Parliament. Elton debates G. L. Harriss and P. Williams over the extent to which the Cromwellian reforms in government can really be said to issue in a modern, bureaucratic government, in *P & P* 25 (1963), 29 (1964), and 31–2 (1965). Elton's thesis has also been questioned by J. J. Scarisbrick, in his biography *Henry VIII* (rev. ed., 1997); and J. Hurstfield, in "Was there a Tudor Despotism after All?," *TRHS* 5th ser., 17 (1967). In an interesting debate, captured in Lamont, Scarisbrick sees Henry as toying with monarchy, and unable to extend beyond the basic medieval idea of the king as the show-piece for pageantry, hunting, warring, and the central progenitor of a dynasty. Still, he argues that Henry, not Cromwell, originated policy. G. W. Bernard has also recently argued that Cromwell was more the king's servant, in *History* 83 (1998).

See also S. G. Ellis, "England in the Tudor State," *HJ* 26 (1983); J. A. Guy, "Thomas Wolsey, Thomas Cromwell and the Reform of Henrician Government," in *The Reign of Henry VIII*, ed. D. MacCulloch (1995); D. Starkey, "Which Age of Reform?," in *Revolution Reassessed*, ed. C. Coleman and Starkey (Oxford, 1986); and A. Fox and J. Guy, eds., *Reassessing the Henrician Age: Humanism, Politics and Reform, 1500–1550* (Oxford, 1986), particularly Guy's essay on the Act in Restraint of Appeals, which shows that the Henrician Revolution involved far more than solely Henry or Cromwell.

DOCUMENTS

2.1   The Paston Letters on the Defense of Norfolk Manors Hellesdon and Drayton (1465)[17]

John Russe sent me word that Barker and Harry Porter told him in counsel that the duke of Suffolk ... maketh a claim [in law] unto Hellesdon. *(Margaret Paston at Caister, Norfolk, to her husband John Paston at London, April 8, 1465)*

Master Philip [agent of the duke of Suffolk] ... let them plainly wit [know] that if you or any of your servants took any distress [legal procedure of taking goods to constrain payment] in Drayton, that were but the value of an hen, they would come to Hellesdon and take there the value of an ox therefore, and if they cannot take the value thereof there, that then they will do [*sic*] break your tenants' houses in Hellesdon, and take as much as they could find therein; and if they be letted thereof – which shall never lie in your power for to do, for the duke of Suffolk is able to keep daily in his house more men than Daubeney [one of Paston's chief "friends and servants," see chapter 1] had hairs in his head if him list [if he desires]. ... Richard Calle [another of Paston's men] asked that parson and Stermyn if they would take an action for their cattle, and the parson said he was aged and sickly and he would not be troubled hereafter; he said he had liefer [rather] lose his cattle, for he wist [knows] well if he did so he should be indicted and so vexed with them that he should never have rest by them. *(Margaret Paston at Hellesdon to John Paston, May 10, 1465)*

[17]   N. Davis, ed., *Paston Letters and Papers of the Fifteenth Century* (Oxford, 1971–6), 1: 292, 296, 301–2, 316, 324, 330, 2: 310–11.

On Saturday last your servants Naunton, Wykes, and others were at Drayton, and there took a distress for the rent. . . . The tenants . . . desired to have their cattle again, and I answered them if they would do pay such duties as they ought for to pay to you that then they should have their cattle delivered again, or else . . . they to find sufficient surety to pay the money at such a day as they might agree with me. . . . And that they said they durst [dared] not for to take upon them for to be bounden. . . . Harleston [retainer of the duke of Suffolk and a steward of the Duchy of Lancaster, part of the Crown lands] was at Norwich and sent for the tenants the said Saturday at afternoon, and there by the means of the bailiff . . . - put the tenants in such fear, saying that if they would pay such duties [that is, pay rent to the Pastons] . . . , that then they would put them out of such lands as they held bondly [by bond] of the lordship [the Duchy] and so to distrain them and trouble them that they should be weary of their part. And that put them such fear that they durst neither pay nor be bounden. . . .

And on Monday next . . . there came Pinchmore to Hellesdon with a replevin [a writ ordering the restitution of distrained goods] which was made in Harleston's name as under-steward of the Duchy [of Lancaster], saying that the beasts were taken upon the Duchy fee [fief, estate]. *(Margaret Paston at Hellesdon to John Paston, May 20, 1465)*

On Monday last past at afternoon ["my Lord of Suffolk's men"] were at Hellesdon, with the number of 300 men. . . . We had 60 men within the place, and guns and such ordnance so that if they had set upon us they had be destroyed. . . .

And I understand there is comen an *oyer [et] determiner* ["hear and determine," a type of law court] to inquire of all riots, and my Lord of Suffolk and Yelverton [Suffolk's steward] be commissioners; and so they say as many of us as can be taken shall be indicted and hanged forthwith. . . .

If my Lord of Norfolk would come, he should make all well, for they fear him above all things; for it is noised here that my Lord of Norfolk hath taken party in this matter, and all the country is glad of it, saying that if he come they will wholly go with him. And meseemeth it were well done to move my lord in it, though you should give him the profits of Hellesdon and Drayton for the keeping, and some money beside; for you must seek some other remedy than you do. *(Richard Calle to John Paston, July 10, 1465)*

As for my coming to you . . . , I hope I shall purvey so for all things ere I come that it shall be safe enough, by the grace of God, till I come again. But at the reverence of God, if you may, purvey a mean that you may come home yourself, for that shall be most profitable to you; for men cut large thongs here of other men's leather. *(Margaret Paston to John Paston, August 18, 1465)*

The lodge [at Hellesdon] and the remnant of your place was beaten down on Tuesday and Wednesday, and the duke [of Suffolk] rode on Wednesday to Drayton, and so forth to Cossey, while the lodge at Hellesdon was in the beating down. And this night at midnight Thomas Sleaford, Green, Porter, and the bailiff of Eye and others had a cart and fetched away feather beds and all the stuff that was left at the parson's and Thomas Water's house to be kept of ours. *(Margaret Paston to John Paston, October 17, 1465)*

I was at Hellesdon upon Thursday last past and saw the place there, and in good faith there will no creature think how foul and horribly it is arrayed but if they saw it. There cometh much people daily to wonder thereupon, both of Norwich and other places, and they speak shamefully thereof.... And they made your tenants of Hellesdon and Drayton, with others, to help to break down the walls of the place and the lodge both....

The duke's [of Suffolk] men ransacked the church and bare away all the goods that was left there, both of ours and of the tenants, and left not so much but that they stood upon the high altar and ransacked the images..., and ransacked every man's house in the town five or six times. *(Margaret Paston to John Paston, October 27, 1465)*

2.2 *A Star Chamber Decree against the Maintenance of Rioters by Lord Grey (November 13, 1471)*[18]

Edward [IV], by the grace of God, king of England and France, and lord of Ireland, to all whom these present letters shall come, greeting. We have inspected the tenor of a certain act before us and our council . . . in the office of the privy seal in our council chamber called the Star Chamber in our palace of Westminster made and issued on 24 October, in these words:

In the matter of the complaint of the mayor, aldermen, and commonalty of the town of Nottingham propounded before the king our sovereign lord and his council against Robert Hamson . . . , and others, about great riots, excesses, and misgovernings, alleged to have been committed by the said Robert and others.... When the answer of the said Robert [etc.], being personally present, had been given to the said complaint, and the said mayor, aldermen, and commons had made their reply, and all that could be alleged by either party in that matter..., had been heard and understood, and when great deliberation had been taken thereon by our sovereign lord, then by the advice of his said council, the 24th day of October... [1471], in the Star Chamber at Westminster, in full council, the king's highness being present, and before him both the parties abovesaid, it was, by the mouth of his chancellor of England, shown, opened, and declared [that Hamson and companions were not to be imprisoned as Nottingham officials had asked, because there was not sufficient proof; but they were each to find surety for good behavior, and to appear again in a year before the king and his council]....

And moreover, our said sovereign lord by his own mouth asked and questioned Henry, Lord Grey, then present, whether all the other persons named in the said complaint and articles of the same were his servants and followers, and whether he would bring them in or not to answer; the same Lord Grey then answering our

---

[18] *W. H. Stevenson, ed., Records of the Borough of Nottingham (1883), 2: 384–6; compared with Myers, English Historical Documents, 1327–1485, 437–8.*

sovereign lord that they were not his servants, and that he could not bring them in to answer. And thereupon our sovereign lord gave the same Lord Grey strict command and injunction that he should not support, favor, nor maintain them . . . contrary to his laws henceforth, as he would answer to our said sovereign lord, and upon the pain that would fall thereon.

2.3   *Richard III's Proclamation against Henry (June 23, 1485)*[19]

King Richard. Greetings. . . . For as much as the king our sovereign lord has certain knowledge that Peter, bishop of Exeter; Jasper Tudor, son of Owen Tudor, calling himself earl of Pembroke; John, late earl of Oxford; and Sir Edward Woodville, with other diverse [men], his rebels and traitors, disabled and attainted by the authority of the high court of Parliament, of whom many [have] been known for open murderers, adulterers, and extortioners, contrary to the pleasure of God and against all truth, honor, and nature, have forsaken their natural country . . . , [and] privily [secretly] departed . . . into France, and there taking themselves to be under the obedience of the king's ancient enemy, Charles [VIII, 1483–98], calling himself king of France; and to abuse and blind the commons of this said realm, the said rebels and traitors have chosen to be their captain one Henry Tudor, son of Edmund Tudor, son of Owen Tudor, who of his ambition and insatiable covetousness encroaches and usurps upon him the name and title of royal estate of this realm of England, whereunto he has no manner of interest, right, title, or color, as every man well knows; for he is descended of bastard blood both of the father's side and of the mother's side. For the said Owen the grandfather was bastard born, and his mother was daughter to John, duke of Somerset, son to John, earl of Somerset, son to Dame Katherine Swynford, and of her in double adultery gotten [born]; whereby it evidently [clearly] appears that no title can or may be in him, who fully intends to enter this realm, purposing a conquest. And if he should achieve this false intent and purpose, everyman's life, livelihood, and goods would be in his hands, liberty, and disposition, whereby [w]ould ensue the disinheriting and destruction of all the noble and worshipful blood of this realm for ever, and to the resisting and withstanding of which every true and natural Englishman born must lay to his hands for our surety and welfare.

And to the intent that the said Henry Tudor might the rather achieve his false intent and purpose by the aid, support and assistance of the king's said ancient enemy of France, he has covenanted and bargained with him and all the council of France to give up and release in perpetuity all the right, title, and claim that the kings of England have, had, and ought to have, to the crown and realm of France, together with the duchies of Normandy, Anjou, and Maine, Gascony, and Guienne, the castles and towns of Calais, Guisnes, and Hammes, with the marches appertaining to the same, and sever and exclude the [heraldic] arms of France out of the arms of England for ever. . . .

---

[19]   H. Ellis, *Original Letters Illustrative of English History* (1827), 2nd ser., 1: 162–6; compared with Pollard, *Reign of Henry VII*, 1: 3–6; and Myers, *English Historical Documents, 1327–1485*, 343–4.

And besides this and the alienation of all these premises into the possession of the king's said ancient enemies, to the greatest destruction, shame, and rebuke that might ever fall to this said land, the said Henry Tudor and others, the king's rebels and traitors aforesaid, have intended at their coming, if they should have the power, to do the most cruel murders, slaughters, and robberies, and disinheritances, that ever were seen in any Christian realm.

For the avoidance of these and other incalculable dangers, and to the intent that the king's said rebels, traitors, and enemies may be utterly put from their said malicious and false purpose, and soon discomfited, if they succeeded in landing by force, the king our sovereign lord desires, wills, and commands all and everyone of the natural and true subjects of this his realm to call the foregoing to their minds, and like good and true Englishmen to fortify themselves with all their powers for the defence of themselves, their wives, their children, and goods and inheritances, against the said malicious purposes and conspiracies which the said ancient enemies have made with the king's said rebels and traitors for the final destruction of this land.

2.4   Henry's Speech to his Army before the Battle of Bosworth Field (August 22?, 1485; from Hall's Chronicle, pub. 1548)[20]

If ever God gave victory to men fighting in a just quarrel, or if He ever aided such as made war for the wealth and tuition [welfare] of their own natural and nutritive country, or if He ever succoured them which adventured their lives for the relief of innocents, suppressing of malefactors and apparent offenders – no doubt, my fellows and friends, but He of his bountiful goodness will this day send us triumphant victory and a lucky journey over our proud enemy and arrogant adversaries. For, if you remember and consider the very cause of our just quarrel, you shall apparently [by appearances, readily] perceive the same to be true, godly, and virtuous. In the which I doubt not but God will rather aid us (yea, and fight for us), than see us vanquished and profligated [put to flight], by such as neither fear Him nor His laws, nor yet regard justice or honesty. Our cause is so just that no enterprise can be of more virtue both by the laws divine and civil; for, what can be a more honest, goodly, or godly quarrel, than to fight against a captain being an homicide and murderer of his own blood and progeny [that is, the murders reported of Clarence, Edward IV, and the princes (Edward V and Richard)]? – an extreme destroyer of his nobility, and to his and our country and the poor subjects of the same, a deadly mall [*malleus*, "hammer," thus, a destroyer], a fiery brand, and a burden untolerable? Besides him, consider who be of his band and company – such as by murder and untruth committed against their own kin and lineage – yea, against their prince and sovereign lord, have disheartened me and you, and wrongfully detain and usurp our lawful patrimony and lineal inheritance. For he that calleth himself king, keepeth from me the crown and regiment [regimen, government] of this noble realm and country, contrary to all justice and equity. Likewise,

---

[20]   *Hall's Chronicle*, 416–17; compared with E. Goldsmid, ed., *A Collection of Historical Documents Illustrative of the Reigns of the Tudor and Stuart Sovereigns* (Edinburgh, 1886), 1: 5–8.

his mates and friends occupy your lands, cut down your woods, and destroy your manors, letting your wives and children range abroad for their living: which persons, for their penance and punishment, I doubt not but God, of His goodness, will either deliver into our hands as a great gain and booty, or cause them, being grieved and compuncted with the prick of their corrupt consciences, cowardly to fly and not abide the battle. Besides this, I assure you that there be yonder in that great battle men brought thither for fear and not for love, soldiers by force compelled and not with good-will assembled – persons which desire rather the destruction than the salvation of their master and captain; and finally, a multitude, whereof the most part will be our friends and the least part our enemies. For truly I doubt which is the greater, the malice of the soldiers toward their captain, or the fear of him conceived by his people. For surely this rule is infallible that as ill men daily covet to destroy the good, so God appointeth the good to confound the ill; and of all wordly goods the greatest is, to suppress tyrants and relieve innocents, whereof the one is ever as much hated as the other is loved. . . . [Richard] hath not only murdered his nephew, being his king and sovereign lord, bastarded his noble brethren, and defamed his virtuous and womanly mother, but also compassed all the means and ways that he could invent how to stuprate [violate] his own niece under the pretence of a cloaked matrimony [Richard reportedly intended to marry Princess Elizabeth, his brother's daughter]: which lady I have sworn and promised to take to my mate and wife, as you all know and believe.

2.5   *Trial and Execution of Perkin Warbeck and Others (November 18–December 4, 1499)*[21]

And upon the Monday [November 18] after [November 16] sat at the Guildhall of London upon an Oyer determyn [*oyer et determiner*, law court] the mayor, with my lord chief judge, with diverse other judges and knights; and there before them was indicted 8 prisoners of the Tower [of London], among the which was Thomas Mashborwth, sometime bowyer [bow and arrow maker] unto King Edward, 2 citizens of the city, that one named Finch, that other Proud, and 6 others, which were servants to M. Digby, marshal of the Tower, intending after the common fame to have slain their said M. [Digby], and to have set at liberty the earl of Warwick and Perkin.

And upon the Tuesday next ensuing was arraigned in the great hall at Westminster the said earl of Warwick, being of the age of 24 years or thereabout; upon whom sat for judge the earl of Oxinford [Oxford], under a cloth of State: where without any process of the law the said earl of Warwick, for treasons by him confessed and done, submitted himself to the king's grace and mercy; and so was there adjudged to be hanged, drawn, and quartered.

And upon the Saturday following next, being Saint Clements day [November 23], was drawn from the Tower unto Tyburn Perkin or Peter Warbeck, and one

---

[21]   Kingsford, *Chronicles of London*, 227–8; compared with Pollard, *Reign of Henry VII*, 1: 211–13.

John a Water, sometime mayor of Cork, as before is said, at which place of execution was ordained a small scaffold, whereupon the said Perkin standing showed to the people there in great multitude being present, that he was a stranger born according unto his former confession; and took it upon his death that he was never the person that he was named for, that is to say the second son of King Edward IV. And that he was forced to take upon him[self], by the means of the said John a Water and other, whereof he asked God and the king of forgiveness; after which confession he took his death meekly, and was there upon the gallows hanged; and with him the said John a Water; and when they were dead, stricken down, and their heads stricken off; and after their bodies brought to the Friars Augustines, and there buried, and their heads set after upon London Bridge.

And upon the Thursday following [November 28], was the earl of Warwick beforesaid brought out of the Tower between two men, and so led unto the scaffold and there beheaded; and after the body with the head laid into a coffin and born again unto the Tower; which execution was done between 2 and 3 of the clock at afternoon. . . .

And at the next tide following the body was conveyed by water unto Byrsam [Bisham Abbey], a place of religion beside Windsor, and there by his ancestors entered and buried.

And upon the Friday next following, being Saint Andrews even [November 29], sat again at the Guildhall the mayor with the chief justice and other judges and knights; before whom was arraigned the forenamed 8 prisoners for life and death, being charged one Quest with 5 prisoners, and that other inquest with 3; of the which said 8 persons, 4 of them named Strangwissh, Blowet, Astwood, and long Roger were adjudged to be hanged, drawn and quartered; which judgment was given upon Saint Andrews day [Saturday, November 30], the mayor and the foresaid judges there again sitting.

And upon Wednesday next ensuing was drawn from the Tower unto Tyburn the forenamed Blewet and Astwood, both upon one hurdle; and there hanged, and after beheaded, and their bodies brought unto the Friars Augustines, and there buried; which forenamed Astwood was, in the year [1494] that Richard Chawry was mayor drawn with other transgressors from Westminster unto the Tower Hill there to have been beheaded; whom the king at that season, of his most bounteous grace, pardoned; wherefore as now his offense was the more heinous and grievous.

2.6 Polydore Vergil's *Anglica Historia, on Henry VII (ca. 1513; pub. in Latin, 1534)*[22]

We have described in the preceding book what Richard [III] did after the death of Edward [IV], and the revolt of the nobles as well as the destruction of Richard himself. After Henry had obtained power, from the very start of his reign he then set

---

[22] *The Anglica Historia of Polydore Vergil, A.D. 1485–1537*, ed. Denys Hay (Camden Society, 74, 1950), 4, 5, 143, 145, 147; compared with C. H. Williams, ed., *English Historical Documents, 1485–1558* (1967), 130.

about quelling the insurrections. Accordingly, before he left Leicester, he despatched Robert Willoughby to Yorkshire with instructions to bring back Edward, the fifteen-year-old earl of Warwick, sole survivor of George duke of Clarence, whom Richard had held hitherto in the castle called Sheriff Hutton. For indeed, Henry, not unaware of the mob's natural tendency always to seek changes, was fearful lest, if the boy should escape and given any alteration in circumstances, he might stir up civil discord. Having made for the castle without delay, Robert received the boy from the commander of the place and brought him to London, where the wretch, born to misery, remained in the Tower until his death, as will be recounted elsewhere. Detained in the same fortress was Elizabeth, elder daughter of King Edward, whom Richard, had kept unharmed with a view to marriage. To such a marriage the girl had a singular aversion. . . . She would repeatedly exclaim, saying, "I will not thus be married, but, unhappy creature that I am, will rather suffer all the torments which St. Catherine is said to have endured for the love of Christ than be united with a man who is the enemy of my family." This girl too, attended by noble ladies, was brought to her mother in London. Henry meanwhile made his way to London like a triumphing general, and in the places through which he passed was greeted with the greatest joy by all. Far and wide the people hastened to assemble by the roadside, saluting him as king and filling the length of his journey with laden tables and overflowing goblets. . . .

After this he summoned a Parliament, as was the custom, in which he might receive the crown by popular consent. His chief care was to regulate well affairs of state and, in order that the people of England should not be further torn by rival factions, he publicly proclaimed that (as he had already promised) he would take for his wife Elizabeth daughter of King Edward and that he would give complete pardon and forgiveness to all those who swore obedience to his name. Then at length having won the good-will of all men and at the instigation of both nobles and people, he was made king at Westminster on 31 October and called Henry, seventh of that name. These events took place in the year[s 1485 and] 1486. . . .

Henry reigned twenty-three years and seven months. He lived for fifty-two years. By his wife Elizabeth he was the father of eight children, four boys, and as many girls. He left three surviving children, an only son Henry prince of Wales, and two daughters, Margaret married to James king of Scotland, and Mary betrothed to Charles prince of Castile. . . . His spirit was distinguished, wise, and prudent. . . . He had a most pertinacious memory. Withal he was not devoid of scholarship. In government he was shrewd and prudent, so that no one dared to get the better of him through deceit or guile. . . . He was most fortunate in war, although he was constitutionally more inclined to peace than to war. He cherished justice above all things; as a result he vigorously punished violence, manslaughter and every other kind of wickedness whatsoever. Consequently he was greatly regretted on that account by all his subjects, who had been able to conduct their lives peaceably, far removed from the assaults and evil doing of scoundrels. . . . But all these virtues were obscured latterly only by avarice, from which . . . he suffered. This avarice is surely a bad enough vice in a private individual, whom it forever torments; in a monarch indeed it may be considered the worst vice, since it is harmful to everyone, and distorts those qualities of trustfulness, justice, and integrity by which the state must be governed.

2.7   *Francis Bacon on the Character of Henry VII (1622)*[23]

He was a prince, sad, serious, and full of thoughts, and secret observations, and full of notes and memorials of his own hand, especially touching persons, as whom to employ, whom to reward, whom to enquire of, whom to beware of, what were the dependencies, what were the factions, and the like; keeping (as it were) a journal of his thoughts. There is to this day a merry tale that his [pet] monkey (set on as it was thought by one of his chamber) tore his principal notebook all to pieces, when by chance it lay forth. Whereat the Court (which liked not those pensive accounts) was almost tickled with sport.

He was indeed full of apprehensions and suspicions. But as he did easily take them, so he did easily check them and master them: whereby they were not dangerous, but troubled himself more than others. It is true, his thoughts were so many, as they could not well always stand together; but that which did good one way, did hurt another. Neither did he at some times weigh them aright in their proportions. Certainly, that rumor which did him so much mischief (that the duke of York should be [had been] saved, and [was] alive) was (at the first) of his own nourishing, because he would have more reason not to reign in the right of his wife. He was affable, and both well and fair spoken, and would use strange sweetness and blandishments of words where he desired to effect or persuade any thing that he took to heart. He was rather studious than learned, reading most books that were of any worth, in the French tongue. Yet he understood the Latin, as appeareth in that Cardinal Hadrian and others, who could very well have written French, did use to write to him in Latin.

For his pleasures, there is no news of them. . . . He did by pleasures, as great princes do by banquets, come and look a little upon them, and turn away. For never prince was more wholly given to his affairs, nor in them more of himself; insomuch as in triumphs of jousts, and tourneys, and balls, and masques (which they then called disguises) he was rather a princely and gentle spectator than seemed much to be delighted.

No doubt, in him as in all men (and most of all in kings) his fortune wrought upon his nature, and his nature upon his fortune. He attained to the crown, not only from a private fortune, which might endow him with moderation, but also from the fortune of an exiled man, which had quickened in him all seeds of observation and industry. And his times being rather prosperous than calm, had raised his confidence by success but almost marred his nature by troubles. His wisdom, by often evading from perils, was turned rather into a dexterity to deliver himself from dangers when they pressed him, than into a Providence to prevent and remove them afar off. . . .

---

[23] Bacon, *The History of the Reign of King Henry VII and Selected Works*, ed. B. Vickers (Cambridge, 1998), 202–4; compared with R. Sharrock, ed., *The Pelican Book of English Prose* (Baltimore, 1970), 1: 181–4.

Yet take him with all his defects, if a man should compare him with the kings his concurrents in France and Spain, he shall find him more *politique* [politically temporizing] than Louis XII of France [1498–1515], and more entire and sincere than Ferdinand of Spain [1479–1516]. But if you shall change Louis XII for Louis XI [1461–83], who lived a little before, then the consort is more perfect. For that Louis XI, Ferdinand, and Henry, may be esteemed for the *tres magi* of kings of those ages. To conclude, if this king did no greater matters, it was long of himself; for what he minded, he compassed.

2.8 Venetian Ambassador Sebastian Giustiniani's Report on Cardinal Wolsey (September 10, 1519)[24]

The cardinal of York . . . is of low origin and has two brothers, one of whom holds an untitled benefice, and the other is pushing his fortune. He rules both the king and the entire kingdom. On my first arrival in England he used to say to me, "His majesty will do so and so." Subsequently, by degrees, he forgot himself, and commenced saying, "We shall do so and so." At this present he has reached such a pitch that he says, "I shall do so and so." He is about forty-six years old, very handsome, learned, extremely eloquent, of vast ability and indefatigable. He transacts alone the same business as that which occupies all the magistracies, offices, and councils of Venice, both and criminal, and all state affairs are managed by him.

He is pensive, and has the reputation of being extremely just. He favors the people exceedingly, and especially the poor, hearing their suits and seeking to despatch them instantly. He also makes the lawyers plead *gratis* for all poor men.

He is in very great repute, seven times more so than if he were pope. He has a very fine palace [York Place or Hampton Court; later taken over by the royal Court], where one traverses eight rooms before reaching his audience chamber.

2.9 John Skelton, "Why come Ye not to Court?" (1523)[25]

> In the Chancery, where he sits,
> But such as he admits,
> None so hardy to speek!
> He saith, "Thou hoddipeke [hod-carrier?, rustic],
> Thy learning is too lewd,
> Thy tongue is not well-thewd [well-mannered]
> To seek before our Grace!"
> And openly, in that place,
> He rages and he raves,
> And calls them "cankered knaves"!
> Thus royally he doth deal
> Under the King's broad seal;

---

[24] *CSP, Venice*, 2: 560; compared with E. P. Cheyney, ed., "The Early Reformation Period in England," in *Translations and Reprints from the Original Sources of European History* (Philadelphia, 1894), 2–3.
[25] Palmer, *Henry VIII*, 92–3, from Skelton, "Why come ye not to court?"

And in the Chequer he them checks
In the Star Chamber he nods and becks,
And beareth him there so stout
That no man dare rowt!
Duke, earl, baron, nor lord,
But to his sentence must accord;
Whether he be knight or squire
All men must follow his desire.....
Why come ye not to court
To which court?
To the King's court,
Or to Hampton Court?
Nay, to the King's court!
The King's court
Should have the excellence
But Hampton Court
Hath the preeminence,
And York's Place,
With my Lord's Grace!
To whose magnificence
Is all the confluence,
Suits and supplications,
Embassades [embassies] of all nations.

2.10   Act in Restraint of Appeals (24 Hen. VIII, c. 12) (1533)[26]

Where by diverse sundry old authentic histories and chronicles it is manifestly
declared and expressed that this realm of England is an empire, and so hath been
accepted in the world, governed by one supreme head and king having the dignity
and royal estate of the imperial crown of the same, unto whom a body politic,
compact of all sorts and degrees of people divided in terms and by names of
spiritualty and temporalty, be bounden and owe to bear next to God a natural
and humble obedience; he being also institute and furnished by the goodness and
sufferance of Almighty God with plenary, whole, and entire power, preeminence,
authority, prerogative, and jurisdiction to render and yield justice and final
determination to all manner of folk resiants [residents] or subjects within this
his realm, in all causes, matters, debates, and contentions happening to occur,
insurge, or begin within the limits thereof, without restraint or provocation to any
foreign princes or potentates of the world; the body spiritual whereof having
power when any cause of the law divine happened to come in question or of

---

[26]   *SR*, 3: 427–8; compared with G. R. Elton, ed., *The Tudor Constitution: Documents and Commentary* (Cambridge, 1968), 344–5.

spiritual learning, then it was declared, interpreted, and showed by that part of the said body politic called the spiritualty, now being usually called the English Church, which always hath been reputed and also found of that sort that both for knowledge, integrity, and sufficiency of number, it hath been always thought and is also at this hour sufficient and meet of itself, without the intermeddling of any exterior person or persons, to declare and determine all such doubts and to administer all such offices and duties as to their rooms spiritual doth appertain. For the due administration whereof and to keep them from corruption and sinister affection the king's most noble progenitors, and the antecessors of the nobles of this realm, have sufficiently endowed the said Church both with honor and possessions. And the laws temporal for trial of propriety of lands and goods, and for the conservation of the people of this realm in unity and peace without ravin [robbery] or spoil, was and yet is administered, adjudged, and executed by sundry judges and administers of the other part of the said body politic called the temporalty, and both their authorities and jurisdictions do conjoin together in the due administration of justice the one to help the other. And whereas the king his most noble progenitors, and the Nobility and Commons of this said realm, at diverse and sundry Parliaments as well in the time of King Edward I, Edward III, Richard II, Henry IV, and other noble kings of this realm, made sundry ordinances, laws, statutes, and provisions [the Statutes of Provisors, 1351, and Praemunire, 1353, 1393] for the entire and sure conservation of the prerogatives, liberties, and preeminences of the said imperial crown of this realm, and of the jurisdictions spiritual and temporal of the same, to keep it from the annoyance as well of the see of Rome as from the authority of other foreign potentates attempting the diminution or violation thereof.... And notwithstanding the said good statutes and ordinances made in the time of the king's most noble progenitors in preservation of the authority and prerogative of the said imperial crown as is aforesaid, yet nevertheless since the making of the said good statutes and ordinances diverse and sundry inconveniences and dangers not provided for plainly by the said former acts, statutes, and ordinances have risen and sprung by reason of appeals sued out of this realm to the see of Rome, in causes testamentary, causes of matrimony and divorces, right of tithes, oblations, and obventions, not only to the great inquietation, vexation, trouble, costs, and charges of the king's highness and many of his subjects and resiants in this his realm, but also to the great delay and let to the true and speedy determination of the said causes, for so much as the parties appealing to the said court of Rome most commonly do the same for the delay of justice; and forasmuch as the great distance of way is so far out of this realm, so that the necessary proofs nor the true knowledge of the cause can neither there be so well known nor the witnesses there so well examined as within this realm, so that the parties grieved by means of the said appeals be most times without remedy.

2.11   Submission of Two Ulster Chiefs
(August 6 and October 1, 1541)[27]

[A] Indenture made 6th August, 1541, between Sir Anthony St. Leger, Deputy, and the Council and Manus O'Donnell....

(1) Manus O'Donnell will recognize and accept the king [Henry VIII] as his liege lord and king.

(2) He will not confederate with the rebels of the king, but persecute them to the utmost of his power.

(3) He will renounce the usurped primacy and authority of the Roman pontiff.

(4) Whenever he shall be called upon by letters of the Lord Deputy and Council, to come to any great hosting, he will come in his own person, with 70 horsemen, 120 kerne [Irish foot-soldier] and as many Scots, or send one of his most powerful men with the same number, for one month at his own expense.

(5) He will appear in the next great Parliament in Ireland, or send to the same some discreet and trusty person authorized by his writing, sealed with his seal.

(6) He will faithfully perform the articles contained in the king's letters sent to him at the time of his receiving pardon.

(7) He will receive and hold his lands from the king, and take such title as the king shall give him.

(8) He offers to send one of his sons into England, to the presence of his majesty, to be there reared and educated according to English manners.

(9) The Lord Deputy and Council promise to assist and defend O'Donnell and his heirs against all who injure him or invade his country.

[B] Articles of the submission of Conn O'Neill.

(1) He utterly forsakes the name of O'Neill.

(2) He and his heirs shall use the English habits, "and to their knowledge the English language."

(3) He shall keep and put such of the lands granted to him as are meet for tillage "in manurance and tillage of husbandry," and cause houses to be builded for such persons as shall be necessary for the manurance thereof.

(4) He shall not take, put, or cess any imposition or charge upon the king's subjects inhabiters of the said lands other than their yearly rent or custom, but such as the deputy shall be content with; nor have any gallowglass [specialized soldiers, usually mercenary] or kerne but such as shall stand with the contentation of the deputy and Council.

---

[27] Maxwell, *Foundations of Modern Ireland*, 35–7. Contrast this with the initial conditions offered to O'Neill in E. Curtis and R. B. McDowell, eds., *Irish Historical Documents, 1172–1922* (1943), 107–9.

(5) He shall be obedient to the king's laws, and answer to his writs, precepts and commandments in the Castle of Dublin, or in any other place where his courts shall be kept.

(6) He shall go with the king's deputy to all hostings, "rodes" [responses to hostile invasions], and journeys, with such a company as the Marchers of the county of Dublin do.

(7) He shall not maintain or succour any of the king's enemies, rebels, or traitors.

(8) He shall hold his lands by whole knight's fees.

CHAPTER THREE

The Old Church Defended and Attacked

The Old Church Criticized and Defended
The New Church Established
Martyrs and the New Church Reestablished

DISCUSSION

Arguably, the most dramatic series of events of the English sixteenth century – and the most controversial among historians – was the Reformation. The drama should be apparent below as we see churchmen, reformers, martyrs, and simple parishioners wrestle with the challenge of Reformation and Counter-Reformation. The controversy hangs on whether the English people were happy with their Church prior to the Reformation, and what proportion of the population was committed either to Reformation or maintenance of the Old Church once key changes began in the 1530s. Both issues prove resistant to a definitive answer. As you read the documents in this chapter, you might ask:

- What aspect of the religion question was most important for each author?
- For whom or what social group did each author speak?

The Old Church Criticized and Defended

What was the Church like on the eve of the Reformation? Historians often rely on recollections of late medieval parish life like that of Roger Martyn (ca. 1527–1615): he described early sixteenth-century religious life in his Suffolk village some 50 to 75 years afterwards, after decades of religious turmoil (document 3.1). How might Church ritual be especially relevant to farming communities? Does Martyn's account suggest that many villagers engaged in the religious ritual described? Further evidence can be gleaned from sources like the churchwardens' accounts from the 1520s and 1530s of Morebath, Devon, which record gifts to a remote parish church. These reveal much simple but determined piety, as in the veneration of a local saint shown in the recorded gifts of one female parishioner in 1529: "Eleanor Nicoll gave to the store of Jesus a little silver cross (of gilt) of value 4d. Item. She gave again to the store of Saint Sidwell her wedding ring in value 8d."[1]

But there were critics within the pre-Reformation Church. When John Colet (1467–1519), dean of St. Paul's, preached at the Convocation of English clerics summoned to discuss how to suppress heresy in 1511, he attacked his audience for their venality and worldliness.

How much greediness and appetite of honor and dignity is nowadays in men of the Church? How run they, yea, almost out of breath, from one benefice to another; from the less to the more, from the lower to the higher? . . . The second secular evil is carnal concupiscence. Hath not this vice so grown and waxen in the Church as a flood of their lust, so that there is nothing looked for more diligently in this most busy time of the most part of priests than that that doth delight and please the senses? They give themselves to feasts and banqueting; they spend themselves in vain babbling; they give themselves to sports and plays; they apply themselves to hunting and hawking; they drown themselves in the delights of this world. . . . Covetousness is the third secular evil, the which Saint John the apostle calleth concupiscence of the eyes. . . . This abominable pestilence hath so entered in the mind almost of all priests, and so hath blinded the eyes of the mind, that we are blind to all things but only unto those which seem to bring unto us some gains. For what other thing seek we nowadays in the Church than fat benefices and high promotions? Yea, and in the same promotions, of what other thing do we pass upon than of our tithes and rents? . . . Of thee, all the suing for tithes, for offering, for mortuaries, for dilapidations, by the right and title of the Church. . . . The fourth secular evil that spotteth and maketh ill favored the face of the Church, is the continual secular occupation, wherein priests and bishops nowadays doth busy themselves, the servants rather of men than of God; the warriors rather of this world than of Christ.[2]

What problems of the Church does Colet lay out? Can they be cured? Who is to blame?

Colet's friend, William Melton (d. 1528), master of Michaelhouse, Cambridge, preaching in Latin to candidates for the clergy (1510), was still more direct.

Everywhere throughout town and countryside there exists a crop of oafish and boorish priests, some of whom are engaged on ignoble and servile tasks, while others abandon themselves to tavern haunting, swilling, and drunkenness. Some cannot get along without their wenches; others pursue their amusement in dice and gambling and other such trifling all day long. . . . Because of such people is the honor of the holy priesthood profaned and defiled.[3]

---

[1] "The Accounts of the Wardens of the Parish of Morebath, Devon, 1520–1573," *Devon and Cornwall Notes and Queries* (Supplement, 1904), 23.

[2] *The Sermon of Doctor Colete made to the Convacacion at Pauls* (English trans. of Colet's *Oratio habita*, 1530), unpag.; compared with C. H. Williams, ed., *English Historical Documents, 1485–1558* (1967), 652–6.

[3] A. G. Dickens and D. Carr, eds., *The Reformation in England to the Accession of Elizabeth I* (1967), 15–16, from English trans. of *Sermo exhortatorius cancelarii Ebor[rum]* (1510), sig. A iii.

Colet and Melton addressed their criticisms to the priesthood; but a young lawyer, Simon Fish (d. 1531), addressed his to the civil authority. His *A Supplication for the Beggars* (1529) framed the attack on the clergy as a plea to Henry VIII (who reportedly was delighted) to curb greedy priests, bishops, pardoners, summoners, and friars. In his view, these clerics were not merely corrupt, but disobedient and disloyal:

And what do all these greedy sort of sturdy, idle, holy thieves [do] with these yearly exactions that they take of the people? Truly nothing, but exempt themselves from the obedience of your Grace [the king]. Nothing, but translate all rule, power, lordship, authority, obedience, and dignity from your Grace unto them.... What remedy: make laws against them? I am in doubt whether ye be able. Are they not stronger in your own Parliament House than yourself?[4]

Do Colet, Melton, and Fish really refute the positive view of parochial religious life portrayed in document 3.1? Alternately, did the vices they describe really affect everyday parochial life? Might both pictures of the pre-Reformation Church be accurate?

The Church did not take such criticism lightly. Late medieval heretics, mostly Lollards, were either burnt by Henry VII and Henry VIII, or made to stand in public penance. For example, on Sunday October 9, 1496,

At Paul's Cross [London] stood four Lollards with the books of their lore hanging about them, which books were, at the time of the sermon, there burnt with the faggots that the said Lollards bore. And among their erroneous opinions one was that the Sacrament of the Altar was but material bread.[5]

While these Lollards predate the Lutheran Reformation, one John Pykas, who confessed before a bishop's court in London (March 7, 1527, document 3.2), may have been either a Lollard or a Lutheran. How might his (and his mother's) views of proper theology and liturgy fit the later Protestant challenge to Catholicism? How would Pykas react to Martyn's views on proper religious belief (compare documents 3.1 and 3.2)? How might everyday life have changed if Pykas's ideas had been put into practice?

Still, Lollards and the likes of Pykas alone would never have made a Reformation without the king. During the 1520s, Henry VIII rejected continental Protestant theology and even wrote *Assertio Septem Sacramentorum* (*Defense of the Seven Sacraments*, 1522) against Martin Luther's *Babylonian Captivity of the Church*:

---

[4] Fish, *A Supplicacyon for the Beggers* (facsimile, Menston, Yorkshire, 1973), sig. A3–3v, 5; compared with G. R. Elton, ed., *The Tudor Constitution: Documents and Commentary* (Cambridge, 1968), 322–4.

[5] C. L. Kingsford, ed., *Chronicles of London* (Oxford, 1905), 211; compared with A. F. Pollard, *The Reign of Henry VII from Contemporary Sources* (1914), 3: 239.

And if there be any who desire to know this strange work of his, I think I have sufficiently made it apparent to them. For seeing by what has been said, it is evident to all men what sacrilegious opinions he has of the sacrament of our Lord's Body, from which the sanctity of all the other sacraments flow: who would have doubted, if I had said nothing else, how unworthily, without scruple, he treats all the rest of the sacraments? Which, as you have seen, he has bandied in such sort that he abolishes and destroys them all, except Baptism alone.[6]

As long as the king opposed Luther, there was little chance that English Lutherans would be any more than a group of vocal intellectuals in Cambridge taverns. But Henry was developing his own positions, in part for non-theological reasons, as his letter (from 1528 or 1529) to Anne Boleyn (1507?–36) suggests:

Mine own sweetheart, this shall be to advertise you of the great elengeness [loneliness] that I find here since your departing. . . . I am right well comforted in so much that my book maketh substantially for my matter; in looking whereof I have spent above four hours this day, which caused me to write the shorter letter to you at this time, because of some pain in my head; wishing myself (especially an evening) in my sweetheart's arms, whose pretty duckys [dugs, breasts] I trust shortly to cusse [kiss].[7]

Henry's "book" was a treatise he was then composing on the unlawfulness, according to Scripture, of his marriage to his dead brother's wife, Catherine of Aragon (1485–1536), a marriage which had not produced the son and heir he desired. His decision to press forward with "the King's Great Matter" by pressuring the pope for an annulment, and intimidating his own clergy into support – ultimately, by employing his Parliament in an arguably revolutionary way – would give former heresies an airing in his kingdom (see Bucholz and Key, chapter 3).

The New Church Established

Lollard anticlericalism, Lutheran theological reforms, and Henry's desire for a new, legitimate heir came together in the Reformation Parliament (1529–36). Edward Hall describes the beginning of that Parliament (pub. 1548, document 3.3). Is Hall, who sat in the Commons, a reliable reporter? Does he take a side? Were the members of the Commons Protestant? What was *their* agenda? In 1532, the Commons petitioned the king, charging the ordinaries (bishops) with a wide array of offenses. These ranged from the usual money grubbing:

the said prelates and ordinaries daily do permit and suffer the parsons, vicars, curates . . . , [etc.], to exact and take of your humble and obedient subjects diverse sums of money for

---

[6]   Henry VIII, *Assertio Septem Sacramentorum: Or an Assertion of the Seven Sacraments against Martin Luther*, trans. T. W., 2nd ed. (trans. of 1522 ed., 1688), 113; compared with W. L. Sachse, *English History in the Making* (1967), 1: 182–3.
[7]   *Harleian Miscellany* (1809), 3: 60; compared with E. Goldsmid, ed., *A Collection of Historical Documents Illustrative of the Reigns of the Tudor and Stuart Sovereigns* (Edinburgh, 1886), 1: 41–2.

the sacraments and sacramentals of Holy Church, sometimes denying the same without [unless] they be first paid the said sums of money;

to too many holy days:

[a]nd also where a great number of holy days which now at this present time, with very small devotion, be solemnized and kept throughout this your realm – upon the which many great, abominable and execrable vices, idle and wanton sports, be used and exercised – which holy days . . . , and specially such as fall in the harvest, might by your majesty . . . , be made fewer in number.[8]

The bishops submitted to the king a spirited reply to the Commons' charges, beginning with the first (1532, document 3.4). What was the charge? How was it related to the Protestant Reformation? To the Tudor Revolution in Government (see chapter 2)? Why did the bishops' argument fall on deaf ears? Henry's angry reaction soon convinced the clergy that the king would accept nothing less than a full submission. On May 15, 1532, they did

offer and promise *in verbo sacerdotii* [on their sacred word] here unto your highness, submitting ourselves most humbly to the same, that we will never from henceforth presume to attempt, allege, claim . . . , or to enact, promulge, or execute any canons, constitution or ordinances provincial, or by any other name whatsoever they may be called in our Convocation in time coming . . . , unless your highness by your royal assent shall license us to make, promulge, and execute the same, and thereto give your most royal assent and authority.[9]

Compare this submission and document 3.4 on the role of the monarch and royal prerogative. What has changed?

In 1533, Henry divorced Catherine of Aragon, prohibited her from appealing to Rome by the Act in Restraint of Appeals (1533, see chapter 2), and married Anne Boleyn. In 1534, the Act of Supremacy (26 Hen. VIII, c. 1) rendered him "the supreme head of the Church of England, and so is recognized by the clergy of the realm in their Convocations . . . , [and] the only supreme head [o]n Earth of the Church of England." In 1536, another Act (28 Hen. VIII, c. 10) extinguished "the pretended power and usurped authority of the bishop of Rome, by some called the pope" in England.[10] Opposition was limited at first, though Sir Thomas More and others would lose their lives for refusing to recognize the king's supremacy. Why, do you suppose, was opposition limited? Did most people realize what was happening?

Only with the Dissolution of the Monasteries did the Reformation affect the world of most English men and women. In 1535, Thomas Cromwell, now vice-

---

[8]   H. Gee and W. J. Hardy, eds., *Documents Illustrative of English Church History* (1896), 145–53; compared with Dickens and Carr, *Reformation in England*, 48–50.
[9]   N. Pocock, *Records of the Reformation: The Divorce, 1527–33* (Oxford, 1870), 2: 257–8; compared with Sachse, *English History*, 185–6; and M. D. Palmer, *Henry VIII*, 2nd ed. (1983), 98–9.
[10]   *SR*, 3: 492, 663; compared with Elton, *Tudor Constitution*, 355–6.

gerent of the Church, sent out a commission to enumerate the practices and the wealth of the religious houses. Their bemused reports included lists of relics:

I send you relics; first, two flowers wrapped in white and black sarcenet, that on Christmas eve..., will spring and burgeon and bear blossoms..., saith the prior of Maiden Bradley..., also...a bag of relics, wherein ye shall see strange things..., as, God's coat, Our Lady's smock, part of God's supper.

They also found immorality and corruption, "another priory called Harwood [Bedfordshire], wherein was 4 or 5 nuns with the prioress, one of them had two fair children, another [had] one." But what the commissioners were really interested in was detailed records of lands, rentals, and moveable property. Although the commissioners clearly had little sympathy for the religious orders in general, they also found much to praise: "I went to Godstow where I found all things well and in good order as well in the monastery."[11] Nevertheless, the government dissolved the lesser monasteries in 1536, the greater in 1539, and seized their properties. The widespread sense of disruption following the abolition of monasteries can be seen in the statement of one John Palmer entered in a Star Chamber complaint from the late 1530s: "Do ye not know that the king's grace hath put down all the houses of monks, friars, and nuns? Therefore now is the time come that we gentlemen will pull down the houses of such poor knaves as ye be."[12]

In the autumn of 1536, popular complaints against the Dissolution of the Monasteries, the changing religious regime, the changing Tudor constitution, and general economic malaise fueled a revolt in the North, the Pilgrimage of Grace. A leader of the Pilgrims, Robert Aske (d. 1537), headed their grievances with

The suppression of so many religious houses as are at this instant time suppressed, whereby the service of our God is not well [performed] but also the [commons] of your realm be unrelieved, the which as we think is a great hurt to the common wealth and many sisters be [put] from their livings and left at large.[13]

Aske and the Pilgrims presented the Pontefract Articles (1536, document 3.5) to members of the king's Council in Yorkshire. Why did the Northern rebels feel so aggrieved by the Dissolution? Were any of their grievances peculiar to the North (that is, far from London and Westminster)? Were there distinct religious, political, and economic demands, or were they all interrelated?

Although the king crushed the Pilgrimage and executed Aske, by the end of his reign, Henry was decidedly ambivalent about religious reform. "An Act Abolish-

---

[11]   Richard Layton and John Tergonwell to Cromwell (Aug.–Dec. 1535), in Dickens and Carr, *Reformation in England*, 94–7, from *Three Chapters of Letters Relating to the Suppression of the Monasteries*, ed. T. Wright (Camden Society, o.s., 26, 1843), 58–9, 91–4.

[12]   R. H. Tawney and E. Power, eds., *Tudor Economic Documents* (1924), 1: 19–24, from PRO, Star Chamber Proceedings, Hen. VIII, 6/181.

[13]   York Articles (Oct. 15, 1536), in A. Fletcher and D. MacCulloch, *Tudor Rebellions*, 4th ed. (1997), 131, from PRO; compared with *Letters and Papers, Foreign and Domestic, of the Reign of Henry VIII* (1888), 11: no. 705.

ing Diversity in Opinions" (1539, 31 Hen. VIII, c. 14), better known as the Act of Six Articles, codified some basic beliefs of the Church in order to squelch the "great discord and variance...arisen as well amongst the clergy...as amongst a great number of vulgar people":

First, that in the most blessed sacrament of the altar, by the strength and efficacy of Christ's mighty word (it being spoken by the priest), is present really, under the form of bread and wine, the natural body and blood of our Savior Jesus Christ, conceived of the Virgin Mary; and that after the consecration there remaineth no substance of bread or wine, nor any other substance but the substance of Christ, God and man. *Secondly*, that communion in both kinds is not necessary *ad salutem*, by the law of God, to all persons; and that it is to be believed, and not doubted of, but that in the flesh under form of bread is the very blood; and with the blood under form of wine is the very flesh, as well apart as though they were both together. *Thirdly*, that priests after the order of priesthood received, as afore, may not marry by the law of God. *Fourthly*, that vows of chastity or widowhood, by man or woman made to God advisedly, ought to be observed by the law of God, and that it exempteth them from other liberties of Christian people, which without that they might enjoy. *Fifthly*, that it is meet and necessary that private masses be continued and admitted in this the king's English Church and congregation, as whereby good Christian people, ordering themselves accordingly, do receive both godly and goodly consolations and benefits; and it is agreeable also to God's law. *Sixthly*, that auricular confession is expedient and necessary to be retained and continued, used and frequented in the Church of God.[14]

How are these articles Catholic in doctrine and practice? How are they Protestant? Which of the sixteenth-century authors of the various documents in this chapter would be most satisfied with these articles?

Edward VI (1547–53) succeeded his father as head of both State and Church. Under the Protectorate of his uncle, Edward Seymour, duke of Somerset (ca. 1506–52), the Edwardian Church moved in a more clearly Protestant direction both in theology and in liturgy, with a campaign against images and the dissolution of the chantries. In 1549, the Act of Uniformity established a single legal form of worship, with punishments reserved for those who did not comply. Further, a committee headed by Thomas Cranmer (1489–1556), archbishop of Canterbury, "concluded, set forth, and delivered to his highness, to his great comfort and quietness of mind, [a new liturgy] in a book entitled, 'The Book of the Common Prayer and Administration of the Sacraments, and other Rites and Ceremonies of the Church, after the Use of the Church of England.'"[15] But the new liturgy and Prayer Book was not uniformly accepted. Somerset told nobles in the countryside to expect disturbances, in part, because "in some places...seditious priests and other evil people set forth to seek restitution of the old bloody

---

[14] *SR*, 3: 739–40; compared with Dickens and Carr, *Reformation in England*, 108–12; and C. Lindberg, ed., *The European Reformations Sourcebook* (Oxford, 2000), 223–4.

[15] G. Bray, ed., *Documents of the English Reformation* (Minneapolis, 1994), 266, from *SR*, 4: 37–9, from 3 Edw. VI, c. 1.

laws."[16] Indeed, Devon rose the day after the Prayer Book became the lawful liturgy for all parish churches. Soon the rebels of Cornwall and Devon issued a list of fifteen demands from their camps outside Exeter. Archbishop Cranmer responded to their manifesto point by point (1549, document 3.6). What did the rebels seek? Which of their demands draws Cranmer's fire most and why? You might compare and contrast the 1549 rebel demands with those from 1536 (documents 3.5 and 3.6).

The government crushed the 1549 rebellion, but by the summer of 1553 Edward was dead, and Mary (1516–58), the Catholic daughter of Catherine of Aragon, became queen. She began the process of returning England, Ireland, and Wales to Rome. The First Statute of Repeal rescinded her half-brother's Acts of Uniformity (a second, more Protestant, one had been passed in 1552), as well as Acts concerning the marriage of priests, and ordered a return by December 1553 to the liturgy as practiced under her father. Many towns and parishes had already returned to the old practice, much to the disgust of one radical Protestant in Ireland:

On the twentieth day of August [1553], was the Lady Mary with us at Kilkenny proclaimed queen of England, France, and Ireland, with the greatest solemnity that there could be devised of processions, musters, and disguisings; all the noble captains and gentlemen thereabout being present. What-a-do I had that day with the prebendaries and priests about wearing the cope, crosier, and miter in procession.... [O]n ... the last day of August, I being absent, the clergy of Kilkenny ... blasphemously resumed again the whole papism, or heap of superstitions of the bishop of Rome; to the utter contempt of Christ and His holy word, of the king and Council of England, and of all ecclesiastical and politic order, without either statute or yet proclamation. They rung all the bells in that cathedral, minster, and parish churches; they flung up their caps to the battlement of the great temple, with smilings and laughings most dissolutely...; they brought forth their copes, candle sticks, holy-water stock, cross, and censers; they mustered forth in general procession most gorgeously, all the town over, with *Sancta Maria, ora pro nobis,* and the rest of the Latin litany; they chattered it, they chanted it, with great noise and devotion; they banqueted all the day after, for that they were delivered from the grace of God into a warm sun.[17]

What does this suggest about Irish opinion on the Edwardian Reformation? Is the author, John Bale (1495–1563), a reliable witness? What aspects of Catholicism arouse his hostility most?

Another witness to the Marian restoration, more pleased by it than Bale, was Robert Parkyn (d. 1570), a Yorkshire Catholic priest, whose narrative of the period (ca. 1555, document 3.7) lamented the former changes under Edward.

---

[16] June 11, 1549, N. Pocock, ed., *Troubles Connected with the Prayer Book of 1549* (Camden Society, 1884), 1–2, from PRO, SPD, Edward VI, 7, art. 31.

[17] *The Vocacyon of Johan Bale to the Bishoprick of Ossorie In Irelande his Persecucuions in the same* (1553), fol. 24, 27–27v; compared with *Harleian Miscellany,* 6: 450, 452; and C. Maxwell, *The Foundations of Modern Ireland: Select Extracts from Sources Illustrating English Rule and Social and Economic Conditions in Ireland in the Sixteenth and Early Seventeenth Century,* part 1, *The Civil Policy of Henry VIII and the Reformation* (1921), 50–1.

What changes did the priest find most objectionable between 1549 and 1553? Which affected the most people? Which did he find most pleasing? Was Mary's Counter-Reformation popular?

Martyrs and the New Church Reestablished

While Parkyn might have been correct to note that changes in the service "came to pass without compulsion," the Marian Injunctions of 1554 set up a standard by which the Catholics could purge the clergy. The touchstone was celibacy:

every bishop, and all the other persons aforesaid, proceeding summarily, and with all celerity and speed, may and shall deprive, or declare deprived . . . all such persons from their benefices and ecclesiastical promotions, who . . . have married and used women as their wives.[18]

As numerous clergymen and a small but significant portion of the laity refused to return to the old liturgy and faith, Mary and her advisers initiated persecution. The fires celebrating the restoration of Catholicism soon had a darker significance.

Friday the 25 of January [1555], being the conversion of St. Paul, there was kept a solemn general procession in London. To which about 11 of the clock the King [Philip] and the Lord Cardinal Pole came riding from Whitehall to Paul's Church. This night also were great bonfires made in every parish within London. The which said procession and fires were done to give God laud and praise for the conversion of this realm to the Catholic faith and church, etc. The 28, 29, 30 of January, the lord chancellor, with other bishops, sat in the [cathedral] church of St. Mary Overie in Southwark for heresies, where was condemned for heresy Mr. Hooper, *quondam* [former] bishop of Gloucester and Worcester; and Rogers, *quondam* vicar of St. Sepulchers in London, and one of the prebendaries of Paul's; and [others]. . . . The sheriffs of London . . . sent Rogers and Hooper to Newgate.[19]

Mary ordered that Bishop John Hooper (1495–1555) be among the first

to be burned according to the wholesome and good laws of our realm . . . in the said city of Gloucester, for the example and terror of such as he hath there seduced and mistaught. . . . And forasmuch also as the said Hooper is, as heretics be, a vain-glorious person, and delighteth in his tongue and having liberty, may use his said tongue to persuade such as he hath seduced . . . , our pleasure is . . . that the said Hooper be neither . . . suffered to speak at large; but thither to be led quietly, and in silence, for eschewing of further infection.[20]

We know about Hooper's final minutes from the *Actes and Monuments* (1563) of John Foxe (1516–87), whose popular book created a Protestant martyrology.

[18] Dickens and Carr, *Reformation in England*, 146; compared with Lindberg, *European Reformations Sourcebook*, 229.
[19] C. Wriothesley, *A Chronicle of England During the Reigns of the Tudors, from A.D. 1485 to 1559*, ed. W. D. Hamilton (Camden Society, 1877), 2: 126; compared with X. Baron, ed., *London, 1066–1914: Literary Sources and Documents* (Mountfield, East Sussex, 1997), 1: 266–7.
[20] Goldsmid, *Collection of Historical Documents*, 2: 16–17, from BL, Cott. Libr. Cloop. E. 5.

When he was black in the mouth, and his tongue swollen that he could not speak, yet his lips went till they were shrunk to the gums; and he knocked his breast with his hands until one of his arms fell off, and then knocked still with the other, while the fat, water, and blood dropped out at his fingers' ends, until by renewing of the fire his strength was gone and his hand did cleave fast in knocking to the iron upon his breast. Then immediately bowing forwards, he yielded up his spirit.[21]

As we shall see (chapter 4, document 4.9), a return to Protestantism would produce martyrs to the Catholic faith as well. One might ask, however, what would be the probable immediate impact of such an incident?

Simon Renard, the Spanish ambassador in London, questioned the efficacy of burning heretics.

The people of this town of London are murmuring about the cruel enforcement of the recent acts of Parliament on heresy which has now begun, as shown publicly when a certain [John] Rogers was burnt yesterday. Some of the onlookers wept, others prayed to God to give them strength..., others gathered the ashes and bones..., yet others threatening the bishops. The haste with which the bishops have proceeded in this matter may well cause a revolt....I do not think it well that your majesty [Philip] should allow further executions to take place unless the reasons are overwhelmingly strong....Tell the bishops that they are not to proceed to such lengths without having first consulted you and the queen....Your majesty will also consider that the Lady Elizabeth has her supporters and that there are Englishmen who do not love foreigners.[22]

Is Renard an eyewitness? Is he convincing? How might his position sway what he reports? Foxe (1563, document 3.8) immortalized one of the most infamous burnings under Mary, that of Bishops Nicholas Ridley (1495–1555) and Hugh Latimer (ca. 1485–1555) at Oxford in October 1555. Foxe was a fervent Protestant, who did not become a Marian martyr, but instead fled to the continent as one of the Marian exiles. On what evidence does he seem to base his account? Is he a convincing historian? Next to the Bible, his *Book of Martyrs*, as it became known, became one of the most popular and influential books in the English language (see also plate 3). How might Foxe's history influence the Elizabethan people's view of themselves?

The accession of Elizabeth on November 17, 1558 (d. 1603) signaled the end of the Marian restoration. Under Mary, Elizabeth may have played her cards close to her chest – but they were Protestant cards. Which Church, Henry's, Edward's, or Mary's, was being reestablished by the Elizabethan Injunctions (document 3.9) of 1559? If parochial practice followed these injunctions, how would ritual change, basically for the last time in the century? Roger Martyn (document 3.1) lived through Elizabeth's reign; what do you think he made of the 1559 changes?

[21] *Fox's Book of Martyrs; or, The Acts and Monuments of the Christian Church*, ed. J. Malham and T. Pratt (Philadelphia, 1830), 2: 310; compared with D. L. Edwards, *Christian England* (1983), 2: 18–19, from Foxe, *Actes and Monuments*.

[22] Feb. 5, 1555, *CSP Relating to...England and Spain..., July 1554–November 1558* (1954), 13: 138–9; compared with J. McGurk, *The Tudor Monarchies, 1485–1603* (Cambridge, 1999), 68.

Plate 3 *Thomas Bilney ejected from the Pulpit.* (*Source*: J. Foxe, *Acts and monuments of these latter and perilous days, touching matters of the Church*, 1563, woodcut, © British Library)

Depicted is Bilney's ejection in 1527; he was executed as a relapsed heretic in 1531 (see document 3.2). What does the pulpit represent in Protestant ideology? Compare Bilney's ejectors with his audience in this woodcut. Foxe's book is famous for portraying the Marian martyrs, although this clearly happened under Henry VIII, just before the Henrician Reformation. How are these the "latter and perilous days" for Foxe (relate to the Book of Revelation)?

Finally, imagine that you were a woman baptized in 1525, confirmed in 1537, married in 1549, bearing two daughters in 1552 and 1556 respectively, widowed in 1560, and buried in 1580. What religion would you hold during your life? How many different types of religious ritual would you experience? How different would be the religious experience of your daughters, born in the 1550s but coming of age in the 1570s and living through the rest of Elizabeth's reign?

HISTORIOGRAPHY

Recent historical debate on the English Reformation is plentiful and exciting. P. Marshall, ed., *The Impact of the English Reformation, 1500–1640* (1997) collects key articles. R. O'Day, *The Debate on the English Reformation*

(1986) maps the contours of the dispute, and the chapter "The Reformation and the People" notes how the debate changed in the 1960s from what-did-the-king-know and when-did-he-know-it, to a dispute over how this played out in the parishes. Another summary of the changing nature of English Reformation historiography is found in G. Redworth, "Whatever Happened to the English Reformation?," *HT* 37 (October 1987).

Overall, historians of the English Reformation can be divided as to whether they believe the major impetus for reform came from above or below, and whether they think the Reformation came quickly or was long resisted. A. G. Dickens was one of the first to use the rich provincial records on the Reformation in his *The English Reformation* (1964; 2nd ed., 1989). His view that the Reformation swept England quickly, pushed by anticlericalism and real grassroots Protestantism among the populace, became the standard. Dickens summarizes his argument in "The Early Expansion of Protestantism in England, 1520–1558" (1987, reprinted in Marshall); and he responds to the revisionist argument that the English people rejected official reformation from above in *JEcclH* 36 (1985). D. M. Palliser, "Popular Reactions to the Reformation, 1530–70," in *Church and Society in England: Henry VIII to James I*, ed. F. Heal and R. O'Day (1977) synthesizes the pre-revisionist view.

After several careful local or circumscribed articles (and the monumental *Henry VIII*, see chapter 2), J. J. Scarisbrick announced that "on the whole, English men and women did not want the Reformation and most of them were slow to accept it when it came." He defended this pithy revisionist thesis at length in *The Reformation and the English People* (Oxford, 1984). E. Duffy buttressed the revisionist argument for the strength of Catholicism on the eve of Henrician, Edwardian, and even Elizabethan reform in *The Stripping of the Altars: Traditional Religion in England c.1400–c.1580* (New Haven, 1992). While neither Scarisbrick nor Duffy condenses his magisterial work elsewhere, the section on Mary's reign of Duffy's *Stripping of the Altars* is reprinted in Marshall; and his brilliant microhistory, *The Voices of Morebath: Reformation and Rebellion in an English Village* (New Haven, 2001), is summarized in "Morebath, 1520–1570: A Rural Parish in the Reformation," in *Religion and Rebellion*, ed. J. Devlin and R. Fanning (*Historical Studies* 20, 1997). C. Haigh, *English Reformations: Religion, Politics, and Society Under the Tudors* (Oxford, 1993) is another important contribution; see also Haigh, ed., *The English Reformation Revised* (Cambridge, 1987), in which Haigh's "The Henrician Reformation and the Parish Clergy" and R. Hutton's "The Local Impact of the Tudor Reformations" (reprinted in Marshall) capture the zeal of early Reformation revisionism.

A post-revisionist examination of popular Protestantism, while acknowledging a popular Catholicism, might be said to emerge in the work of D. MacCulloch. See, for example, his brief survey, *The Later Reformation in England, 1547–1603*, 2nd ed. (Houndmills, Basingstoke, 2001). Other works in this vein are S. Brigden, "Youth and the English Reformation" (1982, reprinted in Marshall); and Brigden, "Popular Disturbance and the Fall of Thomas Cromwell and the Reformers, 1539–1540," *HJ* 24 (1981).

Opponents to the Old Church are reinterpreted in A. Hope, "Lollardy: The Stone the Builders Rejected?," in *Protestantism and the National Church in Sixteenth-Century England*, ed. P. Lake and M. Dowling (1987); and J. F. Davis, "Lollardy and the Reformation in England" (1982, reprinted in Marshall). If Protestantism largely came from above, what was the specific source? The court, suggests M. Dowling, "Anne Boleyn and Reform," *JEcclH* 36 (1985); continental exiles, argues N. M. Sutherland, "The Marian Exiles and the Establishment of the Elizabethan Regime," *Archiv für Reformationsgeschichte* 78 (1987). Was the Pilgrimage of Grace political or religious? Political, argues G. R. Elton, "Politics and the Pilgrimage of Grace," in *Studies in the Tudor and Stuart Politics and Government* (Cambridge, 1974, 1983), vol. 3; religious, answers C. S. L. Davies, "Popular Religion and the Pilgrimage of Grace," in *Order and Disorder in Early Modern England*, ed. A. Fletcher and J. Stevenson (Cambridge, 1985). Iconoclasm is examined in Hutton (above) and M. Aston, "Iconoclasm in England: Official and Clandestine" (1989, reprinted in Marshall). On the so-called Prayer Book Rebellion, J. Youings, "The South-Western Rebellion of 1549," *Southern History* 1 (1979) should be contrasted with Duffy's new findings on Morebath (above). To compare the English with the Irish Reformation, see H. A. Jefferies, "The Early Tudor Reformations in the Irish Pale," *JEcclH* 52, 1 (2001).

Several documents printed in this chapter are reinterpreted in important articles, see: C. Harper-Bill, "Dean Colet's Convocation Sermon and the Pre-Reformation Church in England" (1988, reprinted in Marshall); M. Bowker, "The Commons Supplication against the Ordinaries in the Light of Some Archidiaconal *Acta*," *TRHS* 5th ser., 21 (1971) (though more easily approached in J. Guy, "Law, Lawyers, and the English Reformation," *HT* [November 1985]); W. Ullman, "This Realm of England is an Empire," *JEcclH* 30 (1979) (Act in Restraint of Appeals, see chapter 2); and G. Redworth, "A Study in the Formulation of Policy: The Genesis and Evolution of the Act of Six Articles," *JEcclH* 37 (1986).

Finally, two recent summaries of Reformation research are P. Collinson, "England," in *The Reformation in National Context*, ed. B. Scribner, R. Porter, and M. Teich (Cambridge, 1994); and D. MacCulloch, "England," in *The Early Reformation in Europe*, ed. A. Pettegree (Cambridge, 1992).

DOCUMENTS

3.1 *"The State of Melford Church . . . as I, Roger Martyn, Did Know It" (ca. late sixteenth century)*[23]

At the back of the high altar in the said church there was a goodly mount, made of one great tree, and set up to the foot of the window there, carved very artificially with the story of Christ's passion, representing the horsemen with their swords and the footmen, etc., as they used Christ on the mount of Calvary, all being fair gilt, and lively and beautifully set forth. To cover and keep clean all the which, there were very fair and painted boards, made to shut to, which were opened upon high and solemn feast days, which then was a very beautiful show. Which painted boards were set up again in Queen Mary's time [1553–8]. . . .

There was also . . . at the back of the altar, a table with a crucifix on it, with the two thieves hanging, on every side one, which is in my house decayed; and the same I hope my heirs will repair and restore again one day. . . .

Upon Palm Sunday the blessed sacrament was carried in procession about the churchyard under a fair canopy borne by four yeomen. The procession coming to the church gate went westward, and they with the blessed sacrament went eastward; and when the procession came against the door of Mr. Clopton's aisle, they with the blessed sacrament, and with a little bell and singing, approached at the east end of Our Lady's chapel, at which time a boy with a thing in his hand pointed to it, signifying a prophet as I think, sang standing on the turret . . . , *Ecce Rex tuns venit* [Behold your king comes], etc., and then all did kneel down, and then rising up went and met the sacrament, and so then went singing together into the church. And coming near the porch, a boy or one of the clerks did cast over among the boys flowers and singing cakes, etc.

On Corpus Christi day [Thursday after Sunday after Pentecost] they went likewise with the blessed sacrament in procession about the church green in copes [an outer vestment], and I think also they went in procession on St. Mark's day [April 25] about the said green, with hand-bells ringing before them, as they did about the bounds of the town in Rogation week [Monday through Wednesday after Ascension Day], on the Monday one way, on the Tuesday another way, on the Wednesday another way, praying for rain or fair weather as the time required; having a drinking and a dinner there upon Monday, being fast day; and Tuesday being a fish day [when Catholics were required to abstain from meat] they had a breakfast with butter and cheese, etc., at the parsonage, and a drinking at Mr. Clopton's by Kentwell, at his manor of Lutons, near the ponds in the park, where there was a little chapel, I think of St. Anne, for that was their longest perambulation. Upon Wednesday being fasting day they had a drinking at Melford Hall. All the choir dined there, three times in the year

---

[23] W. Parker, *The History of Long Melford* (1873), 70–3; compared with D. Cressy and L. A. Ferrell, eds., *Religion and Society in Early Modern England: A Sourcebook* (1996), 11–13.

at least: *viz.* St. Stephen's day [December 26], mid-Lent Sunday, and I think upon Easter Monday. On St. James's day [July 25], mass being sung then by note, and the organs going in St. James's chapel (which were brought into my house with the clock and bell that stood there, and the organs that stood upon the rood loft) that was then a little from the road, which chapel had been maintained by my ancestors; and therefore I will that my heirs, when time serve, shall repair, place there and maintain all these things again. . . .

On St. James's eve there was a bonfire, and a tub of ale and bread then given to the poor, and before my door there was made three other bonfires, *viz.* on Midsummer eve [eve before June 24], on the eve of St. Peter and St. Paul [eve before June 29], when they had the like drinkings, and on St. Thomas's eve [eve before December 29], on which, if it fell not on the fish day, they had some long pies of mutton, and pease cods, set out upon boards, with the aforesaid quantity of bread and ale. And in all these bonfires, some of the friends and more civil poor neighbors were called in, and sat at the board with my grandfather, who had at the lighting of the bonfires wax tapers with balls of wax, yellow and green, set up all the breadth of the hall, lighted then and burning there before the image of St. John the Baptist. And after they were put out, a watch candle was lighted, and set in the midst of the said hall upon the pavement, burning all night.

3.2 Confession of John Pykas of Colchester (March 7, 1527)[24]

That about a five years last past, at a certain time, his mother, then dwelling in Bury, sent for him; and moved him that he should not believe in the Sacraments of the Church, for that was not the right way. And then she delivered to this respondent one book of Paul's Epistles in English; and bid him live after the manner and way of the said Epistles and Gospels, and not after the way that the Church doth teach. Also, about a two years last past, he bought in Colchester, of [from] a Lumbard [a North Italian, probably a banker] of London, a New Testament in English, and paid for it four shillings. Which New Testament he kept, and read it thoroughly many times. And afterward, when he heard that the said New Testaments were forbaden, that no man should keep them, he delivered it and the book of Paul's Epistles to his mother again. And so in continuance of time, by the instruction of his mother, and by reading of the said books, he fell into these errors and heresies against the Sacrament of the Altar; that he thought that in the Sacrament of the Altar, after the words of consecration, not the *very body* of Christ, but only *bread* and *wine*.

Which heresy he hath diverse time spoken and taught; not only in the house of Thomas Matthew, in the presence of the said Matthew's wife, William Pykas, and Marion Westden, daughter to Matthew's wife; but also in the houses and presences of John Thompson, fletcher [maker of bows and arrows]; Dorothy Lane, Robert Best, Mistress Swain, John Girling; John Bradley, blacksmith, and his

---

[24]   J. Strype, *Ecclesiastical Memorials: relating chiefly to Religion, and the Reformation of it, and the Emergencies of the Church of England, under King Henry VIII, King Edward VI, and Queen Mary I* (Oxford, 1822), 1.i: 121–3.

wife; Thomas Parker, weaver; Margaret Bowgas, the wife of Thomas Bowgas; Mistress Cambridge, widow, of the town of Colchester: and also in the house and presence of John Hubbert, of East Donyland; Robert Bate, of the same; Richard Collins, alias Jonson, weaver of Boxstead; John Wiley, of Horkesley, weaver. Which all and singular persons, often and many times have had communication of the said articles with him ... and did affirm them to be of truth. ...

Also he saith, that he hath taught, rehearsed, and affirmed, before all the said persons, and in their houses at sundry times, against the sacrament of Baptism, saying that there should be no such things: for there is no baptism, but of the Holy Ghost. ... Also he saith, that he hath in the places and presence aforesaid, spoken against the sacrament of confession, saying, that it was sufficient for a man that had offended to show his sins privily to God, without confession made to a priest. Yet notwithstanding this respondent hath yearly been confessed ..., but for no other cause, but that people should not wonder upon him.

Also he saith, that he hath heard diverse preachers preach, and especially Mr. Bylney [Thomas Bilney, censured in 1527 and executed as a relapsed heretic in 1531, see plate 3] preach at Ipswich, that it was but folly for a man to go on pilgrimages to saints; for they be but stocks and stones; for they cannot speak to a man, nor do him any good. And also that men should pray only to God, and to no saints. For saints can hear no man's prayer, for they are but servants. Which after this respondent heard preached, he did publish and declare it to diverse persons, and set it forward as much as in him was. Moreover he saith, that Mr. Bylney's sermon was most ghostly [spiritual], and made best for his purpose and opinions, as any that ever he heard in his life. ...

Also he confesses, that he hath spoken, rehearsed, and affirmed, in the presence and places aforesaid, and diverse other more; against pardons, saying and affirming, that pardons [indulgences] granted by the pope, or other men of the Church, are of no effect. For they have no authority to grant them. ...

Farther, he saith, that he hath now in his custody a book; called *The Pryck of Conscyence* [*The Directory of Conscience?*, 1527], and another of the *Seven Wise Masters of Rome* [1520]; which he had of a friar of Colchester: also a book which beginneth; *O thou most and excellent Lord, etc.* which he had of old Father Hacker, alias Ebbe. Also he had the copy of a book of communication, *Inter Fratrem et Clericum*, of his brother William Pykas, which he lost by negligence about a twelve months past. [Witnessed] by me John Pekas, of Colchester.

3.3 The Opening of the Reformation Parliament (November 3– December 17, 1529) (from Hall's Chronicle, pub. 1548)[25]

According to the summons the king of England began his high court of Parliament the third day of November. On which day he came by water to his place of Bridewell, and there he and his nobles put on their robes of Parliament, and

---

[25] *Hall's Chronicle; Containing the History of England, During the Reign of Henry the Fourth ... to the End of the Reign of Henry the Eighth. ... Carefully Collated with the Editions of 1548 and 1550* (1809), 764–8; compared with Williams, *English Historical Documents*, 597–602.

so came to the Blackfriars church, where a Mass of the Holy Ghost was solemnly sung by the King's Chapel, and after the Mass, the king with all the Lords of the Parliament and Commons which were summoned to appear at that day came into the Parliament chamber, where the king sat in his throne or seat royal, and Sir Thomas More his chancellor standing on the right hand of the king behind the bar, made an eloquent oration, declaring that like as a good shepherd which not only keepeth and attendeth well his sheep, but also foreseeth and provideth for all things, which either may be hurtful or noisome to his flock, or may preserve and defend the same against all perils that may chance to come, so the king which was the shepherd, ruler, and governor of his realm vigilantly foreseeing things to come considered how diverse laws before this time were made now by long continuance of time and mutation of things, very insufficient and imperfect, and also by the frail condition of man, diverse new enormities were sprung amongst the people, for the which no law was yet made to reform the same, which was the very cause why at that time the king had summoned his high court of Parliament. . . .

When the Commons were assembled in the nether [lower] house, they began to commune of their griefs wherewith the spiritualty [clergy] had before time grievously oppressed them . . . , and in especial they were sore moved with six great causes.

The first for the excess fines, which the ordinaries [bishops, religious officials] took for probate of testaments [wills]. . . .

The second cause was the great polling and extreme exaction [taxation], which the spiritual men used in taking of corpse presents or mortuaries; for the children of the defunct should all die for hunger and go a-begging rather than they would of charity give to them the sely [silly] cow which the dead man ought if he had but only one; such was the charity then.

The third cause was that priests being surveyors, stewards, and officers to bishops, abbots, and other spiritual heads, had and occupied farms, granges, and grazing in every country, so that the poor husbandman could have nothing but of them, and yet for that they should pay dearly. . . .

The fourth cause was that . . . spiritual men . . . bought and sold wool, cloth, and all manner of merchandise. . . .

The fifth cause was because that spiritual persons promoted to great benefices, and having there living of their flock, were living in the court in lords' houses . . . ; so that for lack of residence both the poor of the parish lacked refreshing, and universally all the parishioners lacked preaching and true instruction of God's word. . . .

The sixth cause was to see one priest being little learned to have ten or twelve benefices and to be resident on none, and to know many well learned scholars in the university which were able to preach and teach, to have neither benefice nor exhibition.

These things before this time might in nowise be touched nor yet talked of by no man except he would be made an heretic, or lose all that he had, for the bishops were chancellors, and had all the rule about the king. . . .

But now when God had illuminated the eyes of the king, and that their subtle doings was once espied: then men began charitably to desire a reformation, and so at this Parliament men began to show their grudges.

Whereupon the burgesses of the Parliament appointed such as were learned in the law, being of the common house, to draw one bill of the probates of testaments, another for mortuaries, and the third for non-residence, pluralities, and taking of farms by spiritual men....

But within two days after was sent up the bill concerning probates of testaments, at the which the archbishop of Canterbury in especial, and all other bishops in general both frowned and grunted, for that touched their profit, insomuch as Doctor John Fisher, bishop of Rochester, said openly in the Parliament chamber these words: "My Lords, you see daily what bills come hither from the common house and all is to the destruction of the Church, for God's sake see what a realm the kingdom of Bohemia was, and when the Church went down then fell the glory of the kingdom, now with the Commons is nothing, but down with the Church, and all this me seemeth is for lack of faith only."

When these words were reported to the Commons of the nether house, that the bishop should say that all their doings were for lack of faith, they took the matter grievously, for they imagined that the bishop esteemed them as heretics, and so by his slanderous words would have persuaded the temporal Lords to have restrained their consent from the said two bills, which they before had passed....

Wherefore the Commons after long debate, determined to send the speaker of the Parliament to the king's highness with a grievous complaint against the bishop of Rochester, and so on a day when the king was at leisure, Thomas Audeley, the speaker for the commons, and thirty of the chief of the common house came to the king's presence in his palace at Westminster, which before was called York place [the former palace of Thomas Wolsey, archbishop of York], and there very eloquently declared what a dishonor to the king and the realm it was to say that they which were elected for the wisest men of all the shires, cities, and boroughs within the realm of England should be declared in so noble and open presence to lack faith, which was equivalent to say that they were infidels and no Christians, as ill as Turks or Saracens....

After this the king sent for the archbishop of Canterbury and six other bishops, and for the bishop of Rochester also, and there declared to him the grudge of the Commons, to the which the bishop answered that he meant the doings of the Bohemians was for lack of faith, and not the doings of them that were in the common house, which saying was confirmed by the bishops being present, which had him in great reputation, and so by that only saying the king accepted his excuse, and therefore sent word to the Commons by Sir William Fitzwilliam, knight, treasurer of his household, which blind excuse pleased the Commons nothing at all....

The king ... caused two new bills to be made indifferently, both for the probate of testaments and mortuaries, which bills were so reasonable that the spiritual lords assented to them although they were sore against their minds, and in especial the probate of testaments sore displeased the bishops, and the mortuaries sore displeased the parsons and vicars.

3.4   *Answer of the Ordinaries (1532)*[26]

And where, after the general preface of the said supplication [1532, to which the clerics were responding], your grace's Commons descend to special particular griefs, and first report that the clergy of this your realm, being your highness's subjects, in their convocations by them holden within this your realm, have made and daily make diverse factions of laws concerning temporal things, and some of them be repugnant to the laws and statutes of your realm, not having nor requiring your most royal assent to the same laws so by them made, neither any assent or knowledge of your lay subjects is had to the same, neither to them published and known in their mother tongue, albeit diverse and sundry of the said laws extend, in certain causes, to your excellent person, your liberty and prerogative royal . . . , [etc.]

To this article we say that forasmuch as we repute and take our authority of making of laws to be grounded upon the Scripture of God and the determination of Holy Church. . . .

And as concerning the requiring of your highness's royal assent to the authorizing of such laws as have been by our predecessors, or shall be made by us, in such points and articles as we have by good authority to rule and order by provisions and laws; we, knowing your highness's wisdom, virtue, and learning, nothing doubt but that the same perceiveth how the granting thereunto dependeth not upon our will and liberty, and that we, your most humble subjects, may not submit the execution of our charges and duty, certainly prescribed by God, to your highness's assent; although, of very deed, the same is most worthy for your most princely and excellent virtues, not only to give your royal assent, but also to devise and command what we should, for good order and manners, by statutes and laws, provide in the Church. Nevertheless, considering we may not so, nor in such sort, restrain the doing of our office in the feeding and ruling of Christ's people, your grace's subjects, we – most humbly desiring your grace, as the same has done heretofore, so from henceforth to show your grace's mind and opinion unto us, what your highness's wisdom shall think convenient, which we shall most gladly hear and follow, if it shall please God to inspire us so to do – with all submission and humility . . . to maintain and defend such laws and ordinances as we, according to our calling and by the authority of God shall, for his honor, make to the edification of virtue and the maintaining of Christ's faith, whereof your highness is defender in name, and has been hitherto in deed, a special protector.

3.5   *Pontefract Articles (December 2–4, 1536)*[27]

1. The first touching our faith to have the heresies of Luther, Wycliff, Hus, Malanton [Melanchthon], Ellecumpadus [Oecolampadius], Bucerus, Confes-

---

[26]   Gee and Hardy, *English Church History*, 154–8; compared with Bray, *English Reformation*, 57–70.

[27]   Fletcher and MacCulloch, *Tudor Rebellions*, 135–7; compared with *Letters and Papers . . . of the Reign of Henry VIII*, 11: no. 1246.

sio [Confessa] Gemaniae, Apologia Malanctionis [Melanchthon], the works of Tyndale, of [Thomas] Barnes, of [William] Marshall, of Rastall [Raskell], Saint Germain, and such other heresies of Anabaptists thereby within this realm to be annulled and destroyed.

2. The 2nd to have the supreme head of the Church touching *cure animarum* [cure of souls] to be restored unto the see of Rome as before it was accustomed to be, and to have the consecrations of the bishops from him without any first fruits or pension to him to be paid out of this realm or else a pension reasonable for the outward defense of our faith.

3. Item we humbly beseech our most dread sovereign lord that the Lady Mary may be made legitimate and the former statute therein annulled for the danger of the title that might incur to the crown of Scotland, [and] that to be by Parliament.

4. Item to have the abbeys suppressed to be restored unto their houses, land, and goods.

5. Item to have the tenth and first fruits clearly discharged of the same, unless the clergy will of themselves grant a rent charge [rentcharge] in generality to the augmentation of the crown.

6. Item to have the Friars Observants restored unto their houses again.

7. Item to have the heretics, bishops and temporal, and their sect to have condign punishment by fire or such other, or else to try their quarrel with us and our party takers in battle [that is, trial by fire or trial by battle].

8. Item to have the Lord Cromwell, the Lord Chancellor, and Sir Richard Rich, Kt., to have condign punishment, as the subverters of the good laws of this realm and maintainers of the false sect of those heretics and the first inventors and bringing in of them. . . .

13. Item statute for enclosures and intacks to be put in execution, and that all intacks [and] enclosures since *anno* 4 Henry VII [1488–9] to be pulled down except mountains, forest, and parks.

14. Item to be discharged of the quindene [quinzine] and taxes now granted by Act of Parliament.

15. Item to have the Parliament in a convenient place at Nottingham or York and the same shortly summoned.

16. Item the statute of the declaration of the crown by will, that the same may be annulled and repealed.

17. Item that it be enacted by Act of Parliament that all recognizances, statutes, penalties new forfeit during the time of this commotion may be pardoned and discharged as well against the king as strangers. . . .

20. Item to have the statute "that no man shall will his lands" [Statute of Uses] to be repealed.

21. Item that the statutes of treasons for words and such like made since *anno* 21 [Henry VIII, 1529–30] be in likewise repealed. . . .

23. Item that no man upon subpoena is from [River] Trent north to appear but at York or by attorney unless it be directed upon pain of allegiance and for like maters concerning the king.

3.6 Cranmer's Answer to the Fifteen Articles of the Devon Rebels (1549)[28]

When I first read your request, O ignorant men of Devonshire and Cornwall, straightways came to my mind a request, which James and John made unto Christ; to whom Christ answered: "You ask you wot [know] not what." Even so thought I of you, as soon as ever I heard your articles, that you were deceived by some crafty papist, which devised those articles for you, to make you ask you wist [know] not what.…

Your First Article Is This: "We will have all the general councils and holy decrees of our forefathers observed, kept, and performed: and whosoever shall gainsay them, we hold them as heretics."

First, to begin with the manner of your phrase. Is this the fashion of subjects to speak unto their prince, "We will have?" Was this manner of speech at any time used of the subjects to their prince since the beginning of the world? Have not all true subjects ever used to their sovereign lord this form of speaking, "Most humbly beseecheth your faithful and obedient subjects?" Although the papists have abused your ignorance in propounding such articles, which you understand not, yet you should not have suffered yourselves so much to be led by the nose and bridled by them, that you should clearly forget your duty of allegiance unto your sovereign lord saying unto him, "This we will have"; and that saying with armor upon your backs and swords in your hands. Would any of you that be householders be content that your servants should come upon you with harness unto their backs, and swords in their hands, and say unto you "This we will have?"…

But now, leaving your rude and unhandsome manner of speech to your most sovereign lord, I will come to the point.… You say, you will have all the holy decrees observed and kept. But do you know what they be? The holy decrees, as I told you before, be called the bishop of Rome's ordinances and laws: which how holy and godly soever they be called, they be indeed so wicked, so ungodly, so full of tyranny, and so partial, that since the beginning of the world were never devised or invented the like.…

Your Second Article Is This: "We will have the law of our sovereign lord King Henry VIII concerning the Six Articles to be used again, as in his time they were."

Letting pass your rude style…, First, I examine you of the cause of your willful will, wherefore you will have these six articles: which never were laws in no region but this; nor in this realm also, until…[1539]; and in some things so enforced by the evil counsel of certain papists, against the truth and common judgment both of divines and lawyers, that if the king's majesty himself had not come personally into the Parliament house, those laws had never passed. And yet

[28] J. E. Cox, ed., *Miscellaneous Writings and Letters of Thomas Cranmer* (Cambridge, Parker Society, 1846), 163–5, 168, 172–3, 179–80; compared with Williams, *English Historical Documents*, 361–86.

within a year or little more the same most noble prince was fain to temper his said laws, and moderate them in diverse points: so that the statute of Six Articles continued in his force little above the space of one year. Is this then so great a matter to make these uproars, and to arise against the whole realm? . . .

Your Fourth Article Is This: "We will have the sacrament hang over the high altar, and there to be worshiped, as it was wont to be; and they which will not thereto consent, we will have them die like heretics against the holy catholic faith."

What say you, O ignorant people in things pertaining to God? Is this the holy catholic faith, that the sacrament should be hanged over the altar and worshiped? And be they heretics that will not consent thereto? I pray you, who made this faith? Any other but the bishops of Rome? And that more than a thousand years after the faith of Christ was full, and perfect! Innocent III about 1215 years after Christ did ordain that the sacrament and chrism should be kept under lock and key. But yet no motion is made of hanging the sacrament over the high altar, nor of the worshiping of it. After him came Honorius III and he added further, commanding that the sacrament should be devoutly kept in a clean place and sealed, and that the priest should often teach the people reverently to bow down to the host when it was lifted up in the mass time, and when the priest should carry it to the sick folks. And although this Honorius added the worshiping of the sacrament, yet he made no mention of the hanging thereof over the high altar, as your article purporteth. Nor how long after, or by what means, that came first up into this realm, I think no man can tell. And in Italy it is not yet used until this day. And in the beginning of the Church it was not only not used to be hanged up, but also it was utterly forbid to be kept. . . .

Your Fifth Article Is This: "We will have the sacrament of the altar but at Easter delivered to the lay-people; and then but in one kind."

Methinks you be like a man that were brought up in a dark dungeon that never saw light, nor knew nothing that is abroad in the world. And if a friend of his, pitying his ignorance and state, would bring him out of his dungeon, that he might see the light and come to knowledge, he, being from his youth used to darkness, could not abide the light, but would willfully shut his eyes and be offended both with the light and with his friend also. A most godly prince of famous memory, King Henry VIII, our late sovereign lord, pitying to see his subjects many years so brought up in darkness and ignorance of God by the erroneous doctrine and superstitions of the bishop of Rome, with the counsel of all his nobles and learned men, studied by all means, and that to his no little danger and charges, to bring you out of your said ignorance and darkness unto the true light and knowledge of God's word. And our most dread sovereign lord that now is, succeeding his father, as well in this godly intent as in his realms and dominions, hath with no less care and diligence studied to perform his father's godly intent and purpose. And you, like men that willfully shut their own eyes, refuse to receive the light saying, you will remain in your darkness, or rather you be like men that be so far wandered out of the right way that they can never come to it again without good and expert guides: and yet when the guides would tell them the truth, they would not be ordered by them, but would say unto them, We will have and follow our own ways....

Your Eighth Article Is This: "We will not receive the new service, because it is but like a Christmas game; but we will have our old service of matins, mass, even-song, and procession in Latin, as it was before. And so we the Cornish men, whereof certain of us understand no English, utterly refuse this new English."

As concerning the having of the service in the Latin tongue, is sufficiently spoken of in the answer to your third article. But I would gladly know the reason why the Cornish men refuse utterly the new English, as you call it, because certain of you understand it not; and yet you will have the service in Latin, which almost none of you understand. If this be a sufficient cause for Cornwall to refuse the English service because some of you understand none English, a much greater cause have they, both of Cornwall and Devonshire to refuse utterly the late service; forasmuch as fewer of them know the Latin tongue than they of Cornwall the English tongue. But where you say that you will have the old service because the new is "like a Christmas game," you declare yourselves what spirit you be led withal, or rather what spirit leadeth them that persuaded you that the word of God is but like a Christmas game. It is more like a game and a fond play to be laughed at of all men to hear the priest speak aloud to the people in Latin, and the people listen with their ears to hear; and some walking up and down in the church, some saying other prayers in Latin, and none understandeth other. Neither the priest nor his parish wot [know] what they say. And many times the thing that the priest sayeth in Latin is so fond of itself, that it is more like a play than a godly prayer....

Your Tenth Article Is This: "We will have the Bible and all books of scripture in English, to be called in again. For we be informed that otherwise the clergy shall not of long time confound the heretics."...

Although you savor so little of godliness that you list not to read his word yourselves, you ought not to be so malicious and envious to let them that be more godly and would gladly read it to their comfort and edification. And if there be an English heretic, how will you have him confuted but in English? And whereby else but by God's word? Then it followeth that to confute English heretics we must needs have God's word in English, as all other nations have it in their own native language.

3.7   *Robert Parkyn's Narrative of the Reformation (ca. 1555)*[29]

Then was there a great Parliament held at Westminster at London the same winter, beginning the 4th day of November [actually, November 24, 1548] and there continued and kept to the 14th day of March [1549]..., wherein the holy mass was subdued and deposed by Act of Parliament, and none to be used, but only a communion....

---

[29]   A. G. Dickens, ed., "Robert Parkyn's Narrative of the Reformation" (1947), reprinted in his *Reformation Studies* (1982), 298–311; compared with Cressy and Ferrell, *Religion and Society*, 24–9.

After the feast of the Annunciation of Our Lady (*anno domini* 1549), the king's majesty's acts was proclaimed, declaring how it was lawful by God's law priests to marry women, and so many was married indeed.…

Consequently, followed straight monition, yea, and commandment (according to the king's majesty's acts) at visitations after Easter, that no priest should celebrate or say mass in Latin, or minister any sacrament in Latin words after the feast of Pentecost then next following, but only in English (as they would avoid the king's high displeasure and such penalties as was manifest in the said acts). And so the holy mass was utterly deposed throughout all this realm of England and other of the king's dominions at the said Pentecost, and in place thereof a communion to be said in English without any elevation of Christ's body and blood under form of bread and wine, or adoration, or reservation in the pyx, for a certain English book was set forth in print, containing all such service as should be used in the church of God, and no other (entitled the Book of Common Prayer [1549]).…

In the month of December [1550] all altars of stone was taken away…of the churches and chapels from [River] Trent northwards and a table of wood set in the choir.…

A great Parliament held at Westminster and begun the 23rd day of January and then continued and kept unto the 15th day of April…1552, wherein no goodness towards holy church proceeded, but all things contrary. For in the Parliament was deposed [abolished] by act these three holy days [among others] before accustomed to have been kept holy, *viz.* Conversion of St. Paul [January 25], St. Barnabas [June 11], and Mary Magdalen [July 22]; and that a new communion book in English (called the Book of Common Prayer [1552]) should take effect at All Hallows day next ensuing date hereof (*viz.* first day of November), and so the Communion Book in English (which is above mentioned [1549]) to be of none effect. Oh, note the great instability and newfangledness of the heretic Warwick (alias duke of Northumberland) with his adherents, *viz.* carnal bishops of this realm and very traitors to God. For consequently after that Robert Holgate, archbishop of York, was come from the said Parliament, he sent straight commandment in beginning of June through all his diocese that the table in the choir whereupon the holy communion was ministered, it standing with the ends toward south and north, should be used contrary, *viz.* to be set in the choir beneath the lowest stair or grace, having the ends thereof towards the east and west, and the priest his face towards the north all the communion time, which was nothing seeming nor after any good order.…

The virtuous lady Mary…was proclaimed on the 19th of July [1553]…at which proclamation all good people there being present highly rejoiced, giving thanks, honor, and praise unto Almighty God, and so went singing *Te Deum laudamus* into Paul's church.…

In the meantime in many places of the realm, priests was commanded by lords and knights Catholic to say mass in Latin with consecration and elevation of the body and blood of Christ under form of bread and wine with a decent order as hath been used beforetime, but such as was of heretical opinions might not away therewith but spake evil thereof, for as then there was no act, statute, proclamation or commandment set forth for the same; therefore, many one dared not be bold to celebrate in Latin, though their hearts were wholly inclined that way. Howbeit, in August there was a proclamation set forth declaring how the gracious Queen Mary did license priests to say mass in Latin after the old ancient custom, as was used in her father's days....

Thus through grace of the Holy Ghost, the straight of holy church something began to amend and to arise from the old heresies before used in this realm... [and] in many places of Yorkshire priests unmarried was very glad to celebrate and say mass in Latin with matins and evensong thereto....And so in the beginning of September there was very few parish churches in Yorkshire but mass was sung or said in Latin on the first Sunday of the said month [August] or at furthest, on the feast day of the Nativity of Our Blessed Lady [September 8].

Holy bread and holy water was given, altars was reedified, pictures or images set up, the cross with the crucifix thereon ready to be borne in procession, and with the same went procession. And in conclusion, all the English service of laity used in the church of God was voluntarily laid away and the Latin taken up again (not only with matins, mass, and evensong, but also in ministration of sacraments), and yet all these came to pass without compulsion of any act, statute, proclamation, or law....

So to be brief, all old ceremonies laudably used beforetime in holy church was then revived, daily frequented, and used, after that the right reverend Father in God, the Lord Cardinal Pole, legate *a latere*, was entered this realm in the month of November [1554] bringing with him the pope's power and authority.

3.8 Foxe's Account of the Death of Bishops Latimer and Ridley (October 1555, pub. 1563)[30]

Then the wicked sermon being ended, Dr. Ridley and Master Latimer kneeled down upon their knees to my lord Williams of Tame, the vice-chancellor of Oxford, and diverse other commissioners appointed for that purpose, who sat upon a form thereby; unto whom Master Ridley said, "I beseech you, my lord, even for Christ's sake, that I may speak but two or three words."...The bailiffs and Dr. Marshal, the vice-chancellor, ran hastily unto him, and with their hands stopped his mouth, and said, "Master Ridley, if you will revoke your erroneous opinions, and recant the same, you shall not only have liberty so to do, but also the benefit of a subject, that is, have your life." "Not otherwise?" said Master Ridley. "No," quoth Dr. Marshal.... "Well," quoth Master Ridley, "so long as the breath is in my body I will never deny my Lord Christ, and his known truth: God's will be done in me." And with that he rose up, and said with a loud voice, "Well, then I commit our cause to Almighty God, who will indifferently judge all." To

[30] H. Haydn, ed., *The Portable Elizabethan Reader* (New York, 1955), 335–40; compared with *Fox's Book of Martyrs*, 2: 333–4, from Foxe, *Actes and Monuments*.

whose saying, Mr. Latimer added his old posy, "Well, there is nothing hid but it shall be opened."...

Then Master Ridley, standing as yet in his truss, said to his brother, "It were best for me to go in my truss still." "No," quoth his brother, "it will put you to more pain: and the truss will do a poor man good." Whereunto Dr. Ridley said, "Be it, in the name of God," and so unlaced himself. Then being in his shirt, he stood upon the foresaid stone, and held up his hand and said, "O heavenly Father, I give unto thee most hearty thanks, for that thou hast called me to be a professor of thee, even unto death; I beseech thee, Lord God, take mercy on this realm of England, and deliver the same from all her enemies."

Then the smith took a chain of iron, and brought the same about both Dr. Ridley's and Master Latimer's middle: and, as he was knocking in a staple, Dr. Ridley took the chain in his hand and shaked the same, for it did gird in his belly; and looking aside to the smith, said, "Good fellow, knock it in hard, for the flesh will have his course." Then his brother did bring him a bag of gunpowder, and would have tied it about his neck. Master Ridley asked him what it was; his brother said, "Gunpowder." "Then," said he, "I will take it to be sent of God, therefore I will receive it as sent from him. And have you any," said he, "for my brother?" (meaning Master Latimer). "Yea, sir, that I have," quoth his brother. "Then give it unto him," said he, "betime; lest ye come too late." So his brother went and carried off the same gunpowder to Mr. Latimer....

Then they brought a faggot kindled with fire, and laid the same down at Dr. Ridley's feet. Thereupon Master Latimer said, "Be of good comfort, Master Ridley, and play the man, we shall this day light such a candle, by God's grace, in England, as I trust shall never be put out." And so the fire being given unto them, when Dr. Ridley saw the fire flaming up towards him, he cried with a wonderful loud voice, *In manus teas, Domine, commendo spiritum meum: Domine recipe spiritum meum.* And after, repeated this latter part often in English, "Lord, Lord, receive my spirit." Master Latimer crying as vehemently on the other side, "O Father of heaven, receive my soul!" who received the flame as it were embracing of it. After that he had stroked his face with his hands, and as it were bathed them a little in the fire, he soon died (as it appeareth) with very little pain or none. And thus much concerning the end of this old and faithful servant of God, Master Latimer, for whose laborious travails, fruitful life, and constant death the whole realm hath cause to give thanks to Almighty God.

But Master Ridley, by reason of the evil making of the fire unto him, because the wooden faggots were laid about the gorse, and over-high built, the fire burnt first beneath, being kept down by the wood; which when he felt, he desired them for Christ's sake to let the fire come unto him. Which his brother-in-law heard, but not well understood, intending to rid him out of his pain (for which cause he gave attendance) as one in such sorrow, not well advised what he did, heaped faggots upon him, so that he clean covered him, which made the fire more vehement beneath, that it burned clean all his nether parts, before it touched the upper; and that made him leap up and down under the faggots, and often desire them to let the fire come unto him, saying, "I cannot burn." Which indeed appeared well; for, after his legs were consumed by reason of his struggling through the pain (whereof he had no release, but only his contentation in God) he showed that side toward us clean, shirt and all untouched with flame. Yet in all this torment he forgot not to call unto God still, having in his mouth, "Lord, have mercy upon me," intermingling his cry, "Let the fire come unto me, I cannot burn." In which pangs he labored till one of the standers-by with his bill pulled off the faggots above, and where he saw the fire flame up, he wrested himself unto that side. And when the flame touched the gunpowder, he was seen to stir no more, but burned on the other side, falling down at Master Latimer's feet: which some said, happened by reason that the chain loosed; others said, that he fell over the chain by reason of the poise of his body, and the weakness of the nether limbs.

Some said, that before he was like to fall from the stake, he desired them to hold him to it with their bills. However it was . . . , signs there were of sorrow on every side. Some took it grievously to see their deaths, whose lives they held full dear; some pitied their persons, that thought their souls had no need thereof. His brother moved many men, seeing his miserable case, seeing (I say) him compelled to such infelicity, that he thought then to do him best service when he hastened his end. Some cried out of the fortune, to see his endeavor (who most dearly loved him, and sought his release), turn to his greater vexation, and increase of pain. But whoso considered their preferments in time past, the places of honor that they sometime occupied in this commonwealth, the favor they were in with their princes, and the opinion of learning they had in the university where they studied, could not choose but sorrow with tears to see so great dignity, honor, and estimation, so necessary members sometime accounted, so many godly virtues, the study of so many years, such excellent learning, to be put into the fire, and consumed in one moment.

3.9   *The Elizabethan Injunctions (1559)*[31]

[A]ll deans, archdeacons, parsons, vicars, and other ecclesiastical persons shall faithfully keep and observe . . . all and singular laws and statutes made for the restoring to the Crown the ancient jurisdiction over the state ecclesiastical, and abolishing of all foreign power repugnant to the same. . . .

The persons above rehearsed, shall preach in their churches, and every other cure they have, one sermon, every quarter of the year at the least, wherein they shall purely and sincerely declare the Word of God, and in the same, exhort their hearers to the works of faith, mercy, and charity specially prescribed and commanded in Scripture, and that works devised by men's fantasies, besides Scripture, as wandering to pilgrimages, offering of money, candles or tapers to relics, or images, or kissing and licking of the same, praying upon beads, or such like superstition, have not only no promise of reward in Scripture, for doing of them, but contrariwise, great threats and maledictions of God, for that they be things tending to idolatry and superstition. . . .

---

[31] Lindberg, *European Reformations Sourcebook*, 230–1, from Bray, *English Reformation*, 335–8, 341.

Also that they shall provide within three months next after this visitation one book of the whole Bible, of the largest volume, in English. And within one twelve-months next after the said visitation, the Paraphrasis of Erasmus also in English upon the Gospels, and the same set up in some convenient place, within the said church that they have cure of, whereas their parishioners may most commodiously resort unto the same and read the same, out of the time of common service.

CHAPTER FOUR

Elizabethan Worlds

The First Empire, Ireland, Scotland, and the War with Spain
Between Jesuits and Puritans
The Stage and the Globe

DISCUSSION

Through the second half of the sixteenth century, Queen Elizabeth and her subjects excelled in various arenas: exploration and trade, privateering and colonization, plotting and war, faction and religious division, theater and performance. What did the Elizabethans think they were achieving, and how did this compare with what they actually achieved? Elizabethan foreign policy, domestic politics, religion, and literature were all intertwined; although we have tried to distinguish these arenas and their relevant sources, one should also consider how the documents placed at the beginning, middle, and end of this chapter relate to and inform one another. As you read the documents in this chapter, you might ask:

- What achievements made the Elizabethan authors most proud?
- What issues caused the same authors the most anxiety?

The First Empire, Ireland, Scotland, and the War with Spain

By the end of Gloriana's reign, England's first empire included Wales and Ireland, and her subjects had made their first tentative forays into North America at Virginia, named after the Virgin Queen. English exploration largely began when, a hundred years previously, Henry VII encouraged the voyages of a Venetian-born mariner, John Cabot (d. ca. 1499), who sailed from Bristol. Cabot and later explorers sought an illusory Northwest passage to the East Indies, but they did discover the Grand Banks, seas "swarming with fish, who can be taken not only with the net, but in baskets let down with a stone." Indeed, Cabot's English "companions say that they could bring so many fish that this kingdom would have no further need of Iceland."[1] Consider how an empire based on fishing might differ from one based on mining for gold (the basis of Spain's empire, and the initial rationale for the Virginia colony).

A century later, under Elizabeth, George Best (d. 1584), Sir Humphrey Gilbert (1539?–83), and Richard Hakluyt (ca. 1552–1616) lauded the achievements of English explorers, traders, and privateers and sought to expand their country-men's horizons. As Best noted in his 1578 chronicle of the three voyages of Sir Martin Frobisher (1535?–94), for whom Best served as lieutenant,

the valiant courages of men in this later age, within these 80 years..., have so much enlarged the bounds of the world, that now we have twice and thrice so much scope for our earthly peregrination, as we have had in times past, so that now men need no more contentiously to strive for room to build an house on, or for a little turf of ground.[2]

Now examine Gilbert's claims (1578, document 4.1) for the value of exploration. Which seems most convincing? Which least? Is his rationale for explor-ation entirely economic? How does Hakluyt's source for another exploration narrative (1589, document 4.2) distinguish between the Indians of Wingandacoa (Virginia) and his English countrymen? How might such interactions with New World societies (and their government, social structure, and gender relations) affect the way the English thought about their society? Their own history? Progress?

Despite Best's claim that "there are countries yet remaining without masters and possessors," England's best chance for wealth lay in seizing it from others. A handwritten newsletter from Seville in December 1569 reported on the privateer-ing raids of Sir John Hawkins (1532–95) and Sir Francis Drake (ca. 1543–96):

From Cadiz this morning came the following news and immediately after it Don Melendez. He relates how John Hawkins the Englishman...recently passed Cape St. Vincent with twenty-five well-found ships.... There he intercepted a ship trying to make its way to the Netherlands and carried it off together with its entire cargo. The crew he put on land...to inform Don Melendez...that he was proceeding to India [West Indies] and would await them... [there, to call] them to account for the damage...they had inflicted upon him during the previous year. Every one was utterly horrified at these tidings, than which nothing could be worse for the king and the Indian trade, seeing that with a favorable wind Drake must now be close to the Indian Islands. At this juncture the ships from New Spain would certainly be loaded up and on their way, so that the Englishman would have them at his mercy.... And the most annoying part of this affair is that this Hawkins could not have fitted out so numerous and so well equipped a fleet without the aid and secret

---

[1]   Dec. 18, 1497, n.s.?, Raimondo de Soncino at London to Sforza, duke of Milan, in *CSP...Milan* (1912), 1: 336–8; compared with A. F. Pollard, *The Reign of Henry VII from Contemporary Sources* (1914), 1: 333–6.

[2]   [Best], *A True Discourse of the Late Voyages of Discoverie* (1578), *The Fyrst Booke of the First Voyage*, 13; compared with R. Sharrock, *The Pelican Book of English Prose: From the Beginnings to 1800* (Baltimore, 1970), 1: 121–6.

consent of the queen...of England. It is the nature and habit of this nation not to keep faith, so the queen pretends that all has been done without her knowledge and desire.[3]

Why might one subscribe to such letters? What type of information is included? (Hint: This particular one was subscribed to by the Fuggers, an international banking house.) What is the writer's opinion of Hawkins and Drake? Of Elizabeth? Do you suppose the writer's view was the prevailing one in Europe?

Ireland, though nominally under English control, was the despair of many imperial projectors. Sir Henry Sidney (1529–86), Elizabeth's lord deputy, reported to her on Munster in 1567:

Surely there was never people that lived in more misery than they do, nor as it should seem of worse minds, for matrimony among them is no more regarded in effect than conjunction between unreasonable beasts, perjury, robbery and murder counted allowable; finally I cannot find that they make any conscience of sin and doubtless I doubt whether they christen their children or no, for neither find I place where it should be done, nor any person able to instruct them in the rules of a Christian.[4]

How does Sidney differentiate the Irish from the English? Compare his account with Hakluyt's of the Virginian Indians. Would Ireland be fit for Gilbert's own colonial policy as outlined in document 4.1? Irish opposition to English colonization in Munster provoked harsh martial law by Gilbert, acting as Sidney's subordinate. According to one report, he ordered:

that the heads of all those (of what sort soever they were) which were killed in the day, should be cut off from their bodies and brought to the place where he [Gilbert] encamped at night, and should there be laid on the ground by each side of the way leading into his own tent so that none could come into his tent for any cause but commonly he must pass through a lane of heads which he used *ad terrorem*, the dead feeling nothing the more pains thereby.[5]

Perhaps unsurprisingly, such state terrorism did little to settle the island (although Gilbert was knighted for his service there in 1570). The Elizabethan settlement of Ireland succeeded only in suppressing outright rebellion and only after Elizabeth's own death. As a paper prepared by Robert Devereaux, earl of Essex (ca. 1566–1601), in 1599 (document 4.3) suggests, the Irish situation remained complex to the end of the reign. According to Essex, which Irish problems are to be found within the Pale (the "Englishry," some 30 miles around Dublin), and which problems are endemic outside the Pale? How do the English and Irish in Ireland interact?

Some looked to base future empire more on union with Scotland than on Irish settlement. About 1501, when Henry VII's councilors feared that a projected

---

[3]   Dec. 7, 1569, n.s., in V. Von Klarwill, *The Fugger News-letters 1568–1605*, 2nd ser. (1926), 7–8; compared with S. Doran, *England and Europe, 1485–1603*, 2nd ed. (1996), 97–8. Newsletters preceded newspapers and continued through the end of the seventeenth century.

[4]   N. P. Canny, "The Ideology of English Colonization: From Ireland to America" (1973, reprinted in *Theories of Empire, 1450–1800*, ed. D. Armitage, Aldershot, 1998), 189, from PRO, SP 63/20/66.

[5]   T. Churchyard, *A Generall Rehearsall of Warres* [1579], sig. Q[iv]; compared with Canny, "Ideology," 186.

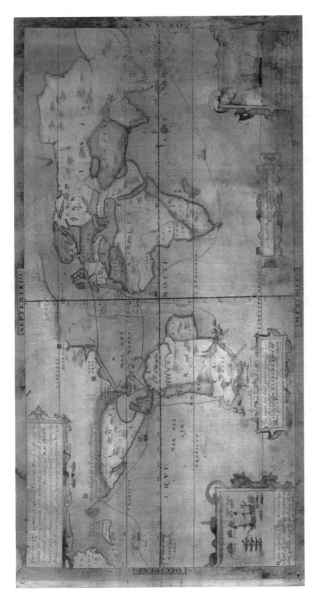

Plate 4 *A True Description of the Naval Expedition of Francis Drake, who with Five Ships Departed from the Western Part of England on 13th December 1577, Circumnavigated the Globe and Returned on 26th September 1580 with One Ship Remaining* (ca. 1587). (*Source*: Yale Center for British Art. Paul Mellon Collection, USA / Bridgeman Art Library)

This map (pen, ink, and wash on vellum, supposedly by Drake himself) was repeatedly reproduced in the sixteenth and seventeenth centuries. What might contemporaries have learned or had confirmed by this map, which plots Drake's privateering circumnavigation? How might this map have been read differently by an English or a Spanish audience? (It may help if you superimpose the Spanish colonial empire in the Americas, Atlantic islands, and Philippines onto this map.) How does this map portray the regions where most sixteenth-century English explorations occurred?

marriage of his eldest daughter, Margaret (1489–1541), to James IV of Scotland (1473–1513) might lead to England's absorption into Scotland, Henry reportedly replied,

what then . . . ? [O]ur realm would not be hurt thereby because England would not come to Scotland but Scotland to England as by far the most superior end of the entire island, since the lesser always is wont for glory and honor to be adjoined to that which is very much greater, after the manner that Normandy formerly came into the dominion and power of our English ancestors.[6]

But "Britain" (England, Wales, and Scotland) remained an unwelcome abstraction for many others. During the last Tudor reign, the longer Elizabeth stayed unmarried, the clearer it became that the line of her cousin, Mary Queen of Scots (reigned 1542–67, d. 1587), would succeed her. If Mary should ascend the English throne, questioned one commentator in 1565,

what should become of us and our country in effect but as bound and subject unto a foreign nation . . . ? Those [Scots] shall be rulers and governors here and we in our country become and made as strangers. . . . And with what mind can we suffer these things of the Scot? [They are] a people by custom and almost nature our enemies, thirsty of our blood, poor and miserable by their country and envious of our welfare.[7]

Compare this English characterization of the Scots with that of the Irish, above. How might the Scots characterize the English?

In 1567, the dynastic problem posed by Mary Queen of Scots became more tangible, as her increasingly Protestant Scottish subjects forced the staunchly Catholic queen first to abdicate (after she married the earl of Bothwell [ca. 1535–78], murderer of her first husband, Henry Darnley [1545–67]), and then to flee to England. As Sir William Cecil (1520–98) wrote to Elizabeth in 1569,

The Queen of Scots indeed is and shall always be a dangerous person to your estate. Yet there be degrees whereby the dangers may be more or less. If you would marry, it should be less; and whilst you do not, it will increase. If her person be restrained either here or at home in her own country, it will be less: if it be at liberty, it will be greater. If she be manifested to be unable by law to have any other husband than Bothwell whilst he liveth [imprisoned on the continent], the peril is the less: if she be esteemed free to marry, it is the greater.[8]

Although Mary was kept under virtual house arrest in the North, she was the touchstone for conspiracies against Elizabeth's rule. Rebellions and conspiracies led by the earls of Northumberland (1528–72) and Westmorland (1543–1601), the duke of Norfolk (1536–72), Robert Ridolfi (1531–1612), Francis

---

[6] M. Levine, *Tudor Dynastic Problems, 1460–1571* (1973), 143, from P. Vergil, *Urbinatis Anglicae Historiae Libri Vigintisex* (Basel, 1546), 608, translated by Levine.

[7] Levine, *Tudor Dynastic Problems*, 180, from BL, Harleian MS. 4627, no. 2, pp. 3–4, 26–7.

[8] Oct. 16, 1569, in D. Starkey, ed., *Rivals in Power: Lives and Letters of the Great Tudor Dynasties* (New York, 1990), 256.

Throckmorton (1554–84), and Anthony Babington (1561–83) dominated dynastic politics from 1569 to 1586. They were fueled by religion, diplomacy, and even the quest for elevated aristocratic status in the face of the Tudor suppression of the nobility. In November 1569, the northern earls, Northumberland and Westmorland, declared their rationale for armed rebellion:

Whereas diverse new set up nobles about the queen's majesty have and do daily, not only go about to overthrow and put down the ancient nobility of this realm but have also misused the queen majesty's own person and have also by the space of twelve years now past set up and maintained a new found religion and heresy.... For the amending and redressing thereof diverse foreign powers do purpose shortly to invade this realm which will be to our utter destruction if we do not speedily forfend [forbid] the same.... These are therefore to will and require you..., for the setting forth of his true and Catholic religion, and as you tender the commonwealth of your country, to come and resort unto us with all speed with all the armor and furniture [equipment] as you or any of you have.... God save the Queen.[9]

What religion do the Northern earls want? What foreign country do they fear? How are these points compatible? Compare and contrast their proclamation with that made by the queen, November 23, 1569:

her majesty manifestly perceiving in what sort these two earls [Northumberland and Westmorland] being both in poverty, the one having but a very small portion of that which his ancestors had and lost, and the other having almost his whole patrimony wasted, do go about through the persuasion of a number of desperate persons..., [to do] certain high treasons against the queen's majesty's person and the realm...: hath thought good that all her good loving subjects should speedily understand, how in this sort the said two earls, contrary to the natural property of nobility (which is instituted to defend the prince being the head, and to preserve peace), have thus openly and traitorously entered into the first rebellion and breach of the public blessed peace of this realm that hath happened ... during her majesty's reign ..., an act horrible against God ... and ungrateful to their sovereign lady, to whom they two particularly have heretofore made sundry professions of their faith.[10]

Are there any points of agreement between rebels and ruler as to the causes of the rebellion? Which case, which interpretation of the rebellion, is more convincing? Though the Northern Rising was crushed, Elizabeth still faced plots and potential risings from English Catholics, as the pope issued a bull excommunicating and deposing the heretical queen the next year (1570). By the 1580s, the English government could demonstrate clear links between domestic conspiracies, Mary Queen of Scots, and projected armed invasion by Spain, all encouraged by Rome.

---

[9]   C. Sharp, ed., *Memorials of the Rebellion of 1569* (1840, reprinted Ilkley, Yorks., 1975), 42–3; compared with J. McGurk, *The Tudor Monarchies, 1485–1603* (Cambridge, 1999), 83; and R. Salter, *Elizabeth I and her Reign* (Basingstoke, 1988), 74–5, from BL, Harleian MS. 6990, f. 44.

[10]   *By the Queene. The Queenes Majestie was Sundry Wayse*...(1569), broadside; compared with A. F. Kinney, *Elizabethan Backgrounds: Historical Documents of the Age of Elizabeth I* (Hamden, Conn., 1990), 103–5.

Thus, when the government arrested Throckmorton for serving as a conduit for letters from Mary Queen of Scots, they discovered

two papers containing the names of certain Catholic noblemen and gentlemen, expressing the havens for landing of foreign forces . . . , [as well as] twelve pedigrees of the descent of the Crown of England, printed and published by the bishop of Ross, in the defense of the pretended title of the Scottish queen his mistress, with certain infamous libels against her majesty [Elizabeth] printed and published beyond the seas.[11]

And in 1585, when Throckmorton implicated the eighth earl of Northumberland (ca. 1532–85, brother of the seventh earl executed for the Northern Rising in 1572), the government felt compelled to reveal his part in an intended foreign invasion, even after the eighth earl committed suicide in prison.

Master attorney showed further, that in summer last, there was taken upon the seas, sailing towards Scotland, a Scottish Jesuit, about whom there was found a discourse written in Italian of a like enterprise to be attempted against England . . . , wherein assurance is made that the earls of Northumberland and Westmorland and . . . all the Catholic lords and gentlemen in the North parts (where the invasion should have been attempted) setting it down . . . that they will join with the foreign forces.[12]

Was there a grand design of foreign and domestic Catholics against Queen Elizabeth? If so, who or what might be the weakest link in any such conspiracy, against which her government might strike? If not, in whose interest was it to say so?

In October 1586, Mary Queen of Scots was tried before a special commission of privy councilors and others at Fotheringhay Castle. When asked to respond to the charges against her, Mary "answered that she was no subject, and rather would she die a thousand deaths than acknowledge herself a subject, considering that by such an acknowledgment she should both prejudice the height of regal majesty, and withal confess herself to be bound by all the laws of England, even in matter of religion." She hit upon the misgivings of Queen Elizabeth herself when she added that answering "should prejudice her own royal majesty, the king of Scots [James VI] her son, her successors, or other absolute princes."[13] The commission convicted Mary. What to do next? Both the House of Commons' as well as Elizabeth's considerations of the problem were printed in one pamphlet (1586, document 4.4). Was the Commons swayed more by religious, diplomatic, domestic political, or personal (that is, their distrust of Mary) reasons? How does

---

[11] *A Discoverie of the Treasons Practised and Attempted Against the Queenes Majestie and the Realme, by Francis Throckemorton* (1584), sig. Aiv–Aii; compared with Kinney, *Elizabethan Backgrounds*, 146–9.

[12] *A True and Summarie Reporte of the Declaration of Some Part of the Earle of Northumberland's Treasons* (1585), 6–7; compared with Kinney, *Elizabethan Backgrounds*, 175.

[13] T. B. Howell, comp., *A Complete Collection of State Trials* (1816), 1: 1169, 1173; compared with J. R. Tanner, *Tudor Constitutional Documents: A.D. 1485–1603* (Cambridge, 1922), 444–5, 447.

the Commons' reasoning compare with that of Elizabeth? (And why is Elizabeth's an "answer answerless"?) One might list the drawbacks for Elizabeth of *any* projected course of action on this issue. Mary was eventually executed on February 8, 1587 at Fotheringhay (see Bucholz and Key, chapter 5). At the place of execution she reportedly said,

Be the bearer of this news, that I die a Catholic, firm in my religion, a faithful Scotch-woman and a true Frenchwoman. God...knows...that I have always desired to see England and Scotland happily united. Commend me to the King my son, and tell him that I have done nothing that could prejudice his kingdom of Scotland.[14]

How did Mary thus define herself and her role at the end? Elizabeth's letter to James VI a few days later focused more on future relations between Scotland and England than on his mother's past:

My dear brother..., I have now sent this kinsman of mine..., to instruct you truly of that which is too irksome for my pen to tell you. I beseech you that – as God and many more know – how innocent I am in this case, so you will believe me that if I had bid aught I would have bid [abide] by it....But as not to disguise fits most a king, so will I never dissemble my actions but cause them show even as I meant them. Thus assuring yourself of me that, as I know this was deserved, yet if I had meant it I would never lay it on others' shoulders, no more will I not damnify myself that thought it not....And for your part, think you have not in the world a more loving kinswoman nor a more dear friend than myself, nor any that will watch more carefully to preserve you and your estate.[15]

Compare this with her response to the Commons. What is Elizabeth claiming and is she believable? Do these sources provide insight into how Elizabeth saw the world? Her style of government?

The trial and execution of the Queen of Scots led to Elizabeth's greatest test: war with Spain. The Anglo-Spanish War had been building since the raids of Hawkins and Drake (see plate 4). It would begin before the intended invasion of England by the Spanish Grand Armada; be fought on three continents; and last until 1604. Thus, it was just as much a test for the seemingly invincible Spanish Empire as it was for England. Both nations hoped God would tilt the balance in their favor. As one senior Spanish officer told a papal diplomat just before the Armada sailed in 1588:

When we meet the English, God will surely arrange matters so that we can grapple and board them, either by sending some strange freak of weather or, more likely, just by depriving the English of their wits. If we can come to close quarters, Spanish valor and

---

[14]   M. M. Maxwell-Scott, *The Tragedy of Fotheringay: Founded on the Journal of D. Bourgoing, Physician to Mary Queen of Scots* (Edinburgh, 1905), 202; compared with L. Yeoman, ed., *Reportage Scotland: History in the Making* (Edinburgh, 2000), 139.

[15]   Feb. 14, 1587, *Elizabeth I: Collected Works*, ed. Leah S. Marcus, Janel Mueller, and Mary Beth Rose (Chicago, 2000), 296; compared with H. Ellis, ed., *Original Letters Illustrative of English History* (1824), ser. 1, 3: 22–5, from BL, MS. Cotton Caligula C.IX, f. 212r.

Spanish steel (and the great masses of soldiers we shall have on board) will make our victory certain. But unless God helps us by a miracle the English, who have faster and handier ships than ours, and many more long-range guns, and who know their advantage just as well as we do, will never close with us at all, but stand aloof and knock us to pieces with their culverins [long-barrel, small-bore cannon].[16]

If Spanish sailors respected English guns, Pope Sixtus V (1585–90) respected Elizabeth:

The pope said he had news from Spain that the Armada was ready. But the English too, are ready. "She certainly is a great queen," he said, "and were she only a Catholic she would be our dearly beloved. Just look how well she governs; she is only a woman, only mistress of half an island, and yet she makes herself feared by Spain, by France, by the Empire, by all. She enriches her kingdom by Spanish booty, besides depriving Spain of Holland and Zealand."[17]

The next three sources discuss England's preparations for the Armada (1588, document 4.5), report on the engagement between the two fleets and its aftermath (pub. 1598, document 4.6), and relate Elizabeth's speech to her troops at Tilbury (1588, document 4.7), respectively. How does the Armada story relate to those of imperial expansion, privateering, the succession, and the Counter-Reformation in England? According to Camden, what is the source of England's strength? According to the Spanish officer? According to Elizabeth? *The Miraculous Victory* (1598), written by a Dutch Protestant in Latin and translated by Hakluyt, was both description and propaganda. What values does it embrace? Why are these actions reported approvingly?

Between Jesuits and Puritans

The Royal Navy and the wind, if not God, disposed of the Spanish at sea, while at home Elizabeth's government sent would-be Catholic conspirators to the unhealthy fenland prison of Wisbech. England was clearly divided in religion, but distinguishing a Catholic from a Protestant remained difficult. By the end of the reign some Protestants as well as Catholics, inside as well as outside the Church of England, disagreed strongly with the religious settlement. The Elizabethan Settlement provoked immediate displays of anti-papist feeling in London, which was perhaps the most enthusiastically Protestant part of the country. For example, on August 24, 1559, during the traditional bonfires at Smithfield fair and elsewhere, crowds burnt Catholic images lately restored under Mary:

against Ironmonger Lane and against St. Thomas Acres, two great [bonfires] of roods and Marys and Johns and other images, there they were burned with great wonder... and the

[16]   G. Mattingly, *The Armada* (Boston, 1959), 216–17; compared with N. A. M. Rodger, *The Safeguard of the Sea: A Naval History of Britain, 660–1649* (New York, 1997), 259.

[17]   April 2, 1588, n.s., *CSP... Venice* (1894), 8: 345–6; compared with J. M. Levine, ed., *Elizabeth I* (Englewood Cliffs, NJ, 1969), 41.

25th day of August, at St. Botolph's without Bishopsgate, the rood, Mary and John, [etc.]..., and books; and there was a fellow within the church[yard?] made a sermon at the burning of the church goods...threw in certain books into the fire, and there they [took away the] cross of wood that stood in the churchyard.[18]

The government encouraged such displays whenever conspiracy loomed. Thus, one Spaniard wrote to Philip (reigned, Spain, 1556–98) on May 14, 1569 that,

They are treating all Catholics with great rigor...and the prisons are full of them. At midnight last night many armed royal officers entered the house of Antonio de Guaras in search of him.... After having taken there from a great number of religious images and crucifixes, as well as figures of Our Lady and the Saints, beautifully carved in bulk and gilded, they carried them through most of the streets in the morning, as if in procession, with great mockery and laughter, saying that these were the gods of the Spaniards.... They burnt half of these images piled on a cart wheel before Guaras's house, and the other half they burnt in the market-place.[19]

Could one use the two preceding comments as evidence for *both* a popular Protestantism *and* a popular Catholicism?

Openly practicing Catholics aside, the restored Protestant Church faced a problem of outward conformity, or, as one manuscript described it, the "Church-Papist; *i.e.* a Papist who attends the Established Church to avoid penalties."[20] Thus Hereford diocese noted that

James Eton of Hereford, chapter clerk to the dean and Chapter and registrar to the dean there, cometh to the church but sitteth so far that, he neither heareth nor can hear, whereat many are offended.... John Vicares, of Hereford, brewer, cometh to St. John's, his parish church...but he walketh up and down in time of divine service in a place so far off that he cannot hear.... John Hareley, of Brompton, Esq., cometh to church, but doth there in the time of divine service read so loud upon his Latin popish primer (that he understandeth not), that he troubleth both the minister and people.[21]

Moreover, outright Catholicism seemed to have revived from the 1570s. By the 1580s, the Jesuits were sending missionary priests into England, trained at colleges at Douai and Rome. The government, which had already prohibited asserting papal authority in England (1563) and importing papal bulls and other instruments from Rome (1571), now outlawed Catholic missionary work (1581, document 4.8), and made all Jesuits in England felonious (1585). Did the 1581 Act, in particular, outlaw Catholicism? What might be the difficulties of enforcing it? The number of Catholic priests executed during Elizabeth's last

[18]   H. N. Birt, *The Elizabethan Religious Settlement: A Study of Contemporary Documents* (1907), 509–10, from BL, Harleian MS. 169, no. 2., f. 32.
[19]   May 9, 1569, n.s., *Calendar of Letters and State Papers...in the [Spanish] Archives of Simancas* (1894), 2: 148; compared with Birt, *Elizabethan Religious Settlement*, 484.
[20]   Birt, *Elizabethan Religious Settlement*, 521, from BL, Harleian MS. 1221, no. 5, f. 65b and 6038, f. 2.
[21]   Nov. 2, 1577, Birt, *Elizabethan Religious Settlement*, 370, from PRO, SPD, Eliz. 118, no. 7i.

decades approached that of the Protestants burned under Mary. William, Cardinal Allen's (1532–94) account of priestly martyrdom (1582, document 4.9) prompted several responses, including one by Lord Treasurer Burghley (Cecil) himself. Why might the English government be so concerned by Allen's publication of the dying words of William Filby?

Strong Protestants had far more reason to be pleased with Elizabeth's accession. John Foxe and others championed her as the English Deborah, leading the English Church out of papist superstition and persecution. But the honeymoon ended by the 1570s: some Protestants saw the Elizabethan Settlement and the Thirty-Nine Articles as just the first step towards further reform, while the queen and some of her bishops viewed further reform as the first step towards anarchy. What was the dispute about? John Field and Thomas Wilcox laid out the Church of England's flaws in a pamphlet in 1572 (document 4.10), and were promptly incarcerated. What type of Church did they want, specifically with regard to Church government (how ministers were chosen), liturgy (how Church services were to be conducted), and Scripture study? Thomas Cartwright (1535–1603), who may have helped compose document 4.10, came to their defense in the *Second Admonition* (1572):

What is there in our books that should offend any that be or would seem to be godly?...The authors...have been, and still are, hardly handled to be sent close prisoners to Newgate, next door to hanging....What, I pray, have they done amiss...? They have published that the ministry of England is out of square. I need not ask what they [the bishops] have answered to that book; for they have answered nothing but that it is a foolish book; but...I trust that will not be taken for a sufficient answer.[22]

This radical or reforming Protestantism took Scripture as its touchstone: "We say the word of God is above the Church; then surely it is above the English Church, and above all the books now rehearsed," that is, above the Book of Common Prayer, the queen's injunctions, and the bishops' canons and articles.[23] Contemporaries labeled them Puritans, as did a German traveling through England in the 1590s:

These according to the doctrine of the Church of Geneva, reject all ceremonies anciently held, and admit of neither organs nor epitaphs in their places of worship, and entirely abhor all difference of rank among ecclesiastics, such as bishops, abbots, etc. They were first named Puritans by the Jesuit Sanders. They do not live separate, but mix with those of the Church of England in the colleges.[24]

The response by some bishops was just as intractable as that of their critics; they wanted the authors removed from London. Whitgift (ca. 1530–1604), who, years

---

[22] [Cartwright], *A Second Admonition to the Parliament* (1572), sig. *iv–*iiv; compared with C. Hampton, *A Radical Reader: The Struggle for Change in England, 1381–1914* (Harmondsworth, Middlesex, 1984), 122–3.
[23] Ibid.
[24] In W. B. Rye, ed., *England as Seen by Foreigners in the Days of Elizabeth & James the First* (1865, reprinted, New York, 1967), 111, from Paul Hentzner, *Travels* (1598).

later, would imprison Cartwright, responded in 1573 to the reformers by identifying them, negatively, as Puritans and, less accurately, as Separatists:

This name Puritan is very aptly given to these men; not because they be pure, no more than were the heretics called Cathari [*katharos*, pure; medieval heretics]; but because they think themselves to be *mundiores ceteris*, "more pure than others," as Cathari did, and separate themselves from all other churches and congregations as spotted and defiled: because also they suppose the Church which they have devised to be without all impurity....For why will they not come to our sermons or to our churches? Why will they not communicate with us in our sacraments, not salute us in the streets, nay, spit in our faces, and openly revile us? Why have they their secret conventicles...? Which if they do, it argueth that they persuade themselves not only of such an outward perfection, but of such an inward purity also, that they may as justly for the same be called Puritans, as the Novatians [third-century schism which rejected concessions to then reigning paganism] were.[25]

Yet the division between reformer and conservative in Elizabeth's Church was never clear. Several bishops, including Edmund Grindal (1519–83), archbishop of Canterbury from the beginning of 1576, supported "prophesyings," gatherings of clergy and laity to discuss Scripture, as a way to ensure both more effective preaching and evangelizing in the provinces. Grindal defended the prophesyings in a letter to Elizabeth, December 20, 1576 (document 4.11), against charges of both "Papistry or Puritanism." Is Grindal's tone appropriate to his audience? Does he say anything that Elizabeth might want to hear? Would you label Grindal a reforming Protestant? A Puritan? Elizabeth did not respond to Grindal until she issued a general letter in May 1577 (document 4.12), but her message was direct. What threats underlie both Grindal's and Elizabeth's statements? (Note that Elizabeth suspended Grindal from his functions as archbishop for five years, forgiving him just before his death.)

As their episcopal support dwindled, Puritans resorted to vicious diatribes against the bishops, led by the pseudonymous Martin Marprelate tracts. A brief excerpt from Marprelate's first *Epistle* (1588) establishes both his mocking tone and his attack on episcopal authority:

Now may it please your Grace, with the rest of your worships to procure that the Puritans may one day have a free disputation with you about the controversies of the Church, and if you be not set at a flat *non plus* and quite overthrown, I'll be a lord bishop myself. Look to yourselves. I think you have not long to reign. Amen. And take heed, brethren, of your reverend and learned brother, Martin Marprelate. For he meaneth in these reasons following, I can tell you, to prove that...those that are petty popes and petty antichrists ought not to be maintained in any Christian commonwealth....They are petty popes and petty antichrists, whosoever usurp the authority of pastors....For none but antichristian

---

[25] *The Defense of the Answer to the Admonition Against the Reply of Thomas Cartwright*, in *The Works of John Whitgift*, ed. J. Ayre (Cambridge, Parker Society, 1851), 1: 171–2; compared with L. B. Smith and J. R. Smith, eds., *The Past Speaks: Sources and Problems in English History*, 2nd ed. (Lexington, Mass., 1993), 1: 298–9.

popes and popelings ever claimed this authority unto themselves; especially when it was gainsaid, and accounted antichristian, generally, by the most churches in the world.[26]

How does the author of this tract want to change the Church of England? Where does he think authority should be vested in the Church? In fact, Church theology at the end of Elizabeth's reign remained Calvinist in doctrine (the preeminence of faith and election or predestination), upon which both Puritans and conservatives could agree. This unity would dissolve only in the seventeenth century.

The Stage and the Globe

In many of the disputes in this chapter – what to do about Mary Queen of Scots, or Catholic priests, or prophesyings – the disputants seem to assume the attitudes of actors, consciously presenting themselves and their arguments to an audience. Self-presentation, artifice, and the cultivation of an appearance of both command and spontaneity were an important part of the training of a Renaissance gentleman, while the Tudor court was the great theater of monarchy, staging numerous set pieces: coronations, marriages, funerals, etc. One contemporary thought that during Elizabeth's coronation pageant "a man ... could not better term the City of London that time than a stage."[27] But Elizabethan London also began to house more permanent stage sets – the first purpose-built theater in 1576; the Globe from 1599. At least 430 different plays were performed in London between 1560 and 1600, and demand was rising (266 of those were presented in the 1590s). Playwrights often wrote about how the world resembled a stage, and how monarchs and politicians were like so many actors with set parts. Witness the following famous excerpts from plays by Shakespeare:

> *Gratiano*: You look not well, Signior Antonio;
>   You have too much respect upon the world:
>   They lose it that do buy it with much care....
> *Antonio*: I hold the world but as the world, Gratiano;
>   A stage where every man must play a part,
>   And mine a sad one. (*Merchant of Venice* [1596–7], 1.1)

> *Northumberland*: And let this world no longer be a stage
>   To feed contention in a lingering act;
>   But let one spirit of the first-born Cain
>   Reign in all bosoms, that, each heart being set
>   On bloody courses, the rude scene may end. (*2 Henry IV* [1597–8], 1.1)

> *Prospero*: Our revels now are ended. These our actors,
>   As I foretold you, were all spirits

[26] *An Epistle to the Terrible Priests of the Convocation House*, in *The Marprelate Tracts, 1588–1589* (Menston, Yorks., facsimile, 1588, 1967), 3–4; compared with Hampton, *A Radical Reader*, 125–6.
[27] L. Manley, ed., *London in the Age of Shakespeare: An Anthology* (University Park, 1986), 285.

> And, like the baseless fabric of this vision,
> The cloud-capp'd towers, the gorgeous palaces,
> The solemn temples, the great globe itself,
> Ye all which it inherit, shall dissolve
> And, like this insubstantial pageant faded,
> Leave not a rack behind. We are such stuff
> As dreams are made on, and our little life
> Is rounded with a sleep. (*The Tempest* [1611–12], 4.1)

It is difficult for us now to think what "all the world's a stage" might mean, because it has become an overused cliché. But consider how the rigid social system of Elizabethan England constrained people to play parts and act suitable to their ranks. Consider the relation between true feelings and acting; or the meaning of the injunction to "act themselves" (Philip Massingham, *The Roman Actor*, 1626). Finally, consider the degree of artifice in Elizabeth's own words and actions. What are her strengths and weaknesses as an actress? Perhaps her most commanding performance was her "Golden Speech" given to members of the House of Commons, November 30, 1601 (document 4.13). While we cannot retrace the full dramatic context of this speech here (see Bucholz and Key, chapter 5), it is important to understand that it followed angry debates in the Commons about monopolies she had given out to her own courtiers, exacerbating a bad economy. So the plot is set in motion. The stage is the queen's own Presence Chamber at court, the audience her loyal Commons – but they are also extras in the drama. The stage directions are that the Speaker of the Commons has just given thanks, and, along with 140 MPs, three low bows to the queen for her proclamation promising to reform the abuse of monopolies, and so the entire cast is kneeling at first. Are there other stage directions within her speech? Do you think this speech was effective? Was her audience charmed? Persuaded? Why or why not?

HISTORIOGRAPHY

Debate on the first British Empire has long been exclusively concerned with the fate of the eventual thirteen colonies huddled between the Alleghenies and the Atlantic, to the relative exclusion of Grand Banks fishing, the West Indies, and Ireland. But chapters by N. Canny and J. C. Appleby in *The Oxford History of the British Empire*, vol. 1, *The Origins of Empire: British Overseas Enterprise to the Close of the Seventeenth Century*, ed. Canny (Oxford, 1998) correct this imbalance. See also essays on early modern Ireland by K. S. Bottigheimer and B. Bradshaw in *The Westward Enterprise: English Activities in Ireland, the Atlantic and America, 1480–1650*, ed. K. R. Andrews, N. P. Canny, and P. E. H. Hair (Detroit, 1979); as well as relevant essays on the Gaelic experience in B. Bradshaw and J. S. Morrill, eds., *The British Problem, 1534–1707* (1996); S. Ellis and S. Barber, eds., *Conquest and Union: Fashioning a British State, 1485–1725* (1995); and

B. Bradshaw and P. Roberts, eds., *British Consciousness and Identity: The Making of Britain, 1533–1707* (Cambridge, 1998).

The empire was, of course, an imaginative construction more than a geographical entity – see D. Armitage, "The New World in British Historical Thought," in *America in European Consciousness, 1493–1750*, ed. K. O. Kupperman (Chapel Hill, 1995); D. B. Quinn, "Renaissance Influences in English Colonization," *TRHS* 5th ser., 26 (1976); and N. P. Canny, "The Ideology of English Colonization: From Ireland to America" (1973, reprinted in *Theories of Empire, 1450–1800*, ed. D. Armitage, Aldershot, 1998). Hakluyt's literary construction is well analyzed in R. Helgerson, "The Voyages of a Nation," in *Forms of Nationhood: The Elizabethan Writing of England* (Chicago, 1992). More tendentious, but useful, counterfoils are advanced in S. Greenblatt, ed., *New World Encounters* (Berkeley, 1993); or K. F. Hall, *Things of Darkness: Economies of Race and Gender in Early Modern England* (Ithaca, 1995).

Essays by I. A. A. Thompson and S. Adams in M. J. Rodriguez-Salgado and Adams, eds., *England, Spain, and the Gran Armada, 1584–1604* (Edinburgh, 1991) put the Armada in the context of 1580s naval warfare; while F. Fernández-Armesto, "Armada Myths: *The* Formative Phase," in *God's Obvious Design: Papers for the Spanish Armada Symposium, Sligo, 1998*, ed. P. Gallagher and D. W. Cruickshank (1990) tries to remove it from constructs written since then. S. Adams also surveys Tudor relations with the world in J. Morrill, ed., *The Oxford Illustrated History of Tudor and Stuart Britain* (Oxford, 1986); and in P. Collinson, ed., *The Sixteenth Century, 1485–1603* (2002). See also K. R. Andrews, "Elizabethan Privateering," in *Raleigh in Exeter 1985: Privateering and Colonisation in the Reign of Elizabeth I*, ed. J. Youings (Exeter, 1985).

Essays by P. Collinson, S. Adams, and P. Williams, reprinted in *The Tudor Monarchy*, ed. J. Guy (1997), detail the ideology, the favorites, and the business of the Elizabethan court. For the construction of Elizabethan politics, see N. Jones, "Elizabeth's First Year: The Conception and Birth of the Elizabethan Political World," in *The Reign of Elizabeth I*, ed. C. Haigh (1984). The brief S. Bassnett, *Elizabeth I: A Feminist Perspective* (Oxford, 1988) is one of a number of similar studies, although it is hard to imagine *not* gendering study of a monarch whose own officers complained (though not, of course, to her face) of serving "a base bastard pissing kitchen woman."[28] F. Teague examines Elizabeth's obvious writing skills in "Queen Elizabeth in Her Speeches," in *Gloriana's Face: Women, Public and Private in the English Renaissance*, ed. S. P. Cerasano and M. Wynne-Davies (Detroit, 1992). C. Levin, "'We shall never have a merry world while

---

[28] 1592, lord deputy in Ireland, in G. B. Harrison, ed., *The Elizabethan Journals* (Ann Arbor, 1938), 126; compared with C. Haigh, *Elizabeth I* (1988), 9.

the Queene lyveth': Gender, Monarchy, and the Power of Seditious Words," and the other articles in *Dissing Elizabeth: Negative Representations of Gloriana*, ed. T. M. Walker (Durham, North Car., 1998), reveal a more clouded contemporary verdict on Elizabeth's strengths. C. Levin, *The Reign of Elizabeth I* (Basingstoke, 2001) and C. Haigh, *Elizabeth I*, 2nd ed. (1998) provide brief, analytical overviews of the queen and her reign.

As we noted in chapter 3, many historians now argue that the change from Catholicism to Protestantism was slow, grudging, and the subject of several Reformations. A synthesis of how the revisionist position has changed our understanding is G. W. Bernard, "The Church of England, *c.*1590–*c.*1642," *History* 75 (1990). D. MacCulloch also discusses the multiple Reformations question directly in "The Impact of the English Reformation," *HJ* 38 (1995). C. Durston and J. Eales, eds., *The Culture of English Puritanism 1560–1700* (Basingstoke, 1996) contains an important essay by P. Collinson, "Elizabethan and Jacobean Puritanism as Forms of Popular Culture." N. Tyacke, ed., *England's Long Reformation, 1500–1800* (1998) includes revisionist essays by Tyacke, E. Duffy (with comment by Collinson), P. Lake and M. Questier, and J. Gregory. On debates within the English Church, historians have differed as to whether or not Puritanism existed. See P. G. Lake, "Calvinism and the English Church, 1570–1635," *P & P* 114 (1987), for a start.

For post-Reformation English Catholic history, see C. Haigh, "From Monopoly to Minority: Catholicism in Early Modern England," *TRHS* 31 (1981). P. McGrath has two responses to Haigh's position, in *JEcclH* 35 (1984) and *JEcclH* 36 (1985). See also *The Reckoned Expense: Edmund Campion and the Early English Jesuits*, ed. T. M. McCoog (1996), especially the essay by M. Questier; and his "What Happened to English Catholicism after the Reformation?," *History* 85 (2000).

DOCUMENTS

4.1 Sir Humphrey Gilbert, A New Passage to Cataia, "What commodities would ensue, this passage once discovered" (1578)[29]

1. First, it were the only way for our princes to possess the wealth of all the East parts (as they term them) of the world, which is infinite ..., which would be a great advancement to our country, wonderful enriching to our prince, and unspeakable commodities to all the inhabitants of Europe.
2. For through the shortness of the voyage, we would be able to sell all manner of merchandise, brought from thence, far better cheap, than either the Portuguese

---

[29] Gilbert, *A Discourse Of a Discoverie for a Newe Passage to Cataia* (Menston, Yorks., facsimile, 1576, 1972), sig. Hi–Hiiv; compared with Sharrock, *English Prose*, 1: 119–21.

or Spaniard doth, or may do: And further, share with the Portuguese in the East, and the Spaniard in the West, by trading to any part of America, through *Mare de Sur* [South Seas, Pacific Ocean], where they can no manner of way offend us.

3. Also we may sail to diverse marvelous rich countries, both civil and others, out of both their jurisdictions, trades, and trafficks, where there is . . . merchandise of an inestimable price. . . .

4. Also we might inhabit some part of those countries and settle there such needy people of our country which now trouble the commonwealth and, through want here at home, are enforced to commit outrageous offenses, whereby they are daily consumed with the gallows. . . .

6. Beside the offering of our country commodities, which the Indians, etc. much esteem . . . , they would have the cloths of this our country, so that there would be found a far better vent [market] for them, by this means, than yet this realm ever had, and that without depending, either upon France, Spain, Flanders, Portugal, Hamburg, Emden, or any other part of Europe.

7. Also, hereby we shall increase both our ships and mariners without burdening of the state.

8. And also have occasion to let poor men's children to learn handicrafts, and thereby to make trifles and such like, which the Indians and those people do much esteem: by reason whereof, there should be no occasion, to have our country encumbered with loiterers, vagabonds, and suchlike idle persons. . . .

Thus have I briefly showed you, some part of the grounds of mine opinion, trusting that you will no longer judge me fantastick in this matter: seeing I have conceived no hope of this voyage, but am persuaded thereunto, by the best cosmographers of our age, the same being confirmed, both by reason and certain experiences.

4.2   Richard Hakluyt, The First English Voyage Made to the Coasts of America (1589)[30]

The second of July [1584], we [including Arthur Barlow, chronicler of this voyage] found shoal water, where we smelt so sweet and so strong a smell . . . , by which we were assured, that the land could not be far distant; and keeping good watch . . . , the fourth of the same month we arrived upon the coast. . . .

We remained by the side of this island two whole days before we saw any people of the country. The third day we espied one small boat rowing towards us having in it three persons. This boat came to the island side, four harquebus-shot from our ships, and there two of the people remaining, the third came along the shoreside towards us. . . . Captain Philip Amadas, myself, and others rowed to the land, whose coming this fellow attended, never making any show of fear or doubt. And after he had spoken of many things not understood by us, we brought him with his own good liking, aboard the ships, and gave him a shirt, a hat and

---

[30]   Hakluyt, *Voyages and Discoveries: The Principall Navigations, Voyages, Traffiques, and Discoveries of the English Nation* (2nd ed., 1598–1600), ed. J. Beeching (Harmondsworth, Middlesex, 1972), 270–2; compared with Sharrock, *English Prose*, 1: 129–35.

some other things, and made him taste of our wine, and our meat, which he liked very well. . . .

The next day there came unto us diverse boats, and in one of them the king's brother, accompanied with forty or fifty men, very handsome and goodly people, and in their behavior as mannerly and civil as any of Europe. His name was Granganimeo, and the king is called Wingina, the country Wingandacoa, and now by her majesty Virginia. . . . After he had made a long speech unto us, we presented him with diverse things, which he received very joyfully, and thankfully. None of the company durst speak one word all the time. . . .

After we had presented this [the king's] brother with such things as we thought he liked, we likewise gave somewhat to the others that sat with him on the mat. But presently he arose and took all from them and put it into his own basket, making signs and tokens, that all things ought to be delivered to him, and the rest were but his servants and followers. A day or two after this, we fell to trading with them, exchanging some things that we had, for chamois, buff [buffalo leather], and deer skins. When we showed him all our packet of merchandise, of all things that he saw, a bright tin dish most pleased him, which he presently took up and clapped it before his breast, and after made a hole in the brim thereof and hung it about his neck, making signs that it would defend him against his enemies' arrows: for those people maintain a deadly and terrible war, with the people and king adjoining. We exchanged our tin dish for twenty skins, worth twenty crowns [100 shillings, five pounds], or twenty nobles [ten pounds?], and a copper kettle for fifty skins worth fifty crowns. They offered us good exchange for our hatchets, and axes, and for knives, and would have given anything for swords, but we would not depart with any. After two or three days the king's brother came aboard the ships and drank wine, and eat of our meat and of our bread, and liked exceedingly thereof. And after a few days overpassed, he brought his wife with him to the ships, his daughter and two or three children. His wife was very well favored, of mean stature, and very bashful. She had on her back a long cloak of leather, with the fur side next to her body, and before her a piece of the same; about her forehead she had a band of white coral, and so had her husband many times; in her ears she had bracelets of pearls hanging down to her middle . . . , and those were of the bigness of good peas. The rest of her women of the better sort had pendants of copper hanging in either ear, and some of the children of the king's brother and other noble men, have five or six in either ear: he himself had upon his head a broad plate of gold, or copper, for being unpolished we knew not what metal it should be, neither would he by any means suffer us to take it off his head, but feeling it, it would bow very easily. His apparel was as his wives, only the women wear their hair long on both sides, and the men but on one. . . .

After that . . . , there came down from all parts great store of people, bringing with them leather, coral, diverse kinds of dies very excellent, and exchanged with us. But when Granganimeo the king's brother was present, none durst trade but himself, except such as wear red pieces of copper on their heads like himself – for that is the difference between the noble men, and the governors of countries, and the meaner sort. And we both noted there, and you have understood since by these men, which we brought home, that no people in the world carry more respect to their king, nobility, and governors, than these do.

4.3 Earl of Essex, "The State of Ireland, as it appeared... during the Rebellion in 1599" (1599)[31]

The chief causes of want [lack] of reformation in Ireland arise,

1. From the [Protestant] Churches for the most part, in general, being decayed so as the laws of God are not in any good sort or order therein ministered.
2. The good instructions delivered to governors from England, not put into execution. . . .
3. No shire halls, nor other places fit for the ordinary administration of justice there.
4. No circuits nor quarter sessions there kept, as becometh.
5. The disorders of soldiers not punished.
6. The disorders of purveyors not corrected.
7. The joining in marriage, fostering, and allying of the Irishry with the English subjects.
8. No English laws or orders put in execution, or administered in Irish countries, where the English do govern.
9. No restitution made to the subjects of the Pale for any spoils on them committed by the Irishry.
10. The selling of horse armor, weapons, munition, and furniture by the English subjects to the Irishry, and paying of great customs and duties in the Irish markets by the English subjects.
11. The great want of English tenants throughout the Pale.
12. The want of armor, weapons, munition, and furniture by the subjects of the Pale, and want of skill for lack of exercise, how to use English weapons.
13. The want of schools throughout the Pale, either to learn younglings the English tongue, or to instruct the elder sort in rules of humanity.
14. The want of gaol-houses for to imprison offenders; by reason whereof private subjects do imprison within their own houses for their particular causes; and likewise upon agreement with the parties, do also enlarge [set free], by which occasion, force is holden in many places for law. . . .
15. A number of idle people – horsemen, kern [poor Irish foot-soldier], galloglass [Irish armed retainer], and such like, with their followers, and dependers – do live traveling the Pale, and consuming the poor inhabitants thereof in eating their meat and drink. . . .
19. Item, The borderers of the Pale bringing up their children after the savage and Irish manner, setting them at liberty at the age of sixteen years, or thereabouts, with companies of kern, to live unbridled by the spoil.
20. The not using English apparel and English behavior by many great gentlemen on the borders, of English birth.

---

[31] H. Harington, ed., *Nugae Antiquae: Being a Miscellaneous Collection of Original Papers in Prose and Verse; Written in the Reigns of Henry VIII, Queen Mary, Elizabeth, King James, &c., By Sir John Harington* (1779), 2: 294–303.

21. Item, The maintaining of Irish harpers, rhymers, bards, poets, and such other their likes, in the Pale together, proving that the Irish behavior is too perfectly learned.
22. Item, The merchants of the Pale do not bring English bows and armor, as by the laws they are appointed. . . .
23. Item, The leaving of English castles and border lands waste by the English subjects, or setting the same to some Irish gentlemen that have made free passages into many places of the Pale for Irishry. . . .
25. Item, The using to parley by borderers with the Irish neighbors privately. . . , and joining with them in great league of friendship; by means whereof the secret service, intended by governors on their appointments, have been . . . made known to the rebels. . . .
26. Item, Loose, idle, and naughty people of the Irish countries, by whom the subjects are most offended, are not answered for, nor brought in by the captains or chieftains of the Irish. . . .
27. The relieving of the Irishry with *aqua vitae* [distilled alcohol], made plentifully in the Pale, and to them conveyed as well in time of peace, as during their rebellion. . . .
28. Item, The want of good laborers, handicraftsmen, and artificers. . . .
29. The black rents [blackmail] and tributes, paid by the English subjects to the Irish neighbors, doth weaken the subject, and strengthen the enemy very much.
30. Item, The hue and cry not followed in form of law, on any robbery or spoils committed by the rebels. . . .
31. Item, The spiritualities and temporalities [bishops and nobles] do not maintain the number of men appointed them by the laws, for the defense of the realm, to the distrengthening thereof.
32. The sheriffs and under-sheriffs of the English counties do use to accompany themselves with kern and suchlike Irish helpers, in . . . doing of their offices. . . .

For all which abuses and defects there are many good laws; yet such hath been the negligent execution of them, that they are at this time little regarded; therefore no hope of reformation, until the said laws are executed, or such as shall be thought necessary, without respect of persons.

4.4 The House of Commons' Report on Mary Queen of Scots and Elizabeth's Reply (November 24, 1586)[32]

A summary report of the second speech, uttered by the speaker of the Lower House, by direction of all the Commons.

That if her majesty should be safe without taking away the life of the Scottish queen, the same were most likely and probably to grow, by one of these means following:

[32] [R. C.], *The Copie of a Letter to the Right Honourable the Earle of Leycester* (1586), 23–8, 32; compared with Kinney, *Elizabethan Backgrounds*, 230–6.

1. First, that happily she might be reclaimed and become a repentant convert, [acknowledging] her majesty's great mercy and favors in remitting her heinous offense....
2. Or else, by a more straight guard be so kept, as there should be no fear of the like attempts hereafter.
3. Or, that good assurance might be given by oath, bonds, or hostages, as cautions for her good and loyal demeanor from henceforth.
4. Or lastly, by banishment, the realm might be voided of her person, and thereby the perils further removed, that grow to her majesty by her presence.

The moments whereof being duly pondered, did yet appear so light in all their judgments, that they [the Council] durst not advise any security to rest in any, no not in all of them.

For touching her conversion, it was considered, that if piety or duty could have restrained her from such heinous attempts, there was cause abundantly ministered to her on her majesty's behalf, when she [Elizabeth] not only protected her against the violence of her own subjects, who pursued her to death by justice, but covered her honor when the same by public fame was touched, and by very heinous and capital crimes objected and proved against her..., more than blemished, and spared her life, when for her former conspiracies and confederacies with the Northern rebels, her highness was with great instance pressed by both the houses in... [1572], to do like justice upon her, as now is desired, and as her treasonable practices then, had most justly deserved....

She hath nevertheless insisted in her former practices, as a person obdurate in malice against her majesty, and irrecoverable....

As for a surer guard, and more strait imprisonment, it was resolved that there was no security therein, nor yet in the other two means propounded of bonds and hostages: forasmuch as the same means that should be practiced to take her majesty's life away (which God forbid) would aptly serve both for the delivery of her person, and release of the bonds and hostages that should be given for cautions in that behalf....

But she will solemnly vow and take an oath that she will not attempt anything to the hurt of her majesty's person: She hath already sundry times falsified her word, her writing, and her oath, and holdeth it for an article of religion, that faith is not to be holden with heretics, of which sort she accounteth your majesty, and all the professors of the Gospel to be....

As for banishment, that were a step *à malo in peius* [growing worse by degrees] to set her at liberty: a thing so greatly desired and thirsted for by her adherents, and by some princes her allies, who sought her enlargement chiefly to make her a head to be set up against her majesty in time of invasion.

To the which were added some few reasons, collected out of her own letters and the confession of Babington, her instrument and chief conspirator.... And in that she directed Babington, in case he failed in the action of her delivery, that he should nevertheless proceed in the residue, which was the death of her majesty.... And therefore, her majesty's death being so earnestly sought, for advancement of this competitor, her highness could not remain in quietness or security, if the Scottish queen should longer continue her life.

The second answer made by the queen's majesty, delivered by her own mouth, to the second speech, uttered in the names of the Lords and Commons of the Parliament. . . .

I have strived more this day than ever in my life, whether I should speak, or use silence. If I speak and not complain, I shall dissemble; if I hold my peace, your labor taken were full vain. . . . Yet such I protest hath been my greedy desire and hungry will, that of your consultation might have fallen out some other means to work my safety joined with your assurance . . . as I protest, I must needs use complaint, though not of you, but unto you, and of the cause: for that I do perceive by your advices, prayers, and desires, there falleth out this accident, that only my injurer's bane, must be my life's surety.

But if any there live so wicked of nature, to suppose, that I prolonged this time only, *pro forma*, to the intent to make a show of clemency, thereby to set my praises to the wire-drawers to lengthen them the more: they do me so great a wrong, as they can hardly recompense. . . . It was of a willing mind and great desire I had, that some other means might be found out, wherein I should have taken more comfort, than in any other thing under the Sun. And since now it is resolved that my surety can not be established without a princess' end, I have just cause to complain, that I, who have in my time pardoned so many rebels, winked at so many treasons, and either not produced them, or altogether slipt them over with silence, should now be forced to this proceeding, against such a person. . . .

And now for your petition, I shall pray you for this present, to content yourselves with an answer without answer. Your judgment I condemn not, neither do I mistake your reasons, but pray you to accept my thankfulness, excuse my doubtfulness, and take in good part my answer answerless. . . . Therefore if I should say, I would not do what you request, it might peradventure be more than I thought: and to say I would do it, might perhaps breed peril of that you labor to preserve, being more than in your own wisdoms and discretions would seem convenient.

4.5 *William Camden,* Annals *(1588)*[33]

Queen Elizabeth . . . prepared with all diligence imaginable as strong a fleet as she could, and all things necessary for war. . . . The command of the whole fleet she gave to Charles Lord Howard of Effingham, lord admiral of England . . . , whom she knew, by his moderate and noble carriage, to be skillful in sea-matters . . . , and of great authority and esteem amongst the sea-men of her navy. Him she sent early to the western parts of England, where Drake, whom she appointed viceadmiral joined with him. The Lord Henry Seymour, second son to the duke of Somerset, she commanded to lie upon the coast of the Low-Countries with 40

---

[33] Camden, *The History of the Most Renowned and Victorious Princess Elizabeth, Late Queen of England* (Chicago, 1970), 311–14, 319, from Camden, *Annals*.

ships, English and Netherlandish [Protestant rebels], and to take care that the prince [duke] of Parma [Spanish regent of the Netherlands] came not out to sea with his forces. Though some there were who earnestly persuaded her to expect the enemy's coming, and to welcome him with a land battle. . . .

For land-service there were disposed along the southern coasts 20,000 men. Besides which two armies were raised of choice well-disciplined and experienced men: the one under the command of the earl of Leicester, consisting of 1,000 horse and 22,000 foot; which encamped at Tilbury, not far from the Thames mouth (for the enemy was fully resolved to set first upon London), the other under the leading of the Lord Hundsdon, consisting of 34,000 foot and 2,000 horse, to guard the queen's person. . . .

In this troublesome season, some beat it many times into the queen's head, that the Spaniards abroad were not so much to be feared as the Papists at home; for the Spaniards would not attempt any hostility against England but upon confidence of help from them: and that therefore, for better security, the heads of that party were upon some pretense or other to be taken off. . . . But the queen, disliking this as cruel counsel, thought it sufficient to commit some of the Papists, and those not of the chief, to custody at Wisbech in the Fens. And having her eyes and mind every way, she by frequent letters excited and quickened the Estates [Lords and Commons], who were not asleep the while. Sir William Fitz-Williams, lord deputy of Ireland, she directed what he should do. The king of Scots she put in mind by her friends in Scotland, and by messengers, to be very wary of the Papists and the Spanish faction. But he, not ignorant how great a tempest and destruction hung overhead, was of his own accord forward and careful, and, according to his continual good affection to the true religion and the queen . . . , had procured a confederacy to be entered into by the Protestants of Scotland for resisting the Spaniards. . . .

On the 16th day [of July] there was a great calm, and a thick fog till noon: then the Northeast wind blew very strongly, and presently after the West wind, till midnight, and then the East-southeast wind; insomuch as the Spanish fleet being dispersed thereby was hardly gathered together again till it came within sight of England on the 19th day. Upon which day the lord admiral of England, being certainly informed . . . that the Spanish fleet was entered into the British Sea (which the sea-men ordinarily call the Channel) and was seen near the point called the Lizard, towed the English fleet forth into the main sea, not without great difficulty, the wind blowing stiffly into the haven. . . .

The next day the English discovered the Spanish fleet with lofty turrets like castles, in front like a half-moon, the wings thereof spreading out about the length of seven miles, sailing very slowly, though with full sails, the winds being as it were tired with carrying them, and the ocean groaning under the weight of them; which they willingly suffered to pass by, that they might chase them in the rear with a fore right wind.

4.6   The Miraculous Victory Atchieved by the English Fleete *(pub. 1598)*[34]

The... 22 July, Sir Francis Drake espied [Don Pedro de] Valdez his ship, where-unto he sent forth his pinnace, and being advertised that Valdez himself was there, and 450 persons with him, he sent him word that he should yield himself. Valdez for his honor's sake caused certain conditions to be propounded unto Drake; who answered Valdez that he was not now at leisure to make any long parle [discussion, parley], but if he would yield himself, he should find him friendly and tractable: howbeit if he had resolved to die in fight, he should prove Drake to be no dastard.

Upon which answer Valdez and his company understanding that they were fallen into the hands of fortunate Drake, being moved with the renown and celebrity of his name, with one consent yielded themselves, and found him very favorable unto them. Then Valdez with 40 or 50 noblemen and gentlemen pertaining unto him, came on board Sir Francis Drake's ship. The residue of his company were carried unto Plymouth, where they were detained a year and an half for their ransom....

Here Valdez began to recount unto Drake... how they were determined first to have put into Plymouth haven, not expecting to be repelled thence by the English ships which they thought could by no means withstand their impregnable forces, persuading themselves that by means of their huge fleet, they were become lords and commanders of the main ocean. For which cause they marveled much how the Englishmen in their small ships durst approach within musket shot of the Spaniards' mighty wooden castles, gathering the wind of them with many other such like attempts....

But it seemeth that the duke of Parma and the Spaniards grounded upon a vain and presumptuous expectation, that all the ships of England and of the Low countries [the Protestants of the Spanish Netherlands, now in revolt] would at the first sight of the Spanish and Dunkirk Navy have betaken themselves to flight, yielding them sea room, and endeavoring only to defend themselves, their havens, and sea coasts from invasion.... They were in good hope also to have met with some rebels against her majesty, and such as were discontented with the present state, as Papists, and others. Likewise they looked for aid from the favorers of the Scottish queen, who was not long before put to death; all which they thought would have stirred up seditions and factions.

Whenas therefore the Spanish fleet rode at anchor before Calais..., the lord admiral of England being admonished by her majesty's letters from the court, thought it most expedient either to drive the Spanish fleet from that place...: and for that cause (according to her majesty's prescription) he took forthwith eight of his worst and basest ships which came next to hand, and disburdening them of

[34]   Kinney, *Elizabethan Backgrounds*, 253–4, 258–9, 263–5, 272–4; compared with Hakluyt, *Voyages and Discoveries*, 321–6, from *The Miraculous Victory Atchieved [sic] by the English Fleete* (translated by Hakluyt for 1598 ed. of *The Principal Navigations*).

all things which seemed to be of any value, filled them with gun-powder, pitch, brimstone, and with other combustible and fiery matter; and charging all their ordnance with powder, bullets, and stones, he sent the said ships upon the 28 of July being Sunday, about two of the clock after midnight, with the wind and tide against the Spanish fleet; which when they had proceeded a good space, being forsaken of the pilots, and set on fire, were directly carried upon the king of Spain's navy; which fire in the dead of the night put the Spaniards into such a perplexity and horror...that cutting their cables whereon their anchors were fastened, and hoisting up their sails, they betook themselves very confusedly unto the main sea.

In this sudden confusion, the principal and greatest of the four galliases [heavy, low-built vessels with both oars and sails] falling foul of another ship, lost her rudder: for which cause when she could not be guided any longer, she was by the force of the tide cast into a certain shoal upon the shore of Calais, where she was immediately assaulted by diverse English pinnaces, hoys, and drumblers [small, fast vessels]....

Likewise upon the Scottish Western Isles of Lewis and Islay, and about Cape Cantyre [Mull of Kintyre] upon the mainland, there were cast away certain Spanish ships, out of which were saved diverse captains and gentlemen, and almost four hundred soldiers, who for the most part, after their shipwreck, were brought unto Edinburgh in Scotland, and being miserably needy and naked, were there clothed at the liberality of the King [James VI] and the merchants, and afterward were secretly shipped for Spain....

Upon the Irish coast many of their noblemen and gentlemen were drowned; and diverse slain by the barbarous and wild Irish....To conclude, there was no famous nor worthy family in all Spain, which in this expedition lost not a son, a brother, or a kinsman.

For the perpetual memory of this matter, the Zealanders [Dutch] caused new coin of silver and brass to be stamped: which on the one side contained the arms of Zealand, with this inscription: "Glory to God Only"; and on the other side, the pictures of certain great ships, with these words: "The Spanish Fleet"; and in the circumference about the ships: "It Came, Went, and Was. Anno 1588." That is to say, the Spanish fleet came, went, and was vanquished this year; for which, glory be given to God only.

Likewise they coined another kind of money; upon the one side whereof was represented a ship fleeing, and a ship sinking: on the other side four men making prayers and giving thanks unto God upon their knees; with this sentence: "Man purposeth; God disposeth, 1588."

4.7   *Queen Elizabeth's Tilbury Speech (August 9, 1588)*[35]

My loving people, I have been persuaded by some that are careful of my safety to take heed how I committed myself to armed multitudes, for fear of treachery. But I tell you that I would not desire to live to distrust my faithful and loving people.

---

[35]   *Elizabeth I: Collected Works*, 296; compared with McGurk, *Tudor Monarchies*, 102; and Levine, *Elizabeth I*, 66–7.

Let tyrants fear: I have so behaved myself that under God I have placed my chiefest strength and safeguard in the loyal hearts and goodwill of my subjects. And therefore I am come amongst you, as you see at this time, not for my recreation and disport, but being resolved, in the midst and heat of the battle, to live or die amongst you all; to lay down for my God and for my kingdom and for my people, my honor and my blood even in the dust. I know I have the body but of a weak and feeble woman, but I have the heart and stomach of a king and of a king of England too – and take foul scorn that Parma or any prince of Europe should dare to invade the borders of my realm. To the which rather than any dishonor shall grow by me, I myself will venture my royal blood; I myself will be your general, judge, and rewarder of your virtue in the field. I know that already for your forwardness you have deserved rewards and crowns, and I assure you in the word of a prince you shall not fail of them. In the meantime, my lieutenant general [Leicester] shall be in my stead, than whom never prince commanded a more noble or worthy subject. Not doubting but by your concord in the camp and valor in the field and your obedience to myself and my general, we shall shortly have a famous victory over these enemies of my God and of my kingdom.

4.8   *An Act to Retain the Queen's Majesty's Subjects in Their Due Obedience (23 Eliz., c. 1) (1581)*[36]

All persons whatsoever which have, or shall have, or shall pretend to have power, or shall by any ways or means put into practice to absolve, persuade, or withdraw any of the queen's majesty's subjects or any within her highness's realms and dominions from their natural obedience to her majesty, or to withdraw them for the intent from the religion now by her highness's authority established within her highness's dominions to the Romish religion, or to move them or any of them to promise any obedience to any pretended authority of the See of Rome . . . , shall be to all intents adjudged to be traitors, and being thereof lawfully convicted shall have judgment, suffer, and forfeit as in case of high treason, and if any person shall, after the end of this session of Parliament, by any means be willingly absolved or withdrawn as aforesaid, or willingly be reconciled, or shall promise any obedience to any such pretended authority . . . , that then every such person, their procurers and counselors thereunto, being thereof lawfully convicted, shall be taken, tried, and judged, and shall suffer and forfeit as in cases of high treason. . . .

And be it likewise enacted, that every person which shall say or sing mass, being thereof lawfully convicted, shall forfeit the sum of two hundred marks [£132] and be committed to prison in the next jail, there to remain by the space of one year, and from thenceforth till he have paid the said sum of two hundred marks; and that every person which shall willingly hear mass shall forfeit the sum of one hundred marks and suffer imprisonment for a year.

---

[36]   P. L. Hughes and R. F. Fries, eds., *Crown and Parliament in Tudor–Stuart England: A Documentary Constitutional History, 1485–1714* (New York, 1959), 121, from *SR*, 4: 657.

4.9   *William Allen on the Martyrdom of William Filby of Oxford (1582)*[37]

On Wednesday being the 30 May these 4 venerable priests [M. William Filby, M. Lucas Kirby, M. Laurence Richardson whose right name was Johnson, and M. Thomas Cottam] were trailed from the Tower of London along the streets to Tyburn, about 7 in the morning, when they were come to the place of execution. William Filby (being the youngest, not above 27 years of age) was first taken from the hurdle, and being lifted into the cart, he blessed himself with the sign of the Cross . . . , and so proceeded with these words: Let me see my brethren, looking to the other which lay on the hurdle and there withal holding forth his hands to them, said, Pray for me. Then speaking to the company, said: I am a Catholic, and I protest before almighty God that I am innocent of all these matters, whereof I am condemned, and I hope to be saved by the merits and death of our Savior Jesus Christ, beseeching him to have mercy on me and to forgive me my offenses. And therewithal a proclamation was read for keeping the peace, and at the end thereof was said, God save the queen, to which he said, Amen.

The people asking him for what queen he prayed for, he answered, for Queen Elizabeth, beseeching God to send her a long and quiet reign, to his good will, and make her his servant, and preserve her from her enemies. With that M. Topcliff and others willed him to say, God save her from the pope. To whom he answered he is not her enemy, therewith the minister of S. Andrews in Holborn said, Note, that he saith the pope is not the queen's enemy. And then a preacher called Charke, yes said he you are a traitor, for you are sworn to the queen's sworn enemy. M. Filby looking aside, said, what do you mean, I never took oath in all my life. What, said Charke, then are you not a priest; you are deceived, said M. Filby, it is a vow and not an oath. After that one of the sheriff's men standing in the cart with M. Filby said unto him, what hast thou there in thy handkerchief, and therewithal taking the handkerchief from him found a little cross of wood with in it, which he holding up in his hands said, O what a villainous traitor is this, that hath a cross, diverse times repeating it, and diverse of the people saying the same. Whereunto M. Filby answered nothing, only smiling at them.

Then the articles, with the preface of the book printed by authority, was read, and his answers unto them. It was replied against him by some urging him further upon the same answer: if you hold this, then you can not be but a traitor to the queen's majesty, for that the pope hath deposed her by his bull. M. Filby said, that that bull was perchance called in again by this Pope Gregory XIII. . . . Then sheriff Martine called upon the hangman to dispatch, and the rope being about his neck, the sheriff said, Filby, the queen is merciful unto you, and we have authority from her to carry you back, if you will ask her mercy, and confess your fault do not

---

[37]   X. Baron, ed., *London, 1066–1914: Literary Sources and Documents*, vol. 1, *Medieval, Tudor, Stuart and Georgian London: 1066–1800* (Mountfield, East Sussex, 1997), 305–6, from *A Briefe Historie of the Glorious Martyrdom of XII Reverend Priests*. Compare with Filby's statements in Howell, *State Trials*, 1: 1081–2.

refuse mercy offered, ask the Q. forgiveness, to whom M. Filby answered, I never offended her, well then said the sheriff make an end, and thus desiring all Catholics to pray for him he prayed, saying his *Pater noster*, and his *Ave*, and *In manus tuas*, etc., and when the cart was trailing away, he said, Lord, receive my soul, and so hanged knocking his breast several times, till some pulled down his hands, and so finished his life.

4.10 *John Field and Thomas Wilcox,* An Admonition to the Parliament *(1572)*[38]

Seeing that nothing in this mortal life is more diligently to be sought for and carefully to be looked unto than the restitution of true religion and reformation of God's Church, it shall be your parts (dearly beloved), in this present Parliament assembled, as much as in you lieth to promote the same, and to employ your whole labor and study, not only in abandoning all popish remnants both in ceremonies and regiment, but also in bringing in and placing in God's Church those things only which the Lord himself in his word commandeth....

Your wisdoms have to remove advowsons, patronages, impropriations, and bishops' authority, claiming to themselves thereby right to ordain ministers, and to bring in that old and true election which was accustomed to be made by the congregation.... Appoint to every congregation a learned and diligent preacher. Remove homilies, articles, injunctions, a prescript [prescribed] order of service made out of the mass-book. Take away the lordship, the loitering, the pomp, the idleness and livings of bishops....

Whereas immediately after the last Parliament [1571]..., the ministers of God's holy word and sacraments were called before her majesty's high commissioners, and enforced to subscribe unto the [Thirty-Nine] Articles, if they would keep their places and livings, and some for refusing to subscribe were... removed: May it please therefore this honorable and high court of Parliament... to take a view of such causes as then did withhold and now doth the foresaid ministers from subscribing and consenting unto those foresaid articles, by way of purgation to discharge themselves of all disobedience towards the Church of God and their sovereign, and by way of most humble entreaty for the removing away... of all such corruptions and abuses as withheld them.... Albeit... we have at all times borne with that which we could not amend in this book [of Common Prayer] and have used the same in our ministry, so far forth as we might..., yet now being compelled by subscription to allow the same and to confess it not to be against the word of God in any point, but tolerable, we must needs say as followeth, that this book is an unperfect book, culled and picked out of that popish dunghill the portuise [portas?, breviary?] and mass-book full of all abominations....

[38] Part in W. L. Sachse, *English History in the Making*, vol. 1, *Readings from the Sources, to 1689* (1967), 207–8; and part in G. W. Prothero, ed., *Select Statutes and other Constitutional Documents Illustrative of the Reigns of Elizabeth and James I*, 4th ed. (Oxford, 1913), 198–9, both from *First Admonition*.

And as for the apparel, though we have been long borne in hand, and yet are, that it is for order and decency commanded, yet we know and have proved that there is neither order nor comeliness nor obedience in using it....Neither is the controversy betwixt them and us (as they would bear the world in hand) for a cap, a tippet or a surplice, but for great matters concerning a true ministry and regiment of the church according to the word....

Amend therefore these horrible abuses and reform God's Church, and the Lord is on your right hand....Is a reformation good for France [the Huguenots], and can it be evil for England? Is discipline meet for Scotland, and is it unprofitable for this realm? Surely God hath set these examples before your eyes to encourage you to go forward to a thorough and a speedy reformation.

4.11 Archbishop Grindal to Elizabeth on Prophesyings (December 20, 1576)[39]

With most humble remembrance of my bounden duty to your majesty....The speeches which it hath pleased you to deliver unto me, when I last attended on your highness, concerning abridging the number of preachers, and the utter suppression of all learned exercises and conferences among the ministers of the church, allowed by their bishops and ordinaries, have exceedingly dismayed and discomforted me....I thought it therefore my duty by writing to declare some part of my mind unto your highness....

By preaching of God's word the glory of God is enlarged, faith is nourished, and charity increased. By it the ignorant is instructed, the negligent exhorted and incited, the stubborn rebuked, the weak conscience comforted, and to all those that sin of malicious wickedness the wrath of God is threatened. By preaching also due obedience to Christian princes and magistrates is planted in the hearts of subjects....So as generally, where preaching wanteth, obedience faileth.

No prince ever had more lively experience hereof than your majesty hath had in your time, and may have daily. If your majesty come to the city of London..., what acclamations and prayers to God for your long life, and other manifest significations of inward and unfeigned love, joined with most humble and hearty obedience, are there to be heard! Whereof cometh this, madam, but of the continual preaching of God's word in that city, whereby that people hath been plentifully instructed in their duty towards God and your majesty? On the contrary, what bred the rebellion in the North [1569]? Was it not papistry, and ignorance of God's word, through want of often preaching? And in the time of that rebellion, were not all men, of all states, that made profession of the Gospel, most ready to offer their lives for your defense? Insomuch that one poor parish in Yorkshire, which by continual preaching had been better instructed than the rest (Halifax I mean) was ready to bring three or four thousand able men into the field to serve you against the said rebels. How can your majesty have a more lively trial

---

[39] *The Remains of Archbishop Grindal*, ed. W. Nicholson (Cambridge, Parker Society, 1843), 376–80, 382–4, 289; compared with D. Cressy and L. A. Ferrell, eds., *Religion and Society in Early Modern England: A Sourcebook* (1996), 93–9.

and experience of the contrary effects of much preaching, and of little or no preaching?...

But it is thought of some, that many are admitted to preach, and few be able to do it well. That unable preachers be removed is very requisite, if ability and sufficiency may be rightly weighed and judged....I, for mine own part..., am very careful in allowing such preachers only, as be able and sufficient to be preachers, both for their knowledge in the scriptures, and also for testimony of their good life and conversation. And besides that, I have given very great charge to the rest of my brethren, the bishops of this province, to do the like. We admit no man to the office, that either professeth papistry or puritanism. Generally, the graduates of the university are only admitted to be preachers....

Now, where it is thought, that the reading of the godly homilies, set forth by public authority, may suffice, I continue of the same mind I was when I attended last upon your majesty. The reading of homilies hath this commodity; but is nothing comparable to the office of preaching....

Now for the second point, which is concerning the learned exercise and conference amongst the ministers of the church: I have consulted with diverse of my brethren, the bishops, by letters; who think the same as I do, *viz.* a thing profitable to the Church, and therefore expedient to be continued. And I trust your majesty will think the like, when your highness shall have been informed of the manner and order thereof; what authority it hath of the scriptures....

The times appointed for the assembly is once a month, or once in twelve or fifteen days, at the discretion of the ordinary. The time of the exercise is two hours: the place, the church....The matter entreated of is...some text of scripture...is interpreted....

These orders following are also observed in the said exercise....No man may speak, unless he first be allowed by the bishop, with this proviso, that no layman be suffered to speak at any time. No controversy of this present time and state shall be moved or dealt withal. If any attempt the contrary, he is put to silence by the moderator. None is suffered...to confute another. If any man utter a wrong sense of the scripture, he is privately admonished thereof, and better instructed by the moderators, and other his fellow-ministers....

Remember, madam, that you are a mortal creature....

And although ye are a mighty prince, yet remember that He which dwelleth in heaven is mightier.

4.12   *Elizabeth to the Bishops on Prophesyings (May 7, 1577)*[40]

Considering it should be the duty of the bishops...to see these dishonors ["unlawful assemblies of a great number of our people out of their ordinary parishes..., in some places called prophesying and in some other places exercises"] against the honor of God and the quietness of the Church reformed...; we

[40]   E. Cardwell, ed., *Documentary Annals of the Reformed Church of England* (Oxford, 1839), 1: 375–6; compared with G. R. Elton, ed., *The Tudor Constitution: Documents and Commentary* (Cambridge, 1968), 443–4.

therefore, according to authority we have, charge and command you... to take order through your diocese... that no manner of public and divine service..., nor any other rites or ceremonies, be in any sort used in the Church but directly according to the orders established by our laws. Neither that any manner of person be suffered within your diocese to preach... but such as shall be lawfully approved and licensed...; and where there shall not be sufficient able persons for learning in any cures to preach or instruct their cures as were requisite, there you shall limit the curates to read the public homilies.... And... we will and straitly charge you that you also charge the same [prophesyings] forthwith to cease and not to be used; but if any shall attempt or continue or renew the same, we will you not only to commit them unto prison as maintainers of disorders, but also to advertise us or our Council of the names and qualities of them.... And in these things we charge you to be so careful and vigilant, as by your negligence, if we shall hear of any person attempting to offend... without your correction or information to us, we be not forced to make some example or reformation of you.

4.13 *Elizabeth's Golden Speech (November 30, 1601)*[41]

Mr. Speaker, We perceive your coming is to present thanks unto me; know it I accept with no less joy than your loves can desire to offer such a present, and more esteem it than any treasure or riches (for that we know how to prize), but loyalty, love, and thanks, I account them invaluable. And though God hath raised me high, yet this I count the glory of my crown – that I have reigned with your loves. This makes [that] I do not so much rejoice that God hath made me to be a queen, as to be a queen over so thankful a people, and to be the means under God to conserve you in safety, and preserve you from danger, yea to be the instrument to deliver you from dishonor, from shame, from infamy, from out of servitude and slavery under our enemies, to keep you from cruel tyranny and vile oppression intended against us. For better withstanding whereof we take very acceptably your intended helps.... Of myself I must say this: I never was any greedy scraping grasper, nor a strait fast-holding prince, nor yet a waster. My heart was never set upon any worldly goods, but only for my subjects' goods [good]. What you do bestow on me, I will not hoard it up, but receive it to bestow on you again. Yea, mine own properties I account yours to be expended for your good....

Mr. Speaker, I would wish you and the rest to stand up, for I fear I shall yet trouble you with longer speech.

Mr. Speaker, you give me thanks, but I am more to thank you, and I charge you, thank them of the Lower House [Commons] from me. For had I not received a knowledge from you, I might have fallen into the lapse of an error, only for lack of true information. For since I was queen, yet did I never put pen to any grant but upon pretext and semblance made to me, that it was for the good and avail of my subjects generally, though a private profit to some of my ancient servants who had

---

[41] *Elizabeth I: Collected Works*, 340–2; compared with S. D'Ewes, ed., *A Compleat Journal of the Votes, Speeches, and Debates* ..., 2nd ed. (1693), 659–60. For other versions, see *Elizabeth I: Collected Works*, 335–40, 342–4.

deserved well. But that my grants shall be made grievances to my people and oppressions to be privileged under color of our patents, our kingly dignity shall not suffer it. And when I heard it, I could give no rest unto my thoughts until I had reformed it. And those varlets, lewd persons, abusers of my bounty, shall know I will not suffer it. And Mr. Speaker, tell the House from me I take it exceeding gratefully that the knowledge of these things is come to me from them. And though amongst them the principal Members are such as are not touched in private, [and] therefore need not speak from any feeling of the grief, yet we have heard that other gentlemen also of the House, who stand as free, have spoken as freely in it, which gives us to know that no respects or interests have moved them other than the minds they bear to suffer no diminution of our honor and our subjects' love unto us. . . . For above all earthly treasure, I esteem my people's love, more than which I desire not to merit. . . .

And in my governing this I have ever had the grace to use – to set the last judgment day before mine eyes, and so to rule as I shall be judged, and to answer before a higher judge, to whose judgment seat I do appeal [in] that never thought was cherished in my heart that tended not to my people's good. And if my kingly bounty have been abused and my grants turned to the hurt of my people, contrary to my will and meaning; or if any in authority under me have neglected or converted what I have committed unto them, I hope God they will not lay their culps [culpabilities] to my charge.

To be a king and wear a crown is a thing more glorious to them that see it than it is pleasant to them that bear it. For myself, I never was so much enticed with the glorious name of a king or royal authority of a queen as delighted that God hath made me His instrument to maintain His truth and glory, and to defend this kingdom from dishonor, damage, tyranny, and oppression. But should I ascribe any of this to myself, or my sexly weakness, I were not worthy to live, and of all, most unworthy of the mercies I have had from God. But to God only and wholly, all is to be given and ascribed. . . . And though you have had and may have many mightier and wiser princes sitting in this seat, yet you never had nor shall have any that will love you better. Thus Mr. Speaker, I commend me to your loyal love, and you to my best care and your further counsels. And I pray you Mr. Comptroller and you of my Councils, that before these gentlemen depart into their countries [counties] you bring them all to kiss my hand.

CHAPTER FIVE

Masterless Men and the Monstrous Regiment of Women

Rough Music, Food Riots, and Popular Rebellions
The Scold, the Witch, and the Almswoman
Poor Laws and the Reform of Popular Culture

DISCUSSION

Order obsessed early modern society in part because its opposite terrified people (see chapter 1). Thus, a government-issued homily (1547, reissued 1559, 1623, etc.) rehearsed a "perfect order," as well as the evils that would befall a society without it:

Every degree of people in their vocation, calling, and office hath appointed to them their duty and order. Some are in high degree, some in low, some kings and princes, some inferiors and subjects, priests and laymen, masters and servants, fathers and children, husbands and wives, rich and poor, and everyone have need of other.... [But] where there is no right order, there reigneth all abuse, carnal liberty, enormity, sin, and Babylonical confusion. Take away kings, princes, rulers, magistrates, judges, and such estates of God's order, no man shall ride or go by the highway unrobbed, no man shall sleep in his own house or bed unkilled, no man shall keep his wife, children, and possessions in quietness: all things shall be common, and there must needs follow all mischief and utter destruction both of souls, bodies, goods, and commonwealths.[1]

This chapter examines late Tudor and early Stuart "Babylonical confusion," from scolding and brawling to violent group actions. The reigns of Elizabeth

---

[1] *Certain Sermons or Homilies Appointed to be Read in Churches, in the Times of the late Queene Elizabeth* (1623 ed., facsimile, Gainesville, 1968), 69–70; compared with *An Exhortation Concerning Good Order, and Obedience to Rulers and Magistrates* (1547), <http://www.anglicanlibrary.org/homilies/bk1hom10.htm>.

and James were not necessarily *more* disorderly than other periods (see Bucholz and Key, chapter 6, for the authors' opinions on this point), but that did not prevent contemporaries from thinking so. As you read the documents in this chapter, you might ask:

- Did violent events such as charivaris, food riots, enclosure riots, popular rebellions, or witchcraft persecutions contribute more to the breaking down or to the reinforcing of social order and values?
- Was there a popular response to social ills and disorder which can be compared or contrasted to the elite response?

Rough Music, Food Riots, and Popular Rebellions

Disorder often began with "angry speeches" or "many outrageous words spoken" (1574).[2] Words were weapons with which to attack reputation. And reputation, in a face-to-face, largely oral culture and society, mattered. Note the following verbal and physical references to horns, the popular symbol of cuckoldry. In 1574, one Arthur Dixson sued Ellen Cordie for defamation, for having "willed him to take a saw and to saw off his horns, which she meant thereby that his wife was not an honest woman." In 1575, one Joan Cooper was charged with slandering her neighbor by "hanging a horn on her neighbor's pale," and, indeed, "she brought in a horn" to the court – an example of gesture operating as speech. Constables, watchmen, and other minor officials took regular verbal abuse. Thus, in 1588, one constable received "evil words" from two blacksmiths he had asked to shoe his horse. Other such officials were subject to "opprobrious and threatening words" when they put a vagrant in the stocks. Since we usually only know about brawling between parishioners or neighbors when they ended up in civil or consistory (Church) court, we might well ask again the question we asked in chapter 1: is this evidence of a lawful or lawless society?

What made words and gestures so threatening was, of course, the specter of real physical violence. ("Assault" and "insult" derive from a common root word.) Note the very real threat made in the following handwritten libel from 1598:

Our most hearty commendation unto you good brethren and apprentices. . . . The cause of our writing to you at this time is for to know whether you will put up this injury or no; for to see our brethren whipped and set on the pillory without a cause . . . is a grief to us. Desiring you to send answer one way or other, for if you will not put it up we do give consent to gather ourselves together upon [St.] Bartholomew's Day [August 24] in the

---

[2]   Quotes in paragraph are from F. G. Emmison, *Elizabethan Life: Morals and the Church Courts* (Chelmsford, 1973), 128 (speeches), 54 (horns); and Emmison, *Elizabethan Life: Disorder* (Chelmsford, 1970), 177 (constables).

fields, some with daggers, some with staves, some with one weapon, some with another, such as may be least mistrusted, and to meet in the fields between Islington and London between three and four... in the afternoon against my lord mayor go[ing] to the wrestling, and there to be revenged of him; but if he go not to the wrestling, then to be revenged of him at his house where he dwells.[3]

Who is being threatened by whom and why?

By the end of Elizabeth's reign, London's dynamic economy brought a steady supply of would-be new citizens from around the country; and the freshly imported, often young and always overcrowded population bred threats of disorder, real and imagined. Document 5.1 (July 7, 1585) suggests that London's sprawl had encouraged organized crime. Why might that be? Was the metropolis more dangerous than the countryside?

Much interpersonal early modern violence involved drink, as it does today, and most crimes prosecuted involved the theft of items of relatively low value. Most of the rest of this chapter, however, seeks to portray disorderly social or group action that appears to represent communal values. Some historians have discovered two concepts of order in early modern society: that of the elite concerned with keeping the lower orders in line versus that of the commoners concerned with keeping the community in general agreement or consensus. Document 5.2 (Trinity or Spring Term 1618) records a charivari or rough music, in which those who have violated social norms were humiliated and, often, forced out of the community by their neighbors. (You might compare this document with plate 5.) What happened during the 1618 affray? What norm might have been violated? Which concept of order does this Wiltshire charivari represent? Did pipes, horns, and cowbells lend a festive atmosphere to this event? In what way does it compare to a lynching?

In fact, the line between the two concepts of order posited above is not always easy to detect. For example, when five London women were convicted in 1529 for "continually using the abominable custom of the foul and detestable sin of lechery and bawdry to the great displeasure of Almighty God and to the great annoyance of their neighbors," the punishment awarded by the lord mayor and aldermen of London resembled that meted out *without* official sanction in rural Wiltshire:

the said persons shall be conveyed from the Compter Prison to Newgate with minstrelsy, that is to say with pans and basins ringing before them and they to wear ray [striped] hoods and to have in their hands white rods in token of common bawds, strumpets, and harlots; and so from thence to be conveyed to the Standard in Cheap[side] and there this proclamation to be made, and so to be conveyed through Cheap into Cornhill and there to stand under the pillory during this proclamation, and from thence to be conveyed to Aldgate and there to be banished the city forever.[4]

---

[3] J. P. Collier, ed., *Trevelyan Papers* (Camden Society, 1863), 2: 101; compared with R. Salter, *Elizabeth I and her Reign* (Basingstoke, 1988), 66.

[4] June 1529, in M. Ingram, "Reformation of Manners in Early Modern England," in *The Experience of Authority in Early Modern England*, ed. P. Griffiths, A. Fox, and S. Hindle (Basingstoke, 1996), 60, from City of London RO, Journal 13, ff. 141v, 143.

Plate 5 *Scenes of a charivari, plaster relief (ca. 1600), Montacute House, Great Hall, Somerset. (Source:* National Trust Photo Library)

The two details from this panel evidently tell a story. What is the cause and what is the effect? Where is private life and where is public life in an early modern village? Charivaris could be very disorderly (we often know about them because the recipients of such popular shaming brought the matter to court). Did charivaris, then, contribute to local order or disorder?

To judge from this example, what underlying assumptions did the two concepts of order have in common? What was the point of this sort of punishment?

There were limits to the consensus between rulers and ruled on what constituted orderly behavior. The elite reacted differently to a grain or enclosure riot than they did to a charivari. William Harrison, in his *Description of England* (1577), complained of the sort of "thriftless poor, as the rioter that hath consumed all, the vagabond that will abide nowhere but runneth up and down from place to place . . . , and finally the rogue and the strumpet."[5] What does Harrison mean by "the rioter that hath consumed all"? Ordinary people who complained and, in some cases, took action, about high grain prices (thus, of bread, the mainstay of most meals) and scarcity, often began their search for redress by petitioning officials to enforce laws against forestalling (buying before grain was brought to market), regrating (purchasing grain to sell again at the same or neighboring market at higher price), and engrossing (purchasing grain wholesale at market). In 1531, the attorney general charged one Mr. Archer of Essex "for keeping in his corn [generic for grain] and consequently for enhancing the price of corn the last year," and, at least one justice presiding over the Star Chamber case decided to make an example of the forestaller:

Justice Harvy delivered his opinion, that whereas it hath pleased God to send a plentiful year, and yet the price of corn continued very high, himself and the rest of the justices of the peace that were in the last Quarter Sessions in Hertfordshire assembled did advise among themselves how they might deal with the country to bring down the price. . . . He was of opinion that this man's [Archer's] punishment and example will do a great deal more good than all their orders which they might have made at the Sessions; and therefore he declared his offense to be very great, and fit to be punished in this Court; and adjudged him to pay 100 marks [£66] fine to the king, and £10 to the poor, and to stand upon the pillory in Newgate Market an hour with a paper, wherein the cause of his standing there was to be written, put upon his hat – For enhancing the price of Corn – and then to be led through Cheapside to Leadenhall Market, and there likewise to stand upon the pillory one hour more with the same paper upon his hat, and after this to be sent to Chelmsford, and there likewise in the market to stand upon the pillory.[6]

Compare Harvy's comment with the 1629 petition from the poor of Blackburn hundred to their JPs:

Not many years ago there was usually sold and bought in open market 30, 40, or 50 measures of meal every market day to the help, nourishment, and relief of your petitioners and other poor distressed people within or near the aforesaid town. But now so it is . . . that there is many licensed badgers [grain middlemen] within this hundred and especially one Lawrence Hargreaves who doth commonly badge, carry, and transport much kind of grain either into foreign parts or for his better profit maketh sale thereof in Burnley not

---

[5]   Harrison, *A Description of Elizabethan England* (New York, 1910), 301; compared with B. Coward, *Social Change and Continuity: England, 1550–1750*, rev. ed. (1997), 119.

[6]   S. R. Gardiner, ed., *Reports of Cases in the Courts of Star Chamber and High Commission* (Camden Society, new ser. 39, 1886), 43–5, from PRO, STAC 2.

frequenting any open market but doth unjustly enrich himself against all equity and good conscience and contrary to the statute in that case provided to the overthrow and impoverishment of your petitioners and many more who cannot buy one half peck [about 1/8 bushel or 1 gallon] of meal or less (if the greatest need required).[7]

Had the nature of the complaint and the form of petitioning changed in the intervening century? How might the badgers' and Mr. Archer's actions be defended today? Would these arguments have carried weight in the sixteenth century?

In times of dearth, when the government either could not or would not act, English townspeople and villagers sometimes took action of their own. Grain or bread rioters would halt exports from a particular region, seize the grain and, often, distribute it at what the rioters considered a just price. (Surprisingly, the yield from the sale was occasionally turned over to the merchants, middlemen, or exporters from whom the grain had been seized.) Document 5.3 (1629) records the examinations of women who participated in a series of grain riots in Essex, which had been experiencing a trade depression for clothworkers and high grain prices. These examinations refer to a riot in March (after a further riot in May, one examinant, Anne Carter, and seven others would be hanged). While men were also involved in the Maldon disturbances, why might women be so heavily involved in the grain riots (consider both their status in law and their role in the household economy)? What were the goals of these women? Were any of them achieved?

A different type of riot was that against enclosure. Enclosure of both open field systems and of common pasturage occurred from the late Middle Ages through the nineteenth century. In 1628 and 1629, rioters attacked workers employed by the Dutch engineer Sir Cornelius Vermuyden (1595?–1683?), who had secured a grant from Charles I to drain the East Anglian Fenlands, and the rioters had to defend themselves against a suit in Star Chamber. The defendants clearly felt aggrieved at what they perceived as a *de facto* enclosure: "they all claimed their common of pasture with all manner of cattle and common of turbary [peat bogs], at all times of the year; that they never agreed with Sir Cornelius Vermuyden; that the country receiveth no profit by the work, the grounds are made rather worse." But the attorney general argued:

that diverse were set on work by Sir Cornelius Vermuyden to make trenches for the draining, that 300 persons came to the workmen, and Harrison, Gibson, and Moody threatened to kill the workmen: and Brown, Stockwell, and William Scott told them if they would leave their work they would appease the multitude; or else they might go on at their peril: that they called the laborers rogues, dogs, and cried out, "Break their legs," and 17 of the laborers were hurt; 8 wheelbarrows, 180 deal boards, planks, many shovels, spades, pickaxes, and other materials and instruments were burnt. That one Mr. Hawthorne was thrown into the river, and kept in with poles a great while; that

[7] R. C. Richardson and T. B. James, eds., *The Urban Experience, A Sourcebook: English, Scottish and Welsh Towns, 1450–1700* (Manchester, 1983), 52–3, from Lancashire RO, Quarter Sessions, QSB/1/61/36.

they cried out, "Drown him! Kill him! Break his arms or legs!" That James Moody, Harrison, Henry Scott, and Edward Gibson did cry out, "Throw him into the river! Break his arms and legs!" Others were beaten with dry blows. Hawthorne's face was hoodwinked with a cloak or coat, and so cast into the river, and Richard Scott and others laid hands on him, and struck and beat him; but bid them not to duck him over head least he should be drowned, but rather to break his arms or his legs, and so let him go; and some of the rioters poured water in at the necks of some of the workmen; and one run at the deponent with a drawn knife and cut his clothes, and some cried out, "Cut his throat! Break his legs!" and made them swear never to come there again. They set up a gallows and threaten to hang such of Sir Cornelius Vermuyden's men as would come thither again. The women assembled themselves to the number of 200 in 1629 diverse days and times, and threw down the banks and works, and burned the instruments and tools.

By the sentence of the court "many of the defendants were found guilty of the several riots charged in the bill . . . were fined £1,000 a piece. . . . And the several women who were proved to be at the said riots 500 marks [£333] a piece."[8] Compare the Fenland riot with the enclosure riots of 1607 (document 5.4). Do those participating in the disturbances see themselves as rioters? Are they? What grievances do they have against the "enclosers and depopulators"? One might compare and contrast the ruling elite's reaction to engrossers of grain (noted earlier in this chapter) and enclosers of land.

Beyond mere riot lay peasant and popular rebellion, although the line dividing one from the other is not always clear. The Cornish Rebellion (1497), the Pilgrimage of Grace (1536, see chapter 3 and documents 1.2, 3.5), the Western Rising (1549, see chapter 3 and document 3.6), Wyatt's Rebellion (1554), and the Rebellion of the Northern Earls (1569, see chapter 4) had decidedly political and religious causes, but Kett's Rebellion (1549) and the Rebellion of 1596 had origins closer to those of enclosure or food riots. At the same time, the solutions suggested by some of the poor rebels aimed higher than destroying a hedge or a deer park. In 1596, one carpenter declared that

after their rising, they would go to Mr. Powers and knock at the gate, and keep him fast that opened the door and suddenly thrust in. And . . . he with his falchion [a short, sickle-like sword] would cut off their heads, and would not bestow a halter on them. And then they would go to Mr. Barry's and despoil him and cut off his head and his daughter's head and from thence they would have gone to Rathbone's house, a yeoman, and despoil him likewise and from thence to Mr. George Whitton and despoil him, and thence to Sir Henry Lee and despoil him likewise, and thence to Sir William Spencer and despoil him. And so to Mr. Frere and so to my Lord Norris and so to London. . . . And . . . when the apprentices hear that we be up, they will come and join with us . . . and he was the rather inclined to think the same by reason of the late intended insurrection in London, and that certain apprentices were hanged [1595].[9]

8 Gardiner, *Reports*, 59–65, from PRO, STAC 9.
9 Examination of Roger Symonds, in J. Walter, "A 'Rising of the People'?: The Oxfordshire Rising of 1596," *P & P* 107 (1985): 90, 107–8; compared with Salter, *Elizabeth I*, 71–2, from PRO, SP12/262/4.

What appears to be the carpenter's goal? What might be the source of his anger?

We know rather more of what motivated Robert Kett (d. 1549) and his East Anglian followers when they encamped outside Norwich in 1549, for they drew up a series of demands of the king:

1. We pray your grace that where it is enacted for enclosing that it be not hurtful to such as have enclosed saffron grounds for they be greatly chargeable to them, and that from henceforth no man shall enclose any more.
2. We certify your grace that whereas the lords of the manors hath been charged with certain free rent, the same lords hath sought means to charge the freeholders to pay the same rent, contrary to right.
3. We pray your grace that no lord of no manor shall common upon the Commons.
4. We pray that priests from henceforth shall purchase no lands ..., and the lands that they have in possession may be let to temporal men, as they were in the first year of the reign of King Henry VII. ...
11. We pray that all freeholders and copyholders may take the profits of all commons, and there to common, and the lords not to common nor take profits of the same. ...
14. We pray that copyhold land that is unreasonably rented may go as it did in the first year of King Henry VII and that at the death of a tenant or of a sale the same lands to be charged with an easy fine as a capon or a reasonable sum of money for a remembrance. ...
16. We pray that all bond men may be made free for God made all free with his precious blood shedding.[10]

Can these demands and the statements of Kett's followers after the rebellion had been crushed (1549–50, document 5.5) be used to explain its causes? What did the rebels want? If they had been successful, would such changes have destroyed the Tudor state? Would they have transformed society? (Consider whether or not a mythological "Golden Age" view of the past can be a revolutionary idea.)

Who was to blame for riot and rebellion? On July 7, 1549, William Paget (1505–63) wrote to Protector Somerset urging stiff penalties for the rebels. Otherwise, he noted, "the foot taketh upon him the part of the head, and commons is become a king, appointing conditions and laws to the governors, saying, 'Grant this, and that, and we will go home.'"[11] On the other hand, in 1550 Robert Crowley (1518?–88) blamed the same risings on "the greedy cormorants," the landlords.

True it is, the poor men (whom ye call peasant knaves) have deserved more [punishment] than you can devise to lay upon them. ... But ... [i]f you charge them with disobedience, you were first disobedient. For without a law to bear you, yea contrary to the law which forbiddeth all manner of oppression and extortion, and ... contrary to conscience ..., ye

---

[10]   A. Fletcher and D. MacCulloch, *Tudor Rebellions*, 4th ed. (1997), 144–6, from BL, Harleian MS. 304, f. 75, signed by Kett, Thomas Cod, Thomas Aldryche, and others.

[11]   Fletcher and MacCulloch, *Tudor Rebellions*, 148, from PRO, SP10/8/4 (*CSPD, Edw. VI*, no. 301); also J. Strype, *Ecclesiastical Memorials: Relating Chiefly to Religion, and the Reformation of It, and the Emergencies of the Church of England, under King Henry VIII, King Edward VI, and Queen Mary I* (Oxford, 1822), 2.ii: 429–37, from BL, Cott. Libr. Titus F. 3.

enclosed from the poor their due commons, levied greater fines than heretofore have been levied, put them from the liberties (and in a manner inheritance) that they held by custom, and raised their rents. Yea, when there was a law ratified to the contrary, you ceased not to find means either to compel your tenants to consent to your desire in enclosing, or else ye found such mastership that no man durst gainsay your doings for fear of displeasure. And what obedience showed you, when the king's proclamations were sent forth, and commissions directed for the laying open of your enclosures, and yet you left not off to enclose still?[12]

What have the landlords done wrong, according to Crowley? Does such a complaint reinforce or contest the Great Chain of Being?

The Scold, the Witch, and the Almswoman

Some contemporaries thought that women could bring the Great Chain into disarray even by non-riotous means. In 1558 John Knox (ca. 1514–72) directed his infamous diatribe, *First Blast of the Trumpet against the Monstrous Regiment of Women*, against the recently departed Catholic rulers Mary Tudor in England and Mary of Guise (1515–60) in Scotland:

To promote a woman to bear rule, superiority, dominion or empire above any realm, nation, or city is repugnant to nature, contumely to God, a thing most contrarious to His revealed will and approved ordinance, and finally it is the subversion of good order, of all equity and justice.[13]

Queen Elizabeth was outraged that such sentiments could be published during *her* reign. But Knox refused to retract the work. Similar sentiments colored the trial of Ann Turner in 1615, who was executed for the murder of Sir Thomas Overbury (1581–1613), when Chief Justice Edward Coke (1552–1634) gave the following summation to the jury:

he ... left to their consideration the seven deadly sins: A strumpet. A bawd. A sorcerer. A conjurer. A Papist. A daughter of Forman [Dr. Simon Forman, a prominent astrologer, magus, and quack doctor, 1552–1611], the foreman of the devil (she ever styled him in her letters, sweet father). A consultor with witches and conjurors. And whether a murderer in the highest degree or not, that was now referred to them to determine.[14]

Regardless of Turner's guilt (the case is too complicated to discuss here, but she had very probably assisted Frances Howard, Lady Essex [1591–1632], in

---

[12] C. H. Williams, *English Historical Documents, 1485–1558* (1967), 309–13, from "The Waie to Wealth," in *The Select Works of Robert Crowley*, ed. J. M. Cowper (E.E.T.S., 1872), 131–50.

[13] *The Works of John Knox*, ed. D. Laing (Edinburgh, 1855), 4: 373; compared with J. Guy, "Tudor Monarchy and its Critiques," in *The Tudor Monarchy*, ed. Guy (1997), 93.

[14] [Nov. 9, 1615] to Sir John Egerton, J. P. Collier, ed., *The Egerton Papers* (Camden Society, 1840), 472–3.

poisoning Overbury), Coke's litany of evil is the classic early modern vision of the viciousness of woman. But discovering whether women were *actually* disorderly (as opposed to that contemporaries *thought* them so) is difficult. A Dutch visitor towards the end of Elizabeth's reign begins a descriptive passage by stressing women's subordinate status and yet concludes by claiming England as "the paradise of married women."

Wives in England are entirely in the power of their husbands, their lives only excepted. Therefore when they marry, they give up the surname of their father and of the family from which they are descended, and take the surname of their husbands, except in the case of duchesses, countesses, and baronesses, who, when they marry gentlemen of inferior degree, retain their first name and title, which, for the ambition of the said ladies, is rather allowed than commended. But although the women there are entirely in the power of their husbands except for their lives, yet they are not kept so strictly as they are in Spain or elsewhere. Nor are they shut up, but they have the free management of the house or housekeeping, after the fashion of those of the Netherlands and others their neighbors. They go to market to buy what they like best to eat. They are well-dressed, fond of taking it easy, and commonly leave the care of household matters and drudgery to their servants. They sit before their doors, decked out in fine clothes, in order to see and be seen by the passers-by. In all banquets and feasts they are shown the greatest honor; they are placed at the upper end of the table, where they are the first served; at the lower end they help the men. All the rest of their time they employ in walking and riding, in playing at cards or otherwise, in visiting their friends and keeping company, conversing with their equals (whom they term *gosseps* [gossip, woman's neighbor and friend]) and their neighbors, and making merry with them at child-births, christenings, churchings, and funerals; and all this with the permission and knowledge of their husbands, as such is the custom. Although the husbands often recommend to them the pains, industry, and care of the German or Dutch women, who do what the men ought to do both in the house and in the shops, for which services in England men are employed, nevertheless the women usually persist in retaining their customs. This is why England is called the Paradise of married women.[15]

These comments best apply to women of what social status? Does the writer approve or disapprove of the condition of women in England? What are the strengths and weaknesses of a foreigner's view for the historian?

One indication of contemporary ambivalence about women is that, at the lowest social levels, courts recorded numerous insults directed towards them, often by other women. During Elizabeth's reign, one Essex man defamed a widow "calling her whore, arrant whore and ridden whore"; another decried his neighbor's wife as a "butter-mouthed whore." One woman called another "harlot," only to be called "witch."[16] Women saw Church and State courts and punishments as just one more arena for their disputes. When one declared to another on a London street in 1613, "Thou art a quean [hussy] and a wrymouth quean and I

---

[15] W. Rye, ed., *England as Seen by Foreigners in the Days of Elizabeth and James I* (1865, reprinted New York, 1967), 72–3, from E. Van Meteren, *Historie der Neder–landschen* (originally 1599, this ed. from 1614), f. 258.

[16] Emmison, *Elizabethan Life: Morals*, 49.

will make thee do penance in a white sheet; and I will have thee carted out of the street," she revealed a knowledge that consistory courts could require someone to do penance for moral infractions by standing them in a public place in a white robe with a tapir (candle), and that quarter sessions could sentence bastard-bearers and others to be tied to the end of a cart and paraded or even whipped around town.[17] One regional study found that of 203 women punished in the early seventeenth century for bearing bastards, 112 (55 percent) were imprisoned and a further 71 (35 percent) were whipped. In the same period 135 men were punished, but only 4 percent were imprisoned and 25 percent whipped. Why the disparity between genders in punishment? As you consider the statutory response to poverty (below), you might contemplate why bastard-bearers, in particular, were punished so harshly. We noted above that Harrison separated the deserving poor from the thriftless poor – the rioter, the vagabond, the rogue, and the strumpet. Consider how the overseers of the poor in Braintree parish, Essex, attempted to distinguish deserving from undeserving poor women (1619–21, document 5.6). How and at what stages in their lives were women particularly prone to poverty? To disorder?

It is not much of a leap from the deserving poor woman to the witch, for historians have found that those executed for witchcraft in the early modern period were women (about 80 percent) and poor. An accusation from Elizabethan Essex exemplifies the charges brought against these women:

Joan Cocke of Kelvedon did lay her hands upon the knees of Richard Sherman, clapping her hand, upon which it is by common report come to our knowledge that he was presently [instantly] lamed and yet halteth. Noble's wife of Kelvedon [Joan Cocke's daughter] is suspected, by reason that she could not have butter according as she was wont to be served by Belfield's wife of Inworth, to have by the craft of witchcraft slain and killed one milch neat [milk cow], and two other to have caused to give milk of all colors, being the beasts of Belfield's wife.[18]

Likewise, John Rivet gave information against Elizabeth Clarke of Suffolk in 1645:

That about Christmas last, his wife was taken sick and lame, with such violent fits that this informant verily conceived that her sickness was something more than merely natural. Whereupon this informant, about a fortnight since, went to a cunning woman, the wife of one Hovye, at Hadleigh in Suffolk, who told this informant that his wife was cursed by two women who were near neighbors to this informant, the one dwelling a little above his house and the other beneath the house, this informant's house standing on the side of an hill. Whereupon he believed his said wife was bewitched by one Elizabeth Clarke, *alias*

---

[17] June 8, 1613, in L. Gowing, "Language, Power and the Law: Women's Slander Litigation in Early Modern London," in *Women, Crime and the Courts in Early Modern England*, ed. J. Kermode and G. Walker (Chapel Hill, 1994), 33, from Greater London RO, DL/C 221, f. 1189v., Cartwright con Hixwell.

[18] Emmison, *Elizabethan Life: Disorder*, 28, undated Elizabethan accusations, from Essex.

Bedinfield, for that the said Elizabeth's mother and some other of her kinsfolk did suffer death for witchcraft and murder.[19]

Successive statutes against witchcraft in 1542, 1563, and 1604 established ever harsher punishments for a wider range of offenses, but also demanded stricter standards of proof until final repeal in 1736. Given that the base of a legal charge against a witch was that she or he had made a pact with the Devil, why were the spells supposedly inflicted – making a person lame, causing milk to spoil – of such a mundane nature? Few contemporaries or historians have given such a plausible answer to this question as Reginald Scot (1538?–99). Can you use his comments (1584, document 5.7), along with the accusations above, to list some popular beliefs about witches? How does he know about the witchcraft cases he discusses? Does Scot think witches exist? Does he think people who *believe* themselves witches exist? Why were witches poor women?

Poor Laws and the Reform of Popular Culture

How did the State and the ruling elite respond to such disorder and potential disorder? Corporal and capital punishments included cucking stools for scolds (in 1579 Oxford ordered a portable cucking stool built "to punish such women as shall undecently abuse any person of this city by words"[20]), carting for prostitutes or bastard-bearers, whipping and, later, branding for vagabonds, and hanging for murderers and repeat offenders.

Curbing everyday disorder was often the business of overworked justices and bureaucrats. They attempted to stifle miscreants and ensure basic economic justice in order to calm would-be rioters. We have already considered how the government attempted to enforce laws against forestalling, regrating, and engrossing in the grain trade during dearths. Similarly, note the Privy Council's questions to London's lord mayor and aldermen concerning the food supply and assize of bread (set price and quality) on March 23, 1574:

(1) First what grain have you of the provision of the city or brought of all sorts and what quantity of every sort and in what garners [granaries?] and where is the same bestowed?...
(7) What medium have you made of the price of the several sorts of the said corn and what assize have you set to the bakers and brewers in that behalf...?

---

[19]   T. B. Howell, comp., *A Complete Collection of State Trials* (1816), 4: 832–3; compared with M. L. Kekewich, ed., *Princes and Peoples: France and the British Isles, 1620–1714* (Manchester, 1994), 131–3, from *Several Examinations and Confessions of Witches* (1645).
[20]   W. H. Turner, ed., *Selections from the Records of the City of Oxford, with Extracts from other Documents Illustrating the Municipal History, Henry VIII to Elizabeth, 1509–1583* (Oxford, 1880), 403, from City of Oxford Council Book, 213.

(11) That the mayor do declare what intention they have hereafter to amend this error in lack of provision of bread corn?[21]

Compare these regulatory actions with William Lambarde's as a JP (1580–8, document 5.8). Can one distinguish between national and local issues? Public and private life? Moral and market economic issues? Using these documents as a guide, what did the English governing classes want to prevent?

Debate raged on the problem of the poor during the last two decades of Elizabeth's reign and the first of James I's (reigned 1603–25). England's economy, particularly the grain and wool trade, had deep systemic flaws by 1580. Writers and politicians began to distinguish not just between the impotent (widows, disabled, orphans) and the thriftless (sturdy beggars) poor, but also to insert a third group: the laboring (and unemployed) poor. Two interrelated lines of response were to insist on a Reformation of Manners to shape the behavior of ordinary people and to reform statutes regarding the poor, vagabonds, apprentices, and workers. Edward Hext's somewhat rambling ideas presented to Lord Burghley (1596, document 5.9) were born of practical experience on petty and quarter sessions. Where does he locate the problems facing the poor relief system, and how does he propose to solve them? One might debate the merit of his ideas, then and now.

Elizabethans turned to a flurry of legislation to restore social order. In 1563, an Act for the Relief of the Poor (5 Eliz. I, c. 3) gave sanction to a system of charitable alms but did nothing to require that parishioners pay them, while a Statute of Artificers (c. 4) kept apprentices and workers hired for a whole year, but limited wages. In the 1570s, an Act for the Punishment of Vagabonds and Relief of the Poor (1572, 14 Eliz. I, c. 5) required that sturdy beggars avoiding work be whipped and burnt through the gristle of the right ear, and that parishes keep a register book of the deserving poor. A further Act for Setting the Poor to Work (1576, 18 Eliz. I, c. 3) required that counties set up a stock of hemp, flax, wool, etc. for the poor to work and earn their own livelihood. But few counties established any such stock before the 1630s, and even then good intentions were evident more than results. The reforms of early Elizabethan Parliaments were dwarfed by the onslaught of legislation in the 1597–8 session, which produced Acts: against decaying towns (39 Eliz. I, c. 1, allowing cottages on the commons for the poor), promoting tillage and limiting enclosure (c. 2), and on poor relief (c. 3, document 5.10), rogues and vagabonds (c. 4), hospitals for the poor (c. 5), and laborers (c. 12). The 1601 session returned to poor relief and revised 39 Eliz. I, c. 3 (43 Eliz. I, c. 2). Finally, James's Parliaments reexamined the 1563 Statute of Artificers (1604, 1 James I, c. 6) and the discouragement of rogues and vagabonds (c. 7, which required the branding of the same with an "R"; and in 1610, 7 & 8 James I, c. 4, which required a house of correction in every county);

---

[21] N. S. B. Gras, *Evolution of the English Corn Market* (Cambridge, Mass., 1915), 450–1; compared with R. H. Tawney and E. Power, eds., *Tudor Economic Documents* (1924), 1: 156–61, from London Guildhall Repertories.

and established laws regarding alehouses (1606, 4 James I, c. 4) and drunkenness (c. 5). How does the 1598 Poor Relief Act (5.10) define the poor? How are they to be relieved? Who should pay for such relief?

As for the Reformation of Manners, attacks on alehouses as centers of prostitution, drunkenness, and prohibited games, as well as on swearing, blasphemy, profaning the Sabbath, dances and revels, pitted a reforming culture against traditional culture (for the Reformation of Manners in the 1690s, see chapter 9). Whether or not such moral earnestness was largely a feature of the "godly" or Puritans, as some historians assert, there was an upsurge of legislation. Between the 1570s and 1610, nine parliamentary bills dealt with bastard-bearing, thirty-five attacked drunkenness, and six swearing; and the statutes passed included both fines and corporal punishment. In 1592, for example, Lancashire sessions banned "unlawful games or disorders in [ale]house, backside, garden or alley [often used for bowls]," as well as "wakes, bullbaitings, bearbaitings, May games, and cockfightings."[22] Also in 1592, the York High Commission proscribed the following Sunday activities, because, they argued,

a great number of evil disposed persons of the younger sort..., being led away with vain and fantastical delights (much more like infidels than Christians)..., have...often and...by great troops...[gone] to rushbearings..., maypoles, May games, morris dances..., Summer games, with other pipings and dancings, bullbaitings, bearbaitings or to some other unlawful or ungodly pastimes, frequenting also feasts, drinkings, stage plays, ridiculous shows, wakes..., and other ethnical and unchristian meetings whereby the Sabbath hath been usually profaned, the resort to the church greatly neglected and sermons and catechizing...highly dishonored.[23]

Assize orders for the Western counties laid down roughly the same rule in 1627, 1628, and 1632:

in regard of the infinite number of inconveniences daily arising by means of revels, church ales, clerk's ales, and other public ales, [they] be utterly from henceforth suppressed. ...And for the further avoiding of the concourse of idle people it is further ordered that minstrels and such other person that usually carry up and down bulls and bears to bait, being rogues by the statute, shall be punished as rogues.[24]

How might reformers react to popular action, such as charivaris, described earlier in this chapter? As we shall see in the following chapter, local cultural divisions would intersect with national political ones by the 1630s.

---

[22] Emmison, *Elizabethan Life: Disorder*, 230.

[23] R. W. Hoyle, "Advancing the Reformation in the North: Orders from York High Commissions, 1583 and 1592," *Northern History* 28 (1992): 225–7; compared with S. Hindle, *The State and Social Change in Early Modern England, 1550–1640* (Houndmills, Basingstoke, 2000), 192, from Yorkshire Archaeological Society, Leeds DD56/5.

[24] J. S. Cockburn, *Western Circuit Assize Orders, 1629–1648* (Camden Society, 4th ser., 17, 1976), 46.

Plate 6 *A morris dance, early seventeenth century.* (*Source: The Thames at Richmond, with the old Royal Palace*, Flemish school, detail, Fitzwilliam Museum, Cambridge)

The morris dance, with its bells and hobby horse, is considered part of traditional English folk culture. Is it part of popular culture? What is the relation suggested between elite and popular culture in this painting (you might distinguish social status by apparel)? From the documents, who wanted to reform popular culture? Why?

HISTORIOGRAPHY

Was early modern England violent? Yes, says L. Stone, "Interpersonal Violence in English Society," *P & P* 101 (1983); no, says A. Macfarlane,

"Violence," in *The Culture of Capitalism* (Oxford, 1987). At the domestic and local level, disorder and violence could be both verbal and brutally physical (see S. D. Amussen, "Punishment, Discipline, and Power: The Social Meanings of Violence in Early Modern England," *JBS* 34, 1, 1995). For the former, see L. Gowing, "Gender and the Language of Insult in Early Modern London," *History Workshop Journal* 35 (1993); for the latter, P. Rushton, "'The Matter in Variance': Domestic Conflict in the Pre-Industrial Economy of North-East England," *Journal of Social History* 25 (1992); or G. Walker, "Rereading Rape and Sexual Violence in Early Modern England," *Gender and History* 10 (1998), which also shows the literary quality of legal records. For Scottish interpersonal violence, see J. Wormald, "Bloodfeud, Kindred and Government in Early Modern Scotland," *P & P* 87 (1980). For communal responses to those perceived as disorderly, see M. Ingram, "Ridings, Rough Music and the 'Reform of Popular Culture' in Early Modern England," *P & P* 105 (1984) (although Ingram and D. Underdown disagree on the meaning of such responses: see below); and J. R. Kent, "'Folk Justice' and Royal Justice in Early Seventeenth-Century England: A 'Charivari' in the Midlands," *Midland History* 8 (1983). S. Hindle, "Custom, Festival and Protest in Early Modern England: The Little Budworth Wakes, St. Peter's Day, 1596," *Rural History* 6 (1995) suggests how revels could shade into rebellion.

Until recently, riots have not been as well served by historians as rebellions. Now, the relevant chapters in R. Manning, *Village Revolts: Social Protest and Popular Disturbances in England, 1509–1640* (Oxford, 1988) may be contrasted with those in B. Sharp, *In Contempt of All Authority: Rural Artisans and the Riot in the West of England, 1586–1660* (Berkeley, 1980); and A. Wall, "Riot," in *Power and Protest in England, 1525–1640* (2000). Food riots are examined in J. Walter, "Grain Riots and Popular Attitudes to the Law: Maldon and the Crisis of 1629," in *An Ungovernable People: The English and their Law in the Seventeenth and Eighteenth Centuries*, ed. J. Brewer and J. Styles (1980); and J. Walter and K. Wrightson, "Dearth and the Social Order in Early Modern England," *P & P* 71 (1976). See J. Walter, "A 'Rising of the People'?: The Oxfordshire Rising of 1596," *P & P* 107 (1985). Who acted in these riots? In part, women, argues R. Houlbrooke, "Women's Social Life and Common Action in England from the Fifteenth Century to the Eve of the Civil War," *Continuity and Change* 1 (1986). In part, adolescents, argue S. Brigden, "Youth and the English Reformation," *P & P* 95 (1982) and S. R. Smith, "London Apprentices as Seventeenth-Century Adolescents," *P & P* 61 (1973). See also I. K. Ben-Amos, *Adolescence and Youth in Early Modern England* (New Haven, 1994). For the overarching constraints of dearth and famine in early modern England, see the work of A. Appleby, and the reexamination of it in J. Walter's and R. Schofield's introduction to *Famine, Disease and the Social Order in Early Modern Society* (Cambridge, 1989).

While no work discusses *all* Tudor and early Stuart rebellions before the Great Rebellion of 1642, Wall, "Rebellion," in *Power and Protest in England*, illuminates the wider context of such disorders; and distinct chapters in A. Fletcher and D. MacCulloch, *Tudor Rebellions*, 4th ed. (1997) describe revolts from the Pilgrimage of Grace to the Northern Rebellion, while their analytic chapters are also recommended. C. S. L. Davies analyzes the role of popular religion in the Pilgrimage of Grace in *Order and Disorder in Early Modern England*, ed. A. Fletcher and J. Stevenson (Cambridge, 1985), and in *Rebellion, Popular Protest and the Social Order in Early Modern England*, ed. P. Slack (Cambridge, 1984). M. E. James analyzes "order" in the Northern Rising of 1569, reprinted in his *Society, Politics and Culture: Studies in Early Modern England* (Cambridge, 1986). Chapters on disorder, cultural conflict, and early Stuart popular politics in D. Underdown, *Revel, Riot and Rebellion: Popular Politics and Culture in England, 1603–1660* (Oxford, 1985) suggest that local participants often better realized the national implications of their actions than is argued in Manning.

Women as madonnas or prostitutes are images repeated in everyday thought both then and now. Historians have often succumbed to this easy labeling, although see B. Harris, "Women and Politics in early Tudor England," *HJ* 33 (1990) for an alternative. B. Capp has recently questioned the applicability of two models for early modern gender roles and relations in two articles: the "double standard" argument (for which see K. Thomas, *Journal of the History of Ideas* 20, 1959), in "The Double Standard Revisited: Plebeian Women and Male Sexual Reputation in Early Modern England," *P & P* 162 (1999); and the "separate spheres" model, in "Separate Domains?: Women and Authority in Early Modern England," in *The Experience of Authority in Early Modern England*, ed. P. Griffiths, A. Fox, and S. Hindle (Basingstoke, 1996). For women's history generally, see articles in J. Kermode and G. Walker, eds., *Women, Crime and the Courts in Early Modern England* (Chapel Hill, 1994), especially Gowing on slander and Ingram on scolds; M. Prior, ed., *Women in English Society 1500–1800* (1985), especially Prior on women in towns; and two strong surveys: A. Laurence, *Women in England, 1500–1760: A Social History* (1995) and S. Mendelson and P. Crawford, *Women in Early Modern England, 1550–1720* (Oxford, 1999). For witches (a gender-related but not gender-specific issue), see A. Gregory, "Witchcraft, Politics and 'Good Neighbourhood' in Early Seventeenth-Century Rye," *P & P* 130 (1991); C. Holmes, "Women: Witnesses and Witches," *P & P* 140 (1993); and J. Sharpe, "Witchcraft and Women in Seventeenth-Century England: Some Northern Evidence," *Continuity and Change* 6 (1991). C. Holmes, "Popular Culture?: Witches, Magistrates, and Divines in Early Modern England," in *Understanding Popular Culture*, ed. S. L. Kaplan (Berlin, 1984) is also useful for the relation between "high" and "low" culture.

Selections from the classic works on the social dimension of witchcraft by A. Macfarlane (1970) and K. Thomas (1972) are available in M. Marwick, ed., *Witchcraft and Sorcery*, 2nd ed. (Harmondsworth, Middlesex, 1986). C. Larner revolutionized thinking on Scottish witchcraft. See her essays on this subject, on the views of James VI and I on witchcraft, and on comparing English and Scottish witch accusations, in *Witchcraft and Religion: The Politics of Popular Belief* (Oxford, 1984). See also L. Jackson, "Witches, Wives and Mothers: Witchcraft Persecution and Women's Confessions in Seventeenth-Century England," *Women's History Review* 4 (1995).

For vagabonds, see A. L. Beier, "Social Problems in Elizabethan London" (1978–9, reprinted in *The Tudor and Stuart Town: A Reader in Urban History, 1530–1688*, ed. J. Barry, 1990); Beier, "The Social Problems of an Elizabethan County Town: Warwick 1580–90," in *Country Towns in Pre-Industrial England*, ed. P. Clark (Leicester, 1981); Beier, "Vagrants and the Social Order in Elizabethan England," *P & P* 64 (1974) (though see debate sparked by this, *P & P* 71, 1976); and P. Slack, "Vagrants and Vagrancy in England, 1598–1664," *EcHR* 28 (1974). Slack's analysis of "Poverty and Social Regulation," in *The Reign of Elizabeth I*, ed. C. Haigh (1984) examines government and intellectual responses (see also his *From Reformation to Improvement*, Oxford, 1999), as does, at the parish level, M. K. McIntosh, "Local Responses to the Poor in Late Medieval and Tudor England," *Continuity and Change* 3 (1988). One government response to the problems is analyzed in S. T. Bindoff, "The Making of the Statute of Artificers," in *English Government and Society*, ed. Bindoff et al. (1961); and D. Woodward, "The Background to the Statute of Artificers: The Genesis of Labour Policy, 1558–63," *EcHR* 33 (1980). A. L. Gillespie, "Negotiating Order in Early Seventeenth-Century Ireland," in *Negotiating Power in Early Modern Society*, ed. M. J. Braddick and J. Alter (Cambridge, 2001) discusses the politics of social issues across the Irish Sea. An important recent work on reactions to disorder is M. K. McIntosh, *Controlling Misbehaviour in England, 1370–1600* (Cambridge, 1998), and a special issue of *JBS* 37, 3 (1998) debates McIntosh's findings. Still useful is K. Wrightson, "Two Concepts of Order: Justices, Constables and Jurymen in Seventeenth-Century England," in Brewer and Styles.

Were many English villages the scene of a struggle in the late Tudor and early Stuart period between a "godly" minority and a less religious and more traditional "multitude"? This is the argument best expressed in K. Wrightson, *English Society, 1580–1680* (1982); K. Wrightson and D. Levine, *Poverty and Piety in an English Village: Terling, 1525–1700* (New York, 1979, rev. ed., Oxford, 1995); and Underdown, *Revel, Riot and Rebellion*. But the "godliness" of the Reformation of Manners movement has been contested by M. Spufford, "Puritanism and Social Control?," in Fletcher and Stevenson; and M. Ingram, in Griffiths, Fox, and Hindle; in *Popular Culture in England, c.1500–1850*, ed. T. Harris (New York,

1995); and in *P & P* (above). For the perennial struggle over the reform of alehouses, see P. Clark's study over a much longer period (1983); K. Wrightson, "Alehouses, Order and Reformation in Rural England, 1590–1660," in *Popular Culture and Class Conflict, 1590–1914: Explorations in the History of Labour and Leisure*, ed. E. and S. Yeo (Hassocks, 1981); and S. K. Roberts, "Alehouses, Brewing and Government Under the Early Stuarts," *Southern History* 2 (1980). Both D. Underdown and S. Amussen contribute to Harris's collection on popular culture as well as that edited by Fletcher and Stevenson. Underdown's "The Taming of the Scold: The Enforcement of Patriarchal Authority in Early Modern England," in Fletcher and Stevenson is particularly recommended, but see also Ingram on scolds in Kermode and Walker. For popular culture as a whole, see the articles in B. Reay, ed., *Popular Culture in Seventeenth-Century England* (1985).

DOCUMENTS

5.1   William Fleetwood, London Recorder, to William Cecil, Lord Treasurer Burghley (July 7, 1585)[25]

Upon Friday last we sat at the Justice Hall at Newgate from 7 in the morning until 7 at night, where were condemned certain horse stealers, cutpurses, and such like, to the number of 10, whereof 9 were executed, and the tenth stayed by a means from the court. These were executed upon Saturday in the morning. There was a shoemaker also condemned for willful murder committed in the Blackfriars, who was executed upon Monday in the morning. The same day my lord mayor being absent ... and also all my lords the justices of the benches ..., we few that were there did spend the same day about the searching out of sundry that were receptors of felons, where we found a great many as well in London, Westminster, Southwark, as in all other places about the same. Amongst our travails this one matter tumbled out by the way, that one Wotton a gentleman born, and sometime a merchant man of good credit, who falling by time into decay, kept an alehouse at Smarts Key near Billingsgate, and after, for some misdemeanor being put down, he reared up a new trade of life, and in the same house he procured all the cutpurses about this city to repair to his said house. There, was a schoolhouse set up to learn young boys to cut purses. There were hung up two devices, the one was a pocket, the other was a purse. The pocket had in it certain counters [counterfeit coins] and was hung about with hawks bells, and over the top did hang a little sacring-bell [rung at the elevation of the host]; and he that could take out a counter without any noise, was allowed to be *a public foister*; and he that could take a piece of silver out of the purse without the noise of any of the bells, he was adjudged *a judicial nipper*. *Nota* that a foister is a pickpocket, and a nipper is termed a pickpurse, or a cutpurse.

[25]   H. Ellis, ed., *Original Letters, Illustrative of English History* (1824; reprinted New York, 1970), 2: 295–9, from BL, MS. Lansdowne 44, art. 38.

5.2 Wiltshire Quarter Sessions, Deposition of Thomas Mills, Cutler, and his Wife Agnes (Trinity [Spring] Term, 1618)[26]

Upon Wednesday [27] May [1618], about eight or nine . . . in the morning, there came to Quemerford a young fellow of Calne named Croppe, playing upon a drum, accompanied with three or four men and ten or twelve boys; and Ralph Wellsteede of Quemerford, this examinate's landlord, and himself came to them as far as the bridge in Quemerford, and asked them what they meant, and they answered that there was a skimmington dwelling there, and they came for him. . . . About noon came again from Calne to Quemerford another drummer named William Wiatt, and with him three or four hundred men, some like soldiers armed with pieces and other weapons, and a man riding upon a horse, having a white night cap upon his head, two shoeing horns hanging by his ears, a counterfeit beard upon his chin made of a deer's tail, a smock upon the top of his garments, and he rode upon a red horse with a pair of pots under him, and in them some quantity of brewing grains, which he used to cast upon the press of people, rushing over thick upon him in the way as he passed; and he and all his company made a stand when they came just against this examinant's house, and then the gunners shot off their pieces, pipes and horns were sounded, together with lowbells and other smaller bells which the company had amongst them, and rams' horns and bucks' horns, carried upon forks, were then and there lifted up and shown. . . . Thomas Mills . . . locked the street door and locked his wife into his chamber where she lay . . . and presently the parties abovementioned and diverse others rushed in upon him into his entry, and thence into his hall, and broke open his chamber door upon his wife . . . and . . . took her up by the arms and the legs, and had her out through the hall into the entry, where being a wet hole, they threw her down into it and trod upon her and buried her filthily with dirt and did beat her black and blue in many places.

5.3 Examination of Anne Carter and Others Regarding the Maldon Riot (1629)[27]

The examination of Anne wife of John Carter of Maldon butcher taken the 28th day of April *anno* 1629. . . . The said examinate confesseth touching the late assembling of many women and their taking away of corn out of the ships at Burrow Hills in Totham that before the said assembly, herself heard one Phillip Ewdes a hoyman [hoy, a small sloop] of Lee complain that the owners of the said vessel were Dunkirks [Dunkirk merchants] and that it was pity they were suffered to lie there, by occasion of which speech and of other men sailors, herself and diverse other women to the

---

[26] M. Ingram, "Ridings, Rough Music and the 'Reform of Popular Culture' in Early Modern England," *P & P* 105 (1984): 105; compared with Coward, *Social Change*, 109–10, from Wiltshire RO, Trowbridge, Quarter Sessions Great Rolls, Trinity 1618, no. 168.

[27] P. Crawford and L. Goring, *Women's Worlds in Seventeenth-Century England: A Sourcebook* (2000), 247–9, from Maldon Court Leet Records, Essex RO, D/B 3/3 208, m. 14, 18.

number of above a hundred of Maldon, Heybridge, and Witham and from the heath called Totham Heath assembled together to the said Burrow Hills in the parish of Greater Totham where the said vessels did lie in the channel and she and the rest of the women entered into one of the said ships, and the Flemings who were therein filled the rye which was therein into the aprons and coats of many of the women and some children who were in the company which they carried away but that herself took not any whit thereof. And she denieth that she did draw any company of women from Witham to the said Burrow Hills.

Anne the wife of Thomas Speareman of Maldon fisherman examined the fourth day of May before his majesty's bailiffs and justice of the said borough: The said examinate confesseth that she with others (because she could not have corn in the market and certain Flemish ships lying at Borrow Hills in the parish of Little Totham there to receive in corn to carry beyond sea) did go down about the 23rd day of March last past and there being assembled diverse women to the number of about seven score they did enter into one of the said ships and did take away a quantity of corn which was therein but how much she knoweth not, and denieth that any did set her on the said action, and being demanded why she stayed not when she was required and charged by one of the bailiffs of the said town to depart home she saith she saw the rest go and she followed them.

Elizabeth the wife of Samuel Sturgion of Maldon laborer examined the said fourth day of May saith that she being in poverty and wanting victual for her children and being called out of her house by Anne the wife of Thomas Spearman of Maldon and Dorothy the wife of John Berry of the same town about the said 23rd of March she went with them and other women to . . . Burrow Hills in Little Totham where the said Flemish ships did lie where there were a great many of women met and they entered into one of the same ships and took out a quantity of corn whereof herself had about half a bushel and she denieth that any did set her on but only the two women aforesaid. . . .

Dorothy wife of John Berry of Maldon shepherd examined the day and year abovesaid saith that there being want of corn in the market and she being a poor woman and hearing that there were Flemish vessels at Burrow Hills at Little Totham which lay to carry away corn she with other women went to the said place where they entered into one of the said Flemish vessels where they had filled into their aprons a quantity of rye and being demanded who procured her thither she answereth the cry of the country and her own want.

5.4 Sir Roger Wilbraham on Enclosure Riots in the East Midlands (ca. mid-June–December 6, 1607)[28]

Beggars and vagrants in the town of Northampton, angered at the enclosures made near the town, in bands during the night threw down a part thereof. And in as much as they are not put down – their numbers increase, both from this town

[28] H. S. Scott, ed., *Journal of Sir Roger Wilbraham* (*Camden Miscellany* 10, Camden Society, 3rd ser., 4, 1902), 91–4; compared with B. W. Clapp, H. E. S. Fisher, and A. R. J. Jurica, eds., *Documents in English Economic History* (1977), 132–3, original in French.

and diverse towns in the county and in the counties of Warwick, Leicester, etc., and for 20 days their numbers continue to increase, till 300 or more in one place night and day are throwing down the new enclosures; nor do they desist in spite of two proclamations made by the king on different occasions that they should have justice and mercy if they desisted. And yet they continue until Sir A[ntony] Mildmay with some horsemen using force slay some ten in hot blood; and thus they were put down. Afterwards at the assizes of the before mentioned several counties, two or three were hanged as an example. So that, as the king says, the punishment of a few may impress the majority with fear. Moreover the proclamation says that it is not a legal course for subjects to remedy their grievances by force, but that they should petition the king to be relieved according to justice. And the judges of assize in order to satisfy the common people inveigh against enclosers and depopulators; and inquire concerning them and promise reformation at the hands of justice. And this puts courage into the common people, so that with mutterings they threaten to have a more violent revenge if they cannot be relieved. On this the [Privy] Council appoints select commissioners, learned in the law, in the six counties; to inquire concerning the acts of depopulation and conversion of arable into pasture land. And they report to the Council on December 6, 1607, to this effect. That in the counties of Lincoln, Leicester, Northampton, Warwick, Huntingdon, Bedford and Buckingham about 200 or 300 tenements have been depopulated, and a great number of acres have been converted from arable into pasture land. To wit, 9,000 acres in Northamptonshire and a great number in the other counties....

On this directions were given to the learned counsel that the most notorious enclosers in each county should be summoned this Christmas for Hilary Term before the Star Chamber and justice and mercy shown to them, so that they should not despair, nor should the common people insult them or be incited to make rebellion, whereof they are greatly suspected. Also the mayor of Northampton, the sheriff, and the neighboring justices who did not repress the outrages at the beginning should also be brought before the Star Chamber by reason of their remissness. And it is hoped that this public example may stay the fury of the common people. These deliberations I reported to the king at Newmarket on December 8th by order of the Council. And he seems to approve of this course.

5.5 Depositions Taken Before the Mayor and Aldermen of Norwich after Kett's Rising (1549–50)[29]

Made 21 September [1549]. Edmund Warden and Thomas Dorye churchwardens of the parish of St. Gregory demanded certain ornaments out of the hands of Robert Burnam being our parish clerk ..., and did advise him to turn his heart and become a new man. And he said he had offended no man but that he was able to answer. Then said I unto him that I heard a gentleman say when he was in prison that he was

---

[29] W. Rye, ed., *Depositions Taken Before the Mayor and Aldermen of Norwich* (Norwich, 1905), 18, 20–2; compared with Tawney and Power, *Tudor Economic Documents*, 1: 47–53, from Norwich Municipal Archives.

not afraid of his life of no man but of the said Burnam. Then answered the said Burnam and said: "There are too many gentlemen in England by five hundred." Then said I again, if thou speakest such a word again thou shalt go to prison. . . .

The examination of John Redhead before Thomas Cod, mayor of the city of Norwich, and others the 12th day February [1550]. John Redhead of Norwich, of the parish of St. Marten, worsted weaver, sayeth and confesseth: that upon a market day not a month passed . . . , being in the market upon his business to buy his victual, walking there he saw two or three persons men of the countryside standing together having conversation betwixt themselves. He heard the one of them speak to the other looking upon Norwich castle toward Kett [his corpse now hanging there in chains] these words, *viz.*: "Oh Kett, God have mercy upon thy soul, and I trust in God that the king's majesty and his Council shall be informed once betwixt this and Midsummer even, that of their own gentleness thou shall be taken down by the grace of God and buried, and not hanged up for Winter store, and set a quietness in the realm, and that the ragged staff [John Dudley's, then earl of Warwick's, badge displayed on prominent houses] shall be taken down also of their own gentleness from the gentlemen's gates in this city, and to have no more King's Arms but one within this city under Christ but King Edward VI, God save his Grace"; which persons he saith he never knew them, nor cannot name them. . . .

Examination of Nicholas Lowe of Norwich, worsted weaver, 22 June [1550], as to Robert Burnam; and deposes that while watching in W. Wymer Ward with deponent and two others, by order of the constables, grumbling at having to watch and saying that if Sir Richard Southwell, Sir Thomas Woodhouse, Mr. Roger Woodhouse, and Mr. Corbett were not offenders, they would not have such a band of men about them – for they fear bad measure, and said further if the camp [of Kett] had taken them four they would never have fought one stroke and that if the gentlemen do go forward as they have begun they would destroy the realm. . . .

[July 2, 1550, before Mayor Robert Rug and other justices.] William Stedde of Norwich, innholder, of the age of 40 years, sworn and examined saith and deposeth upon his oath: that . . . he was at Saxlingham at a marriage and there was one William Cowper of St. Margaret parish in Norwich, cooper, and diverse others; and as they sat at their dinner there amongst other words in communication . . . Cowper said: "That as sheep or lambs are a prey to the wolves or lions so are the poor men to the rich men or gentlemen." And moreover . . . Cowper said that there are more merchants now at this present time than there were wont [needed] to be by a hundred thousand, in carrying and conveying of vittles and such other things.

5.6 *Women Receiving Poor Relief, Braintree Parish, Essex (1619–21)*[30]

August 2, 1619, *Imprimis* [Firstly] at this meeting it was agreed that the widow Browne and her son if she do live and recover shall be removed to the almshouse at Braintree bridge, where we the last day did appoint Eliot should be.

---

[30] Crawford and Goring, *Women's Worlds*, 110–11, from Braintree Parish Records, Essex RO, D/P 284/8/3, ff. 3v–33 (extracts).

September 6, 1619, *Imprimis* order was taken at this meeting that Anne Gay shall be warned with all speed to provide her a service, or else that she shall be sent to the house of correction. . . .

Item notice is given us by William Stebbing of a wench entertained at John Beckwith's dwelling on Cursing Green, that is supposed to have a great belly [with child]; which the constables have warning to look after, and to take order to remove her if they find the report to be true.

February 8, 1620, *Imprimis* it was agreed that widow Gay be placed in the almshouse with Howell, and the widow Coe shall be put into the house where she is. . . .

February 5, 1621, [On the disposition of five shillings which had been received from the constables for the use of the poor:] It was agreed that Richard Loveday shall have two shillings of this money, in regard of the extraordinary charge he hath been at for the washing of his wife being lame.

It is agreed that the widow Gay shall have 12d. of the said money for pains taken with the widow Eliot and that for the time to come she shall have 6d. a week for attendance given upon the said widow, during the time the overseers shall think fit.

Item it is agreed that Margery Pierson shall be provided of an almshouse at the discretion of the overseers, because she is [a] helpful woman at their request to those that are sick. . . .

March 5, 1621, It is agreed that the widow Coe shall be provided of an almshouse in the Hyde at the discretion of the overseers and that the widow Gay shall be displaced out of the almshouse.

October 8, 1621, Item it is agreed that the widow Boltwood shall have 2s. 6d. allowed her out of the poor man's box and that she shall have an almshouse offered her which if she refuse she shall have no more allowance.

November 5, 1621, *Imprimis* it was agreed that widow Ingram's boy that should be taken from her and put into the hospital and that she being incorrigible in her idle and vicious course that she shall be sent to the house of correction.

5.7 *Reginald Scot,* The Discoverie of Witchcraft *(1584)*[31]

The Epistle. To the right worshipful Sir Thomas Scot, Kt., etc. Sir, I see among other malefactors many poor old women convented [brought] before you [as a judge] for working of miracles, otherwise called witchcraft, and therefore I thought you also a meet [fitting] person to whom I might commend my book. . . . I therefore (at this time) do only desire you to consider . . . the evidence that is commonly brought before you against them. See first whether the evidence be not frivolous, and whether the proofs brought against them be not incredible, consisting of guesses, presumptions, and impossibilities contrary to reason, scripture, and nature. See also what persons complain upon them, whether they be not of the basest, the unwisest, and most faithless kind of people. Also, may it please

[31] Scot, *Discoverie*, ed. B. Nicholson (Totowa, New Jersey, 1973), xiii–xv, 5–7, 10; compared with H. Haydn, ed., *The Portable Elizabethan Reader* (New York, 1955), 320–3.

you to weigh what accusations and crimes they lay to their charge, namely: "She was at my house of late, she would have had a pot of milk, she departed in a chafe [rage] because she had it not, she railed, she cursed, she mumbled and whispered, and finally she said she would be even with me; and soon after my child, my cow, my sow, or my pullet died, or was strangely taken. Nay (if it please your worship) I have further proof: I was with a wise woman, and she told me I had an ill neighbor, and that she would come to my house yet it were long, and so did she; and that she had a mark above her waste, and so had she: and God forgive me, my stomach hath gone against her a great while. Her mother before her was counted a witch, she hath been beaten and scratched by the face till blood was drawn upon her, because she hath been suspected, and afterwards some of those persons were said to amend." These are the certainties that I hear in their evidences.

Note also how easily they may be brought to confess that which they never did, nor lieth in the power of man to do: and then see whether I have cause to write as I do. . . .

Your loving cousin, Reg. Scot. . . .

Book 1, Chapter 3. One sort of such as are said to be witches, are women which be commonly old, lame, bleary-eyed, pale, foul, and full of wrinkles; poor and sullen, superstitious, and papists; or such as know no religion: in whose drowsy minds the Devil hath gotten a fine seat; so as, what mischief, mischance, calamity, or slaughter is brought to pass, they are easily persuaded the same is done by themselves; imprinting in their minds an earnest and constant imagination hereof. They are lean and deformed, showing melancholy in their faces, to the horror of all that see them. They are doting, scolds, mad, devilish; and not much differing from them that are thought to be possessed with spirits. . . .

These miserable wretches are so odious unto all their neighbors, and so feared, as few dare offend them, or deny them anything they ask: whereby they take upon them; yea, and sometimes think, that they can do such things as are beyond the ability of human nature. These go from house to house, and from door to door for a pot full of milk, yeast, drink, pottage, or some such relief; without the which they could hardly live: neither obtaining for their service and pains, nor by their art, nor yet at the Devil's hands (with whom they are said to make a perfect and visible bargain) either beauty, money, promotion, wealth, worship, pleasure, honor, knowledge, learning, or any other benefit whatsoever.

It falleth out many times, that neither their necessities, nor their expectation is answered or served, in those places where they beg or borrow; but rather their lewdness is by their neighbors reproved. And further, in tract of time the witch waxeth odious and tedious to her neighbors; and they again are despised and despited of her: so as sometimes she curseth one, and sometimes another; and that from the master of the house, his wife, children, cattle, etc., to the little pig that lieth in the sty. Thus in process of time they have all displeased her, and she hath wished evil luck unto them all; perhaps with curses and imprecations made in form. Doubtless (at length) some of her neighbors die, or fall sick; or some of their children are visited with diseases that vex them strangely: as apoplexies, epilepsies, convulsions, hot fevers, worms, etc. Which by ignorant parents are supposed to be the vengeance of witches. Yea and their opinions and conceits are confirmed and maintained by unskillful physicians. ... Also some of their cattle perish, either by disease or mischance. Then they, upon whom such adversities fall, weighing the fame that goeth upon this woman (her words, displeasure, and curses meeting so justly with their misfortune) do not only conceive, but also are resolved, that all their mishaps are brought to pass by her only means.

The witch on the other side expecting her neighbors' mischances, and seeing things sometimes come to pass according to her wishes, curses, and incantations ... being called before a justice, by due examination of the circumstances is driven to see her imprecations and desires, and her neighbors harms and losses to concur, and as it were to take effect: and so confesseth that she (as a goddess) hath brought such things to pass. ...

Another sort of witches there are, which be absolutely cozeners [cheats]. These take upon them, either for glory, fame, or gain, to do anything, which God or the Devil can do: either for foretelling of things to come, betraying of secrets, curing of maladies, or working of miracles. ...

Chapter 6. Alas! What an inept instrument is a toothless, old, impotent, and unwieldy woman to fly in the air? Truly, the Devil little needs such instruments to bring his purposes to pass.

5.8   William Lambarde's "Ephemeris" of his Actions as a Justice of the Peace (1580–8)[32]

October [1580] The 3 of October my father-in-law and I bound Walter Pelsant ... from keeping an alehouse any more; his sureties were Reignold Pelsant and Nicholas Miller of Wrotham, yeomen.

The 4 October I certified at the quarter sessions the said recognizances of Walter Pelsant, Thomas Chambers, William Cosin, and Thomas Norham for not keeping alehouses, and the said recognizances of James Hawkes, Thomas Pigeon, and George Colt for the keeping of good rule in their alehouses, and the said recognizance of John Sone for his appearance aforesaid, the said Walter Pelsant and John Usiner of Wrotham, butchers, being his sureties, which recognizance was then forfeit by his default of appearance.

The 25 October I delivered to the Lord Chief Baron the said examination of John Sone aforesaid.

My father-in-law and I entreated Nordashe of Kemsing to give over [cease] aleselling because no alehouse had been kept there within the memory of any man. ...

21 May [1583] There was holden at Maidstone a special session of the peace for the rogues, where diverse were bound and whipped.

I have signed a license for Thomas Godfrey to beg till Allhallowtide [November 1] (for his house burnt) within the limits of the Lord Cobham [alehouse?] only. ...

[32]   C. Read, ed., *William Lambarde and Local Government: His "Ephemeris" and Twenty-Nine Charges to Juries and Commissions* (Ithaca, 1962), 17–18, 29, 50–1, from Folger Library, MS. X.d. 249.

6–7 June [1588] Mr. Leveson and I took order for John Vaughan, a bastard child, begotten at Birling by Thomas Vaughan of Snodland, miller, on Marion Gorby, widow, of Birling also, which Thomas, with John Coveney and William Elfye, all of Birling, were bound, in £30, to save the parish harmless. Mr. Leveson hath the bond.

He and I took order also for Agnes Cumber, a bastard begotten on Agnes Cumber of East Malling by John Crowhurst of Aylesford, with the like bond of them and of Thomas Reynes of Burham, yeoman, for discharge of East Malling. And we ordered all the said four offenders to be whipped in the open market of West Malling, 8 June 1588.

5.9 Edward Hext, Somerset JP, to Lord Burghley on the Increase of Rogues and Vagabonds (September 25, 1596)[33]

Having long observed the rapines and thefts committed within this county where I serve, and finding they multiply daily to the utter impoverishing of the poor husbandman that beareth the greatest burthen of all services..., [I] do think it my bounden duty to present unto your honorable and grave consideration these calendars enclosed of the prisoners executed and delivered this year past in this county of Somerset, wherein your Lordship may behold 183 most wicked and desperate persons to be enlarged. And of these very few come to any good, for none will receive them into service....

I do not see how it is possible for the poor countryman to bear the burdens duly laid upon him, and the rapines of the infinite numbers of the wicked wandering idle people of the land, so as men are driven to watch their sheepfolds, their pastures, their woods, their cornfields, all things growing too too [sic] common. Others there be... that stick not to say boldly, "they must not starve, they will not starve." And this year there assembled 80 in a company and took a whole cart load of cheese from one driving it to a fair and dispersed it amongst them, for which some of them have endured long imprisonment and fine by the judgment of the good Lord Chief Justice at our last Christmas Sessions; which may grow dangerous by the aid of such numbers as are abroad, especially in this time of dearth, who no doubt animate them to all contempt both of noble men and gentlemen, continually buzzing into their ears that the rich men have gotten all into their hands and will starve the poor. And I may justly say that the infinite numbers of the idle wandering people and robbers of the land are the chiefest cause of the dearth, for though they labor not, and yet they spend doubly as much as the laborer doth, for they lie idly in the alehouses days and night eating and drinking excessively. And within these 3 months I took a thief that was executed this last assizes, that confessed unto me that he and two more lay in an alehouse three weeks, in which time they ate 20 fat sheep whereof they stole every night one, besides they breaks many a poor man's plough by stealing an ox or two from

---

[33] Tawney and Power, *Tudor Economic Documents*, 2: 339–46; compared with Salter, *Elizabeth I*, 68–70, from BL, MS. Lansdowne 81, art. 6, ff. 161–2.

him, and [he], not being able to buy more, leaseth a great parts of his tillage that year.... And such numbers being grown to this idle and thievish life, there are scant sufficient to do the ordinary tillage of the land, for I know that some having had their husbandmen sent for soldiers they have lost a great parts of their tillage that year, and others are not to be gotten by reason so many are abroad practicing all kind of villainy.

And when these lewd people are committed to the jail, the poor country that is robbed by them are enforced there to feed them, which they grieve at. And this year there hath been disbursed to the relief of the prisoners in the jail above £73, and yet they are allowed but 6d. a man weekly. And if they were not delivered at every quarter sessions, so much more money would not serve, nor too such jails would not hold them, but if this money might be employed to build some houses adjoining to the jail for them to work in; and every prisoner committed for any cause and not able to relieve himself compelled to work, and as many of them as are delivered upon their trials, either by acquittal of the grand jury or petty jury, burning in the hand, or whipping, presently transferred thence to the houses of correction to be kept in work..., the 10th felony will not be committed that now is. And if some like course might be taken with the wandering people they would easily be brought to their places of abode. And being abroad they all in general are receivers of all stolen things that are portable, as namely the tinker in his budget, the peddler in his hamper, the glassman in his basket, and the lewd proctors which carry the broad seal and green seals in their bags, covers infinite numbers of felonies, in such sort as the tenth felony cometh not to light, for he hath his receiver at hand in every alehouse in every bush. And these last rabble are very nurseries of rogues....

The corn that is wastefully spent and consumed in alehouses by the lewd wandering people will find the greatest parts of the poor, for it is most certain if they light upon an alehouse that hath strong ale they will not depart until they have drunk him dry. And it falleth out by experience that the alehouses of this land consumeth the greatest parts of the barley. For upon a survey taken of the alehouses only of the towns of Wells, [Somerset,] leaving out the taverns and inns, it appeared by their own confessions that they spent this last year twelve thousand bushels of barley malt, which would have afforded to every market of this shire 10 bushels weekly, and would have satisfied a great parts of the poor, a great part whereof is consumed by these wandering people, who being reduced to conformity, corn no doubt will be much more plentiful.

5.10   *Poor Relief Act (39 Eliz. I, c. 3) (1598)*[34]

Be it enacted by the authority of this present Parliament that the churchwardens of every parish, and four substantial householders there...who shall be nominated yearly..., under the hand and seal of two or more justices of the peace in the same county...dwelling in or near the same parish, shall be called overseers of

---

[34]   *SR*, 4, part 2: 896–9; compared with Tawney and Power, *Tudor Economic Documents*, 2: 346–54.

the poor.... And they...shall take order from time to time by and with the consent of two or more such justices of peace for setting to work of the children of all such whose parents shall not by the said persons be thought able to keep and maintain their children; and also all such persons married or unmarried as having no means to maintain them use no ordinary and daily trade of life to get their living by; and also to raise weekly or otherwise (by taxation of every inhabitant and every occupier of lands in the said parish...) a convenient stock of flax, hemp, wool, thread, iron, and other necessary ware and stuff to set the poor on work. And also competent sums of money for and towards the necessary relief of the lame, impotent, old, blind, and such other among them being poor and not able to work, and also for the putting out of such children to be apprentices, to be gathered out of the same parish.... Which said churchwardens and overseers..., or such of them as shall not be let by sickness or other just excuse to be allowed by such two justices of peace or more, shall meet together at the least once every month in the church of the said parish, upon the Sunday in the afternoon after divine service, there to consider of some good course to be taken and of some meet order to be set down in the premises...; upon pain that every one of them absenting themselves without lawful cause as aforesaid from such monthly meeting..., or being negligent in their office..., to forfeit for every such default twenty shillings.

2. And be it also enacted, that if the said justices of peace do perceive that the inhabitants of any parish are not able to levy among themselves sufficient sums of money for the purposes aforesaid, that then the said justices shall and may tax, rate, and assess as aforesaid any other of other parishes, or out of any parish within the hundred where the said parish is, to pay such sum and sums of money to the churchwardens and overseers of the said poor parish for the said purpose as the said justices shall think fit....

3. And that it shall be lawful for the said churchwardens and overseers...to levy as well the said sums of money of everyone that shall refuse to contribute according as they shall be assessed by distress and sale of the offenders' goods....

4. And be it further enacted that it shall be lawful for the said churchwardens and overseers or the greater part of them, by the assent of any two justices..., to bind any such children as aforesaid to be apprentices where they shall see convenient, till such man-child shall come to the age of four and twenty years, and such woman-child to the age of one and twenty years....

5. And to the intent that necessary places of habitation may more conveniently be provided for such poor impotent people, be it enacted...that it shall and may be lawful for the said churchwardens and overseers or the greater part of them, by the leave of the lord or lords of the manor whereof any waste or common within their parish is...to erect, build, and set up in fit and convenient places of habitation in such waste or common, at the general charges of the parish or otherwise of the hundred or county..., to be taxed, rated, and gathered in manner before expressed, convenient houses of dwelling for the said impotent poor; and also to place inmates or more families than one in one cottage or house....

10. And be it further enacted...that from the first day of November...no person or persons whatsoever shall go wandering abroad [outside their parish] and beg in any place whatsoever, by licence or without, upon pain to be esteemed, taken, and punished as a rogue....

12. And forasmuch as all begging is forbidden by this present act, be it further enacted...that the justices of peace for every county or place corporate, or the more part of them, in their general Sessions to be holden next..., shall rate every parish to such a weekly sum of money as they shall think convenient, so as no parish be rated above the sum of 6d. nor under the sum of an half-penny weekly to be paid, and so as the total sum of such taxation of the parishes in every county amount not above the rate of twopence for every parish in the said county; which sums so taxed shall be yearly assessed by the agreement of the parishioners..., or in default thereof by the churchwardens and constables of the same parish..., or in default of their agreement by the order of such justice or justices of peace as shall dwell in the same parish or... in the parts next adjoining. And if any person shall refuse or neglect to pay any such portion of money so taxed, it shall be lawful for the said churchwardens and constables or in their default for the justices of the peace, to levy the same by distress and sale of the goods of the party so refusing or neglecting..., and in default of such distress it shall be lawful... to commit such persons to prison....

13. And be it also enacted that the said justices of the peace at their general quarter sessions... shall set down what competent sum of money shall be sent quarterly out of every county or place corporate for the relief of the poor prisoners of the King's Bench and Marshalsea, and also of such hospitals and almshouses as shall be in the said county....

17. Provided always that this act shall endure no longer than to the end of the next session of Parliament. [It was prolonged by numerous Acts, revised in 1601, and made permanent in 1640.]

CHAPTER SIX

Early Stuart Church and State

Divine Right of Kings and Ancient Constitutionalism

The Crisis of Parliaments in the 1620s

Laudianism, Puritanism, and the Personal Rule

The Constitution Reformed or Deformed?

DISCUSSION

It is difficult to read about England during the first four decades of the seventeenth century without focusing on the divisions within the political nation over Church and State. After all, in the 1640s rival armies would fight gruesome civil wars over just these issues. The victorious Parliament would execute first an archbishop and then a king on the way to abolishing both episcopacy and monarchy. But it is just as true that there was *no* civil war in 1604, nor in 1629, nor in 1640. We should be able to explain the time before 1642 in its own terms before determining if the seeds of the bitter disputes of the 1640s lie in that period. As you read the documents in this chapter, you might ask:

- How did religious and constitutional struggles interact? How were they distinct?
- How were the issues of James's reign and those of Charles's different? How were they related?

Divine Right of Kings and Ancient Constitutionalism

One place to learn about the relationship of the English people to their monarch ca. 1603 is in their literature. Shakespeare's *Macbeth* rehearses Stuart conceptions of the Divine Right of hereditary kings to rule, and the divinely sanctioned responsibility of subjects to obey. The real Macbeth ruled Scotland more than five centuries before Shakespeare lived, but Raphael Holinshed's *Chronicles of England, Scotlande, and Irelande* (1577, 1587) had recently described how the noble Scottish thane slew the "soft and gentle" Duncan to assume the throne for himself. Holinshed (d. ca. 1580) distinguishes between Macbeth's first decade of justice and good rulership followed by seven years of cruelty which led to his overthrow in 1057. But Shakespeare's play does not portray ten years of good rule under Macbeth. He does not portray ten minutes. The very night that Macbeth murders Duncan, Nature itself rebels against the usurpation and Scotland begins to decay.

Lennox: The night has been unruly. Where we lay
 Our chimneys were blown down, and, as they say,
 Lamentings heard i' th' air, strange screams of death. (Act II, scene iii, 54–6)

Ross: And Duncan's horses – a thing most strange and certain –
 Beauteous and swift, the minions of their race,
 Turned wild in nature, broke their stalls, flung out,
 Contending 'gainst obedience, as they would
 Make war with mankind.
Old Man: 'Tis said they eat each other. (Act II, scene iv, 14–18)

Compare these metaphors of order and disorder with those in chapter 1.

Shakespeare wrote *Macbeth* at the beginning of James's reign, and it may have been performed at Hampton Court before the king on August 7, 1606. James I of England (1603–25) was also James VI of Scotland (1567–1625) – the latest of a long line of Stuarts ruling Scotland, as Shakespeare foreshadowed in Act IV, scene i. But kingship had a divine mystique long before James (see, for example, the 1559 homily excerpted in chapter 5). *The Homily of Obedience* (1547) states "[w]e may not withstand, nor in any wise hurt, an anointed king, which is God's lieutenant, vice-gerent, and highest minister in the country."[1] *The Homily against Disobedience* (1570) portrays God's understandable reaction to the rebellions of first Lucifer and then of Adam and Eve.

After this breach of obedience to God and rebellion against his majesty..., God forthwith...not only ordained that in families and households the wife should be obedient unto her husband, the children unto their parents, the servants unto their masters, but also, when mankind increased and spread itself more largely over the world, [God] did constitute and ordain in cities and countries several and special governors and rulers, unto whom the residue of his people should be obedient.[2]

---

[1] *Certain Sermons or Homilies Appointed to be Read in Churches, in the Times of the late Queene Elizabeth* (1623 ed., facsimile, Gainesville, 1968), 73l; compared with *An Exhortation Concerning Good Order, and Obedience to Rulers and Magistrates* (1547), <http://www.anglicanlibrary.org/homilies/bk1hom10.htm>.

[2] *The Second Tome of Homilies* (1623 ed., facsimile, Gainesville, 1968), 276; compared with D. Wootton, ed., *Divine Right and Democracy: An Anthology of Political Writing in Stuart England* (Harmondsworth, Middlesex, 1986), 95.

What analogies or metaphors make the abstract link between God, ruler, and subject more concrete? In *The Trew Law of Free Monarchies* (1598, document 6.1) James likewise mentions various "similitudes," analogies for kingly power and the relation between kings and subjects. What are they? What other analogies might symbolize the relationship? Which seem most compelling? Why might certain "similitudes" not work as well as others? (For example, don't children grow up? Don't we owe allegiance to both mother and father?)

In fact, where obedience to a monarch was previously conditional on his godliness, James added the idea of indefeasibility – that the people could not reject or resist a lawful king, just because of his bad behavior. According to James, who was a lawful king? Where does royal power, authority, and legitimacy come from? What are the implications of this idea? If, as James argues, the next person in strict primogeniture succession is God's choice to be the lawful king, then that person, not merely the office of king, was divine. By the same token, regicide inverts all order. (If you know the play, consider how Lady Macbeth's role inverts order.) What options were there for the people to resist a bad but rightful king, even a tyrant (reexamine document 6.1)? James clarified his answer in an address to Parliament in 1610: "That as to dispute what God may do is blasphemy...; so is it sedition in subjects to dispute what a king may do in the height of his power."[3] He elaborated further when he spoke to his judges in 1616: "It is atheism and blasphemy to dispute what God can do. Good Christians content themselves with his will revealed in his word. So it is presumption and high contempt in a subject to dispute what a king can do, or say that a king cannot do this or that."[4] Is this absolutism? How might nobles, bishops, gentry, and lawyers react to such a claim?

Why might James have been so fearful of resistance to monarchs? To put it another way, upon what grounds did people resist monarchs in the late sixteenth and early seventeenth centuries? For example, upon what justifications had there been attempts on Elizabeth's life? Why had French kings been assassinated – Henry III in 1589 and Henry IV in 1610? Why, in part, had James's own mother, Mary Queen of Scots, been harried out of that land? And why did Catholic conspirators – Roger Catesby, Guy Fawkes, and others – stuff gunpowder in a room under Westminster Palace in an attempt to blow up Lords, Commons, and James himself in late 1605 (see below, plate 8)? Did God's law (revealed religion) ever justify regicide, or did it always forbid it?

Divine Right had many strengths: it had Biblical support; its emphasis on hierarchy was analogical to familial, social, even natural (Aristotelian) hierarchy; it had "proof" in courtly splendor and in the widely held belief that the royal touch could cure certain diseases (consider what eyewitness "proof" might uphold the modern "sovereignty of the people"). But it could be criticized on two grounds: (1) the difference between the theory of Divine Right and the all-

---

[3]   March 21, 1610, *The Workes of the Most High and Mighty Prince, James ..., Kinge of Great Brittaine, France & Ireland* (1616), 531; compared with S. J. Houston, *James I* (1973), 116–18.

[4]   June 20, 1616, James, *Workes*, 557; compared with G. W. Prothero, ed., *Select Statutes and other Constitutional Documents Illustrative of the Reigns of Elizabeth and James I*, 4th ed. (Oxford, 1913), 400.

too-earthly lives and characters of the Stuarts in practice; and (2) the countervailing contemporary belief in an Ancient Constitution – that kingly prerogative did not abrogate parliamentary rights.

Just a few months into James's reign, Sir Roger Wilbraham (1553–1616, see also document 5.4), a judge at the Court of Requests under both Elizabeth and James, addressed the first of these issues by comparing his two masters:

The queen solemn and ceremonious, and requiring decent and disparent [unequal] order to be kept convenient in each degree; and although she bare a greater majesty, yet would she labor to entertain strangers, suitors, and her people with more courtly courtesy and favorable speeches than the king used, who although he be indeed of a more true benignity and ingenious nature, yet the neglect of those ordinary ceremonies – which his variable and quick wit cannot attend – makes common people judge otherwise of him.[5]

Compare Wilbraham's description of James's traits with that written by minor courtier and future Parliamentarian (see chapter 7) Sir Anthony Weldon, published a year after his death (1650, document 6.2). Weldon discusses James's public and personal traits – he was sloppy, timid, he showered his young male favorites with gifts and titles. For the latter, we have James's own statement to his Privy Council about the wealth and power he lavished on George Villiers, duke of Buckingham (1592–1628), from 1614:

I, James, am neither a god nor an angel, but a man like any other. Therefore I act like a man, and confess to loving those dear to me more than other men. You may be sure that I love the earl of Buckingham [created 1617, duke from 1623] more than anyone else, and more than you who are here assembled. I wish to speak in my own behalf, and not to have it thought to be a defect, for Jesus Christ did the same and therefore I cannot be blamed. Christ had his John and I have my George.[6]

Compare this with Elizabeth's defense of gifts to her courtiers in 1601 (document 4.13). How might the attributes described by Weldon and others add to or detract from the aura of Divine Right kingship? Comparing him to Henry VIII or Elizabeth, do you think that you would have liked King James or disliked him? Respected or disrespected him?

As Wilbraham notes, one part of kingship (and diplomacy) was courtly splendor, hospitality, and entertainment. In the summer of 1606, James's brother-in-law, Christian IV, king of Denmark (reigned 1596–1648), visited the new English king at his favorite hunting estate, Theobalds, north of London (document 6.3). Christian IV was a notorious drunk, and the whole English court seems to have tried to make him feel right at home. Might such behavior seem to disprove

---

[5] H. S. Scott, ed., *Journal of Sir Roger Wilbraham* (*Camden Miscellany* 10, Camden Society, 3rd ser., 4, 1902), 59; compared with L. B. and J. R. Smith, eds., *The Past Speaks: Sources and Problems in English History*, 2nd ed. (Lexington, Mass., 1993), 1: 327–8.

[6] S. R. Gardiner, *History of England . . . , 1603–1642* (1901), 3: 98; compared with D. Wilkinson, "George Villiers, Duke of Buckingham," in *Statesmen and Politicians of the Stuart Age*, ed. T. Eustace (Houndmills, Basingstoke, 1985), from Gondomar, Madrid Palace Library.

Divine Right? What do you suppose contemporaries made of it? Was a "divine" king entitled to privacy, peccadilloes, or a personal life?

Charles I (lived 1600–49) had more sense of kingly propriety than his father. This propriety, however, sometimes meant that the public was kept at arm's length. Edward Hyde, earl of Clarendon (1609–74), first a critic then a chief minister for both Charles and his son (see chapter 8), remembered Charles I's public persona as follows:

> His kingly virtues had some mixture and allay that hindered them from shining in full luster, and from producing those fruits they should have been attended with. He was not in his nature very bountiful, though he gave very much. This appeared more after the duke of Buckingham's death, after which those showers fell very rarely; and he paused too long in giving, which made those to whom he gave less sensible of the benefit. He kept state to the full, which made his court very orderly; no man presuming to be seen in a place where he had no pretense to be. He saw and observed men long, before he received them about his person; and did not love strangers; nor very confident men.[7]

Compare public access to Elizabeth, James, and Charles. Does access or lack thereof affect a claim to rule by Divine Right?

Some members of Parliament insisted that Divine Right coexisted with Ancient Constitutionalism – the theory that the coronation oath served as a compact; and that Parliament, especially the Commons, predated the Norman Conquest, and, thus, did not exist solely at the whim of the monarch. They made such an argument, at least in committee, as early as 1604 (document 6.4). What "fundamental privileges" do they assert? What did they offer in return? What does "the voice of the people . . . is . . . the voice of God" (in Latin, "*Vox Populi, Vox Dei*") mean? Did the Commons' arguments threaten Divine Right? Or could both sets of beliefs be held simultaneously?

By the end of the 1620s, Sir Robert Filmer (1588?–1653) would defend at length Divine Right and kingly power in *Patriarcha* (document 6.5). (After reading the next section, one might ask what provoked such a strident defense of royal prerogative.) Compare the writings of Filmer and James. How is absolutism, or "the absolutest dominion of any monarch," based on God's law? James and others referred to the Bible to defend Divine Right. How does focusing on Adam and his descendants strengthen Filmer's argument?

The Crisis of Parliaments in the 1620s

What happened when a Divine Right king encountered an uncooperative Parliament? At the opening of the wartime Parliament of 1628, King Charles warned both houses that,

---

[7] Clarendon, *The History of the Rebellion and Civil Wars in England* (Oxford, 1702–4, 1888 ed.), ed. W. D. Macray, 4: 490 (book 11, 240); compared with Smith and Smith, *The Past Speaks*, 1: 354.

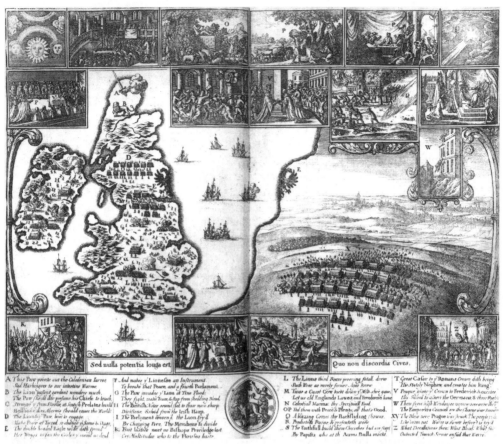

Plate 7 John Rushworth, *Historical Collections.... Remarkable Proceedings in five Parliaments. Beginning the sixteenth year of King James, anno 1618. And ending the fifth year of King Charl[e]s, anno 1629*, 2nd ed. (1659), frontispiece. (*Source*: © British Library)

The main picture includes the "double-headed eagle" (E) of the Catholic Habsburgs overlooking both Britain and the battle of White Mountain (1620), while the poem below and insets (V–Y) refer to Frederick and the throne of Bohemia. Overall, the engraving is a history of the British kingdoms and of the continent from the late 1610s to the 1640s. What types of scenes and issues does the engraver emphasize? What link between the continent and the British Isles is suggested? What events of the 1620s or 1630s might also have been included in the insets?

A. This paw points out the Caledonian jaws,
 Sad harbingers to our intestine wars....

C. Strange, that from stools at Scottish prelates hurl'd,
 Bellona's dire alarms should rouse the World....

E. The double-headed eagle wide doth spread
 The wings to fan the coals, that seemed as dead....

H. The British notes sound flat, to those more sharp
 Divisions, echoed from the Irish harp.

I. The Parliament convened, the lion tried
 By charging five, the Members to divide....

V. Prague gives the crown to Frederick and excites
 His sword to assert the Germans and their rights.

W. Then from high windows unawares were thrown
 The emperor's council, 'ere the charge was known.

X.Y. The blow near Prague was struck, the people ride,
 Like Jehu out. War's sweet before 'tis tried.

Z. What decollations then: What blood: What far
 Outacted tragick scenes ensu'd that war.

if to maintain ... the true religion, the laws, liberties of this state, and the just defense of our true friends and allies, be not sufficient [a cause for parliamentary cooperation], no eloquence of men or angels will prevail ... if you ... should not do your duties in contributing what [money] this state at this time needs, I must ... use those other means which God has put into my hands.

Charles's linking of the issues of religion and the powers of the State to an implied threat to "use those other means" to raise money should Parliament prove recalcitrant caused Sir Benjamin Rudyerd to argue, in the opening debate on grievances in the Commons on March 22: "This is the crisis of Parliaments; by this we shall know whether Parliament will live or die."[8] In fact, it could be argued that the entire decade had seen a "crisis of Parliaments" from James's 1621 clash with the Lower House until the dissolution of Charles's 1629 Parliament (see plate 7).

One source of the crisis was foreign policy. James's aspiration to be a *Rex Pacificus* (document 6.2) collapsed at the outset of the Thirty Years' War (see Bucholz and Key, chapter 7). By 1620, James's son-in-law, the Protestant Frederick, Elector Palatine (lived 1596–1632), had been driven, first, from the throne of Bohemia and, then, even from his own Rhine Palatinate by the Catholic Habsburgs and their allies. Frederick and James's daughter, Elizabeth, were reduced to exile under the sarcastic titles the Winter King and Queen, because they had only managed to rule Bohemia for one brief season. In 1621, many MPs saw threats to Protestantism domestically and abroad and, by the November–December 1621 session, raised the issue of an expedition to relieve the Palatinate. James, however, worried that such a discussion threatened to boil over into a call for war against Habsburg Spain. James still hoped to position himself as peacemaker by arranging the marriage of his son into the Spanish royal family to balance that of Elizabeth to Frederick. No wonder he warned Parliament not to meddle in "princes' prerogatives," like foreign policy. But many in the Commons saw this as another struggle for Parliament's ancient rights and liberties, and, on December 18, the House entered into their *Journal* a protestation

that the arduous and urgent affairs concerning the king, state, and the defense of the realm, and of the Church of England, and the maintenance and making of laws, and redress of mischiefs and grievances, which daily happen within this realm, are proper subjects and matter of counsel and debate in Parliament.[9]

---

[8]   R. C. Johnson and M. J. Cole, eds., *Commons Debates, 1628* (New Haven, 1977), 2: 58 (with two versions of Rudyerd's speech); compared with B. D. Henning, A. S. Foord, and B. L. Mathias, eds., *Crises in English History, 1066–1945: Select Problems in Historical Interpretation* (New York, 1949), ch. 10.

[9]   J. Rushworth, *Historical Collections* (1659, 1721), 1: 53; compared with J. R. Tanner, ed., *Constitutional Documents of the Reign of James I, A.D. 1603–1625: With a Historical Commentary* (Cambridge, 1930), 288–9.

James responded not only by sending Parliament packing but also, as the *Journals of the Commons* records, "King James in council with his own hand rent out this protestation." Why did the Commons' statement outrage James?

Support for international Protestantism continued at home. Note the following news from the London Inns of Court in early 1623:

The lieutenant of Middle Temple played a game this Christmas time, whereat his majesty was highly displeased.... [B]eing at supper, [he] took a cup of wine in one hand, and held his sword drawn in the other, and so began a health to the distressed Lady Elizabeth [the Winter Queen of Bohemia], and having drunk, kissed his sword, and laying his hand upon it, took an oath to live and die in her service; then delivered the cup and sword to the next, and so the health and ceremony went round.[10]

Why might James have been disconcerted by the public support shown to his daughter and her cause?

By 1624, the attempt by Prince Charles to woo the Spanish *infanta* had failed, ending the possibility of a marital, diplomatic alliance with Spain. Charles and Buckingham had returned to London disgusted with the Spanish, but, ironically, hailed as Protestant heroes. One report noted 108 bonfires in part of London alone, celebrating England's delivery from a Spanish match. (To help understand why Spain loomed so large in popular demonology, see plate 8.) And a Spanish diplomat described reaction to an anti-Spanish play by Thomas Middleton in August 1624.

[D]uring these last four days more than 12,000 persons have all heard the play of *A Game at Chess*, for so they call it, including all the nobility still in London. All these people come out of the theater so inflamed against Spain that, as a few Catholics have told me who went secretly to see the play, my person would not be safe in the streets.[11]

What arenas existed for popular political discussion in England? The Parliament of 1624 witnessed what is sometimes called a "blessed revolution," or change, as both court and country seemed to unite to prepare for war with Spain. But this unity soon fell apart and to understand that, we need to look to Buckingham, Charles, and public reaction to both.

Unlike many favorites, the duke made a successful transition to the new reign. By the time of James's death he had gained the trust and affections of Prince Charles, as an Italian observer noted in 1625:

The duke of Buckingham, although deeply grieved by the loss of the late king, his ever liberal master, may feel assured that the countenance and favor of the new king will be extended to him to a greater degree if it be possible.... He is with his majesty all day; he sleeps in a room contiguous to the royal chamber; he has been confirmed in all his offices

---

[10] Jan. 25, 1623, J. Meade to M. Stuteville, in H. Ellis, ed., *Original Letters, Illustrative of English History* (1824), 3: 118–19, from BL, Harleian MS. 389.

[11] To the count-duke of Olivares in Madrid, G. E. Bentley, *The Jacobean and Caroline Stage* (Oxford, 1956), 4: 872; compared with Houston, *James I*, 125–7.

Plate 8 Samuel Ward, "The Double Deliverance: 1588, 1605" (1621), detail. (*Source:* Bridgeman Art Library)

Ward (1577–1640) was a Puritan pamphleteer and preacher. Why do you think he chose to portray the Armada on the left, the Gunpowder Plot of November 5, 1605 on the right, and the pope in consultation with the Devil in the center? The Spanish ambassador Gondomar protested the publication of this print and the Privy Council responded by imprisoning Ward. In what way is this print Puritan (see next section of discussion)?

which are numerous and of the highest importance; and he has also been made Gentleman of the Bedchamber, and has received the golden key, the emblem of his office, so that he can, whenever he pleases, and at any hour, enter that chamber as well as any other part of the palace occupied by his majesty. In fine, nothing is done without him.[12]

Though Buckingham's key and proximity to the king were perfectly consistent with his duties as an officer of the Bedchamber, why might such a close working relationship between king and favorite alarm many in Parliament?

If Charles saw Buckingham's strengths and virtues, some MPs saw only his incompetence and corruption. In March 1626, six articles against Buckingham were presented in the Commons preparatory to impeachment proceedings in the Lords: his failure as admiral, "the unreasonable, exorbitant, and immense gifts of money and land bestowed on the duke and his kindred," "the multiplicity of offices conferred upon the duke, and others depending upon him," the allowances made to his Catholic relatives, the sale of honors and offices through him, and the failure of the costly Cadiz expedition the previous year.[13] Were these allegations mainly personal, ideological, or practical? The duke's opponents, one pamphleteer wrote in 1626, sought only "the debasing of this free monarchy."[14] Were attacks on Buckingham fueled by a desire to limit the power of the monarchy or just the influence of a favorite? What is the difference? Many feared that if the king were forced to choose between the favorite and the Parliament, he would choose the former. In May 1626, one letter-writer thought

His majesty's affection no whit abates toward him [Buckingham], but seems rather to increase. Lord help us, what will come of these things? ... The duke being in the bedchamber, private with the king, his majesty was overheard ... to use these words. "What can I do more? I have engaged mine honor to mine uncle of Denmark and other princes. I have in manner lost the love of my subjects. And what wouldst thou have me do?" Whence some think the duke moved the king to dissolve the Parliament, etc.[15]

How did such rumors portray the relationship between Charles and Buckingham?

Charles responded by reminding Parliament pointblank of his power over them. "Remember, that Parliaments are altogether in my power for their calling, sitting, and dissolution. Therefore, as I find the fruits of them good or evil, they are to continue, or not to be."[16] Indeed, Charles dissolved this Parliament within

[12]   April 11, Tuscan Ambassador Salvetti, HMC *Eleventh Report, Appendix I, The Manuscripts of Henry Duncan Skrine, Esq. Salvetti Correspondence* (1887), 3; compared with B. Quintrell, *Charles I, 1625–1640* (1993), 93.

[13]   Rushworth, *Historical Collections*, 1: 217; compared with Quintrell, *Charles I*, 98.

[14]   P. Lake, "Anti-Popery: The Structure of a Prejudice," in *Conflict in Early Stuart England*, ed. R. Cust and A. Hughes (1989), 84; compared with G. E. Seel and D. L. Smith, *The Early Stuart Kings, 1603–1642* (2001), 74.

[15]   May 13, [1626], Mr. Mead to Sir Martin Stutevill, in Ellis, *Original Letters, Illustrative*, 3: 225–8, from BL, Harleian MS. 390.

[16]   Rushworth, *Historical Collections*, 1: 225; compared with R. Lockyer, *Buckingham: The Life and Political Career of George Villiers, First Duke of Buckingham, 1592–1628* (1981), 316.

the year, which left him with no subsidy to pay for the war effort. Worse, in 1627, the war effort expanded as Buckingham encouraged military action against *both* France and Spain. In 1626 and 1627, therefore, the king turned to raising the money without parliamentary sanction: "We had resolved, [he announced in October 1626,] for the necessary defense of our honor, our religion, and kingdoms, to require the aid of our loving subjects in that way of loan..., [though] this course, which at this time is thus enforced upon us by that necessity..., shall not in any wise be...made a precedent for after times."[17] Anglican preachers supported the forced loan from the pulpit, such as Robert Sybthorpe's timely assize sermon of February 1627, "showing the duty of subjects to pay tribute and taxes to their princes."[18] In 1628 John Pym (ca. 1584–1643) described sermons justifying the forced loan of 1626–7 as evil because they "infuse into his majesty that which was most unfit for his royal breast – an absolute power not bounded by law."[19] What is the connection between God's law and civil law on this issue?

When Parliament was summoned again in 1628, the Commons, furious about wartime failures (such as Buckingham's unsuccessful attempt to relieve the Huguenots at La Rochelle), extraparliamentary taxation, and arbitrary arrest of loan resisters, began discussions that led to the Petition of Right, which they presented to the Lords as a draft in early May (June 2–7, 1628, document 6.6). Before examining reactions to the Petition, consider the Petition as a history of the past decade. How accurate was it? In the Petition, how were the king's actions proved to be illegal? What did the Commons believe their function to be? What was the connection between grievances and supply?

The king responded with a royal address to the Lords on May 12.

We find it still insisted on, that, in no case whatsoever, should it never so nearly concern matters of state and government, we or our Privy Council have power to commit [to prison] any man without the cause showed; whereas it often happens that should the cause be showed, the service itself would thereby be destroyed and defeated....

Wherefore..., my Lords, we have thought good to let you know, that, without overthrow of sovereignty, we cannot suffer this power to be impeached. Notwithstanding, to clear our conscience and just intentions..., we do hereby declare...that neither we nor our Privy Council shall or will, at any time hereafter, commit or command to prison, or otherwise restrain, the person of any, for the not lending of money unto us, or for any other cause which in our conscience doth not concern the State, the public good, and safety of us and our people.[20]

---

[17]   Oct. 7, 1626, J. F. Larkin, ed., *Stuart Royal Proclamations* (Oxford, 1983), 2: 110–11; compared with Seel and Smith, *Early Stuart Kings*, 78.

[18]   Sibthorpe, *Apostolike Obedience* (1627), title page.

[19]   R. C. Johnson and others, eds., *Commons Debates, 1628* (1977), 3: 408; compared with J. P. Sommerville, *Royalists and Patriots: Politics and Ideology in England, 1603–1640*, 2nd ed. (1999), 231.

[20]   *LJ*, 3: 789–90; compared with C. Petrie, ed., *The Letters, Speeches and Proclamations of King Charles I* (1935, 1968), 61–2.

Why do you think Charles delivered this address to the Lords? How did the king and the Commons differ? After much prevarication on Charles's part, king and Parliament assembled again on June 7, and "the clerk of the crown read the said Petition of Right...and pronounced the king's answer, *viz.*: '*Soit droit fait come est desiré*'" ("Let right be done as desired").[21]

With the Petition in hand, Parliament returned to criticizing Buckingham, resolving that "the principal cause" of a host of "evils and dangers" to be "the excessive power of the duke of Buckingham, and the abuse of that power."[22] Who was the audience for such petitions and remonstrances? What impact do you think it had on Charles's view of Buckingham? In any case, Buckingham's planning for another expedition in defense of La Rochelle was cut short on August 23 when John Felton sank "a tenpenny knife" into the duke's chest, killing him instantly. Felton was an officer in the last expedition who had been denied a place (and pay) in the new one. Upon his arrest, he said that "it came into his mind" to kill the favorite after reading both a pamphlet suggesting that Buckingham had poisoned James I as well as the Commons' Remonstrance against Buckingham and "that in committing the act of killing the duke, he should do his country great good service." One report noted that as Felton passed under guard through Kingston-upon-Thames, "an old woman bestowed this salutation upon him: 'Now God bless thee, little David,' quoth she; meaning he had killed Goliath."

In contrast to Felton's popularity, Buckingham's funeral was a shambles.

[L]ast night at ten of the clock his funeral was solemnized in as poor and confused a manner as hath been seen, marching from Wallingford House over against Whitehall to Westminster Abbey; there being not much above an hundred mourners, who attended upon an empty coffin born upon six men's shoulders; the duke's corpse itself being there interred yesterday; as if it had been doubted the people in their madness might have surprised it. But to prevent all disorder the trained bands kept a guard on both sides of the way, all along..., beating up their drums loud, and carrying their pikes and muskets upon their shoulders as in a march, not trailing them at their heels, as is usual at a mourning. As soon as the coffin was entered the Church [Abbey], they came all away without giving any volley of shot at all. And this was the obscure catastrophe of that great man.[23]

Why such an ignominious end for the favorite of two kings and patron of politicians, clergymen, and merchants? What do the ends of Wolsey, Buckingham, and, later, Clarendon tell you about a courtier's power?

---

[21]   *LJ*, 3: 843–4; compared with C. Stephenson and F. G. Marcham, *Sources of English Constitutional History: A Selection of Documents from A.D. 600 to the Present* (New York, 1937), 1: 453. Even then, Charles continued to show his disapproval by ordering the Petition issued without the usual statute number, thus leaving its standing in law questionable.

[22]   Rushworth, *Historical Collections*, 1: 625; compared with Lockyer, *Buckingham*, 269.

[23]   Ellis, *Original Letters, Illustrative*, 3: 254–67, esp. 264–5 (Sept. 19, 1628), from BL, Harleian MS. 390.

Parliament's end was just as chaotic as Buckingham's, culminating, in March 1629, with the Speaker of the House of Commons being forcibly held in his chair to prevent dissolution while they voted articles against "Popery or Arminianism," and "tonnage and poundage [customs], not being granted by Parliament."[24] Before turning to the religious issue, how does the constitutional and financial point of the 1629 Protestation relate to the events of the 1620s?

A week later, Charles issued a Declaration showing his reasons for dissolving Parliament, in which he noted:

No sooner...was the Parliament set down [in January 1629] but...ill-affected men began to sow and disperse their jealousies....The sincerer and better part of the House [of Commons] was overborne by the practices and clamors of the other, who, careless of their duties, and taking advantage of the times and our necessities, have enforced us to break off this meeting.[25]

Can you find proof of his reasons in other documents in this chapter? Whom would you blame for the end of Parliaments and the beginning of eleven years of Personal Rule? Why?

Laudianism, Puritanism, and the Personal Rule

During the Personal Rule, 1629–40, struggles over the constitution of the State were paralleled by those over the constitution of the Church. Were these religious divisions due to the innovations of the Arminians or Laudians from the 1620s, or were they continuations of struggles over the direction of the Elizabethan Church (see chapter 4)?

Certainly those who wanted the Church changed bombarded James with advice at the very beginning of his reign. They presented the Millenary Petition to him in April 1604.

We, the ministers of the gospel in this land, neither as factious men affecting a popular parity in the Church, nor as schismatics aiming at the dissolution of the State ecclesiastical..., desiring and longing for the redress of diverse abuses of the Church, [petition:] (1)...that the cross in baptism..., may be taken away...; the cap and surplice not urged...; no ministers charged to teach their people to bow at the name of Jesus...; (2)...that none hereafter be admitted into the ministry but able and sufficient men, and those to preach diligently...; that non-residency be not permitted...; (3)...that double-

---

[24] W. Notestein and F. H. Relf, eds., *Commons Debates for 1629* (Minneapolis, 1921), 101–2; compared with B. Tierney and J. W. Scott, eds., *Western Societies: A Documentary History*, 2nd ed. (Boston, 2000), 2: 40–1.

[25] Rushworth, *Historical Collections*, 1: appendix, 7, 10; compared with S. R. Gardiner, ed., *The Constitutional Documents of the Puritan Revolution, 1625–1660*, 3rd ed. (Oxford, 1906), 91, 97.

beneficed men be not suffered to hold some two, some three benefices with cure...; (4)...that none be excommunicated without consent of his pastor.[26]

Who were these "ministers of the gospel"? Why might they think that James would be amenable to their Petition? In fact, James had already identified the authors of "public invectives against the state ecclesiastical," as he described the Petition in October, in his advice-book to his son, *Basilikon Doron* (1599):

Some fiery-spirited men in the ministry...begouth [began] to fantasize to themselves a democratic form of government....I was ofttimes calumniated in their popular sermons..., informing the people, that all kings and princes were naturally enemies to the liberty of the Church....Take heed therefore...to such Puritans, very pests in the Church and Commonwealth....Cherish no man more than a good pastor, hate no man more than a proud Puritan.[27]

Did Puritans (see also chapter 4) really threaten to change the Commonwealth (State) as well as the Church? (Why, in the Form of Apology, document 6.4, did the Commons try to distinguish itself from Puritans?) James nevertheless agreed to a conference between leading Puritans and bishops to be held at Hampton Court, for which we have the somewhat tendentious account of William Barlow (d. 1613), the dean of Chester and later bishop of Rochester (1604, document 6.7). Can you tell from the document how Barlow reacted to Reynolds's proposition and James's response? Why did James say "No bishop, no king"?

How did those who were called Puritan define themselves? About 1621, attacks on Puritans had been made in the Commons; in response, Sir Robert Harley, MP (1579–1656) penned a positive "Character" of a Puritan (document 6.8; see also Richard Baxter's defense of Puritan practice in Bucholz and Key, chapter 6). From the opponents of Puritanism, we have the character of "A She-Puritan," published by the young John Earle (1600–65) in 1628:

She is a Nonconformist in a close stomacher and ruff of Geneva print, and her purity consists much in her linen. She has heard of the rag of Rome, and thinks it a very sluttish religion, and rails at the whore of Babylon for a beastly woman....She loves preaching better than praying....She doubts of the Virgin Mary's salvation, and dares not saint her, but knows her own place in heaven as perfectly as the pew she has a key to....She overflows so with the Bible, that she spills it upon every occasion, and will not cudgel her maids without Scripture....Nothing angers her so much, as that women cannot preach....She is more fiery against the maypole than her husband.[28]

---

[26] H. Gee and W. J. Hardy, eds., *Documents Illustrative of English Church History* (New York, 1896), 508–11; compared with Seel and Smith, *Early Stuart Kings*, 27–8.

[27] Oct. 1604, R. Lockyer, *The Early Stuarts: A Political History of England, 1603–1642*, 2nd ed. (1999), 100, from J. F. Larkin and P. L. Hughes, eds., *Stuart Royal Proclamations* (Oxford, 1973), 1: 62; and *Basilikon*, book 2, James, *Workes*, 160–1; compared with S. Davies, ed., *Renaissance Views of Man* (New York, 1979), 160–1.

[28] Earle, *The Autograph Manuscript of Microcosmographie* (1628, facsimile, Leeds, 1966), 115–21; compared with L. A. Sasek, ed., *Images of English Puritanism: A Collection of Contemporary Sources, 1589–1646* (Baton Rouge, 1989), 279–80.

Using these contrasting documents, could you pen a portrait of a Puritan (such "Characters" were a popular pastime in early modern England)?

The comment on maypoles reveals another religious struggle over popular culture: if the "She-Puritan" attacked maypoles, there were others who would defend May games, Whitsun ales, wakes, and Sunday sports (see Bucholz and Key, chapter 6). Note the pastoral nostalgia of the anonymous *Pasquils Palinodia* (1619).

> Happy the age and harmlesse were the dayes,
> (For then true love and amity was found,)
> When every village did a May-pole raise,
> And Whitson-ales, and May-games did abound:
> And all the lusty Yonkers in a rout
> With merry Lasses daunc'd the rod about,
> Then friendship to their banquets bid the guests,
> And poore men far'd the better for their feasts....
> But since the Sommer-poles were overthrowne,
> And all good sports and merryments decayed,
> How times and men are chang'd.[29]

It was not only Puritans who sought a Reformation of Manners, however. Justices and others of all stripes often saw church-ales and May festivities as little different from unlicensed alehouses, equally prone to disorder and violence. A struggle ensued over the unlikely issue of popular Sunday pastimes. First, under James in the 1610s and then again under Charles in the 1630s, local JPs launched campaigns to curtail or regulate such practices. But James in 1618 and Charles in 1633 reacted by issuing a proclamation which became known as the "Book of Sports" (1633, document 6.9). What are the arguments in favor of Sunday sport? Are these anti- or irreligious arguments? Why might Puritans oppose dancing? May games? Maypoles? Whitsun ales? Rushes for decorating the Church? Why did two kings think "sports" so important? The Book of Sports provoked a Puritan outcry about desecrating the Sabbath (1636, document 6.10). From Henry Burton's (1578–1648) examples of evils that befell those profaning the Sabbath, can you detect two sides of a cultural and religious war in the localities? Who supported Charles? Who were against him? Which is the "popular" side?

Official opposition to Puritanism or Calvinism from the late 1620s came largely from a group of clergymen associated with William Laud (1573–1645), bishop of St. David's in Wales from 1621, of Bath and Wells from late 1626, of London from 1628, and archbishop of Canterbury from 1633. These Laudians or Arminians (see Bucholz and Key, chapter 7) promoted ceremonial religious practice, the sacred role of clergy and bishops, and the necessity of a well-ordered Church for all in preference to a sermon-based, lay-dominated Church focused on

---

[29] P. Collinson, "Elizabethan and Jacobean Puritanism as Forms of Popular Religious Culture," in *The Culture of English Puritanism, 1560–1700*, ed. C. Durston and J. Eales (1996), 41–2.

true believers. Why might the early Stuart kings welcome sentiments like those of Laud's sermon at the opening of the 1626 Parliament excerpted below?

Would you keep the State in unity? In any case, take heed of breaking the peace of the Church. The peace of the State depends much upon it.... They, whoever they be, that would overthrow *sedes ecclesiae*, the seats of ecclesiastical government, will not spare, if ever they get power, to have a pluck at the throne of David. And there is not a man that is for parity, all fellows in the Church, but he is not for [that is, he is against] monarchy in the State.[30]

What is Church "parity" that Laud decries? Why might some members react to Laud's ideas by drawing up a remonstrance against him in 1628? Laud's position had a political component, but he felt deeply about Church practice. "His altar," he noted in June 1637, "is the greatest place of God's residence upon earth....I say the greatest, yea, greater than the pulpit; for there 'tis *Hoc est corpus meum*, 'This is My body'; but in the pulpit 'tis at most but *Hoc est verbum meum*, 'This is My word.' And a greater reverence, no doubt, is due to the body than to the word of our Lord."[31] When he became archbishop, Laud ordered changes in ceremony and the liturgy, such as "setting up pictures in the windows of his chapels at Lambeth and Croydon..., according to the Roman missal, his bowing towards the table or altar, and using copes at the Sacrament," and he used a new ecclesiastical Court of High Commission and the Court of Star Chamber to enforce use of the new practice. Why might many ministers refuse to comply?

In the last years of the Personal Rule, lawyers and clergy were prosecuted for writing against the Laudian bishops, and former MPs brought to trial for refusing to pay extraparliamentary taxes. As a result, the Personal Rule is sometimes called, perhaps unfairly, the "Eleven Years' Tyranny." In 1637, the court of Star Chamber sentenced William Prynne (1600–69), Henry Burton (see document 6.10), and John Bastwick (1593–1654) to a gruesome punishment. Prynne had already been punished in 1634 for writing *Histrio-Mastix* (1633), a work denouncing plays and actresses (the latter had only appeared so far in court masques, and had included Queen Henrietta Maria, 1609–69). For this, Prynne had suffered his ears to be cropped, only to have them trimmed further along with those of Burton and Bastwick in 1637, for writing tracts denouncing Laud and his clerical allies. At their sentencing in 1637,

Mr. Prynne...showed the disparity between the times of Queen Mary and Queen Elizabeth, and the times [now], and how far more dangerous it was now to write against a bishop or two than against a king or queen: there at the most there was but six months imprisonment in ordinary prisons, and the delinquent might redeem his ears for £200...; here they are fined £5,000 a piece, to be perpetually imprisoned in the remotest castles, where no friends must be permitted to see them, and to lose their ears without

---

[30] *The Works of the Most Reverend Father in God, William Laud, D.D.*, ed. W. Scott and J. Bliss (Oxford, 1847–60), 1: 71, 83; compared with Quintrell, *Charles I*, 97.

[31] *The Works of William Laud*, 6: 57; compared with Lockyer, *The Early Stuarts*, 311.

redemption....He said, if the people but knew into what times they were cast, and what changes of laws, religion and ceremonies had been made of late by one man [Archbishop Laud], they would look about them. They might see that no degree or profession was exempted from the prelates' malice; here is a divine [Burton] for the soul, a physician [Bastwick] for the body, and a lawyer [Prynne] for the estates, and the next to be censured in Star Chamber is likely to be a bishop....The executioner cut off [Burton's] ears deep and close, in a cruel manner, with much effusion of blood, an artery being cut, as there was likewise of Dr. Bastwick. Then Mr. Prynne's cheeks were seared with an iron made exceeding hot; which done, the executioner cut off one of his ears and a piece of his cheek with it; then hacking the other ear almost off, he left it hanging and went down; but being called up again he cut it quite off.[32]

What, do you think, was the effect of such punishments?

Finally, Ship Money, an old tax on maritime counties to provide protection from pirates now extended to inland counties in order to pay for the Navy, provoked opposition. Although the first writs from 1634 aroused little excitement and brought in full tax returns, by 1636 it was clear that this was to be a permanent tax, and the country divided upon the issue of the king's prerogative versus Parliament's right to approve or reject taxation. From previous disputes, can you predict which groups would plump for which side of the Ship Money debate and why? When MP John Hampden (1594–1643) refused payment of a mere 20 shillings, he was brought before the Court of the Exchequer and his relatively lengthy trial became a test case (1638, document 6.11). The decision went against Hampden by a vote of seven to five; Robert Berkeley's explanation for the majority and Sir George Crooke's explanation for the minority are excerpted below. Upon what bases did they make their decisions? To what extent did these theoretical debates about the constitution affect everyday lives? What problems might a seven-to-five decision pose for the Crown? In any case, by this time Charles was faced with a new problem, the rebellion in Scotland against the Laudian Scottish Prayer Book (see chapter 8). Scottish troops were poised to invade England and Charles had little military means to oppose them. In December 1639, Wentworth, Laud, and "those lords that were all this while most averse to Parliaments, did now begin to advise the king's making trial of his people in Parliament."[33] And so, a new Parliament was called for April 1640.

The Constitution Reformed or Deformed?

Between 1640 and 1642 the Short Parliament (April–May 1640) and the Long Parliament (November 1640–April 1653 and May 1659–March 1660) took up the issues of the 1620s, added the grievances of the 1630s, as well as the crises of

---

[32] Rushworth, *Historical Collections*, abridged ed. (1706), 2: 293–4. For a similar report of Prynne's speech, see T. B. Howell, comp., *A Complete Collection of State Trials* (1816), 3: 746–9.

[33] Dec. 12, 1639, earl of Northumberland to earl of Leicester; Quintrell, *Charles I*, 111, from A. Collins, ed., *Letters and Memorials of State* (1746), 2: 623.

the three British Kingdoms (see chapter 7). Both Houses of Parliament united in dismantling the expedients of the Personal Rule, abolishing the courts of Star Chamber and High Commission (used by the Laudian bishops to chastise outspoken opponents), fines for distraint of knighthood and the regulation of royal forests, and, as Sir Simonds D'Ewes, MP wrote to his wife on December 10, 1640, "on last Monday morning..., we utterly damned ship monies."[34] It should be obvious how the Act abolishing Ship Money (16 Car. I, c. 14) related to issues discussed in the previous two sections:

that the said charge imposed upon the subject for the providing and furnishing of ships commonly...called ship money..., and writs commonly called the ship-writs are against the laws of the realm, the right of property, the liberty of the subjects, and contrary to former resolutions in Parliament, and to the Petition of Right [document 6.6].[35]

But other issues, particularly religion, were more divisive. Public demonstrations on this score were stage-managed by parliamentarian leaders such as John Pym, but more spontaneous demands for action also came from beyond Parliament's doors. In December 1640, for example, some 1,500 Londoners presented a petition to the Commons on behalf of over 15,000 people, raising what D'Ewes told his wife was "the weightiest matter that ever was yet handled in the House."[36]

That whereas the government of archbishops and lord bishops, deans, and archdeacons, etc., with their courts and ministrations in them, have proved prejudicial and very dangerous both to the Church and Commonwealth..., We therefore most humbly pray, and beseech this honorable assembly, the premises considered, that the said government with all its dependencies, roots and branches, may be abolished, and all laws in their behalf made void, and the government according to God's word may be rightly placed amongst us.[37]

The petition blamed a long list of "evils" on the bishops: suppressing discussion of predestination, suppressing preaching and lectureships (preaching ministries) funded by lay purchase of benefices, the publishing of Arminian tracts and suppressing those attacking Arminianism, requiring Catholic-seeming liturgical practices such as praying towards the East, bowing at the name of Jesus, using the cross in baptism, and turning the communion table "altar-wise." This petition led to a Root and Branch Bill in May 1641, but divisions in the Commons caused them to abandon the legislation in August.

---

[34]   H. Ellis, ed., *Original Letters of Eminent Literary Men of the Sixteenth, Seventeenth, and Eighteenth Centuries* (Camden Society, 23, 1843), 165.
[35]   Rushworth, *Historical Collections*, 4: 88; compared with Stephenson and Marcham, *Sources*, 1: 482.
[36]   Dec. 14, Ellis, *Original Letters of Eminent Literary Men*, 167.
[37]   Rushworth, *Historical Collections*, 4: 93; compared with Gardiner, *Constitutional Documents*, 137–44; and Gee and Hardy, *English Church History*, 537–45.

That is, many members of the ruling elite found such measures too radical. For example, Sir Thomas Aston of Cheshire attacked their authors: "Under pretext of reforming the Church, the true aim of such spirits is to shake off the yoke of all obedience, either to ecclesiastical, civil, common, statute or customary laws of the kingdom, and to introduce a mere arbitrary government."[38] Counter-petitions defending episcopacy were also produced, such as this one from almost 4,000 knights, gentlemen, and freeholders of Herefordshire:

That episcopacy being the ancient and primitive government of the Church, renowned for successes, victorious against schisms, and heresies; and especially, of late years, against that *Hydra* of heresies, the Roman papacy, glorious for the ancient and late martyrdoms, happy before the corruption of Popery, and since the Reformation in the plantation and preservation of truth and peace, eminently serviceable to this Commonwealth, most compliable with the civil government . . . : may for the future (as formerly) by your great authority be continued and maintained, for the glory of God, the preservation of order, peace, and unity, the reformation and suppression of wickedness and vice, and the mature prevention of schisms, factions, and seditions; that cathedrals, the monuments of our forefathers' charity, the reward of present literature and furtherance of piety, be also continued.[39]

In December 1641, the leaders of the Commons pulled their various fears and grievances together in the Grand Remonstrance, a grab-bag of no fewer than 204 numbered complaints about bishops, Catholics, monopolies, and the king's advisers. The Petition accompanying the Remonstrance suggested their proposed solution to the faults laid out (document 6.12). It was printed and published in addition to being presented to the king. Did the parliamentary leaders see themselves as radicals or conservatives? Compare the Petition with the king's Answer later that month (document 6.13). Which seems more reasonable and accommodating? Upon what arguments does each side make its case? Which arguments, those of the remonstrators or those of the king, do you think would appeal more to Sir Edward Dering, who made the following speech during debate on the Remonstrance?

Mr. Speaker, when I first heard of a Remonstrance, I presently imagined that like faithful councilors, we should hold up a glass unto his majesty. I thought to represent unto the king the wicked counsels of pernicious councilors; the restless turbulency of practical Papists; the treachery of false judges; the bold innovations and some superstition brought in by some pragmatical bishops and the rotten part of the clergy. I did not dream that we should remonstrate downward, tell stories to the people and talk of the king as of a third person. The use and end of such Remonstrance I understand not; at least, I hope I do not.[40]

---

[38] J. Morrill, *The Revolt of the Provinces: Conservatives and Radicals in the English Civil War, 1630–1650* (1976), 49; compared with Seel and Smith, *Early Stuart Kings*, 122.

[39] S. Taylor, ed., *From Cranmer to Davidson: A Church of England Miscellany* (2002), 148, from *A Collection of Sundry Petitions* (1642).

[40] Rushworth, *Historical Collections*, 4: 425; compared with A. Hughes, ed., *Seventeenth-Century England: A Changing Culture*, vol. 1, *Primary Sources* (Totowa, New Jersey, 1980), 73.

Why do you think the Commons passed the Remonstrance by only a small margin (159 to 148)?

By the spring of 1642, the political nation (the petitioners and others from jurymen, to JPs, to MPs, and Lords) had fractured. Parliamentary leaders and the king each attempted to form a militia under their respective oversight, and scoured the countryside for war *matériel*. Lucy Hutchinson (1620–ca. 1680) later described the situation in her *Memoirs* of her late husband, a Parliamentarian and regicide:

Before the flame of the war broke out in the top of the chimneys, the smoke ascended in every county. The king had sent forth commissions of array, and the Parliament had given out commissions for their militia, and sent off their members into all counties to put them in execution. Between these, in many places, there was fierce contests and disputes, almost to blood, even at the first; for in the progress every county had more or less the civil war within itself. Some counties were in the beginning so wholly for the Parliament that the king's interest appeared not in them; some so wholly for the king, that the godly, for those generally were the Parliament's friends, were forced to forsake their habitations and seek other shelters: of this sort was Nottinghamshire.[41]

But there was one more round of words. Parliament and Charles I made their case towards each other and towards the public in June 1642, when the *Nineteen Propositions* (document 6.14) and the king's *Answer to the Nineteen Propositions* (document 6.15) were printed. What does Parliament want? How does the king respond? Which side is defending the English Constitution? Which is calling for change? In what ways is either of them compromising or moderate? What is each side's greatest fear? To whom (which social groups) might these arguments appeal? Were these arguments worth fighting over?

HISTORIOGRAPHY

Writing on the early Stuart period once focused resolutely on constitutional struggle. From the end of Elizabeth's reign, if not earlier, it was argued, Parliament (meaning the Commons) struggled with the monarch, a struggle which led inexorably to civil war. Revisionists, beginning with G. R. Elton and C. Russell, questioned this Whiggish focus and its conclusions by confronting the Whigs on their home turf, parliamentary history. (Marxists also questioned these conclusions, but, by emphasizing economic and social struggles, largely conceded the point about the Commons' "initiative.") The revisionist argument is most easily followed in Russell's essays, collected in *Unrevolutionary England, 1603–1642* (1990); as well as those in K. Sharpe, ed., *Faction and Parliament: Essays*

---

[41] L. Hutchinson, *Memoirs of the Life of Colonel Hutchinson*, ed. N. H. Keeble (1995), 84; compared with M. Bennett, *The English Civil War, 1640–1649* (1995), 115–16.

on Early Stuart History (1978). Although there is now a self-proclaimed "post-revisionist" school, best exemplified by R. Cust, A. Hughes, and T. Cogswell (for example, Cust and Hughes, eds., *Conflict in Early Stuart England: Studies in Religion and Politics, 1603–1642*, Harlow, 1989), revisionist scholars, such as Sharpe, Russell, and G. Burgess, continue unbowed. Seminal articles in this debate are collected in M. Todd, ed., *Reformation to Revolution: Politics and Religion in Early Modern England* (1995). C. Hill, D. Hirst, and T. K. Rabb react to revisionism in *P & P* 92 (1981); and post-revisionists have reinvigorated study of the Commons: see T. Cogswell, "A Low Road to Extinction: Parliament and Supply," *HJ* 33 (1990). Revisionist and post-revisionist political history has also moved beyond the history of the Commons to reemphasize politics in the court, the Lords, and the country. Articles by N. Cuddy and K. Sharpe in D. Starkey, ed., *The English Court: From the Wars of the Roses to the Civil War* (1987); as well as those in L. L. Peck, ed., *The Mental World of the Stuart Court* (Cambridge, 1991); and R. M. Smuts, ed., *The Stuart Court and Europe* (Cambridge, 1996), reflect this shift of focus. (For "country" historiography, see chapter 7.) A broader conception of political culture can also be found in P. Lake and K. Sharpe, eds., *Culture and Politics in Early Stuart England* (1993); and S. Amussen and M. Kishlansky, eds., *Political Culture and Cultural Politics in Early Modern England* (1995). The confusing alarms of early Stuart historiography in general are laid out briefly in R. Lockyer, "Postscript: The Causes of the Civil War," in *The Early Stuarts: A Political History of England, 1603–1642*, 2nd ed. (1999); and J. Kenyon, "Revisionism and Post-Revisionism in Early Stuart History," *JMH* 64, 4 (1992).

Turning to the ideas supposedly behind the constitutional struggle, J. P. Sommerville and G. Burgess have clashed over the meaning, or even the existence, of early Stuart constitutional debates. See Sommerville's "The Ancient Constitution Reassessed: The Common Law, the Court and the Languages of Politics in Early Modern England," in Smuts; and his "James I and the Divine Right of Kings: English Politics and Continental Theory," in Peck; as well as Burgess's *The Politics of the Ancient Constitution: An Introduction to English Political Thought, 1603–1642* (1992); and his review essay in "Revisionism, Politics and Political Ideas in Early Stuart England," *HJ* 34, 2 (1991). An overview, albeit one that reveals its own colors, is Sommerville's "Revisionism Revisited: A Retrospect," in his *Royalists and Patriots: Politics and Ideology in England, 1603–1640*, 2nd ed. (1999). Russell has continued to insist that there was a high degree of consensus about "Divine Rights in the Early Seventeenth Century," in *Public Duty and Private Conscience in Seventeenth-Century England*, ed. J. Morrill, P. Slack, and D. Woolf (Oxford, 1993). Relating Divine Right to the British problem is J. Wormald, "James VI & I, *Basilike Doron* and *The Trew Law of Free Monarchies*: The Scottish Context and the English Translation," in Peck. For constitutional ideas beyond Divine Right, see A. G. R. Smith,

"Constitutional Ideas and Parliamentary Developments in England, 1603–25," in *The Reign of James VI and I*, ed. Smith (1973).

Early Stuart historians have also divided on whether or not there was a crisis in the 1620s and, if there was, what were its causes. Besides the important work of Cogswell, Cust, and Russell (above), see R. Lockyer's biography of *Buckingham* (1981), which argues against the traditionally negative view of his significance, though this should be compared with G. E. Aylmer, "Buckingham as an Administrative Reformer?," *EHR* 105 (1990). For 1628 and the Petition of Right, see R. Cust, "Charles I, the Privy Council and the Parliament of 1628," *TRHS* 6th ser., 2 (1992); J. A. Guy, "The Origins of the Petition of Right Reconsidered," *HJ* 25 (1982); and L. J. Reeve, "The Legal Status of the Petition of Right," *HJ* 29 (1986). How government policy was (or was not) implemented in the localities is examined in D. Hirst, "The Privy Council and Problems of Enforcement in the 1620s," *JBS* 18 (1978); K. Sharpe, "Crown, Parliament and Locality: Government and Communication in Early Stuart England," *EHR* 101 (1986); P. Lake, "Puritans, Popularity and Petitions: Local Politics in National Context, Cheshire, 1641," in *Politics, Religion and Popularity in Early Stuart Britain*, ed. T. Cogswell, R. Cust, and Lake (Cambridge, 2003); and, at the parish level, K. Wrightson, "Two Concepts of Order: Justices, Constables and Jurymen in Seventeenth-Century England" (see chapter 5). The relation between finances, the localities, and constitutional issues is discussed in R. Cust, "Charles I, the Privy Council, and the Forced Loan," *JBS* 24 (1985). Regarding the continent, see T. Cogswell, "Foreign Policy and Parliament: The Case of La Rochelle, 1625–1626," *EHR* 99 (1984); and S. Adams, "Spain or the Netherlands?: The Dilemmas of Early Stuart Foreign Policy," in *Before the Civil War*, ed. H. Tomlinson (1983).

Jacobean and Caroline Calvinists and Laudians/Arminians, or "anti-Calvinists," have generated a rich but exceedingly complex historiography of their own. Historians continue to debate the relationship between "Puritans" and "Anglicans," or, indeed, whether one can meaningfully use the former word at all. Combatants include: P. Collinson, in *Godly People: Essays on English Protestantism and Puritanism* (1993), or his more accessible essay for students, *English Puritanism* (1983), or his "A Comment: Concerning the Name Puritan," *JEcclH* 31 (1980); and P. G. Lake, "Calvinism and the English Church, 1570–1635" (1987), reprinted in Todd; though Lake is approached more easily through his review article, "The Impact of Early Modern Protestantism," *JBS* 28 (1989). For defining Puritanism, see also C. Durston and J. Eales, eds., *The Culture of English Puritanism, 1560–1700* (1996); W. Lamont, *Puritanism and Historical Controversy* (1996); and J. Spurr, "Defining Puritans," *English Puritanism, 1603–1689* (New York, 1998). Regarding Arminianism, N. Tyacke, "Puritanism, Arminianism and Counter-Revolution" (1973, reprinted in Todd) is the pioneering prelude to his

Anti-Calvinists: The Rise of English Arminianism, c.1590–1640 (Oxford, 1987). It is questioned by P. White, "The Rise of Arminianism Reconsidered," *P & P* 101 (1983). The dispute is summarized in a debate by White, Tyacke, and Lake in *P & P* 115 (1987). The formal Church is examined in useful essays in K. Fincham, ed., *The Early Stuart Church* (1993), especially Tyacke's "Archbishop Laud" (which you might contrast with Sharpe's "Archbishop Laud," *HT* 1983, reprinted in Todd). It has been suggested that what Calvinist consensus existed in the early Stuart Church was undermined not only from without by Arminianism but also from within by Puritan, even Antinomian, fissions. See, especially, P. Lake and D. Como, "'Orthodoxy' and Its Discontents: Dispute Settlement and the Production of 'Consensus' in the London (Puritan) 'Underground,'" *JBS* 39, 1 (2000). For the Catholic community, see chapter 4, and articles mentioned there; and C. Hibbard, "Early Stuart Catholicism: Revisions and Re-Revisions," *JMH* 52 (1980). C. Hill's important "Puritans and the 'Dark Corners of the Land,'" in his *Continuity and Change in Seventeenth-Century England* (1974) shows either a continuing attempt to reform those who did not want Reformation, or the tendency of the hotter sort of Protestants to always view themselves as a beleaguered minority whatever their success.

DOCUMENTS

6.1   *James VI and I,* Trew Law of Free Monarchies *(1598)*[42]

The king towards his people is rightly compared to a father of children, and to a head of a body composed of diverse members; for as fathers the good princes and magistrates of the people of God acknowledged themselves to their subjects. And for all other well-ruled commonwealths, the style [title] of *pater patriae* [father of the fatherland] was ever, and is, commonly used to kings. And the proper office of a king towards his subjects agrees very well with the office of the head towards the body and all members thereof; for from the head, being the seat of judgment, proceeds the care and foresight of guiding, and preventing all evil that may come to the body or any part thereof. The head cares for the body: so does the king for his people. . . .

So . . . if the children may, upon any pretext that can be imagined, lawfully rise up against their father, cut him off, and choose any other whom they please in his room, and if the body for the weal of it may, for any infirmity that can be in the head, strike it off, then I cannot deny that the people may rebel, control, and displace or cut off their king at their own pleasure, and upon respects moving them. And whether these similitudes represent better the office of a king, or the offices of masters or deacons of crafts, or doctors in physic . . . , I leave it also to the reader's discretion. . . .

---

[42]   James, *Workes*, 204–9, 201; compared with Wootton, *Divine Right*, 99–100, 102–3; and I. Carrier, *James VI and I: King of Great Britain* (Cambridge, 1998), 79.

I grant indeed that a wicked king is sent by God for a curse to his people, and a plague for their sins. But that it is lawful to them to shake off that curse at their own hand, which God has laid on them, that I deny. . . .

It is certain . . . that patience, earnest prayers to God, and amendment of their lives, are the only lawful means to move God to relieve them of that heavy curse. . . .

And the last objection is grounded upon the mutual paction [contract] . . . betwixt the king and his people at the time of his coronation . . . , although I deny any such contract to be made then . . . , yet I confess that a king at his coronation, or at the entry to his kingdom, willingly promises to his people to discharge honorably and truly the office given him by God over them. But, presuming that thereafter he breaks his promise unto them never so inexcusably, the question is, who should be judge of the break . . . ?

The kings . . . in Scotland were before any estates or ranks of men . . . , before any Parliaments were holden, or laws made: and by them was the land distributed (which at first was wholly theirs), states erected . . . , and forms of government devised and established. And so it follows of necessity that the kings were the authors and makers of the laws, and not the laws of the kings. . . .

6.2   Anthony Weldon on the Character of James I (1650)[43]

He was very witty, and had as many ready witty jests as any man living, at which he would not smile himself, but deliver them in a grave and serious manner. He was very liberal, of what he had not in his own grip, and would rather part with £100 he never had in his keeping, than one twenty shillings piece within his own custody. He spent much, and had much use of his subjects' purses, which bred some clashings with them in Parliament, yet would always come off, and end with a sweet and plausible close; and truly his bounty was not discommendable, for his raising favorites was the worst. Reward[ing] old servants and relieving his native country-men, was infinitely more to be commended.

He was so crafty and cunning in petty things, as circumventing any great man, the change of a favorite, [etc.,] insomuch as a very wise man was wont to say he believed him the wisest fool in Christendom, meaning him wise in small things, but a fool in weighty affairs. . . .

He was infinitely inclined to peace, but more out of fear than conscience, and this [fear] was the greatest blemish this king had through all his reign, otherwise [he] might have been ranked with the very best of our kings.

In a word, take him altogether and not in pieces, such a king I wish this kingdom have never any worse, on the condition, not any better; for he lived in peace, died in peace, and left all his kingdoms in a peaceable condition, with his own motto: *Beati Pacifici* [Blessed are the Peacemakers].

---

[43]   A. W[eldon], *The Court and Character of King James* (1650), 184, 186–9; compared with Houston, *James I*, 113–14.

6.3   *Sir John Harington on the Entertainment at Theobalds for Christian IV, King of Denmark (1606)*[44]

One day, a great feast was held, and, after dinner, the representation of Solomon his Temple and the coming of the queen of Sheba was made, or (as I may better say) was meant to have been made, before their majesties [that is, of Denmark and England]. . . . But alas! . . . The lady who did play the queen's part, did carry most precious gifts to both their majesties; but, forgetting the steps arising to the canopy, overset her casket into his Danish majesty's lap, and fell at his feet, though I rather think it was in his face. Much was the hurry and confusion. Cloths and napkins were at hand, to make all clean. His majesty [Christian IV] then got up and would dance with the queen of Sheba; but he fell down and humbled himself before her, and was carried to an inner chamber and laid on a bed of state; which was not a little defiled with the presents of the queen which had been bestowed on his garments, such as wine, cream, jelly, beverage, cakes, spices, and other good matters.

The entertainment and show went forward, and most of the presenters went backward, or fell down; wine did so occupy their upper chambers. Now did appear, in rich dress, Hope, Faith, and Charity. Hope did assay to speak, but wine rendered her endeavors so feeble that she withdrew. . . . Faith was then all alone . . . , and left the court in a staggering condition. Charity came to the king's feet, and . . . in some sort she made obeisance. . . . She then returned to Hope and Faith, who were both sick and spewing in the lower hall. Next came Victory, in bright armor, and . . . , by a strange medley of versification, did endeavor to make suit to the king. But Victory did not triumph long; for, after much lamentable utterance, she was led away like a silly captive, and laid to sleep in the outer steps of the antechamber. Now did Peace make entry, and strive to get foremost to the king; but I grieve to tell how great wrath she did discover unto those of her attendants; and, much contrary to her semblance, most rudely made war with her olive branch, and laid on the pates of those who did oppose her coming.

I have much marveled at these strange pageantries, and they do bring to my remembrance what passed of this sort in our queen's [Elizabeth's] days: of which I was sometime an humble presenter and assistant. But I never did see such lack of good order, discretion, and sobriety, as I have now done.

6.4   Form of Apology and Satisfaction of the Commons *(June 20, 1604)*[45]

The form of apology and satisfaction to be presented to his majesty, penned and agreed by a former select committee, was now reported and delivered into the House. . . .

---

[44]   J. Harington, *Nugae Antiquae* (1804), 1: 348–52; compared with P. Williams, "Court and Polity under Elizabeth I," in *The Tudor Monarchy*, ed. J. Guy (1997), 370; and Carrier, *James VI and I*, 104.

[45]   *CJ*, 1: 243 (for the beginning); and Stephenson and Marcham, *Sources*, 418–20, 422–4; compared with Tanner, *Constitutional Documents*, 217–30, from PRO, SPD, James I, 8, f. 60ff.

Seeing no human wisdom, how great soever, can pierce into the particularities of the rights and customs of people, or of the sayings and doings of particular persons, but by tract of experience and faithful report of such as know them ..., what grief, what anguish of mind hath it been unto us at some times in presence to hear and see, in other things to find and feel by effect, your gracious majesty, to the extreme prejudice of this house of the Commons, thereof so greatly wronged by information! ...

Now concerning the ancient right of the subjects of this realm, chiefly consisting in the privileges of this house of the Parliament, the misinformation openly delivered to your majesty hath been in three things: first, that we hold not our privileges of right, but of grace only, renewed every Parliament by way of donative upon petition, and so to be limited; secondly, that we are no court of record, nor yet a court that can command view of records, but that our proceedings here are only to acts and memorials, and that the attendance with the records is courtesy, not duty; and, lastly, that the examination of the returns of writs for knights and burgesses is without our compass, and due to the Chancery. Against which assertion ..., tending directly and apparently to the utter overthrow of the very fundamental privileges of our house – and therein of the rights and liberties of the whole commons of your realm of England – we, the knights, citizens, and burgesses in the house of Commons assembled in Parliament ..., do expressly protest, as being derogatory in the highest degree to the true dignity, liberty, and authority of your majesty's high courts of Parliament, and consequently to the right of all your majesty's said subjects, and the whole body of this your kingdom; and desire that this our protestation may be recorded to all posterity. And contrariwise ... [w]e most truly avouch, first, that our privileges and liberties are our rights and due inheritance no less than our very lands and goods. Secondly, that they cannot be withheld from us, denied, or impaired, but with apparent wrong to the whole state of the realm.

From these [aforementioned] misinformed positions ... the greatest part of our troubles, distrust, and jealousy have arisen. ... For although it may be true that in the latter times of Queen Elizabeth some one privilege now and then were by some particular act attempted against ..., yet was not the same ever by so public speech nor by positions in general denounced against our privileges. Besides that in regard to her sex and age which we had great cause to tender, and much more upon care to avoid all trouble, which by wicked practice might have been drawn to impeach the quiet of your majesty's right in the succession, those actions were then passed over, which we hoped, in succeeding times of freer access to your highness' so renowned grace and justice, to redress, restore, and rectify. ...

What cause we your poor Commons have to watch over our privileges is manifest in itself to all men. The prerogatives of princes may easily and do daily grow; the privileges of the subject are for the most part at an everlasting stand. ...

The right of the liberty of the Commons of England in Parliament consisteth chiefly in these three things: first, that the shires, cities, and boroughs ... have free choice of such persons as they shall put in trust to represent them; secondly, that the persons chosen...be free from restraint, arrest, and imprisonment; thirdly, that in Parliament they may speak freely their consciences without check or controlment....

Let your majesty be pleased to receive public information from your Commons in Parliament as well of the abuses in the church as in the civil estate and government; for private informations pass often by practice. The voice of the people in things of their knowledge is said to be as the voice of God.

6.5   *Robert Filmer,* Patriarcha *(ca. 1630, pub. 1680)*[46]

For as Adam was lord of his children, so his children under him had a command and power over their own children, but still with subordination to the first parent, who is lord-paramount over his children's children to all generations, as being the grandfather of his people.

I see not then how the children of Adam, or of any man else, can be free from subjection to their parents. And this subjection of children being the fountain of all regal authority, by the ordination of God himself. It follows that civil power not only in general is by divine institution, but even the assignment of it specifically to the eldest parent, which quite takes away that new and common distinction which refers only power universal as absolute to God, but power respective in regard of the special form of government to the choice of the people. Nor leaves it any place for such imaginary pactions between kings and their people as many dream of.

This lordship which Adam by creation had over the whole world, and by right descending from him the patriarchs did enjoy, was as large and ample as the absolutest dominion of any monarch which hath been since the creation....

It may seem absurd to maintain that kings now are the fathers of their people, since experience shows the contrary. It is true, all kings be not the natural parents of their subjects, yet they all either are, or are to be reputed the next heirs to those progenitors who were at first the natural parents of the whole people, and in their right succeed to the exercise of supreme jurisdiction. And such heirs are not only lords of their own children, but also of their brethren, and all others that were subject to their fathers....

Many will be ready to say it is a slavish and a dangerous condition to be subject to the will of any one man who is not subject to the laws. But such men consider not:

That the prerogative of a king is to be above all laws, for the good only of them that are under the laws, and to defend the people's liberties – as his majesty graciously affirmed in his speech after his last answer to the Petition of Right.

---

[46]   Filmer, *Patriarcha and Other Writings*, ed. J. P. Sommerville (Cambridge, 1991), 6–7, 10, 12, 44; compared with Tierney and Scott, *Western Societies*, 2: 13.

6.6 *Petition of Right (3 Charles I, c. 1) (June 2–7, 1628)*[47]

Humbly show unto our sovereign lord the king, the Lords spiritual and temporal and Commons in Parliament assembled, that, whereas it is declared and enacted by a statute made in the time of the reign of King Edward [I], commonly called *Statutum de Tallagio non Concedendo* [not a statute but a petition from the parliamentary opposition of 1297] that no tallage or aid should be laid or levied by the king or his heirs in this realm without the goodwill and assent of the archbishops, bishops, earls, barons, knights, burgesses, and other the freemen of the commonalty of this realm; and, by authority of Parliament holden [25] King Edward III [1351], it is declared and enacted that from thenceforth no person should be compelled to make any loans to the king against his will.... And by other laws of this realm it is provided that none should be charged by any charge or imposition, called a benevolence [also abolished by Richard III, 1483], nor by such like charge, by which the statutes before mentioned, and other the good laws and statutes of this realm, your subjects have inherited this freedom, that they should not be compelled to contribute to any tax, tallage, aid, or other like charge not set by common consent in Parliament.

Yet, nevertheless, of late diverse commissions directed to sundry commissioners in several counties with instructions have issued, by means whereof your people have been in diverse places assembled and required to lend certain sums of money unto your majesty; and many of them, upon their refusal so to do, have had an oath administered unto them, not warrantable by the laws or statutes of this realm....

And where...in [28] King Edward III [1354] it was declared and enacted by authority of Parliament that no man, of what estate or condition that he be, should be put out of his land or tenements, nor taken, nor imprisoned, nor disherited, nor put to death, without being brought to answer by due process of law.

Nevertheless, against the tenor of the said statutes and other the good laws and statutes of your realm to that end provided, diverse of your subjects have of late been imprisoned without any cause showed....

And whereas of late great companies of soldiers and mariners have been dispersed into diverse counties of the realm, and the inhabitants against their wills have been compelled to receive them into their houses....

They do therefore humbly pray your most excellent majesty that no man hereafter be compelled to make or yield any gift, loan, benevolence, tax, or such like charge without common consent by act of Parliament; and that none be called to make answer, or take such oath, or to give attendance, or be confined, or otherwise molested or disquieted concerning the same, or for refusal thereof; and that no freeman, in any such manner as is before mentioned, be imprisoned or detained.

---

[47] *SR*, 5: 23–4; compared with Stephenson and Marcham, *Sources*, 1: 450–2.

6.7 *William Barlow,* The Summe and Substance of the Conference...at Hampton Court *(January 16–18, 1604)*[48]

Second Day (16 January 1604): Dr. [John] Reynolds...desired that...they of the clergy might have meetings once every three weeks, first in rural deaneries, and therein to have prophesying [meetings to discuss the Scriptures, see documents 4.11 and 4.12]..., [and] that such things as could not be resolved upon there might be referred to the archdeacon's visitation, and so from thence to the episcopal synod, where the bishop with his presbyteri [clergy] should determine all such points as before could not be decided.

At which speech his majesty was somewhat stirred..., thinking that they aimed at a Scottish presbytery [includes laymen], "which," said he, "as well agreeth with a monarchy, as God and the Devil. Then Jack and Tom, and Will and Dick, shall meet, and at their pleasure censure me and my Council and all our proceedings...."

And then putting his hand to his hat, his majesty said, "My lords the bishops. I may thank you, that these men [Dr. Reynolds, etc.] do thus plead for my supremacy....But if once you were out, and they in place, I know what would become of my supremacy. No bishop, no king, as before I said...." And rising from his chair, as he was going to his inner chamber, "If this be all," quoth he, "that they have to say, I shall make them conform themselves, or I will harry them out of the land, or else do worse."

Third Day (18 January 1604):...[His] majesty shut up all with a most pithy exhortation to both sides for unity....To which they all gave their unanimous assent....Finally, they jointly promised to be quiet and obedient, now they knew it to be the king's mind to have it so.

6.8 *Sir Robert Harley's Character of a Puritan (ca. 1621)*[49]

A Puritan is he that desires to practice what others profess. Is one that dares do nothing in the worship of God or course of his life but what God's word warrants him and dares not leave undone anything that that word commands him.

His sins are more than other men's because he sees them and greater because he feels them.

He is the best instructor of a prince and the best councilor to a king. The one he will teach first to know God that he may in time be the worthier to bear his great name. The other he will ever persuade that God's word, the perfect rule of good government, is best for him, on whom he hath set his own name, which makes him honored, but his word makes him wise.

---

[48] Barlow, *The Summe and Substance of the Conference* (1604), 78–9, 82–3, 9[7]–8, 103; compared with Carrier, *James VI and I*, 56.

[49] J. Eales, "Sir Robert Harley, K.B. (1579–1656) and the 'Character' of a Puritan," *British Library Journal* 15, 2 (1989): 150–2, from BL, Add. MS. 70, 212 (sections have been rearranged based on Harley's own marginal numbers).

He honors and obeys his superiors as children should their parents in the Lord, not for fear but for [con]science sake and as the civil magistrate bears the name of God so he esteems him next to God *ordine et autoritate* [by order and authority].

To things indifferent he thinks himself not born a bondman and wonders why he is styled a man of disorder when he is so willing to obey all law[ful] commands....

He thinks the making of the cross made between the Holy Sacrament of baptism and the humble thanksgiving of the congregation is like the placing of the Apocrypha between the Old and New Testaments, which being a stream without a fountain is unworthy to be joined with the living water of life.

He says a dumb [silent] minister is a dry nurse, one not able to feed God's children, a man not sent by God....

He heartily desires discipline in the Church according to God's word.

Join discretion with his zeal, he is a man without compare and most unlike his description which I have seen in print.

6.9 *Charles I's* Declaration to his Subjects Concerning Lawful Sports to be Used *(1633)*[50]

By the king [Charles]. Our dear father of blessed memory, in his return from Scotland coming through Lancashire, found that his subjects were debarred from lawful recreations upon Sundays...and upon holy days; and he prudently considered, that if these times were taken from them, the meaner sort who labor hard all the week should have no recreations at all to refresh their spirits. And...did therefore in his princely wisdom publish a Declaration to all his loving subjects concerning lawful sports to be used at such times, which was printed and published by his royal commandment in [1618]...which hereafter followeth:

"*By the king* [James].... Whereas we did justly in our progress through Lancashire rebuke some Puritans and precise people, and took order that the like unlawful carriage should not be used by any of them hereafter, in the prohibiting and unlawful punishing of our good people for using their lawful recreations and honest exercises upon Sundays and other holidays after the afternoon sermon or service, we now find that two sorts of people, wherewith that country is much infected (we mean Papists and Puritans) have maliciously traduced and calumniated those our just and honorable proceedings....

"The report of this growing amendment amongst them made us the more sorry, when with our own ears we heard the general complaint of our people that they were barred from all lawful recreation and exercise upon the Sunday afternoon, after the ending of all divine service, which cannot but produce two evils: the one the hindering of the conversion of many, whom their priests will take occasion hereby to vex, persuading them that no honest mirth or recreation is lawful on those days, which cannot but breed a great discontent in our people's hearts,

---

[50] E. Cardwell, *Documentary Annals of the Reformed Church of England* (Oxford, 1839), 2: 188–93; compared with P. E. More and F. L. Cross, eds., *Anglicanism: The Thought and Practice of the Church of England, Illustrated from the Religious Literature of the Seventeenth Century* (1935), 565–8.

especially of such as are peradventure upon the point of turning; the other inconveniency is that this prohibition barreth the common and meaner sort of people from using such exercises as may make their bodies more able for war, whenever we or our successors shall have occasion to use them; and in place thereof, set up filthy tiplings and drunkenness, and breed a number of idle and discontented speeches in their alehouses. For when shall the common people have leave to exercise, if not upon Sundays and holidays...?

"Our express pleasure therefore is...that no lawful recreations shall be barred to our good people, which shall not tend to the breach of the...laws and canons of our Church....And...that after the end of divine service our good people be not disturbed, letted, or discouraged from any lawful recreation, such as dancing, either men or women, archery for men, leaping, vaulting, or any other such harmless recreation, nor from having of May-games, Whitsun ales, and morris dances, and the setting up of maypoles, and other sports...; and that women shall have leave to carry rushes to church for the decoring of it....But withal we do here account still as prohibited all unlawful games to be used on Sundays only as bear and bull baitings, interludes, and at all times in the meaner sort of people by law prohibited bowling...."

Now..., we [Charles] do ratify and publish this our blessed father's declaration, the rather because of late in some counties of our kingdom we find, that under pretense of taking away abuses there hath been a general forbidding not only of ordinary meetings, but of the feasts of the dedication of the churches, commonly called "wakes." Now our express will and pleasure is, that the feasts with others shall be observed, and that...all neighborhood and freedom with manlike and lawful exercises be used.

6.10   Henry Burton, A Divine Tragedie Lately Acted, or, A Collection of Sundrie Memorable Examples of Gods Judgments upon Sabbath-Breakers *(1636, reprinted 1641)*[51]

These examples of God's judgments hereunder set down, have fallen out within the space of these few years, eve[r] since the Declaration of Sports (tolerated on the Lord's day) was published and read by many ministers in their congregations; for hereupon ill-disposed people...were so encouraged, if not enraged, as taking liberty dispensed, thereby so provoked God, that his wrath in sundry places, hath broken out to the destruction of many....

Example 3. 1634. A maid at Enfield near London, hearing of the liberty which was given by the Book which was published for sports, would needs go dance with others on the Lord's day, saying she would go dance so long as she could stand on her legs; she danced so long that thereof within two or three days she died....

[51]   Burton, *A Divine Tragedie Lately Acted* (written 1635, pub. 1636, taken from first full ed., 1641).

Example 5. On January 25, 1634, being the Lord's day, in the time of the last great frost 14 young men presuming to play at football upon the ice on the river Trent, near to Gainsborough, coming all together..., the ice suddenly broke and they were all drowned....

Example 15. One Wright at Kingston, being a scoffer of religion and rejoicing at the suspending of his minister and others for not reading the Book of Sports in the churches, saying he hoped to see them all so served shortly, was within a day or two after struck with a dead palsy all over the one side and with blindness and dumbness that he could neither go, nor see, nor speak, and so lay in a miserable manner for a fortnight and then died....

Example 42. At Topudle in Dorset, one John Hooper *alias* Cole, upon the promulgation of the said Book, was let down into a well to cleanse it, for to brew beer for at Whitsun ale by [three] churchwardens..., which John Hooper fell from the rope into the well whereof he died.

Example 43. At Glassenbury in Somersetshire, at the setting up of a maypole, it miscarrying fell upon a child and slew it and it is reported that it was the churchwarden's child, who was the chief stickler in the business. Also when the maypole in the same town was again the second time a setting up, a fire took in the town so as all the people about the maypole were forced to leave it and to run to the quenching of the fire.

Example 44. A May-lord of misrule, not far from thence became mad upon it [May day].

Example 45. Also at Battersea near London, the last year a notable example of God's judgment befell a fiddler. The young of the town of both sexes, being assembled solemnly to set up a garland upon their maypole and having got a tabor [drum] and pipe for the purpose, he with the pipe in his mouth fell down dead and never spake [a] word.

6.11 The King v. John Hampden in the Case of Ship Money (1638)[52]

Sir Robert Berkeley:...The grand question is shortly this: whether...in this special case...the charges imposed by the king upon his subjects for provision of shipping, without common consent in Parliament, be good in law – yea or no?...

It is to be observed that the principal command in the shipping-writ is not to levy money; it is to provide a ship – which ship being to be provided at the charge of a multitude..., the thing cannot be done any manner of way but by...money....

Mr. Holbourne [Hampden's counsel] supposed a fundamental policy in the creation of the frame of this kingdom that, in case the monarch of England should be inclined to exact [money] from his subjects at his pleasure, he should be

---

[52] Howell, *State Trials*, 3: 1089, 1095, 1098, 1144; compared with Stephenson and Marcham, *Sources*, 1: 459–62.

restrained, for that he could have nothing from them but upon a common consent in Parliament.

He is utterly mistaken herein. I agree the Parliament to be a most ancient and supreme court, where the ... peers and commons may ..., amongst other things, make known their grievances (if there be any) to their sovereign and humbly petition him for redress.

But the former fancied policy I utterly deny. The law knows no such king-yoking policy. The law is of itself an old and trusty servant of the king's; it is his instrument or means which he useth to govern his people by. I never read nor heard that Lex [law] was Rex [king]; but it is common and most true that Rex is Lex, for he is ... a living, a speaking, an acting law. ...

Sir George Crooke: ... [I] declare my opinion to be that, as this case is, judgment ought to be given for the defendant. My reasons and grounds that I shall insist upon are these: (1) that the command by this writ ... for to have ships at the charge of the inhabitants of the county ... is illegal and contrary to the common laws, not being by authority of Parliament; (2) that, if at the common laws it had been lawful, yet now this writ is illegal, being expressly contrary to diverse statutes prohibiting a general charge to be laid upon the commons in general without consent in Parliament; (3) that it is not to be maintained by any prerogative or power royal, nor allegation of necessity or danger; (4) admitting it were legal to lay such a charge upon maritime ports, yet to charge any inland county, as the county of Bucks [Hampden was from Buckinghamshire] is, with making ships and furnishing them with masters, mariners, and soldiers at their charge ... is illegal and not warranted by any former precedent.

6.12 The Petition Accompanying the Grand Remonstrance Presented to Charles I (December 1, 1641)[53]

Your majesty's most humble and faithful subjects, the Commons in this present Parliament assembled, do with much thankfulness and joy acknowledge the great mercy and favor of God, in giving your majesty a safe and peaceable return out of Scotland into your kingdom of England ..., to give more life and power to the dutiful and loyal counsels and endeavors of your Parliament for the prevention of that eminent ruin and destruction wherein your kingdoms of England and Scotland are threatened. The duty which we owe to your majesty and our country, cannot but make us very sensible and apprehensive, that the multiplicity, sharpness, and malignity of those evils under which we have now many years suffered, are fomented and cherished by a corrupt and ill-affected party, who amongst other their mischievous devices for the alteration of religion and government, have sought by many false scandals and imputations, cunningly insinuated and dispersed amongst the people, to blemish and disgrace our proceedings in this Parliament, and to get themselves a party and faction amongst your subjects, for

---

[53] Rushworth, *Historical Collections*, 4: 437–8; compared with Gardiner, *Constitutional Documents*, 202–32.

the better strengthening themselves in their wicked courses, and hindering those provisions and remedies which might, by the wisdom of your majesty and counsel of your Parliament, be opposed against them.

For preventing whereof, and the better information of your majesty, your Peers, and all other your loyal subjects, we have been necessitated to make a declaration of the state of the kingdom, both before and since the assembly of this Parliament, unto this time. . . .

And because we have reason to believe that those malignant parties, whose proceedings evidently appear to be mainly for the advantage and increase of Popery, is composed, set up, and acted by the subtle practice of the Jesuits and other engineers and factors for Rome, and to the great danger of this kingdom, and most grievous affliction of your loyal subjects, have so far prevailed as to corrupt diverse of your bishops and others in prime places of the Church, and also to bring diverse of these instruments to be of your Privy Council, and other employments of trust and nearness about your majesty, the prince, and the rest of your royal children.

And by this means have had such an operation in your counsel and the most important affairs and proceedings of your government, that a most dangerous division and chargeable preparation for war betwixt your kingdoms of England and Scotland [from 1638, see chapter 7], the increase of jealousies betwixt your majesty and your most obedient subjects, the violent distraction and interruption of this Parliament, the insurrection of the Papists in your kingdom of Ireland [from October, see chapter 7], and bloody massacre of your people, have been not only endeavored and attempted, but in a great measure compassed and effected.

For preventing the final accomplishment whereof, your poor subjects are enforced to engage their persons and estates to the maintaining of a very expensive and dangerous war, notwithstanding they have already since the beginning of this Parliament undergone the charge of £150,000 sterling, or thereabouts, for the necessary support and supply of your majesty in these present and perilous designs. And because all our most faithful endeavors and engagements will be ineffectual for the peace, safety, and preservation of your majesty and your people, if some present, real, and effectual course be not taken for suppressing this wicked and malignant party:

We, your most humble and obedient subjects, do with all faithfulness and humility beseech your majesty,

1. That you will be graciously pleased to concur with the humble desires of your people in a parliamentary way, for the preserving the peace and safety of the kingdom from the malicious designs of the popish party:

   For depriving the bishops of their votes in Parliament, and abridging their immoderate power usurped over the clergy, and other your good subjects, which they have perniciously abused to the hazard of religion, and great prejudice and oppression to the laws of the kingdom, and just liberty of your people . . . :

For uniting all such your loyal subjects together as join in the same fundamental truths against the Papists, by removing some oppressive and unnecessary ceremonies by which diverse weak consciences have been scrupled, and seem to be divided from the rest, and for the due execution of those good laws which have been made for securing the liberty of your subjects.

2. That your majesty will likewise be pleased to remove from your council all such as persist to favor and promote any of those pressures and corruptions wherewith your people have been grieved; and that for the future your majesty will vouchsafe to employ such persons in your great and public affairs, and to take such to be near you in places of trust, as your Parliament may have cause to confide in; that in your princely goodness to your people you will reject and refuse all mediation and solicitation to the contrary, how powerful and near soever.

3. That you will be pleased to forbear to alienate any of the forfeited and escheated lands in Ireland which shall accrue to your Crown by reason of this rebellion, that out of them the Crown may be the better supported, and some satisfaction made to your subjects of this kingdom for the great expenses they are like to undergo [in] this war.

6.13   The King's Answer to the Petition Accompanying the Grand Remonstrance (December 23, 1641)[54]

We having received from you, soon after our return out of Scotland, a long petition consisting of many desires of great moment, together with a declaration of a very unusual nature annexed thereunto, [and]..., much against our expectation, finding...the said declaration is already abroad in print, by directions from your House as appears by the printed copy, we must let you know that we are very sensible of the disrespect....

To the petition, we say that although there are diverse things in the preamble of it which we are so far from admitting that we profess we cannot at all understand them..., yet, notwithstanding, we are pleased to give this answer to you.

To the first, concerning religion, consisting of several branches, we say that, for preserving the peace and safety of this kingdom from the design of the Popish party, we have, and will still, concur with all the just desires of our people in a parliamentary way. That, for the depriving of the bishops of their votes in Parliament, we would have you consider that their right is grounded upon the fundamental law of the kingdom and constitution of Parliament....

Unto that clause which concerneth corruptions (as you style them) in religion, in Church government, and in discipline, and the removing of such unnecessary ceremonies as weak consciences might check [balk at]: that for any illegal innov-

---

[54] Rushworth, *Historical Collections*, 4: 452–3; compared with Hughes, *Seventeenth-Century England*, 78–80.

ations which may have crept in, we shall willingly concur in the removal of them...; but we are very sorry to hear, in such general terms, corruption in religion objected, since we are persuaded in our consciences that no Church can be found upon the earth that professeth the true religion with more purity of doctrine than the Church of England doth..., which, by the grace of God, we will with constancy maintain...in their purity and glory, not only against all invasions of Popery, but also from the irreverence of those many schismatics and separatists, wherewith of late this kingdom and this city abounds....

To the second prayer of the petition, concerning the removal and choice of councilors, we know not any of our Council to whom the character set forth in the petition can belong. That by those whom we had exposed to trial, we have already given you sufficient testimony that there is no man so near unto us in place or affection, whom we will not leave to the justice of the law, if you shall bring a particular charge and sufficient proofs against him....

That for the choice of our councilors and ministers of state, it were to debar us that natural liberty all freemen have; and as it is the undoubted right of the Crown of England to call such persons to our secret counsels, to public employment and our particular service as we shall think fit, so we are, and ever shall be, very careful to make election of such persons in those places of trust as shall have given good testimonies of their abilities and integrity.

6.14   The Nineteen Propositions *(June 1, 1642)*[55]

Your majesty's most humble and faithful subjects, the Lords and Commons in Parliament, having nothing in their thoughts and desires more precious and of higher esteem (next to the honor and immediate service of God) than the just and faithful performance of their duty to your majesty and this kingdom: and being very sensible of the great distractions and distempers, and of the imminent dangers and calamities which those distractions and distempers are like to bring upon your majesty and your subjects; all which have proceeded from the subtle insinuations, mischievous practices and evil counsels of men disaffected to God's true religion, your majesty's honor and safety, and the public peace and prosperity of your people, after a serious observation of the causes of those mischiefs, do in all humility and sincerity present to your majesty their most dutiful petition and advice, that...you will be pleased to grant and accept these their humble desires and propositions, as the most necessary effectual means...of removing those jealousies and differences which have unhappily fallen betwixt you and your people, and procuring both your majesty and them a constant course of honor, peace, and happiness....

1. That the lords and others of your majesty's Privy Council, and such great officers and ministers of State, either at home or beyond the seas, may be put

---

[55]   *LJ*, 5: 97–9; compared with Gardiner, *Constitutional Documents*, 249–54 (perhaps not delivered to Charles I until June 3), later published as *XIX Propositions Made by Both Houses of Parliament*.

from your Privy Council, and from those offices and employments, excepting such as shall be approved of by both houses of Parliament....

2. That the great affairs of the kingdom may not be concluded or transacted by the advice of private men, or by any unknown or unsworn councilors, but that such matters as concern the public, and are proper for the high court of Parliament..., may be debated, resolved, and transacted only in Parliament, and not elsewhere...:

3. That the lord high steward of England, lord high constable..., lord keeper of the Great Seal, lord treasurer, lord privy seal, earl marshal, lord admiral, warden of the Cinque Ports, chief governor of Ireland, chancellor of the Exchequer, master of the Wards, secretaries of State, two chief justices and chief baron, may always be chosen with the approbation of both houses of Parliament....

4. That he or they unto whom the government and education of the king's children shall be committed shall be approved of by both houses of Parliament..., in such manner as is before expressed in the choice of councilors....

5. That no marriage shall be concluded or treated for any of the king's children, with any foreign prince, or other person whatsoever, abroad or at home, without the consent of Parliament....

6. That the laws in force against Jesuits, priests, and Popish recusants, be strictly put in execution....

7. That the votes of popish lords in the house of Peers may be taken away....

8. That your majesty will be pleased to consent that such a reformation be made of the Church government and liturgy, as both houses of Parliament shall advise....

9. That your majesty will be pleased to rest satisfied with that course that the Lords and Commons have appointed for ordering of the militia, until the same shall be further settled by a bill....

10. That such members of either house of Parliament as have... been put out of any place and office, may either be restored to that place and office, or otherwise have satisfaction for the same....

11. That all Privy Councilors and judges may take an oath, the form whereof to be agreed on and settled by Act of Parliament, for the maintaining of the Petition of Right [document 6.6]....

12. That all the judges, and all the officers placed by approbation of both houses of Parliament, may hold their places *quamdiu bene se gesserint* ["during good behavior," as opposed to "at pleasure" of the king].

13. That the justice of Parliament may pass upon all delinquents, whether they be within the kingdom or fled out of it....

14. That the general pardon offered by your majesty may be granted, with such exceptions as shall be advised by both houses of Parliament.

15. That the forts and castles of this kingdom may be put under the command and custody of such persons as your majesty shall appoint, with the approbation of your Parliament....

16. That the extraordinary guards and military forces now attending your majesty, may be removed and discharged....

17. That your majesty will be pleased to enter into a more strict alliance with the States of the United Provinces, and other neighboring princes and states of the Protestant religion, for the defense and maintenance thereof...; whereby your Majesty will obtain a great access of strength and reputation, and your subjects be much encouraged and enabled, in a parliamentary way, for your aid and assistance, in restoring your royal sister [Elizabeth, the Winter Queen] and her princely issue to those dignities and dominions which belong unto them....

18. That your majesty will be pleased, by Act of Parliament, to clear the Lord Kimbolton and the five members of the house of Commons [whom Charles attempted to seize, January 4, 1642], in such manner that future Parliaments may be secured from the consequence of that evil precedent.

19. That your majesty will be graciously pleased to pass a bill for restraining peers made hereafter, from sitting or voting in Parliament, unless they be admitted thereunto with the consent of both houses of Parliament.

And these our humble desires being granted by your majesty, we shall forthwith apply ourselves to regulate your present revenue in such sort as may be for your best advantage; and likewise to settle such an ordinary and constant increase of it, as shall be sufficient to support your royal dignity in honor and plenty, beyond the proportion of any former grants of the subjects of this kingdom to your majesty's royal predecessors.

6.15 *Charles I's* Answer to the Nineteen Propositions of Both Houses of Parliament *(1642)*[56]

We call to God to witness that, as for our subjects' sake these rights are vested in us so for their sakes, as well as for our own, we are resolved not to quit them, nor to subvert (though in a parliamentary way) the ancient, equal, happy, well-poised, and never enough commended constitution of the government of this kingdom; nor to make ourself of a king of England, a duke of Venice; and this of a kingdom, a republic.

There being three kinds of government among men (absolute monarchy, aristocracy, and democracy), and all these having their particular conveniences and inconveniences, the experience and wisdom of your ancestors has so molded this out of a mixture of these as to give to this kingdom (as far as human prudence can provide) the conveniences of all three, without the inconveniences of any one, as long as the balance hangs even between the three states.... The ill of absolute monarchy is tyranny; the ill of aristocracy is faction and division; the ills of democracy are tumults, violence, and licentiousness. The good of monarchy is the uniting a nation under one head to resist invasion from abroad and

---

[56] Rushworth, *Historical Collections*, 4: 731–2; compared with Wootton, *Divine Right*, 171–4.

insurrection at home; the good of aristocracy is the conjunction of council in the ablest persons of a state for the public benefit; the good of democracy is liberty, and the courage and industry which liberty begets.

In this kingdom, the laws are jointly made by a king, by a house of Peers, and by a house of Commons chosen by the people, all having free votes and particular privileges. The government, according to these laws, is trusted to the king. Power of treaties, of war and peace; of making peers, of choosing officers and councilors for state, judges for law, commanders for forts and castles; giving commissions for raising men to make war abroad, or to prevent or provide against invasions or insurrections at home; benefit of confiscations, power of pardoning, and some more of the like kind, are placed in the king. And this kind of regulated monarchy, having this power to preserve that authority, without which it would be disabled to preserve the laws in their force, and the subjects in their liberties and proper-ties, is intended to draw to him such a respect and relation from the great ones as may hinder the ills of division and faction; and such a fear and reverence from the people as may hinder tumults, violence, and licentiousness.

Again, that the prince may not make use of this high and perpetual power to the hurt of those for whose good he has it, and make use of the name of *public necessity* for the gain of his private favorites and followers to the detriment of his people, the house of Commons (an excellent conserver of liberty, but never intended for any share in government, or the choosing of them that should govern) is solely entrusted with the first propositions concerning the levies of moneys (which is the sinews as well of peace as of war), and the impeaching of those who, for their own ends, though countenanced by any surreptitiously gotten command of the king, have violated that law which he [the king] is bound (when he knows it) to protect; and to the protection of which they were bound to advise him, at least not to serve him in the contrary. And the Lords, being trusted with a judicatory power, are an excellent screen and bank between the prince and people, to assist each against any encroachments of the other, and by just judgments to preserve that law which ought to be the rule of every one of the three. For the better enabling them in this, beyond the examples of any of our ancestors, we were willingly contented to oblige our self both to call a Parliament every three years, and not to dissolve it in fifty days, and for the present exigency, the better to raise money, and avoid the pressure (no less grievous to us than them) our people must have suffered by a longer continuance of so vast a charge as two great armies, and for their greater certainty of having sufficient time to remedy the inconveniences arisen during so long an absence of Parliaments, and for the punishment of the causers and ministers of them, we yielded up our right of dissolving this Parliament, expecting an extraordinary moderation from it, in gratitude for so unexampled a grace....

Since as great an one [change] in the church must follow this of the kingdom, since the second estate would in all probability follow the fate of the first, and by some of the same turbulent spirits jealousies would be soon raised against them, and the like propositions for reconciliation of differences would be then sent to them as they now have joined to send to us, till (all power being vested in the house of Commons, and their number making them incapable of transacting affairs of state with the necessary secrecy and expedition, those being retrusted to some close committee) at last the common people … discover this *arcanum imperii* [mysteries of state], that all this was done by them, but not for them, grow weary of journey-work, and set up for themselves, call parity and independence liberty, devour that estate which had devoured the rest; destroy all rights and properties, all distinctions of families and merit; and by this means this splendid and excellently distinguished form of government end in a dark equal chaos of confusion, and the long line of our many noble ancestors in a Jack Cade or a Wat Tyler [peasant rebellion leaders, 1450 and 1381, respectively].

For all these reasons to all these demands our answer is *nolumus leges Angliae mutari* [we do not wish to change the English laws]; but this we promise, that we will be as careful of preserving the laws in what is supposed to concern wholly our subjects, as in what most concerns our self. For, indeed, we profess to believe that the preservation of every law concerns us, those of obedience being not secure when those of protection are violated; and we being most of any injured in the least violation of that by which we enjoy the highest rights and greatest benefits, and are therefore obliged to defend no less by our interest than by our duty, and hope that no jealousies to the contrary shall be any longer nourished in any of our good people by the subtle insinuations and secret practices of men who, for private ends, are disaffected to our honor and safety, and the peace and prosperity of our people.

CHAPTER SEVEN

Civil War and Revolution

War and Reaction in the Three British Kingdoms
Trial of the King and the New State Envisioned
Radicals, Sectaries, and the Second Coming

DISCUSSION

It might be argued that the British Civil Wars and Interregnum are the central and most dramatic events of the early modern period. Why? One place to begin is with the lives they cost: according to a recent calculation, while 3 percent of the population of the British Isles died from "war-attributable" causes in World War I, over 11 percent did so during the Civil Wars. Another measure of their significance is their effect on speech and culture: after years of Church-imposed censorship, printing and pamphleteering flourished in the 1640s and 1650s. One collection alone, that of London bookseller George Thomason, contains over 20,000 items from these decades. Finally, at no other time in the history of the Isles was the monarch tried and executed by his own people; nor monarchy, the Lords, and the bishops abolished; nor as many new political and religious groups, such as the Quakers, formed. As you read the documents in this chapter, you might ask:

- What impact did civil war have on the lives and psyches of the English people? How did this impact differ between men and women?
- To what extent were the political, religious, and social ideas of the 1640s and 1650s new or unique? To what extent were they based on ideas from the late Tudor and early Stuart periods?

War and Reaction in the Three British Kingdoms

Scotland

The violence which tore Scotland, England, and Ireland began with the Edinburgh "Prayer Book" riots of 1637. As will be recalled, Charles I had attempted to impose on Anglican-style Prayer Book on largely Presbyterian Scotland (see Bucholz and Key, chapter 7). Walter Balcanquall (1586?–1645), dean of Durham, published a government-approved denunciation of the rioters:

On the twenty third day of July 1637, being Sunday, according to the public warning given the Sunday before, the service book was begun to be read in Edinburgh in St. Giles's church.... No sooner was the book opened by the dean of Edinburgh, but a number of the meaner sort, who used to keep places for the better sort, most of them women, with clapping of their hands, cursings, and outcries, raised such a barbarous hubbub in that sacred place, that not any one could either hear or be heard. The bishop of Edinburgh, who was to preach, stepped into the pulpit..., intending to appease the tumult, by putting them in mind that the place, in which they were, was holy ground, and by entreating them to desist from that fearful and horrible profanation of it. But...if a stool, aimed to be thrown at him, had not by the providence of God been diverted by the hand of one present, the life of that reverend bishop, in that holy place, and in the pulpit, had been endangered, if not lost. The archbishop of St. Andrews, lord chancellor, and diverse others offering to appease the multitude, were entertained with such bitter curses and imprecations, as they not being able to prevail with the people, the provost, bailiffs, and diverse others of the council of that city were forced to come down from the gallery..., and..., in a very great tumult and confusion, thrust out of the church these disorderly people, making fast the church doors. After all which, the dean devoutly read service.... Yet the outcries, rapping at the church doors, throwing of stones at the church windows by the tumultuous multitude without, was so great as the bailiffs of the city were once more put to...use their best endeavors for the appeasing of the rage and fury of those who were without.[1]

How did Balcanquall discredit the rioters? Does he sound like an Arminian or a Puritan?

The opposition organized. At the end of February 1638, Presbyterian Scots nobles approved a National Covenant, and others sought signatures to the "national oath and subscription" across the country:

to adhere unto and to defend the foresaid true religion ["which now is...revealed to the world...and is received, believed, and defended by many and sundry notable kirks and realms, but chiefly by the Kirk of Scotland, the king's majesty, and three estates of this realm"], and (forbearing the practice of all [in]novations already introduced in the matters of the worship of God..., till they be tried and allowed in free assemblies and in Parliaments) to labor, by all means lawful, to recover the purity and liberty of the Gospel.[2]

What do the subscribers of the Covenant want? What do they abhor? Why do they invoke "the king's majesty" against his own bishops?

---

[1] K. Lindley, *The English Civil War and Revolution: A Sourcebook* (1998), 45–6, from Balcanquall, *A Large Declaration Concerning the Late Tumults in Scotland* (1639), 23–5.

[2] J. Rushworth, *Historical Collections* (1721), 2: 734–5, 739–70; compared with S. R. Gardiner, ed., *The Constitutional Documents of the Puritan Revolution, 1625–1660*, 3rd ed. (Oxford, 1906), 124–34.

Soon a Scottish army took the field in defense of the Kirk and Covenant; by 1640, these soldiers, many battle-hardened from mercenary service in the Thirty Years' War, occupied the northern counties of England. Presbyterian divine Robert Baillie (1602–62), serving as a chaplain to the Scottish army in what came to be called the Bishops' Wars, recalled that "every company had, flying at the captain's tent-door, a brave new color stamped with the Scottish arms, and this motto, 'For Christ's Crown and Covenant,' in golden letters."[3] Three decades later, Lucy Hutchinson remembered that many English people refused to fight the Scots in the king's cause (ca. 1664–71, document 7.1). Remember (see chapter 6) that the widow Hutchinson wrote to defend her deceased Parliamentarian husband. What biases appear in her description of 1639–41? How does Hutchinson relate the Bishops' Wars to divisions within English politics and religion?

By the fall of 1642, those divisions had erupted into the first English Civil War. Within a year, Scots and English Parliamentarian commissioners had made common cause, swearing a Solemn League and Covenant (September 25, 1643), to:

endeavor...the preservation of the reformed religion in the Church of Scotland...against our common enemies; the reformation of religion in the kingdoms of England and Ireland ...according to the word of God, and the example of the best reformed Churches; and shall endeavor to bring the Churches of God in the three kingdoms to the nearest conjunction and uniformity in religion, confessio[n] of faith, form of church government, directory for worship and catechizing.

This recalls the Scottish National Covenant. But adherents of the Solemn League went on to swear to:

endeavor, with our estates and lives, mutually to preserve the rights and privileges of the Parliaments, and the liberties of the kingdoms; and to preserve and defend the king's majesty's person and authority, in the preservation and defense of the true religion and liberties of the kingdoms.[4]

By 1645 the Scots had come to doubt the will of many of the English "to pursue actively the ends expressed in the Covenant."[5] How might the Scots view the different post-war factions *within* the English Parliamentarians (see Bucholz and Key, chapter 8)? In December 1647, many Scots, dismayed at the growing radicalism of the English Revolution, subscribed the Engagement to force the English Parliament to accept Charles I's terms; following the Rump's execution of the king in 1649, the Scots proclaimed his son Charles II. Parliamentarian armies defeated the Scots at Preston (August 1648) and again at Dunbar and Worcester

---

[3] Sept. 2, 1639, *The Letters and Journals of Robert Baillie, A.M.* (Edinburgh, 1841), 1: 212; compared with R. Sharrock, ed., *The Pelican Book of English Prose: From the Beginnings to 1800* (Baltimore, 1970), 1: 202–5.

[4] Rushworth, *Historical Collections*, 5: 478; compared with Gardiner, *Constitutional Documents*, 267–70.

[5] June 21, 1645, HMC, *Thirteenth Report, Appendix I, Portland I* (1891), 229.

(September 3, 1650 and September 3, 1651). As a result, on April 12, 1654, the Protectorate issued an Ordinance uniting England and Scotland. Did union achieve the desires of James VI and I, or Charles I, or of the Covenanters (see Bucholz and Key, chapters 6–8)?

England

The first bloodshed of the English Civil Wars was not until July 1642; the king did not raise his standard at Nottingham until August; and the first major battle was not fought until October, at Edgehill. Yet, the Venetian ambassador's dispatches from August through October reveal a frantic search for arms and soldiers by both the Royalist and the Parliamentarian side (document 7.2). What else do the reports sent back to Venice reveal? Is the ambassador a reliable witness? Why or why not?

How did individuals decide whether to fight with the king or with Parliament? Some knew clearly where their duty lay. For example, Sir Edmund Verney is supposed to have said "my conscience is only concerned in honor and gratitude to follow my master. I have eaten his bread and served him near thirty years, and will not do so base a thing as to forsake him."[6] Others decided their allegiance through a more tortuous process. Compare Verney's reasoning with that of Richard Baxter (1615–91), a Puritan minister, whose posthumously published autobiography is an insightful narrative of the 1640s–80s (document 7.3). First, note how Baxter distinguishes Royalists from Parliamentarians by class, by religion, and by constitutional viewpoint. How does he link allegiances in 1642 with struggles of the 1620s and 1630s? Then, consider Baxter's own allegiance: how did he come to make it? What issues loomed largest for him? Finally, consider that Baxter wrote some time *after* the Restoration of monarchy in 1660. How might that affect his reliability as a guide to choices made in 1640–2?

Thomas Knyvett (1596–1658) would later join the Royalist side; but in May 1642 he wrote from London to his wife in Norfolk about the difficulties of trying to remain neutral:

Oh, sweetheart, I am now in a great strait what to do. Walking this other morning at Westminster, [Parliamentarian MP] Sir John Potts...saluted me with a commission...to take upon me, by virtue of an ordinance of Parliament, my company and command [as a captain in the Norfolk county militia] again. I was surprised what to do, whether to take or refuse. 'Twas no place to dispute, so I took it and desired some time to advise upon it. I had not received this many hours, but I met with a Declaration point blank against it by the king [Proclamation Condemning the Militia Ordinance]. This distraction made me to advise with some understanding men what condition I stand in.... What further commands we shall receive to put this ordinance in execution, if they run in a way that trenches upon my obedience against [to] the king, I shall do according to my conscience.... In the

---

[6]   F. P. Verney, *Memoirs of the Verney Family during the Civil War* (1892), 2: 126; compared with A. Stroud, *Stuart England* (1999), 90.

meantime I hold it good wisdom and security to keep my company as close to me as I can in these dangerous times, and to stay out of the way of my new masters till these first musterings be over.[7]

Was Knyvett's neutrality a principled stance or a survival mechanism?

For all the war preparations, the violence of actual civil war came as a shock. A Parliamentarian army officer described his part in the first large set-piece battle, that of Edgehill:

On Sunday 23 October [1642] about one o'clock in the afternoon the battle did begin and continued until it was very dark; the field was very great and large and the king's forces came down a great and long hill, he had the advantage of the ground and the wind, and they gave a brave charge and did fight very valiantly. . . . My lord general [Robert Devereaux, third earl of Essex (1591–1646), commander of the parliamentary forces] did give first charge, presenting them with two pieces of ordnance which killed many of their men, and then the enemy did shoot one to us which fell twenty yards short in ploughed land and did no harm; our soldiers did many of them run away. . . and there did run away 600 horse . . . and when I was entering the field I think 200 horse came by me with all the speed they could out of the battle, saying that the king hath the victory and that every man cried "God and King Charles." I entreated, prayed, and persuaded them to stay and draw up in a body with our troops, for we saw them fighting and the field was not lost, but no persuasion would serve, and then turning to our three troops, two of them were run away [and] of my troop I had not six and thirty men left. . . . I stayed with those men I had . . . and diverse of the enemy did run that way, both horse and foot. I took away about ten or twelve horse, swords and armor. I could have killed 40 of the enemy [but] I let them pass, disarming them and giving spoil to my troopers. . . . The armies were both in confusion. . . . The enemy ran away as well as our men.[8]

How do you explain the responses of the men on the battlefield?

As in all wars, some rose to the occasion. Among the best sources on the Civil Wars and the religious politics of the army are the letters of Oliver Cromwell (1599–1658). Cromwell was an obscure fenland farmer who became, first, an MP in the Short and Long Parliaments; then, from early 1643, a captain in the regional parliamentary army (the Eastern Association); and from early 1644, a lieutenant-general (1643–4, document 7.4). What do the letters of September 11, 1643 and March 10, 1644 reveal about the staffing, logistics, and expenses of such an army? Why was the issue of the soldiers' religion so volatile? The letter of July 5, 1644 is a famous letter of condolence informing a father that his son has died in battle. Note the structure and the message(s). Do you think this letter was effective? Why or why not? This letter also describes the battle of Marston Moor.

---

[7]   May 18, 1642, B. Schofield, ed., *The Knyvett Letters, 1620–1644* (Norfolk Record Society, 20, 1949), 102–3; compared with J. S. Morrill, *The Revolt of the Provinces: Conservatives and Radicals in the English Civil War, 1630–1650* (1976), 136.

[8]   Stroud, *Stuart England*, 100, from *A Full and True Relation of the Battle between the King's Army and His Excellency the Earle of Essex . . . sent in a letter from Capt. Edward Knightley* (Oct. 23, 1642).

According to Cromwell, why were the Parliamentarians victorious? Can you suggest other reasons? We will return to Cromwell; in the meantime, what do these letters reveal about his nature?

Set-piece Civil War battles were less common than the many sieges of towns and fortified houses. According to the description of the Colchester siege (August 18, 1648, document 7.5), who suffered what in a siege? Was siege warfare more or less humane than that of pitched battle? How would you characterize the fighting of the Civil War?

Even the churches were battlefields in the 1640s. In October 1642, a Parliamentarian army officer described the behavior of his soldiers in Hereford Cathedral after seizing the Royalist stronghold.

Sabbath day, about the time of morning prayer, we went to the Minster [Hereford Cathedral], when the pipes played and the puppets sang so sweetly, that some of our soldiers could not forbear dancing in the holy choir; whereat the Baalists [believers in a false god – in this case, Anglicans] were sore displeased. The anthem ended, they fell to prayer, and prayed devoutly for the king, the bishops, etc.; and one of our soldiers, with a loud voice, said, "What! never a bit for the Parliament?" which offended them much more.[9]

Were the soldiers religious? Might there be any theological point to such sacrilege? The parliamentary government encouraged such popular demonstrations against church practices with an August 1643 order to demolish altars and "superstitious objects." William Dowsing's report shows the activity of one man appointed to do just this in East Anglian churches on just one day:

–At Babraham in Cambridgeshire, January 5, 1644. We brake down 3 crucifixes and 60 superstitious pictures, and brake in pieces the rails.

– January 5. At Linton, we took up 8 inscriptions, we beat down 3 crucifixes and 80 superstitious pictures and brake the rails, and gave order to deface 2 grave stones, with "pray for our souls."

– At Horseheath January 5. We brake down 2 crucifixes, 6 prophets' pictures – Malachi, Daniel, Ezekiel, and Sophany [Zephaniah], and 2 more – and 40 superstitious pictures.

– January 5. At Withersfield [Suffolk], we brake down 3 crucifixes and 80 superstitious pictures.[10]

Not everyone supported such actions. A nostalgic view of the Anglican Church arose in response to radical Puritanism during the 1640s and 1650s. Numerous

---

[9] J. Adair, *By the Sword Divided: Eyewitness Accounts of the English Civil War* (Stroud, Glos., 1998), 47; compared with R. Shoesmith, *The Civil War in Hereford* (Little Logaston, Herefordshire, 1995), 39–40, from H. Ellis, ed., "Letters of Sergeant Nehemiah Wharton," *Archaeologia* 25 (1853).

[10] T. Cooper, *The Journal of William Dowsing* (Woodbridge, Suffolk, 2001), 210–11; compared with Lindley, *English Civil War and Revolution*, 127–8.

Plate 9 Francis Quarles, *The Shepherds Oracles* (1644), frontispiece. (*Source:* © British Library)

Who is watering and defending the tree of religion, and who is lopping off branches or attempting to uproot it? (Hints: who wields a sword against its enemies? Radical religious clergy often preached outside, thus were known as tub-preachers – as soap-box speakers today.) What documents or sources might this comment on?

images (1644, plate 9) reveal the Church of England under threat. Which groups might be least amenable to the changes pushed by the Puritan Parliamentarians?

As the war continued opposition to *both* sides mounted. A women's peace demonstration in Westminster, August 8–9, 1643, ended in mayhem and violence. Clergyman John Lightfoot (1602–75) noted in his journal "a tumultuous company of women," who came on August 8 "to the Parliament Houses, and cried for peace, and they would have peace, whatsoever came on it." Knyvett described more fully the two days of protest.

Dear Heart, this day's tragedy makes me at my wits end what to advise thee concerning coming up. We had fair hopes on Saturday last of some overture for peace, six propositions drawn up by the Lords sent down to the house of Commons, very honorable. The consideration of them, after a great debate was voted to be referred 'till Monday. Monday morning being come, there came down a great concourse of people out of the city, and filled all passages, crying to the Lords and Commons "No Peace," "Remember their late oath and covenant," "We'll die in the cause," and such like acclamations. . . . That night it was carried by the major vote against these propositions. Tuesday morn' a multitude of women came and made an outcry for peace. Some verbal satisfaction they had, and no hurt done that day. This day they came again in a far greater number, and fell to be more unruly, which occasioned a sadder spectacle, diverse men and women being slain by the trained guard. Such a combustion hath been today, and likely to be worse, that, as well as I love thee, I cannot wish thee here yet.[11]

Lightfoot's less sympathetic comment was that, on August 9, "the tumult of women grew outrageous; and many men, and they Papists, were mingled amongst; so that the Parliament guards were forced to violent resistance, and they slew two men and one woman."[12] From Knyvett and Lightfoot, can you reconstruct a balanced narrative and explanation of the events between August 7 and 10? What do you think most caused the women to fight for peace?

The most violent protest against war was by the clubmen of various counties who banded together, ostensibly, to fight off both Royalist and Parliamentarian troops and plunderers from their respective counties. The Sussex clubmen complained in September 1645:

ii) For three years we have through much labor and God's blessing gained the fruit of the earth, and had hoped to enjoy the same, but by free quarter [billeting] and plunder of soldiers our purses have been exhausted, corn eaten up, catttle plundered, persons frighted from our habitations. . . .

iii) The insufferable, insolent, arbitrary power that hath been used among us, contrary to all our ancient known laws.[13]

---

[11] Aug. 9, Schofield, *Knyvett Letters*, 126; compared with W. M. Lamont and S. O. Oldfield, eds., *Politics, Religion, and Literature in the Seventeenth Century* (1975), 181–2.

[12] *The Whole Works of Rev. John Lightfoot, D.D.*, ed. J. R. Pitman (1824), 13: 9.

[13] Sept. 26, 1645, Morrill, *Revolt of the Provinces*, 198, from BL, Tanner MS. 60, f. 254.

The Desires and Resolutions of the Clubmen of the Counties of Dorset and Wiltshire (1645), bemoaned that "the true worship of almighty God and our religion are almost forgotten, and that our ancient laws and liberties, contrary to the great charter of England and the petition of right [1628, document 6.6], are altogether swallowed up in the arbitrary power of the sword." Its signatories swore "to join with and assist one another in the mutual defense of our liberties and properties against all plunderers, and all other unlawful violence whatsoever."[14] How were the clubmen's desires similar to those of the Royalists? To the Parliamentarians? To neither?

Ireland

As we have seen through the memoirs of Lucy Hutchinson and Richard Baxter (documents 7.1 and 7.3), the rising of Irish Catholics from October 23, 1641 convinced many in England to side with Parliament and not the king. The rising seemed to confirm a widespread belief in a royal conspiracy uniting Popery with prelacy. The letters of support from Charles I brandished by the Irish rebels, though in fact forged, only corroborated this suspicion. In truth, many of the "facts" of the Irish rising, in particular the claim of 200,000 Protestants murdered, were wildly exaggerated (see Bucholz and Key, chapter 7). Nevertheless, by the early 1640s, Ireland, too, descended into civil war. Gaelic and Old English Catholics came together with the Confederation of Kilkenny and petitioned the king

That all acts made against the professors of the Roman Catholic faith, whereby any restraint, penalty, mulet [mule bit, bridle], or incapacity may be laid upon any Roman Catholic within the kingdom of Ireland may be repealed, and the said Catholics to be allowed the freedom of the Roman Catholic religion.

And that

the offices and places of command, honor, profit and trust within that kingdom be conferred upon Roman Catholic natives of that kingdom, in equality and indifference with your majesty's other subjects.[15]

How do these demands compare to the sources you have read on the Irish rebellion of 1641? How do they compare with Parliamentarian demands of Charles I?

Parliament's war against the Irish could not begin in earnest until the wars against the king were over in England. On August 15, 1649, Oliver Cromwell

[14] *The Desires, and Resolutions of the Club-men* (1645), 1, 3; compared with Lindley, *English Civil War and Revolution*, 133–4.

[15] E. Curtis and R. B. McDowell, eds., *Irish Historical Documents, 1172–1922* (1943), 152–3; compared with M. L. Kekewich, ed., *Princes and Peoples: France and the British Isles, 1620–1714* (Manchester, 1994), 38–9, from J. T. Gilbert, *History of the Irish Confederation and the War in Ireland* (1882–91), 3: 128–33.

landed in Ireland, and led his troops in the siege and sack of Drogheda (September 11, document 7.6) and Wexford (October 11). Do these sieges seem more vicious and bloody than those in the English Civil Wars? What was Cromwell's explanation for his actions in the sacking of Drogheda? Did it matter to him that most of the Irish defenders of Drogheda were Old English and not native Irish, and that it had been the latter who had actually risen in October 1641? Should it matter to historians? Whatever its morality, the violence was effective: towns like Ross soon submitted to terms, and, thus, Ireland submitted to Cromwell and Parliament.

Trial of the King and the New State Envisioned

The king lost the first English Civil War, but there was a good chance he could win the peace. First the Scots and the English disputed the settlement, and then the English themselves divided between moderate parliamentary Presbyterians and more radical parliamentary Independents and their allies in the army. Here it is important to remember that the Self-Denying Ordinance of April 3, 1645 had removed virtually every peer or MP from any military command, and so the Parliamentarian government was largely distinct from the army officers. After the war, the Rump sought to curry favor with the landowning classes by disbanding the army in order to lower taxes or by sending them to subdue the Irish rebellion. The army responded with a series of addresses airing their grievances. The April 1647 address from Col. Edward Harley's regiment raised "bread-and-butter" issues of pay and indemnity against prosecution for actions taken during wartime:

1. We have been credibly informed...that the Parliament hath suddenly resolved to disband us without any provision made for the stating of our accounts and payment of our arrears which we have so dearly purchased with the loss of our friends, trades, hard service, and hazard of our lives.
2. We are under many fears and jealousies that notwithstanding we have faithfully served the Parliament and freely engaged ourselves against the common enemy...we shall after our disbanding be forced against our will to serve as soldiers out of this kingdom.
3. Although we have long harkened for it we cannot hear of a sure security made to preserve us from the common law which a time of peace would not allow us the liberty of many actions which the exigency of the war hath forced us unto.[16]

The army came to see its victory over the king as God-ordained and its size and openness as endowing it with a legitimacy independent of the Rump Parliament. In June 1647, the army elected political agitators (or "ajutators") from each regiment. On June 10, the army high command gave Parliament the following notice:

we are drawing near your city; professing sincerely from our hearts, we intend not evil towards you; declaring, with all confidence and assurance, that if you appear not against us in these our just desires, to assist that wicked party that would embroil us and the

[16]   C. Firth and G. Davies, *The Regimental History of Cromwell's Army* (Oxford, 1940), 360–3.

Kingdom, nor we nor our soldiers shall give you the least offense. . . . And we shall here wait, or remove to a farther distance there to abide, if once we be assured that a speedy settlement of things be in hand. . . . Which done, we shall be most ready, either all of us, or so many of the army as the Parliament shall think fit, to disband, or go for Ireland.[17]

Is this a threat? Who was "that wicked party that would embroil us and the Kingdom"?

In August 1647, the leadership of the army, principally Cromwell's son-in-law Henry Ireton (1611–51) and Lieutenant-Colonel John Lambert (1619–84), offered a blueprint for a settlement entitled the *Heads of the Proposals* (document 7.7). If the *Heads of the Proposals* represents the majority of army officer opinion, what issues in the settlement were most important to them? Which issues discussed have come up before and which are new? What is their attitude toward the king?

Two months later, the army agitators and the political Levellers drafted their own plan, the *Agreement of the People* (late October 1647, document 7.8). How have their grievances and suggested solutions changed since Harley's regiment's address? While the *Agreement* never had the backing of more than a minority of the army, it had support among the cavalry and from London citizens. Compare and contrast the settlement envisioned in the *Heads* and that in the *Agreement* (especially compare "Head" 5 with article I of the *Agreement*). To what extent did the latter move into new territory? According to the *Agreement*, who is sovereign in England? The *Agreement*, particularly the first article on the franchise, became the basis of the first day's discussion when the army met for three days at Putney Church (ominously close to Westminster) for what became known as the Putney Debates (October 29, 1647: William Clarke, secretary to the Army Council, recorded the Debates in shorthand, document 7.9). The second day's debate focused both on the franchise and the redistribution of seats in the Commons. There were essentially two types of seats: those for the counties and those for boroughs (town corporations). Traditionally, all freeholders with land worth 40 shillings (£2) per annum could vote for the county representatives (also known as knights of the shire). This was a small amount of land, but it effectively excluded the landless and the farmers who only rented land. The borough franchise varied: in some towns it was fairly open, including all freemen or all who did not receive alms. Other towns restricted the vote more severely, sometimes just to the town council (often only thirty-two voters). And new towns and cities, such as Manchester, did not return any members to Parliament, because they had no medieval charter. One protagonist in the debate on this issue was Ireton, a Nottinghamshire country gentleman, general, MP, and Cromwell's son-in-law. Opposing him was Col. Thomas Rainsborough (1610?–48), also an MP. Rainsborough, an obscure figure before Putney, appears to have been much influenced by Leveller ideas (see below). Over what issue do Ireton and Rainsborough

[17]   *The Writings and Speeches of Oliver Cromwell*, ed. W. C. Abbott (Oxford, 1937, 1988), 1: 460; compared with *The Letters and Speeches of Oliver Cromwell*, ed. T. Carlyle and S. C. Lomas (1904), 1: 266–9.

disagree? Where would they stand on older disputes over Divine Right and the Ancient Constitution? If traditional arguments about political authority had been based on the law of God (the Bible) and law of Man (the civil constitution), upon what *new* basis does Rainsborough make his claim? That is, how does he justify change? Cromwell took the moderator's chair when General Fairfax refused to participate. Why might Fairfax refuse? From this brief excerpt, where do you think Cromwell stood on the issues?

The Putney Debates ended without a decision, so at the end of April 1648 army officers and agitators met again at Windsor to pray and discuss the future. But on May 1 word came of the risings which erupted into the Second Civil War. One agitator reported the dark talk at the meeting:

The Lord...did direct our steps, and presently we were led, and helped to a clear agreement amongst ourselves, not any dissenting, that it was the duty of our day...to go out and fight against those potent enemies, which that year in all places appeared against us..., also enabling us then, after serious seeking His face, to come to a very clear and joint resolution...that it was our duty, if ever the Lord brought us back again in peace, to call Charles Stuart, that man of blood, to an account, for that blood he had shed, and mischief he had done.[18]

What was the significance of calling the king "Charles Stuart, that man of blood?"

By the end of the Second Civil War, the Army Council was bent on trying the king. In early November, King Charles fled to the Isle of Wight, which was governed by Col. Robert Hammond, Cromwell's friend and cousin, but a moderate and so reluctant to imprison the king, let alone try him. Cromwell wrote to steel Hammond's courage – and perhaps his own – on November 25, 1648 (document 7.10). What is his argument? What does Cromwell mean by "fleshly reasonings" and "providences"? Why are the latter to be preferred to the former? What do they indicate about whether or not to try the king in November 1648?

By December, it was clear that the trial would take place. On the morning of the 6th, Col. Thomas Pride and his men occupied the entrances to Parliament and allowed in only those MPs who refused to negotiate with the king. The resulting Rump Parliament set up a High Court of Justice, and, on January 20, the trial began with Lord President Bradshaw's address to the prisoner:

Charles Stuart, king of England, the Commons of England assembled in Parliament, being deeply sensible of the calamities that have been brought upon this nation...have resolved to make inquisition for blood, and according to that debt and duty they owe to justice, to God, the kingdom, and themselves, and according to the fundamental power that rests in themselves, they have resolved to bring you to trial and judgment, and for that purpose have constituted this High Court of justice before which you are brought.[19]

---

[18] W. Allen, *A Faithful Memorial of that Remarkable Meeting of Many Officers of the Army in England, at Windsor Castle, in the Year 1648* (1659), 4–5; compared with Lindley, *English Civil War and Revolution*, 167.

[19] D. Iagomarsino and C. J. Wood, eds., *The Trial of Charles I: A Documentary History* (Hanover, New Hampshire, 1989), 60.

There followed the reading of a lengthy charge against the sovereign which recounted much of the history of the Civil Wars from a parliamentary perspective (January 20, 1649, document 7.11). Why? How could the king be responsible for all "the calamities that have been brought upon this nation"? Why did the king refuse to plead (7.11)? Why does he distinguish between "authority" and "lawful authority"? How could he claim to "stand more for the liberty of my people than any here that come to be my pretended judges"? How does Bradshaw, previously a provincial judge, justify the court's legitimacy? The verdict a foregone conclusion, King Charles was executed on January 30, 1649. On March 17, the Commons abolished "the kingly office in England and Ireland." And, on January 2, 1650, they passed an Act for Subscribing the Engagement.

[T]he Parliament now assembled do enact and ordain . . . , that all men whatsoever within the Commonwealth of England, of the age of eighteen years and upwards, shall . . . take and subscribe this Engagement following; *viz.* "I do declare and promise, that I will be true and faithful to the Commonwealth of England, as it is now established, without a king or House of Lords."[20]

Numerous pamphlets debated the merits or even the legality of taking such a brief oath; why do you think the Engagement bothered so many Englishmen? Why was it so brief? Did this settle the government of the English republic?

Radicals, Sectaries, and the Second Coming

Civil War opened the floodgates of pamphleteering, and between 1644 and 1653 the press was probably the freest it had ever been. Milton, in his pamphlet in favor of such freedom, *Areopagitica* (1644), celebrated the London printers during this period:

Behold now this vast city, a city of refuge, a mansion house of liberty . . . , the shop of war hath not there more anvils and hammers waking, to fashion out the plates and instruments of armed justice in defense of beleaguer'd truth, than there be pens and heads there, sitting by their studious lamps, musing, searching, revolving new notions and ideas wherewith to present, as with their homage and their fealty, the approaching Reformation: others as fast reading, trying all things, assenting to the force of reason and convincement.[21]

Not everyone appreciated the cacophony of the press, with its competing news and ballad sellers. Thomas Jordan (ca. 1612–85) ridiculed the new political ideas dreamed up by the lower classes and the new religious sects:

[20] C. H. Firth and R. S. Rait, eds., *Acts and Ordinances of the Interregnum, 1642–1660* (1911), 2: 325.
[21] *Complete Prose Works of John Milton* (New Haven, 1959), 2: 553–4.

Come clownes and boyes, come hoberdehoys,
Come Females of each degree,
Stretch your throats, bring in your Votes,
And make good the Anarchy.
Sure I have the truth, sayes Numphs,
Nay, I have the truth, sayes Clem,
Nay, I have the truth, sayes reverend Ruth,
Nay, I have the truth, sayes Nem....
We're fourscore Religions strong
Then take your choice, the Major voice
Shall carry it right or wrong;
Then let's have King Charles, sayes George,
Nay, we'll have his Son, sayes Hugh;
Nay, then let's have none says gabbering Jone,
Nay, wee'l be all Kings, sayes Prue.[22]

Thomas Edwards (1599–1647), in his popular *Gangraena* (1646), portrayed the many Protestant religious sects as a sickness in the body politic, first spread by the parliamentary army:

[O]f that army, called by the sectaries, [it is] ... made up and compounded of Anabaptism, Antinomianism, Enthusiasm, Arminianism, Familism; all these errors and more too sometimes meeting in the same persons, strange monsters, having their heads of Enthusiasm, their bodies of Antinomianism, their thighs of Familism, their legs and feet of Anabaptism, their hands of Arminianism, and Libertinism as the great vein going through the whole; in one word, the great religion of that sort of men in the army, is liberty of conscience, and liberty of preaching.[23]

Compare Edwards's views with the varieties of sects categorized in "The Discription [*sic*] of the severall Sorts of Anabaptists" (1645, plate 10). Given that our knowledge of these sects comes from the attacks of conservative Puritans, can we be certain that they were really so radical; or that they even existed?

For all those who feared new ideas, there remained a vocal minority pushing for political, social, and religious change. We have already seen basic Leveller political ideas in the *Agreement of the People* (document 7.8). The Levellers continued to advocate reformed elections and a written constitution in their third *Agreement of the Free People of England* (1649):

That the supreme authority of England and the territories therewith incorporate, shall be and reside henceforward in a representative of the people consisting of four hundred

---

[22] *Rump: or an Exact Collection of the Choycest Poems and Songs Relating to the Late Times* (1662), 1: 291–2; compared with C. V. Wedgwood, *Poetry and Politics under the Stuarts* (Ann Arbor, 1964), 91–2.
[23] Edwards, *Gangraena: or a Catalogue and Discovery of Many of the Errours, Heresies, Blasphemies and Pernicious Practices of the Sectaries of this Time, Vented and Acted in England in These Four Last Years* (Feb. 16, 1646), 1st part, 16–17; compared with A. Hughes, ed., *Seventeenth-Century England: A Changing Culture*, vol. 1, *Primary Sources* (Totowa, New Jersey, 1980), 131–3.

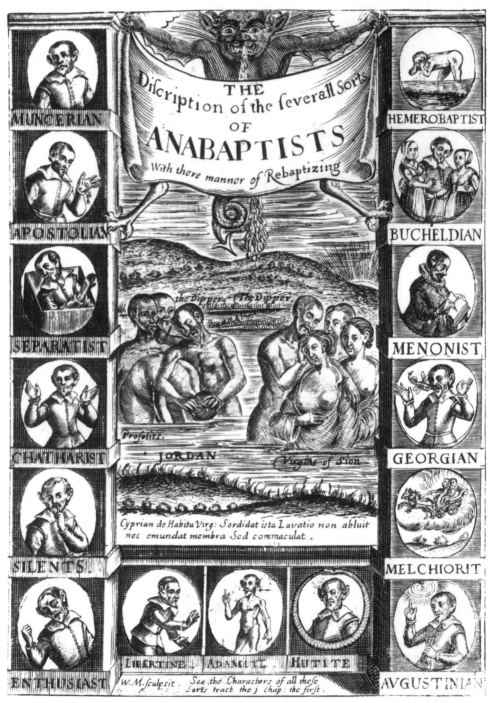

Plate 10 "The Discription of the severall Sorts of Anabaptists with there [*sic*] manner of Rebaptizing." (*Source*: Daniel Featley, *Katabaptistai kataptüstoi: The dippers dipt, or, The anabaptists duck'd and plung'd over head and eares, at a disputation in Southwark*, 1645, Bridgeman Art Library)

"Anabaptists" was the contemporary name given to various groups ranging from what are modern-day Mennonites to Calvinist Baptists whose one common trait was a belief in adult baptism. What is wrong with adult baptism according to the central image of this woodcut (the sun appears to be setting)? What appear to be the beliefs of the "Separatist"? The "Silents"? The "Hemerobaptist"? The "Adamite"? Is this a positive or negative image of these groups? Did all these groups exist?

persons, but no more; in the choice of whom (according to natural right) all men of the age of one and twenty years and upwards (not being servants, or receiving alms, or having served the late king in arms or voluntary contributions) shall have their voices.[24]

Is this the Sovereignty of the People? Is this more or less inclusive than Rainsborough's demands? Why exclude servants, the poor, and former Royalists? When the authors of the third Agreement were thrown in prison, a group of Leveller women in London petitioned for their relief. The protesting women suggested that political and legal rights should be extended to themselves as well:

That since we are assured of our creation in the image of God, and of an interest in Christ, equal unto men, as also of a proportionable share in the freedoms of this Commonwealth, we cannot but wonder and grieve that we should appear so despicable in your eyes, as to be thought unworthy to petition or represent our grievances to this honorable House. Have we not an equal interest with the men of this nation in those liberties and securities contained in the Petition of Right and other the good laws of the land? Are any of our lives, limbs, liberties, or goods to be take from us more than from men, but by due process of law?[25]

What do you suppose was the source of these ideas? How radical and how united were the Levellers between 1647 and 1649?

The Levellers sought to distance themselves from other groups, especially from the Diggers, or self-styled "True Levellers." The government received the following report on their activities in the Thames Valley, not far from London, in mid-April 1649:

One Everard, once of the army but was cashiered, who termeth himself a prophet, one Stewer and Colten, and two more, all living at Cobham, came to St. George's Hill in Surrey, and began to dig on that side the hill next to Camp Close, and sowed the ground with parsnips and carrots and beans. On Monday following they were there again, being increased in their number. . . . On Friday last they came again, between 20 and 30, and wrought all day at digging. They did then intend to have two or three ploughs at work, but that they had not furnished themselves with seed corn, which they did on Saturday at Kingston. They invite all to come in and help them, and promise them meat, drink and clothes. They do threaten to pull down and level all park pales [fences], and lay open, and intend to plant there very shortly. They give out they will be four or five thousand within ten days.[26]

What did this group want? Which social groups would feel most threatened by the Diggers? The Diggers' leader, Gerrard Winstanley (1609?–76?), was arrested at Kingston at least twice in the summer of 1649. In *The True Levellers' Standard*

[24] D. M. Wolfe, ed., *Leveller Manifestoes of the Puritan Revolution* (New York, 1944), 402–3; compared with G. E. Aylmer, ed., *The Levellers in the English Revolution* (Ithaca, 1975), 162, 167.

[25] *To the Supreme Authority of England, The Commons Assembled in Parliament* (May 5, 1649), broadside; compared with P. Crawford and L. Gowing, eds., *Women's Worlds in Seventeenth-Century England: A Sourcebook* (2000), 254.

[26] *The Clarke Papers* (Camden Society, n.s. 54, 1894), 2: 210–11; compared with C. Hill and E. Dell, eds., *The Good Old Cause: The English Revolution of 1640–1660*, 2nd ed. (1949, 1969), 383–4.

Advanced (ca. April 1649), he explained why they had begun to "dig up, manure, and sow corn [grain] upon George Hill":

> In the beginning of time, the great Creator, Reason, made the Earth to be a common treasury, to preserve beasts, birds, fishes, and man, the lord that was to govern this creation.... But not one word was spoken in the beginning, that one branch of mankind should rule over another.[27]

He also accompanied his masterpiece, *The Law of Freedom in a Platform*, with a long prefatory letter to Oliver Cromwell (1652, document 7.12). Upon what basis does Winstanley argue for socioeconomic change? Is this revolutionary?

Diggers attempted to distance themselves from Ranters just as Levellers attempted to distance themselves from Diggers:

> Beware you women of the ranting crew
> And call not freedom those things that are vain.
> For if a child you get, by ranting deeds
> The man is gone and leaves the child your gain:
> Then you and yours are left by such free-men,
> For other women are as free for them.[28]

Who were "the ranting crew"? Unfortunately, most of our evidence for the Ranters comes from anti-Ranter pamphlets. But several writers of the period did develop an extensive theology that could be called Ranter. Lawrence Clarkson (1615–67), like many of the radicals during the Civil Wars and Interregnum, drifted from Presbyterianism to Independency, to Baptism, and beyond. His autobiography suggests how his questioning of Scripture changed his life.

> Now observe at this time my judgment was this, that there was no man could be freed from sin, till he had acted that so called sin, as no sin, this a certain time had been burning within me, yet durst not reveal it to any.... I pleaded the words of Paul, *That I know and am persuaded by the Lord Jesus, that there was nothing unclean, but as man esteemed it*, unfolding that was intended all acts, as well as meats and drinks, and therefore till you can lie with all women as one woman, and not judge it sin, you can do nothing but sin: now in Scripture I found a perfection spoken of; so that I understood no man could attain perfection but this way, at which Mr. Rawlinson was much taken, and Sarah Kullin, being then present, did invite me to make trial of what I had expressed, so as I take it, after we parted she invited me to Mr. Wats in Rood Lane, where was one or two more like herself; and as I take it, lay with me that night.[29]

How did the Ranters put their theology into practice? What was the relation between that theology and Puritanism? Finally, examine the *Fiery Flying Roll*

[27]   *The Works of Gerrard Winstanley*, ed. G. H. Sabine (New York, 1965), 76–95.
[28]   Ibid., 392; compared with G. E. Aylmer, ed., "England's Spirit Unfoulded, or an Incouragement to Take the Engagement: by Jerrard Winstanley: A Newly Discovered Pamphlet," *P & P* 40 (1968): 14.
[29]   B. Coward, *Social Change and Continuity: England, 1550–1750*, rev. ed. (1997), 125, from Clarkson, *The Lost Sheep Found* (1660).

(January 1650, document 7.13) of Abiezer Coppe (1619–72), a former Oxford undergraduate. Coppe contrasts his own "blood-life-spirit levelling" with "sword levelling" and "digging levelling": how does his argument relate to those of the Levellers and the Diggers described above? Coppe explores at length a story (2 Samuel 6: 12–22) in which David danced uncovered in celebration before his handmaidens, to the chagrin of his wife Michal. Coppe justifies David's actions with 1 Corinthians 1: 27–8, "God hath chosen the ... base things of the world, and things which are despised ..., to bring to nought things that are." How does he apply this to the recent history of England? Who might Coppe's ideas most upset? Is he a revolutionary? The Rump Parliament condemned Coppe's *Fiery Flying Roll* to be burnt by the common hangman and passed the Blasphemy Act of August 1650 to outlaw similar tracts and the behavior they inspired.

A religious group that arose in the 1650s but exhibited greater staying power were the Quakers. Today we view Quakers as benign: pacifists of few words, reliable in negotiations, searching within for guidance from the Spirit. But, in the 1650s, that search took them out into the world and led them to criticizing its Great Ones in a manner not unlike Coppe. We see them first through the eyes of their enemies, such as Presbyterian minister Immanual Bourne (1590–1672) writing in 1656:

there is another sort of people which travel up and down the nation, under the name of Quakers, as the Jesuits and seminary priests have used to do secretly, so these now openly, dissuading and seducing our people all they can from coming to our churches or meeting houses, calling our churches idols' temples. All our services to God in prayer, preaching of the word and other Christian exercises, ordinary and extraordinary, when we seek the face of God for the peace and welfare of the nation, for the prosperity of our navy and armies..., or our praising God for his mercies we do enjoy – all these, say the Quakers, are but idol-worship, and beastly services; and all the faithful and godly ministers of Christ, without exception, are thieves; our maintenance by tithes, anti-Christian and unlawful. Yea, they call us conjurors, Antichrists, witches, devils, liars, a viperous and serpentine generation, blasphemers, scarlet-colored beasts, Babylon's merchants, whited walls, painted sepulchers; and whatsoever the true prophets of God, or Christ our savior, did justly call the false prophets, wicked priests, and scribes and pharisees, those names do these railing and reviling Quakers give to the godly, painful, learned, and faithful ministers of Christ in the nation..., disturbing us in our public ministry.[30]

One further symbolic action which brought notoriety and infamy upon early Quaker women was "going naked for a sign," usually wearing sackcloth with hair undone and uncovered rather than actual nakedness, in order to demonstrate humility and purity of Spirit (May 3, 1655, document 7.14). What was the reaction of the Bristol city officers to the Quakers? Parliament was more severe with James Nayler (ca. 1617–60), a prominent Quaker preacher and apostle who was imprisoned for impersonating Christ as he entered Bristol in the fall of 1656

---

[30] Bourne, *A Defence of the Scriptures*, sig. A2; compared with Hughes, *Seventeenth-Century England*, 148.

(see Bucholz and Key, chapter 8). In his own writings he sounds just like one of Bourne's "railing and reviling Quakers."

All your hirelings [paid ministers] are strangers to Christ, and he knows them not: for though they may prophesy in his name, and in his name cast out devils, yet if they be workers of iniquity, Christ knows them not and such know not Christ. *For he that sayeth I know him and keeps not his commandments is a liar* [1 John 2: 4]. Now all people, cease from your strange guides and outside lights and return to the light of Christ in you, that which shows you sin and evil and the deeds of darkness. For whatever makes manifest is light; and this is that light which shines into the conscience, which tells you that lying, swearing, pride, envy, covetousness, backbiting, and dissembling leads to condemnation. And this light checks you for sin and would have you to do to all men as you would be done to. And this light is not a chapter without you, in a book, but it is that light that revealed that to the saints, in their several measures, which they spoke forth and which thou readest in the chapter.[31]

If we are to seek Christ's light (the Holy Spirit) within us, what is the point of a Directory of worship or Book of Common Prayer? Of the Bible? Of ministers? Of organized Churches? Were Quakers revolutionary?

One can understand how the trial and execution of the king, the abolition of the monarchy, of the House of Lords, of episcopacy (the bishops) and the Book of Common Prayer might encourage people to anticipate (and others to fear) further political, economic, and spiritual change. While most of the groups seeking change were fairly marginal, either in numbers or in power, one sect saw its role expand in the early 1650s, especially when Cromwell and the army forcibly dissolved the Rump and tried a brief experiment of godly rule with the Assembly of Saints (nicknamed Barebones Parliament) in April 1653. This was the millenarian group of Fifth Monarchists. Following Revelation's cryptic prophecies, millenarians believed that Christ's thousand-year reign was about to be established on earth. Of course Revelation is part of the Bible, in which everyone believed; throughout the early seventeenth century, clergy and gentry alike scoured its text for hints of the future and looked to current events for signs, providences and other indications of God working out his plan. By the Interregnum, most hard-headed English men and women came to reject millenarianism as a basis for political action. But the Fifth Monarchists (the most prominent of whom, Major-General Thomas Harrison, d. 1660, was a member of the Council of State) influenced Cromwell directly in the period 1652–3. Drawing on the Book of Daniel, Fifth Monarchists believed that there had been four great world monarchies so far. The fourth, the Roman, included the papacy and, by similar reasoning, episcopal government in England. Each had fallen in turn, and, as episcopacy had fallen most recently, the fifth monarchy, Christ's kingdom on earth, would be erected soon, by force of arms if necessary.

---

[31] Nayler, *The Power and Glory of the Lord Shining out of the North* (1656), 2; compared with Hughes, *Seventeenth-Century England*, 146.

Know therefore that the uttermost dura[tion] of Antichrists' dominion, will be in the year 1673.... 'Ere which time it will be necessary that the ten horns, or kings, which are the strength of the Best, be broken off, which work is already begun in the beheading of Charles, late king of the three kingdoms, anno 164[9], according to that in Dan. 7.11.24.26, and the rest of the horns are to continue but a little longer, v. 12. Now this kingdom of Christ which I call the fifth monarchy, shall begin a little before the fourth monarchy be destroyed.... But to come yet a little nearer to the first rise of this monarchy, it is said, that judgment was given to the saints ... Dan. 7.22.26, which was fulfilled 164[9], and this is not the beginning of the fifth monarchy, but it comes near it.... [W]hen God awakens the saints and witnesses to hearken to a voice from Heaven, that is, from the churches, saying *Come up hither*, Rev. 11.12. When they are content to forget their old forms of government, civil and ecclesiastical, called the *first Heavens, and first Earth* Rev. 21.1, Isa. 65.17. When I say the saints are come to this pitch, and they will have no laws, statutes, or rules of government in the Church or civil State, but what Christ hath given in his word, even from thenceforth does this fifth monarchy begin, which Peter calls the *new Heavens, and new Earth, wherein dwells righteousness* 2 Pet. 3.13. Of this Paul prophesies, Heb. 12.27, that not only the earth, but also the heaven, to wit, the government, civil and ecclesiastical, should be shaken towards the end of the fourth monarchy.... And by shaking he means removing of them.... And verily there has been a great shaking already, and more yet remains, for the work will not be wholly finished until the Jews be called, and the fullness of the nations come in. For which let all saints pray, *Come Lord Jesus, come quickly, and let thy Kingdome come* ..., Rev. 22.17, Mat. 6.10.[32]

In fact, the Fifth Monarchists' moment, and with it the Assembly of Saints, came and went very quickly, with plenty of shaking but no Second Coming (see Bucholz and Key, chapter 8). By the end of 1653, the Assembly had been dissolved and, from December 16, 1653, by the Instrument of Government,

the supreme legislative authority of the Commonwealth of England, Scotland, and Ireland, and the dominions thereunto belonging, shall be and reside in one person, and the people assembled in Parliament; the style of which person shall be the Lord Protector of the Commonwealth of England, Scotland, and Ireland.[33]

Despite the term "Lord Protector," the Instrument of Government had placed a king-like power in Cromwell's hands. England had taken its first step back from the radical political and religious experiments of the Interregnum.

HISTORIOGRAPHY

Two dramatically different views on the Civil Wars era have been advanced by two prolific historians: C. Hill and C. Russell. Both critiqued an earlier

---

[32] W. Aspinwall, *A Brief Description of the Fifth Monarchy, or Kingdome, That shortly is to Come into the World* (1653), 14; compared with D. Newton, *Papists, Protestants and Puritans, 1559–1714* (Cambridge, 1998), 59–60.

[33] *American Historical Documents, 1000–1904* (New York, 1910), 106; compared with C. Blitzer, ed., *The Commonwealth of England: Documents of the English Civil Wars, the Commonwealth and Protectorate* (New York, 1963), 151.

Whig view that a long-standing struggle for constitutional and religious liberties reached its climax in the wars, regicide, and revolution. Hill's early works, such as the pamphlet *The English Revolution, 1640* (1940) and *Puritanism and Revolution* (1958), agreed that there was a struggle with long-term causes, but argued that it was primarily a social struggle with economic roots. For sympathetic explorations of this Marxian view, see G. Eley and W. Hunt, eds., *Reviving the English Revolution: Reflections and Elaborations on the Work of Christopher Hill* (1988). Russell succinctly expressed his view in the title of his collected essays, *Unrevolutionary England, 1603–1642* (1990): elite, factional politics played more of a role in the largely accidental, or at least short-term causes, of the first Civil War, than any long-term ideological or social causes. See also his "Why Did Charles I Fight the Civil War?," *HT* (June 1984); and T. Cogswell, R. Cust, and P. Lake, "Revisionism and Its Legacies: The Work of Conrad Russell," in *Politics, Religion and Popularity in Early Stuart Britain*, ed. Cogswell, Cust, and Lake (Cambridge, 2002). J. S. A. Adamson extends Russell's viewpoint in "The English Context of the British Civil Wars," *HT* (November 1998) and "The Baronial Context of the English Civil War," *TRHS* 5th ser., 40 (1990). Contrasting with both Russell and Hill is A. Hughes, *The Causes of the English Civil War*, 2nd ed. (1998).

During the Civil War, as before, most English people lived and worked in the provinces. The county community approach once dominated Stuart social and political history. See articles in E. W. Ives, ed., *The English Revolution, 1600–1660* (New York, 1968); J. Morrill, *The Revolt of the Provinces: Conservatives and Radicals in the English Civil War, 1630–1650* (1976), revised as *Revolt in the Provinces: The People of England and the Tragedies of War, 1630–1648* (1999); and more recent county community studies: A. Fletcher, "National and Local Awareness in County Communities," in *Before the English Civil War*, ed. H. Tomlinson (1983); A. Hughes, "Local History and the Origins of the Civil War," in *Conflict in Early Stuart England: Studies in Religion and Politics, 1603–1642*, ed. Hughes and R. Cust (1989); and articles in R. C. Richardson, ed., *Town and Countryside in the English Revolution* (Manchester, 1992). But the concept has been attacked in C. Holmes, "The County Community in Stuart Historiography," *JBS* 19, 2 (1980, reprinted in R. Cust and A. Hughes, eds., *The English Civil War*, 1997).

Beyond the provinces, the War in the Three British Kingdoms is contextualized in J. Morrill, ed., *The Scottish National Covenant in its British Context* (Edinburgh, 1990); J. Ohlmeyer, ed., *Ireland from Independence to Occupation* (Cambridge, 1995), especially N. Canny, "What Really Happened in Ireland in 1641?"; B. MacCuarta, ed., *Ulster, 1641: Aspects of the Rising* (Belfast, 1993); J. R. Young, ed., *Celtic Dimensions of the British Civil Wars* (Edinburgh, 1997); as well as, more broadly, B. Bradshaw and J. S. Morrill, eds., *The British Problem, 1534–1707* (1996). Russell, *The Causes of the English Civil War* (Oxford, 1990) makes the British context the key to understanding the event. War and reaction are studied in C. Carlton, *Going to the Wars: Experience of the British Civil Wars, 1638–1651* (1992); I. Roy, "England Turned Germany?: The Aftermath of the Civil War in its European Context," *TRHS* 5th ser., 28 (1978); and J. Morrill, ed., *The Impact of the English Civil War* (1991). Biography is emphasized in I. Gentles et al., eds., *Soldiers, Writers and Statesmen of the English Revolution* (Cambridge, 1998). M. Bennett, *The Civil Wars in Britain and Ireland, 1638–1651* (Oxford, 1997) is brief and lucid.

Analysis of popular politics and allegiance during the wars and Interregnum should start with D. Underdown, "The Problem of Popular Allegiance," *TRHS* 31 (1981); and his *Revel, Riot, and Rebellion: Popular Politics and Culture in England, 1603–1660* (Oxford, 1985), chs. 6–10; to be contrasted with J. Morrill, *The Nature of the English Revolution* (1993), chs. 8–11, which focus on the diversity of allegiance; A. Hughes, "King, Parliament and Localities" (1985, reprinted in Cust and Hughes, *English Civil War*); and M. Stoyle, *Loyalty and Locality: Popular Allegiance in Devon During the English Civil War* (Exeter, 1994). An intriguing aspect of popular allegiance is that of the clubmen, for which see D. Underdown, "The Chalk and the Cheese: Contrasts among the English Clubmen," *P & P 85* (1979); and P. Gladwish, "The Herefordshire Clubmen: A Reassessment," *Midland History* 10 (1985).

Who, where, and when were the radicals in the English revolution? Many historians have pointed to the religious radicalization of the soldiers and officers of the parliamentary army. But M. Kishlansky, in "Ideology and Politics in the Parliamentary Armies, 1645–9," in *Reactions to the English Civil War, 1642–1649*, ed. J. Morrill (1982); his *The Rise of the New Model Army* (Cambridge, 1979); and elsewhere has questioned this link by noting the basic pay and legal issues that motivated the soldiers in the aftermath of the first Civil War. Kishlansky has been challenged, in turn, by I. Gentles, *The New Model Army* (Oxford, 1992) and by A. Woolrych, *Soldiers and Statesmen* (Oxford, 1987). G. E. Aylmer, ed., *The Levellers in the English Revolution* (Ithaca, 1975), "Introduction," opens up the Putney Debates; they are also dissected in M. Mendle, ed., *The Putney Debates of 1647: The Army, the Levellers and the English State* (Cambridge, 2001).

The role and intentions of Oliver Cromwell in the 1640s and 1650s continue to excite interest. Students approaching this question for the first time should consider C. Hill, *God's Englishman: Oliver Cromwell and the English Revolution* (New York, 1970); B. Coward, *Oliver Cromwell* (1991); and, still useful, C. Firth, *Oliver Cromwell and the Rule of the Puritans in England* (New York, 1903); as well as articles in J. Morrill, ed., *Oliver Cromwell and the English Revolution* (1990); and in I. Roots, ed., *Cromwell: A Profile* (New York, 1973), especially H. R. Trevor-Roper's "Oliver Cromwell and His Parliaments."

A good introduction to radical voices in print is T. N. Corns, "Radical Pamphleteering," in *The Cambridge Companion to Writing on the English Revolution*, ed. N. H. Keeble (Cambridge, 2001). One of the best works on Quaker (and women's) history is P. Mack, *Visionary Women: Ecstatic Prophecy in Seventeenth-Century England* (Berkeley, 1992); or Mack, "Women as Prophets During the English Civil War," *Feminist Studies* 8, 1 (1982). (For women generally, see also P. Crawford, "The Challenges to Patriarchalism: How Did the Revolution Affect Women?," in *Revolution and Restoration: England in the 1650s*, ed. J. Morrill, 1992; A. M. McEntree, " 'The [Un]Civill-Sisterhood of Oranges and Lemons': Female Petitioners and Demonstrators, 1642–53," in *Pamphlet Wars: Prose in the English Revolution*, ed. J. Holstum, 1992; and E. Hobby, "Prophecy, Enthusiasm and Female Pamphleteers," in Keeble, *Cambridge Companion*.) But the radical Hydra is still best approached first through C. Hill, *The World Turned Upside Down: Radical Ideas During the English Revolution* (1975); chapters on individual sects in B. Reay and I. McGregor, eds., *Radical Religion in the English Revolution* (Oxford, 1984); and B. Reay's work: *The Quakers and the English Revolution* (1985), and, especially, his "Popular Hostility Towards Quakers in Mid-Seventeenth-Century England," *Social History* 5 (1980). Was the Digger Gerrard Winstanley a radical? See the debate among C. Hill, L. Mulligan, J. K. Graham, and J. Richards, on "The Religion of Gerrard Winstanley," *P & P* 89 (1980). Hill's view of the Interregnum as a window of liberation has been questioned by J. C. Davis, "Religion and the Struggle for Freedom in the English Revolution," *HJ* 35 (1992). Davis has also questioned the very existence of the Ranters in *Fear, Myth and History* (Cambridge, 1986). The fascinating debate over the Ranters – see *P & P* 129 (1990) and 140 (1993) – has wider implications for what historians study and why. Before celebrating the possibilities for religious change during the Interregnum, one might temper one's enthusiasm by reading Morrill, "The Church in England," in *Reactions to the English Civil War*, which finds a continuing strong Anglican presence.

After all is said and done, was it a revolution? Hill has never had any doubt. His "The Word 'Revolution,' " in *A Nation of Change and Novelty*, rev. ed. (1993) suggests that contemporaries did use the term in the modern sense of a radical, abrupt political change (as opposed to what has been taken to be the usual early modern sense of cyclical change). But a revisionist critique is found in J. Morrill, "Christopher Hill's Revolution," in *The Nature of the English Revolution*. And there is an introductory debate by J. Morrill, B. Manning, and D. Underdown on "What Was the English Revolution?," in *HT* 34, 3 (1984). G. E. Aylmer, *Rebellion or Revolution?: England from Civil War to Restoration* (Oxford, 1986) and A. Woolrych, *Britain in Revolution, 1625–1660* (Oxford, 2002) are, despite the titles, analytic narratives, but none the worse for that.

The overall situation of the Commonwealth and Protectorate is surveyed briefly in T. Barnard, *The English Republic*, 2nd ed. (1997); R. Hutton, *The British Republic, 1649–1660*, 2nd ed. (2000); and I. Roots, ed., *"Into Another Mould": Aspects of the Interregnum*, 2nd ed. (Exeter, 1998). But see also B. Worden, "Marchamont Nedham and the Beginnings of English Republicanism, 1649–1656," in *Republicanism, Liberty, and Commercial Society, 1649–1776*, ed. D. Wootton (Stanford, 1994); Worden, "Providence and Politics in Cromwellian England," *P & P* 109 (1985); and, for the British context, F. O. Dow, *Cromwellian Scotland, 1651–1660* (Edinburgh, 1979); and T. C. Barnard, *Cromwellian Ireland: English Government and Reform in Ireland, 1649–1660*, 2nd ed. (Oxford, 2000). The lengthy D. Underdown, *Pride's Purge: Politics in the Puritan Revolution* (Oxford, 1971) and B. Worden, *The Rump Parliament, 1648–53* (Cambridge, 1974) are classics, still crucial for the revolutionary years.

DOCUMENTS

7.1   Lucy Hutchinson, Memoirs of the Life of Colonel Hutchinson, ca. 1640s (written ca. 1664–71, pub. 1806)[34]

About the year 1639, the Scots having the English service-book obtruded upon them violently refused it and took a national covenant against it, and entered England with a great army to bring their complaints to the king, which his unfaithful ministers did much, as they [the Scots] supposed, misreport. The king himself levied an army against them, wherein he was assisted . . . most of all by the prelates, insomuch that the war got the name of *Bellum Episcopale* [Bishops' War(s)]; but the commonality of the nation, being themselves under grievous bondage, were loath to oppose a people that came only to claim their just liberties. . . .

While the king was in Scotland, that cursed rebellion in Ireland broke out [October 23, 1641], wherein about 200,000 were massacred in two months' space, being surprised, and many of them most inhumanely butchered and tormented; and besides the slain, abundance of poor families stripped and sent naked away out of all their possessions; and had not the providence of God miraculously prevented the surprise of Dublin Castle the night it should have been seized, there had not been any remnant of the Protestant name left in that country. As soon as this sad news came to the Parliament, they vigorously set themselves to the work of relieving them; but then the king returned from Scotland, and being sumptuously welcomed home by the city, took courage thereby against the Parliament, and obstructed all their proceedings for the effectual relief of Ireland. Long was he before he could be drawn to proclaim those murderers rebels, and when he did, by special command there were but 40 proclamations printed, and care taken that they should not be much dispersed;

---

[34]   L. Hutchinson, *Memoirs of Colonel Hutchinson*, ed. N. H. Keeble (1968, 1995), 71, 73–4.

which courses afflicted all the good Protestants in England, and confirmed that this rebellion in Ireland received countenance from the king and queen of England.

7.2 A Venetian Ambassador's Reports on England's Preparations for Civil War (August 1–October 10, 1642)[35]

(August 1, 1642) The visitation which his majesty is carrying out in the northern counties appears to be most successful. In every place that he has visited so far he has been received by the whole of the nobility, the people flocking to meet him in crowds, and his entry has been accompanied by loyal acclamations and blessings. . . . They offered him their fortunes and their services in his cause. The town of Niuarch [Newark] in particular and Lincoln also have bound themselves by spontaneous promises to maintain under present conditions at their own expense, some companies of cavalry. . . .

In this city [London] they do not relax their efforts for the completion of the levies [Parliamentarian] of horse and foot reported. Every day they hold reviews and make demonstrations for the purpose of magnifying their warlike preparation, and by the trick of these shows to keep the common people of London more and more determined against the king. The rebels have based all their hopes upon the unreasoning opinions of these folk, but it is a support which may perchance prove insufficiently strong, for so great a superstructure. . . .

(August 15, 1642) Four thousand apprentices attracted by the advantageous terms and by the offers of high pay have taken service under the standard of the Parliament, many others are disposed to do the same, and they hope in a short time to have a considerable number of this sort of folk. They are for the most part of tender age, entirely without discipline and unaccustomed to hardship or the handling of weapons. On this account it is not reasonable to expect great proofs of valor or of loyalty from their services. . . .

(August 29, 1642) After the failure of all his majesty's attempts to bring back the dissident Parliamentarians to the path of duty, he has decided, out of consideration for his own safety, to appeal to the sword. He has announced by proclamation that on Monday the 1st of next month he will proceed to the town of Nottingham . . . , and there display the royal standard. . . . He invites all true Protestants, specially those who live more than thirty miles from this city, to supply him with men, money, and arms and bring them speedily to his camp. He enlarges upon the justice of his cause, which he protests is bound up with that of religion, the public liberty, and the privileges of Parliament. . . .

(September 5, 1642) In conformity with the declaration reported, the king left York on Tuesday in this week with a following of fifteen hundred horse and of a few bands of infantry. . . . On arriving at Nottingham and perceiving at a glance the scant inclination of the people there to follow his fortunes, he made up his

---

[35] *CSP and Manuscripts, Relating to English Affairs, Existing in the Archives . . . of Venice*, 26, *1642–1643*, ed. A. B. Hinds (1925), 111–13, 123, 134, 139–40, 147, 154–5, 161, 171; compared with P. Razzell, ed., *The English Revolution: A Contemporary Study of the English Civil War* (1999), 160–73.

mind not to make a halt there but to push on to the town of Coventry..., with the idea of subsequently unfurling the royal standard in that place....

But on arriving within a short distance of the town he found the bridges closed and the people there not less contumacious than the others, with a determination not to permit him to enter unless on the condition that he would not bring inside the walls the warlike forces accompanying him. The king refused to agree to this and filled with resentment he tried to force a way in with a bomb. The garrison, for its part, having evaded the perils of this first blow, sallied out from the town and attacking the royal troops without any compunction, they threw them into disorder and compelled them to retreat in manifest rout, with the loss of three pieces of artillery and of some soldiers as well. After this unfortunate incident his majesty betook himself once more to Nottingham....

(September 12, 1642) They send word from Wales that when the harvest is gathered in the king will receive important succors, and from other quarters as well.... Meanwhile Parliament... [has] sent orders to Holland for the transport of arms, since the mechanics here cannot cope with the demand, with the number of the troops, which every day it is gathering under its flag....

(September 18, 1642) In consequence of the overtures made by the Scots for the union of the two Churches of England and Scotland, it was proposed on Monday in the lower House to do away altogether with the bishops and every other ecclesiastical dignity, and to leave the care of the Church of England to the sole direction of the preachers, in accordance with the doctrine of Calvin, and the practice of Holland and of the Huguenots in France. There was a prolonged discussion, and much feeling was aroused.... But... it was finally carried by a majority that in future there shall be no bishops or other prelates in this kingdom....

(September 26, 1642) Before leaving Nottingham the king took away the arms of many of the inhabitants of that county and of the town of Leicester as well, who are strenuous professors of Calvinism, and whom he suspected of being likely to support the interests of the other side, owing to their unchangeable bias....

(October 10, 1642) News comes that it is now a common saying among the [Parliamentarian] troops that they took service under this flag on condition of serving the king no less than Parliament, both equally, from which men of experience foresee that it will not be easy for the general [Essex] to lead them to fight against the troops of his majesty if that becomes necessary.

7.3 Richard Baxter on Royalists and Parliamentarians (written ca. 1664, pub. 1696)[36]

But of all the rest there was nothing that with the people wrought so much as the Irish massacre and rebellion. The Irish Papists did, by an unexpected insurrection,

---

[36] *Reliquiae Baxterianae* (1696), 1, part 1: 28–31, 33, 39; compared with *The Autobiography of Richard Baxter*, ed. N. H. Keeble (1974), 31–7.

rise all over Ireland at once, and seized upon almost all the strengths of the whole land, and Dublin wonderfully escaped..., which was to have been surprised with the rest, October 23, 1641. Two hundred thousand persons they murdered (as you may see in... Sir John Temple's *History*, who was one of the resident justices). Men, women, and children were most cruelly used, the women ripped up and filthily used when they killed them, and the infants used like toads or vermin. Thousands of those that escaped came stripped and almost famished to Dublin, and afterwards into England to beg their bread. Multitudes of them were driven together into rivers, and cast over bridges and drowned. Many witnesses swore before the lords justices that at Portdown Bridge a vision every day appeared to the passengers of naked persons standing up in the middle in the river and crying out, "Revenge! Revenge!" In a word, scarce any history mentioneth the like barbarous cruelty as this was....

This filled all England with a fear both of the Irish and of the Papists at home, for they supposed that the priests and the interest of their religion were the cause; insomuch that when the rumor of a plot was occasioned at London, the poor people, all the countries [counties] over, were ready either to run to arms or hide themselves, thinking that the Papists were ready to rise and cut their throats. And when they saw the English Papists join with the king against the Parliament, it was the greatest thing that ever alienated them from the king....

It is of very great moment here to understand the quality of the persons which adhered to the king and to the Parliament, with their reasons.

A great part of the Lords forsook the Parliament, and so did many of the House of Commons, and came to the king; but that was, for the most of them, after Edgehill fight, when the king was at Oxford. A very great part of the knights and gentlemen of England in the several counties (who were not Parliament-men) adhered to the king.... And most of the tenants of these gentlemen, and also most of the poorest of the people, whom the other call the rabble, did follow the gentry and were for the king.

On the Parliament's side were (besides themselves) the smaller part (as some thought) of the gentry in most of the counties, and the greatest part of the tradesmen and freeholders and the middle sort of men, especially in those corporations and countries which depend on clothing and such, manufactures....

But though it must be confessed that the public safety and liberty wrought very much with most, especially with the nobility and gentry who adhered to the Parliament, yet was it principally the differences about religious matter that filled up the Parliament's armies and put the resolution and valor into their soldiers, which carried them on in another manner than mercenary soldiers are carried on.... But the generality of the people through the land... who were then called Puritans, precisians, religious persons, that used to talk of God, and heaven, and Scripture, and holiness.... I say, the main body of this sort of men, both preachers and people, adhered to the Parliament. And on the other side [the Royalists], the gentry that were not so precise and strict against an oath, or gaming, or plays, or drinking nor troubled themselves so much about the matters of God and the world to come, and the ministers and people that were for the King's Book [of

Sports, 1633, document 6.9], for dancing and recreations on the Lord's days, and those that made not so great a matter of every sin, but went to church and heard Common Prayer, and were glad to hear a sermon which lashed the Puritans, and which ordinarily spoke against the strictness and preciseness in religion . . . , these were against the Parliament. . . .

And abundance of the ignorant sort of the country, who were civil, did flock in to the Parliament, and filled up their armies afterward, merely because they heard men *swear* for the Common Prayer and bishops, and heard others *pray* that were against them; and because they heard the king's soldiers with horrid oaths abuse the name of God, and saw them live in debauchery and the Parliament's soldiers flock to sermons and talking of religion, and praying and singing Psalms together on their guards. And all the sober men that I was acquainted with, who were against the Parliament, were wont to say, "The king hath the better cause, but the Parliament hath the better men." . . .

For my own part . . . I freely confess that, being astonished at the Irish massacre, and persuaded fully both of the Parliament's good endeavors for reformation and of their real danger, my judgment of the main cause much swayed my judgment in the matter of the wars.

7.4   Oliver Cromwell's Letters about the English Civil War (1643–4)[37]

(September 11, 1643, Oliver Cromwell with the Parliamentarian Eastern Association army to Oliver St. John, Esq., at London) Of all men I should not trouble you with money matters, did not the heavy necessities my troops are in, press me beyond measure. I am neglected exceedingly!

I am now ready for my march towards the enemy; who hath entrenched himself over against Hull, my Lord Newcastle having besieged the town. Many of my lord of Manchester's troops are come to me: very bad and mutinous, not to be confided in; they paid to a week almost; mine no ways provided for to support them, except by the poor sequestrations of the county of Huntingdon. My troops increase. I have a lovely company; you would respect them, did you know them. They are no Anabaptists, they are honest sober Christians: they expect to be used as men.

If I took pleasure to write to the House in bitterness, I have occasion. Of the £3,000 allotted me, I cannot get the part of Norfolk nor Hertfordshire: it was gone before I had it. I have minded your service to forgetfulness of my own and soldiers' necessities. I desire not to seek myself, but I have little money of my own to help my soldiers. My estate is little. I tell you, the business of Ireland and England hath had of me, in money, between eleven and twelve hundred pounds; therefore my private can do little to help the public. You have had my money: I hope in God I desire to venture my skin. So do mine. Lay weight upon their

---

[37]   *Writings and Speeches of Cromwell*, ed. Abbott, 1: 258–9, 277–8, 287–8; compared with *Letters and Speeches of Cromwell*, ed. T. Carlyle (1845, 1907).

patience; but break it not. Think of that which may be a real help. I believe £5,000 is due. . . .

(March 10, 1644, Oliver Cromwell at Cambridge to Major-General Crawford) [Regarding t]he complaints you preferred to my lord [Manchester] against your lieutenant-colonel, both by Mr. Lee and your own letters. . . .

Surely you are not well advised thus to turn off one so faithful to the cause, and so able to serve you as this man is. . . .

Ay, but the man is an Anabaptist. Are you sure of that? Admit he be, shall that render him incapable to serve the public? He is indiscreet. It may be so, in some things, we have all human infirmities. I tell you, if you had none but such indiscreet men about you, and would be pleased to use them kindly, you would find as good a fence to you as any you have yet chosen.

Sir, the State, in choosing men to serve them, takes no notice of their opinions, if they be willing faithfully to serve them, that satisfies. I advised you formerly to bear with men of different minds from yourself; if you had done it when I advised you to it, I think you would not have had so many stumblingblocks in your way. It may be you judge otherwise, but I tell you my mind. I desire you would receive this man into your favor and good opinion. I believe, if he follow my counsel, he will deserve no other but respect from you. Take heed of being sharp, or too easily sharpened by others, against those to whom you can object little but that they square not with you in every opinion concerning matters of religion.

(July 5, 1644, Oliver Cromwell, before York to his brother-in-law Col. Valentine Walton) It's our duty to sympathize in all mercies; that we may praise the Lord together in chastisements or trials, that so we may sorrow together.

Truly England and the Church of God hath had a great favor from the Lord in this great victory given unto us, such as the like never was since this war began. It had all the evidences of an absolute victory obtained by the Lord's blessing upon the godly party principally. We never charged but we routed the enemy. The left wing, which I commanded, being our own horse, saving a few Scots in our rear, beat all the prince's [Rupert's] horse. God made them as stubble to our swords; we charged their regiments of foot with our horse, routed all we charged. The particulars I cannot relate now, but I believe, of twenty thousand the prince hath not four thousand left. Give glory, all the glory, to God.

Sir, God hath taken away your eldest son by a cannon-shot. It brake his leg. We were necessitated to have it cut off, whereof he died.

Sir, you know my trials this way, but the Lord supported me with this: that the Lord took him into the happiness we all pant after and live for. There is your precious child full of glory, to know sin nor sorrow any more. He was a gallant young man, exceeding gracious. God give you His comfort. Before his death he was so full of comfort that to Frank Russell and myself he could not express it, it was so great above his pain. This he said to us. Indeed it was admirable. A little after, he said one thing lay upon his spirit. I asked him what that was. He told me that it was that God had not suffered him to be no more the executioner of His enemies. At his fall, his horse being killed with a bullet, and as I am informed three horses more, I am told he bid them open to the right and left, that he might see the rogues run. Truly, he was exceedingly beloved in the army, of all that knew him. But few knew him, for he was a precious young man, fit for God. You have cause to bless the Lord. He is a glorious saint in Heaven, wherein you ought exceedingly to rejoice. Let this drink up your sorrow; seeing these are not feigned words to comfort you, but the thing is so real and undoubted a truth. You may do all things by the strength of Christ. Seek that, and you shall easily bear your trial. Let this public mercy to the Church of God make you to forget your private sorrow. The Lord be your strength.

7.5 *The Parliamentarian Siege of Colchester (August 18, 1648)*[38]

We hope that hunger will necessitate the people to something which may occasion the soldiers to join with them, which may facilitate our work in gaining the town. The honest and well-affected people that are there, we very much pity their condition; and could we single them out from the rest, they might have passes from the general; but [the Royalist general] Goring will let no well-affected come out, unless some that are ill-affected, may come out with them.

Yesterday there came out a woman and five children, one sucking at her breast; she fell down at our guards, beseeching them to pass beyond the line; the people in the town looking to see if they had admittance, resolving to follow them; but the guards were necessitated to turn them back again, or otherwise hundreds will come out, which would much prejudice the service.

The soldiers and the woman said, "that could they get but dogs and cats to eat, it were happy for them, but all the dogs and cats, and most of the horses are near eaten already." Some sad thing of necessity must befall the town suddenly....

A mother is stolen out of town, who saith, that this day the women and children were at the Lord Goring's door for bread; that he told them, "They must eat their children if they wanted"; the women . . . told him, "They would pull out his eyes rather than starve," and were in a high discontent; and that all the inhabitants set the women on, and some soldiers dislike it not.

7.6 *Oliver Cromwell at Dublin to William Lenthall, Esq., Speaker of the Parliament of England (September 17, 1649)*[39]

Your army came before the town [Tredah, Drogheda] upon [September 3], where having pitched, as speedy course was taken as could be to frame our batteries.... Upon [September 10] . . ., the batteries began to play. Whereupon I sent Sir Arthur Ashton, the then governor, a summons to deliver the town to the use of the Parliament of England. To the which I received no satisfactory answer, but

---

[38] Rushworth, *Historical Collections*, 7: 1232–3; compared with Lamont and Oldfield, *Politics, Religion, and Literature*, 185–6.

[39] *Writings and Speeches of Cromwell*, ed. Abbott, 2: 125–8; compared with *Letters and Speeches of Cromwell*, ed. Carlyle and Lomas, 1: 466–71.

proceeded that day to beat down the steeple of the church on the south side of the town, and to beat down a tower not far from the same place....

Upon [September 11]..., about five o'clock in the evening, we began the storm, and after some hot dispute we entered about seven or eight hundred men, the enemy disputing it very stiffly with us. And indeed, through the advantages of the place, and the courage God was pleased to give the defenders, our men were forced to retreat quite out of the breach, not without some considerable loss....

Although our men that stormed the breaches were forced to recoil..., yet, being encouraged to recover their loss, they made a second attempt, wherein God was pleased [so] to animate them that they got ground of the enemy, and by the goodness of God, forced him to quit his entrenchments. And after a very hot dispute..., they gave ground, and our men became masters both of their retrenchments and the church; which indeed, although they made our entrance the more difficult, yet they proved of excellent use to us, so that the enemy could not now annoy us with their horse....

The enemy retreated, diverse of them, into the Mill-Mount: a place very strong and of difficult access, being exceedingly high, having a good graft, and strongly palisadoed. The governor, Sir Arthur Ashton, and diverse considerable officers being there, our men getting up to them, were ordered by me to put them all to the sword. And indeed, being in the heat of action, I forbade them to spare any that were in arms in the town, and, I think, that night they put to the sword about 2,000 men, diverse of the officers and soldiers being fled over the bridge into the other part of the town, where about one hundred of them possessed St. Peter's church-steeple, some the west gate and others a strong round tower next the gate called St. Sunday's. These being summoned to yield to mercy, refused, whereupon I ordered the steeple of St. Peter's Church to be fired, where one of them was heard to say in the midst of the flames: "God damn me, God confound me; I burn, I burn."

The next day, the other two towers were summoned, in one of which was about six or seven score; but they refused to yield themselves, and we knowing that hunger must compel them, set only good guards to secure them from running away until their stomachs were come down. From one of the said towers, notwithstanding their condition, they killed and wounded some of our men. When they submitted, their officers were knocked on the head, and every tenth man of the soldiers killed, and the rest shipped for the Barbados. The soldiers in the other tower were all spared, as to their lives only, and shipped likewise for the Barbados.

I am persuaded that this is a righteous judgment of God upon these barbarous wretches, who have imbrued their hands in so much innocent blood; and that it will tend to prevent the effusion of blood for the future, which are the satisfactory grounds to such actions, which otherwise cannot but work remorse and regret. The officers and soldiers of this garrison were the flower of all their army, and their great expectation was, that our attempting this place would put fair to ruin us....

I believe all their friars were knocked on the head promiscuously but two; the one of which was Father Peter Taaff, (brother to the Lord Taaff), whom the soldiers took the next day and made an end of; the other was taken in the round tower, under the repute of lieutenant, and when he understood that the officers in that tower had no quarter, he confessed he was a friar; but that did not save him....

I do not think we lost one hundred men upon the place, though many be wounded.

7.7 The Heads of the Proposals Agreed Upon by his Excellency Sir Thomas Fairfax and the Council of the Army *(August 1, 1647)*[40]

I. That the things hereafter proposed, being provided for by this Parliament, a certain period may by Act of Parliament be set for the ending of this Parliament (such period to be put within a year at most). And in the same Act provision to be made . . . as followeth:

1. That Parliaments may biennially be called and meet at a certain day, with such provision for the certainty thereof, as in the late Act was made for triennial Parliaments [1641]. . . .

2. Each biennial Parliament to sit 120 days certain (unless adjourned or dissolved sooner by their own consent), afterwards to be adjournable or dissolvable by the king, and no Parliament to sit past 240 days from their first meeting. . . .

3. The king, upon advice of the Council of State, in the intervals between biennial Parliaments, to call a Parliament extraordinary, provided it meet above 70 days before the next biennial day, and be dissolved at least 60 days before the same; so as the course of biennial elections may never be interrupted. . . .

5. That the elections of the Commons for succeeding Parliaments may be distributed to all counties, or other parts or divisions of the kingdom, according to some rule of equality or proportion, so as all counties may have a number of Parliament members allowed to their choice, proportionable to the respective rates they bear in the common charges and burdens of the kingdom, according to some other rule of equality or proportion, to render the House of Commons (as near as may be) an equal representative of the whole; and in order thereunto, that a present consideration be had to take off the elections of burgesses for poor, decayed, or inconsiderable towns, and to give some present addition to the number of Parliament members for great counties that have now less than their due proportion, to bring all (at present), as near as may be, to such a rule of proportion as aforesaid.

6. That effectual provision be made for future freedom of elections, and certainty of due returns. . . .

40 Rushworth, *Historical Collections*, 7: 731–4; compared with Gardiner, *Constitutional Documents*, 316–26.

10. That the right and liberty of the Commons of England may be cleared and vindicated as to a due exemption from any judgment, trial, or other proceeding against them by the house of Peers, without the concurring judgment of the house of Commons....

XI. An Act to be passed to take away all coercive power, authority, and jurisdiction of bishops and all other ecclesiastical officers whatsoever....

XII. That there be a repeal of all Acts or clauses in any Act enjoining the use of the Book of Common Prayer, and imposing any penalties for neglect thereof; as also of all Acts or clauses of any Act, imposing any penalty for not coming to church, or for meetings elsewhere for...religious duties..., and some other provision to be made for discovering of Papists and popish recusants, and for disabling of them....

XIII. That the taking of the Covenant be not enforced upon any, nor any penalties imposed on the refusers....

XVI. That there may be a general Act of Oblivion to extend unto all (except the persons...in exception as before), to absolve from all trespasses, misde-meanors, etc. done in prosecution of the war.

7.8 An Agreement of the People for a Firm and Present Peace, upon Grounds of Common-right and Freedoms; as it Was Proposed by the Agents of the Five Regiments of Horse; and since by the General Approbation of the Army, Offered to the Joint Concurrence of All the Free Commons of England (*ca. late October, 1647*)[41]

Having by our late labors and hazards made it appear to the world at how high a rate we value our just freedoms, and God having so far owned our cause, as to deliver the enemies thereof into our hands: We do now hold ourselves bound in mutual duty to each other, to take the best care we can for the future, to avoid both the danger of returning into a slavish condition, and the chargeable remedy of another war. For as it cannot be imagined that so many of our country-men would have opposed us in this quarrel, if they had understood their own good; so may we safely promise to ourselves, that when our common rights and liberties shall be cleared, their endeavors will be disappointed, that seek to make them-selves our masters: since therefore our former oppressions, and scarce yet ended troubles have been occasioned, either by want of frequent national meetings in council, or by rendering those meetings ineffectual. We are fully agreed and resolved, to provide that hereafter our representatives be neither left to an uncer-tainty for the time, nor made useless to the ends for which they are intended. In order whereunto we declare:

---

[41] Aylmer, *Levellers*, 89–91; compared with Lindley, *English Civil War and Revolution*, 148–50.

I. That the people of England being at this day very unequally distributed by counties, cities, and boroughs, for the election of their deputies in Parliament, ought to be more indifferently proportioned, according to the number of the inhabitants: the circumstances whereof, for number, place, and manner, are to be set down before the end of this present Parliament.

II. That to prevent the many inconveniences apparently arising from the long continuance of the same persons in authority, this present Parliament be dissolved upon the last day of September... 1648.

III. That the people do of course choose themselves a Parliament once in two years....

IV. That the power of this, and all future representatives of this nation, is inferior only to theirs who choose them, and doth extend...to the enacting, altering, and repealing of laws; to the erecting and abolishing of offices and courts; to the appointing, removing, and calling to account magistrates, and officers of all degrees; to the making war and peace, to the treating with foreign states: and generally, to whatsoever is not expressly, or impliedly reserved by the represented to themselves.
Which are as followeth,

1. That matters of religion, and the ways of God's worship, are not at all intrusted by us to any humane power, because therein we cannot go remit or exceed a tittle of what our consciences dictate to be the mind of God, without willful sin: nevertheless the public way of instructing the nation (so it be not compulsive) is referred to their discretion.

2. That the matter of impressing and constraining any of us to serve in the wars, is against our freedom; and therefore we do not allow it in our representatives....

3. That after the dissolution of this present Parliament, no person be at any time questioned for anything said or done, in reference to the late public differences....

4. That in all laws made, or to be made, every person may be bound alike, and that no tenure, estate, charter, degree, birth, or place, do confer any exemption....

5. That as the laws ought to be equal, so they must be good, and not evidently destructive to the safety and well-being of the people.

These things we declare to be our native rights, and therefore are agreed and resolved to maintain them with our utmost possibilities, against all opposition whatsoever, being compelled thereunto...by our own woeful experience, who having long expected, and dearly earned the establishment of these certain rules of government are yet made to depend for the settlement of our peace and freedom, upon him that intended our bondage, and brought a cruel war upon us.

7.9 The Putney Debates of the General Council of the Army (October 29, 1647)[42]

The paper called the *Agreement* read. Afterwards the first article read by itself.

Commissary General Henry Ireton: The exception that lies in it is this. It is said, they are to be distributed according to the number of the inhabitants: "The people of England, etc." And this doth make me think that the meaning is, that every man that is an inhabitant is to be equally considered, and to have an equal voice in the election of those representers, the persons that are for the general representative; and if that be the meaning, then I have something to say against it. But if it be only that those people that by the civil constitution of this kingdom, which is original and fundamental, and beyond which I am sure no memory of record does go.

Commissary General Nicholas Cowling, interrupting: Not before the Conquest.

Ireton: But before the Conquest it was so. If it be intended that those that by that constitution that was before the Conquest, that hath been beyond memory, such persons that have been before by that constitution the electors, should be still the electors, I have no more to say against it.

Colonel Thomas Rainsborough: Moved, That others might have given their hands to it [that is, the Army was already committed to support the *Agreement*].

Captain Richard Denne: Denied that those that were set of their regiment were their hands.

Ireton: Whether those men whose hands are to it, or those that brought it, do know so much of the matter as to know whether they mean that all that had a former right of election are to be electors, or that those that had no right before are to come in.

Cowling: In the time before the Conquest. Since the Conquest the greatest part of the kingdom was in vassalage.

Mr. Maximilian Petty [a civilian Leveller]: We judge that all inhabitants that have not lost their birthright should have an equal voice in elections.

Rainsborough: I desired that those that had engaged in it [might be included]. For really I think that the poorest he that is in England hath a life to live, as the greatest he; and therefore truly, sir, I think it's clear, that every man that is to live under a government ought first by his own consent to put himself under that government. And I do think that the poorest man in England is not at all bound in a strict sense to that government that he hath not had a voice to put himself under. And I am confident that, when I have heard the reasons against it, something will be said to answer those reasons, insomuch that I should doubt whether he was an Englishman or no, that should doubt of these things.

Ireton: That's this.

---

[42] Aylmer, *Levellers*, 99–119; compared with D. Wootton, ed., *Divine Right and Democracy: An Anthology of Political Writing in Stuart England* (Harmondsworth, Middlesex, 1986), 285–93.

Give me leave to tell you, that if you make this the rule I think you must fly for refuge to an absolute natural right, and you must deny all civil right; and I am sure it will come to that in the consequence.... For my part, I think it is no right at all. I think that no person hath a right to an interest or share in the disposing of the affairs of the kingdom, and in determining or choosing those that shall determine what laws we shall be ruled by here, no person hath a right to this, that hath not a permanent fixed interest in this kingdom, and those persons together are properly the represented of this kingdom, and consequently are also to make up the representers of this kingdom, who taken together do comprehend whatsoever is of real or permanent interest in the kingdom. And I am sure otherwise I cannot tell what any man can say why a foreigner coming in amongst us – or as many as will coming in amongst us, or by force or otherwise settling themselves here, or at least by our permission having a being here – why they should not as well lay claim to it as any other. We talk of birthright. Truly by birthright there is thus much claim. Men may justly have by birthright, by their very being born in England, that we should not seclude them out of England, that we should not refuse to give them air and place and ground, and the freedom of the highways and other things, to live amongst us – not any man that is born here, though by his birth there come nothing at all that is part of the permanent interest of this kingdom to him. That I think is due to a man by birth. But that by a man's being born here he shall have a share in that power that shall dispose of the lands here, and of all things here, I do not think it a sufficient ground.... [T]hat those that choose the representers for the making of laws by which this state and kingdom are to be governed, are the persons who, taken together, do comprehend the local interest of this kingdom; that is, the persons in whom all land lies, and those in corporations in whom all trading lies. This is the most fundamental constitution of this kingdom and that which if you do not allow, you allow none at all.... It is true, as was said by a gentleman near me, the meanest man in England ought to have a voice in the election of the government he lives under – but only if he has some local interest. I say this: that those that have the meanest local interest – that man that hath but forty shillings a year, he hath as great voice in the election of a knight for the shire as he that hath ten thousand a year, or more if he had never so much; and therefore there is that regard had to it. But this local interest, still the constitution of this government hath had an eye to (and what other government hath not an eye to this?).... And if we shall go to take away this, we shall plainly go to take away all property and interest that any man hath either in land by inheritance, or in estate by possession, or anything else – I say, if you take away this fundamental part of the civil constitution.

Rainsborough: Truly, sir, I am of the same opinion I was, and am resolved to keep it till I know reason why I should not. I confess my memory is bad, and therefore I am fain to make use of my pen. I remember that, in a former speech which this gentleman brought before this meeting, he was saying that in some cases he should not value whether there were a king or no king, whether lords or no lords, whether a property or no property. For my part I differ in that. I do very much care whether there be a king or no king, lords or no lords, property or no property; and I think, if we do not all take care, we shall all have none of these very shortly. But as to this present business. I do hear nothing at all that can convince me, why any man that is born in England ought not to have his voice in election of burgesses. ... I do think that the main cause why almighty God gave men reason, it was that they should make use of that reason, and that they should improve it for that end and purpose that God gave it them. And truly, I think that half a loaf is better than none if a man be an-hungry. This gift of reason without other property may seem a small thing, yet I think there is nothing that God hath given a man that any one else can take from him. And therefore I say, that either it must be the law of God or the law of man that must prohibit the meanest man in the kingdom to have this benefit as well as the greatest. I do not find anything in the law of God, that a lord shall choose twenty burgesses, and a gentleman but two, or a poor man shall choose none. I find no such thing in the law of nature, nor in the law of nations. ...

And truly I have thought something else: in what a miserable distressed condition would many a man that hath fought for the Parliament in this quarrel, be! I will be bound to say that many a man whose zeal and affection to God and this kingdom hath carried him forth in this cause, hath so spent his estate that, in the way the state and the army are going, he shall not hold up his head, if when his estate is lost, and not worth forty shillings a year, a man shall not have any interest ..., so that a man cannot lose that which he hath for the maintenance of his family but he must also lose that which God and nature hath given him! ...

Ireton: ... I think I agreed to this matter, that all should be equally distributed. But the question is, whether it should be distributed to all persons, or whether the same persons that are the electors now should be the electors still, and it be equally distributed amongst them. I do not see anybody else that makes this objection; and if nobody else be sensible of it I shall soon have done. ... All the main thing that I speak for, is because I would have an eye to property. I hope we do not come to contend for victory – but let every man consider with himself that he do not go that way to take away all property. For here is the case of the most fundamental part of the constitution of the kingdom, which if you take away, you take away all by that. ... Why now I say then, if you, against the most fundamental part of the civil constitution ..., will plead the law of Nature, that a man should ... have a power of choosing those men that shall determine what shall be law in this state, though he himself have no permanent interest in the state, but whatever interest he hath he may carry about with him – if this be allowed, because by the right of nature we are free, we are equal, one man must have as much voice as another, then show me what step or difference there is, why I may not by the same right take your property, though not of necessity to sustain nature. It is for my better being, and the better settlement of the kingdom? ...

Rainsborough: I shall now be a little more free and open with you than I was before. ... For my part, as I think, you forgot something that was in my speech, and you do not only yourselves believe that some men are inclining to anarchy, but you would make all men believe that. And, sir, to say because a man pleads that every man hath a voice by right of nature, that therefore it destroys by the same argument all property – this is to forget the law of God. That there's a property, the law of God says it; else why hath God made that law, Thou shalt not steal? I am a poor man, therefore I must be oppressed: if I have no interest in the kingdom, I must suffer by all their laws be they right or wrong. Nay thus: a gentleman lives in a country and hath three or four lordships, as some men have (God knows how they got them); and when a Parliament is called he must be a Parliament-man [MP]; and it may be he sees some poor men, they live near this man, he can crush them. . . . And therefore I think that to that it is fully answered: God hath set down that thing as to propriety with this law of his, Thou shalt not steal. And for my part I am against any such thought, and, as for yourselves, I wish you would not make the world believe that we are for anarchy.

Cromwell: I know nothing but this, that they that are the most yielding have the greatest wisdom; but really, sir, this is not right as it should be. No man says that you have a mind to anarchy, but that the consequence of this rule tends to anarchy, must end in anarchy; for where is there any bound or limit set if you take away this limit, that men that have no interest but the interest of breathing shall have no voice in elections? Therefore I am confident on it, we should not be so hot one with another.

Rainsborough: I know that some particular men we debate with believe we are for anarchy.

Ireton: I profess I must clear myself as to that point. I would not desire, I cannot allow myself, to lay the least scandal upon anybody. And truly, for that gentleman that did take so much offense, I do not know why he should take it so. We speak to the paper – not to persons – and to the matter of the paper. And I hope that no man is so much engaged to the matter of the paper – I hope that our persons, and our hearts and judgments, are not so pinned to papers but that we are ready to hear what good or ill consequence will flow from it.

7.10   Oliver Cromwell at Knottingley, Yorkshire, to Colonel Robert Hammond, Isle of Wight (November 25, 1648)[43]

I find some trouble in your spirit; occasioned first, not only by the continuance of your sad and heavy burden, as you call it, upon you, but [also] by the dissatisfaction you take at the ways of some good men whom you love with your heart, who through this principle, that it is lawful for a lesser part, if in the right, to force "a numerical majority," etc. . . .

Dear Robin, our fleshly reasonings ensnare us. These make us say, heavy, sad, pleasant, easy. . . .

You say: "God hath appointed authorities among the nations, to which active or passive obedience is to be yielded. This resides in England in the Parliament. Therefore active or passive," etc. . . .

---

[43]   *Writings and Speeches of Cromwell*, ed. Abbott, 1: 696–9; compared with *Letters and Speeches of Cromwell*, ed. Carlyle and Lomas, 1: 393–9.

To this I shall say nothing, though I could say very much; but only desire thee to see what thou findest in thy own heart as to two or three plain considerations. First, whether *Salus Populi* [*salus populi suprema lex esto*, let the welfare of the people be the final law] be a sound position? Secondly, whether in the way in hand, really and before the Lord, before whom conscience must stand, this be provided for, or the whole fruit of the war like to be frustrated, and all most like to turn to what it was, and worse? And this, contrary to engagements, declarations, implicit covenants with those who ventured their lives . . . ? Thirdly, whether this army be not a lawful power, called by God to oppose and fight against the king upon some stated grounds; and being in power to such ends, may not oppose one name of authority, for those ends, as well as another, the outward authority that called them, not by their power making the quarrel lawful, but it being so in itself? . . .

My dear friend, let us look into providences; surely they mean somewhat. They hang so together; have been so constant, so clear and unclouded. . . . God's people, now called saints . . . , by providence, having arms, and therein blessed with defense and more. I desire, he that is for a principle of suffering [passive obedience] would not too much slight this. . . .

What think you of providence disposing the hearts of so many of God's people this way, especially in this poor army, wherein the great God has vouchsafed to appear? I know not one officer among us but is on the increasing hand [that is, is coming to the opinion that the king should be tried]. And let me say it is here in the North, after much patience, we trust the same Lord who hath framed our minds in our actings, is with us in this also. . . .

And to conclude. . . . Dear Robin, beware of men, look up to the Lord. . . .

Dost thou not think this fear of the Levellers (of whom there is no fear) that they would destroy nobility, had caused some to rake up corruption; to find it lawful to make this ruining hypocritical agreement [Treaty at Newport], on one part? Hath not this biased even some good men? I will not say, their fear will come upon them; but if it do, they will themselves bring it upon themselves. Have not some of our friends, by their passive principle . . . , been occasioned to overlook what is just and honest?

7.11   *The Charge and King Charles's Refusal to Plead at His Trial (January 20, 1649)*[44]

That . . . Charles Stuart, being admitted king of England, and therein trusted with a limited power to govern by and according to the laws of the land, and not otherwise, and by his trust, oath, and office, being obliged to use the power committed to him for the good and benefit of the people, and for the preservation of their rights and liberties, yet nevertheless out of a wicked design to erect and uphold in himself an unlimited and tyrannical power to rule according to his will, and to overthrow the rights and liberties of the people, yea, to take away and make

---

[44]   Iagomarsino and Wood, *Trial of Charles I*, 64–5; compared with Rushworth, *Historical Collections*, 7: 1396–8 (for the charge).

void the foundations thereof, and of all redress and remedy of misgovernment, which by the fundamental constitutions of this kingdom were reserved on the people's behalf in the right and power of frequent and successive Parliaments, or national meetings in council; he . . . , for accomplishment of such his designs, and for the protecting of himself and his adherents in his and their wicked practices, to the same ends hath traitorously and maliciously levied war against the present Parliament, and the people therein represented, particularly upon or about the 30th day of June . . . 1642, at Beverley, in the county of York . . . ; and upon or about the 24th day of August in the same year, at the county of the town of Nottingham, where and when he set up his standard of war; and also on or about the 23rd day of October in the same year, at Edgehill or Keynton field, in the county of War-wick . . . , [etc.]. At which several times and places, or most of them, and at many other places in this land . . . , and in . . . 1646, he . . . hath caused and procured many thousands of the free people of this nation to be slain; and by divisions, parties, and insurrections within this land, by invasions from foreign parts, endeavored and procured by him, and . . . he . . . hath not only maintained and carried on the said war both by land and sea, during the years before mentioned, but also hath renewed, or caused to be renewed, the said war against the Parliament and good people of this nation in . . . 1648, in the counties of Kent, Essex, Surrey, Sussex, Middlesex, and many other counties and places in England and Wales, and also by sea. And particularly he . . . hath for that purpose given commission to his son the prince, and others, whereby, besides multitudes of other persons, many such as were by the Parliament entrusted and employed for the safety of the nation . . . , have had entertainment and commission for the continuing and renewing of war and hostility against the said Parliament and people as aforesaid. . . . And for further prosecution of his said evil designs, he . . . doth still continue his commissions to the said prince, and other rebels and revolters, both English and foreigners, and to the earl of Ormond, and the Irish rebels and revolters associated with him; from whom further invasions upon this land are threatened. . . .

All which wicked designs, wars, and evil practices of . . . Charles Stuart, have been, and are carried on for the advancement and upholding of a personal interest of will, power, and pretended prerogative to himself and his family, against the public interest, common right, liberty, justice, and peace of the people of this nation, by and from whom he was entrusted as aforesaid.

By all which it appeareth that the said Charles Stuart hath been, and is the occasioner, author, and continuer of the said unnatural, cruel and bloody wars; and therein guilty of all the treasons, murders, rapines, burnings, spoils, desolations, damages and mischiefs to this nation, acted and committed in the said wars, or occasioned thereby. . . .

Lord president [John Bradshaw]: Sir, you have now heard your charge read, containing such matter as appears in it. You find that in the close of it, it is prayed to the court in the behalf of the Commons of England that you answer to your charge. The court expects your answer.

The king: I would know by what power I am called hither. I was not long ago in the Isle of Wight. How I came there is a longer story than I think is fit at this time for me to speak of. But there I entered into a treaty [at Newport] with both Houses of Parliament with as much public faith as it's possible to be had of any people in the world. I treated there with a number of honorable lords and gentlemen, and treated honestly and uprightly; I cannot say but they did very nobly with me. We were upon a conclusion of the treaty. Now, I would know by what authority – I mean lawful – there are many unlawful authorities in the world – thieves and robbers by the highways – but I would know by what authority I was brought from thence and carried from place to place, and I know not what. And when I know what lawful authority, I shall answer. Remember, I am your king – your lawful king – and what sins you bring upon your heads and the judgment of God upon this land, think well upon it – I say think well upon it – before you go further from one sin to a greater. Therefore let me know by what lawful authority I am seated here and I shall not be unwilling to answer. In the meantime, I shall not betray my trust. I have a trust committed to me by God, by old and lawful descent [by hereditary right]. I will not betray it to answer to a new unlawful authority. Therefore, resolve me that, and you shall hear more of me.

Lord president: If you had been pleased to have observed what was hinted to you by the court at your first coming hither, you would have known by what authority. Which authority requires you – in the name of the people of England, of which you are elected king – to answer them.

The king: No, sir, I deny that.

Lord president: If you acknowledge not the authority of the court, they must proceed.

The king: I do tell them so – England was never an elective kingdom but an hereditary kingdom for near these thousand years. Therefore, let me know by what authority I am called hither. I do stand more for the liberty of my people than any here that come to be my pretended judges. And, therefore let me know by what lawful authority I am seated here, and I will answer it. Otherwise I will not answer it.

Lord president: Sir, how really you have managed your trust is known. Your way of answer is to interrogate the court, which beseems not you in this condition. You have been told of it twice or thrice.

The king: . . . I do not come here as submitting to the court. I will stand as much for the privilege of the House of Commons, rightly understood, as any man here whatsoever. I see no House of Lords here that may constitute a Parliament, and the king too should have been. Is this the bringing of the king to his Parliament? Is this the bringing an end to the treaty in the public faith of the world?

7.12 Gerrard Winstanley, "To His Excellency Oliver Cromwell, General of the Commonwealth's Army" (1652)[45]

God hath made you a successful instrument to cast out that conqueror, and to recover our land and liberties again, by your victories, out of that Norman hand.

---

[45] Winstanley, *The Law of Freedom in a Platform, or, True Magistracy Restored*, in *Gerrard Winstanley: Selections from His Works*, ed. L. Hamilton (1944), 109, 112–14; compared with *The Law of Freedom*, ed. R. W. Kenny (New York, 1973), 49–55.

That which is yet wanting on your part to be done, is this, to see the oppressor's power to be cast out with his person; and to see that the free possession of the land and liberties be put into the hands of the oppressed commoners of England....

Now you know sir, that the kingly conqueror was not beaten by you only as you are a single man, nor by the officers of the army joined to you; but by the hand and assistance of the commoners, whereof some came in person, and adventured their lives with you; others stayed at home, and planted the earth, and paid taxes and free-quarter to maintain you that went to war.

So that whatsoever is recovered from the conqueror is recovered by a joint consent of the commoners. Therefore it is all equity, that all the commoners who assisted you should be set free from the conqueror's power with you....

I have asked diverse soldiers what they fought for; they answered, they could not tell; and it is very true, they cannot tell indeed, if the monarchial law be established without reformation. But I wait to see what will be done; and I doubt not but to see our commonwealth's government to be built upon his own foundation....

If we look into parishes, the burdens there are many.

First, for the power of lords of manors remains still over their brethren, requiring fines and heriots [customary payment upon death of tenant]; beating them off the free use of the common land, unless their brethren will pay them rent; exacting obedience, as much as they did, and more, when the king was in power....

Secondly, in parishes where commons lie, the rich Norman freeholders, or the new (more covetous) gentry, over-stock the commons with sheep and cattle; so that inferior tenants and poor laborers can hardly keep a cow, but half starve her; so that the poor are kept poor still, and the common freedom of the earth is kept from them....

Thirdly, in many parishes two or three of the great ones bears all the sway, in making assessments, over-awing constables and other officers....

Fourthly..., country people cannot sell any corn or other fruits of the earth in a market town, but they must either pay toll, or be turned out of town....

Now saith the whisperings of the people, the inferior tenants and laborers bears all the burdens, in laboring the earth, in paying taxes and free-quarter beyond their strength, and in furnishing the armies with soldiers, who bear the greatest burden of the war; and yet the gentry, who oppress them, and that live idle upon their labors, carry away all the comfortable livelihood of the earth.

For is not this a common speech among the people, we have parted with our estates, we have lost our friends in the wars, which we willingly gave up, because freedom was promised us; and now in the end we have new taskmasters, and our old burdens increased? And though all sorts of people have taken an Engagement to cast out kingly power, yet kingly power remains in power still in the hands of those who have no more right to the earth than ourselves.

7.13 *Abiezer Coppe*, A Fiery Flying Roll: a Word from the Lord to All the Great Ones of the Earth *(January 1650)*[46]

Thus saith the Lord, *I inform you, that I overturn, overturn, overturn.* And as the bishops, Charles, and the lords, have had their turn, overturn, so your turn shall be next (ye surviving great ones by what name or title soever dignified or distinguished) who ever you are, that oppose me, the eternal God, who am universal love, and whose service is perfect freedom, and pure libertinism.

But afore I proceed any further, be it known to you, that although that excellent Majesty, which dwells in the writer of this roll, hath reconciled all things to himself, yet this hand (which now writes) never drew sword, or shed one drop of any man's blood. (I am free from the blood of all men) though (I say) all things are reconciled to me, the eternal God (in Him) yet sword levelling, or digging-levelling, are neither of them his principle. . . .

Though you can as little endure the word Levelling, as could the late slain or dead Charles (your forerunner, who is gone before you) and had as live hear the Devil named, as hear of the Levellers (Men-Levellers) which is, and who (indeed) are but shadows of most terrible, yet great and glorious good things to come. . . .

Not by sword; we (holy) scorn to fight for anything; we had as live be dead drunk every day of the week, and lie with the whores i'the market place, and account these as good actions as taking the poor abused, enslaved ploughman's money from him. . . .

I am confounding, plaguing, tormenting nice, demure, barren Michal, with David's unseemly carriage, by skipping, leaping, dancing, like one of the fools; vile, base fellows, shamelessly, basely, and uncovered too before handmaids,

Which thing was St. Paul's tutor, or else it prompted him to write, God hath chosen Base things, and things that are despised, to confound the things [that] are.

Well! family duties are no base things, they are things that are: Churches, ordinances, etc., are no base things, though indeed Presbyterian Churches begun to live i'th womb, but died there, and rot and stink there to the death of the mother and child. . . .

Grace before meat and after meat, are no base things; these are things that are. But how long Lord, holy and true, etc.

Fasting for strife and debate, and to smite with the fist of wickedness, (and not for taking off heavy burdens, breaking every yoke, [Isaiah] 58) and thanksgiving days for killing of men for money, are no base things, these are things that are.

Starting up into the notion of spirituals, scorning history, speaking nothing but mystery, crying down carnal ordinances, etc. is a fine thing among many, it's no base thing (nowadays) though it be a cloak for covetousness, yea, though it be to maintain pride and pomp; these are no base things.

---

[46] Coppe, *Fiery Flying Rolle* (Jan. 4, 1650), 1–2, 5; and *A Second Fiery Flying Rolle* (1650), 8–9 (both facsimile, Exeter, 1973).

These are things that are, and must be confounded by base things, which St. Paul saith, not God hath connived at, winked at, permitted, tolerated, but God hath chosen etc. base things.

What base things? Why Michal took David for a base fellow, and thought he had chosen base things, in dancing shamelessly uncovered before handmaids.

And barren, demure Michal thinks (for I know her heart saith the Lord) that I chose base things when I sat down, and eat and drank around on the ground with gypsies, and clip't, hug'd, and kiss'd them, putting my hand in their bosoms, loving the she-gypsies dearly. O base! saith mincing Michal, the least spark of modesty would be as read as crimson or scarlet, to hear this.

I warrant me, Michal could better have borne this if I had done it to ladies: so I can for a need, if it be my will, and that in the height of honor and majesty, without sin. But at that time when I was hugging the gypsies, I abhorred the thoughts of ladies, their beauty could not bewitch mine eyes, or snare my lips, or entangle my hands in their bosoms; yet I can if it be my will, kiss and hug ladies, and love my neighbor's wife as myself, without sin.

7.14   Quaker Women Going "Naked" for a Sign (May 1655)[47]

On the 3d of the 3d month [May: Quakers did not believe in pagan names for days of the week nor for months], 1655, Sarah Goldsmith, being moved to put on a coat of sackcloth of hair next her, to uncover her head, and put earth thereon, with her hair hanging down about her, and without any other clothes upon her, excepting shoes on her feet, and in that manner to go to every gate, and through every street within the walls of the city, and afterward to stand at the High-Cross in the view of the town and market, as a sign against the pride of Bristol, and to abide so in that habit seven days, in obedience thereto, though in great self-denial, and in a cross to her natural inclinations, she cheerfully prepared her garment, being long and reaching to the ground; and on the 5th of the 3rd month early in the morning, two friends accompanying her, passed through the streets to the several gates, some people following them, but doing no harm: then she returned home. And about the ninth hour came to the High-Cross, and one friend with her, a great multitude of people following; there she stood about half an hour, till the tumult grew so violent, that some bystanders, in compassion, forced them into a shop, out of which the multitude called to have them thrown, that they might abuse them; but by the intervention of the chamberlain kept out of their hands, and carried to the Tolzey [tolbooth, guildhall]. The mayor came thither, and asked her, why she appeared in the city in that habit? She answered, "in obedience to the light in my conscience." "What if you," said the mayor, "in your obedience had been killed by the rude multitude?" She replied, "I am in the hands of Him that ruleth all things. I have harmed none, yet have I been harmed; neither have I broken any law by which I can be brought under just censure; if I had appeared in

[47]   Crawford and Gowing, *Women's Worlds*, 256, from London, Friends House Library, The Great Book of Sufferings, 1: 548, and Abstract of the Sufferings, 1: 15.

gay clothing you would [not?] have been troubled." In conclusion, the mayor, at the instigation of Joseph Jackson one of the aldermen sent her to Bridewell [prison], and with her Anne Gunnicliffe and Margaret Wood, for owning and accompanying her.

CHAPTER EIGHT

Religion, Restoration, and Revolution

Comprehension, Toleration, and Antipopery
Whig and Tory Ideas and Actions
James II, William of Orange, and the Revolution

DISCUSSION

In 1656, Edward Harley, a Presbyterian and Parliamentarian officer in the Civil Wars who had distanced himself from the regicide and the Cromwellian regime, wrote to his mentor, Richard Baxter (see chapter 7), asking for advice "how to move in this ensuing Parliament for the service of the distressed Church." Harley was "sure that only *Fata Ecclesiae* can *auspiciat Fata Imperii*."[1] His prediction that the fate of the Church would foretell that of the State remained valid for more than thirty years. The Restoration religious settlement of the 1660s, Charles II's Declaration of Indulgence in 1672 and the backlash of the Test Act in 1673, the fear of Popery and of Dissent during the Exclusion Crisis, and James II's Declarations of Indulgence in 1687 and 1688 – all involved struggles over the Church which rocked the English government. As you read the documents in this chapter, you might ask:

- To what degree did *Fata Ecclesiae* (the fate of the Church) *auspiciat Fata Imperii* (foretell the fate of the State)? Likewise, how did the State's fortunes determine the destiny of the Church?
- To what degree were changes in political culture and ideologies between the Restoration and the Glorious Revolution truly revolutionary? To what degree did they continue older struggles dating back to the early Stuarts?

---

[1] R. Schlatter, *Richard Baxter and Puritan Politics* (New Brunswick, New Jersey, 1957), 45.

Comprehension, Toleration, and Antipopery

In 1659, as the Protectorate crumbled and a series of *ad hoc* and short-lived governments came and went, many hoped to restore pre-war forms of Church and State. Out of the chaos emerged General George Monck (1608–70), established by Cromwell as overseer of Scotland, who marched south in early January 1660 to seize London with a well-paid army purged of sectarians and radicals. Monck closely guarded his own preferences, but in Parliament on February 21 he advocated a "moderate not rigid Presbyterian government, with a sufficient liberty for consciences truly tender."[2] While Monck and others debated religious options for England, Charles I's eldest son, the exiled Charles II of Scotland, prepared the way for his return to the English throne with a Declaration made at Breda on the continent in April 1660 (document 8.1). What is the overall purpose of this document? How does it relate to Monck's discussions? What are "tender consciences"? What particular promises does Charles II make? Why? Does he hint at his future relationship to Parliament? Finally, why does Charles claim to be "king of England," etc., if he has not yet been restored?

The "liberty to tender consciences" promised by Charles II at his Restoration, vague as it was, set in motion talks between Presbyterians and Anglicans about a possible Church settlement. Perhaps the closest they came to a Church that would "comprehend" or include both groups was Charles II's Declaration of October 25, 1660. This would have limited the role of bishops by "the advice and assistance of the presbyters," and that of the Book of Common Prayer: "we will appoint...learned divines of both persuasions to review the [Book] and to make such alterations as shall be thought most necessary...and that it be left to the minister's choice to use one or other at his discretion."[3] Why might this appeal to Presbyterians? The opportunity for such comprehension and agreement between the two groups, however, faded at the Savoy Conference in March 1661. And the new Parliament elected in 1661 contained fewer Presbyterians than the 1660 Convention and more Anglican Royalists or sons of Royalists from the Civil Wars.

This "Cavalier Parliament" (1661–78) ignored Charles II's request for religious toleration or comprehension and, instead, restored the bishops and passed a series of laws forcing religious uniformity and punishing those who would not conform. As you read the Corporation, Uniformity, and Five Mile Acts (below, and document 8.2), consider what might be the response not only of radical Puritans and Independents, but of the Presbyterians and moderate churchmen to the statutes. One of the first laws forcing uniformity was the Corporation Act of 1661 (13 Car.

---

[2] J. Thirsk, *The Restoration* (1976), 41, from *The Parliamentary or Constitutional History of England by Several Hands* (1760), 12: 142.

[3] E. Cardwell, ed., *A History of Conferences...Connected with the Revision of the Book of Common Prayer* (Oxford, 1840), 292, 294; compared with J. Miller, *Restoration England: The Reign of Charles II* (1985), 89–90.

II, St. II, c. 1), which required municipal officeholders "to take the oaths of allegiance and supremacy" as well as the following:

I, A. B., do declare and believe that it is not lawful upon any pretense whatsoever to take arms against the king and that I do abhor that traitorous position of taking arms by his authority against his person or against those that are commissioned by him. So help me God.[4]

Borough corporations concerned the government for at least three reasons: Protestant sects had proliferated among urban groups like artisans and tradesmen; corporations had their own legal jurisdiction, outside that of country JPs; and incorporated boroughs often returned two MPs to Parliament. How might these concerns have influenced the supporters of the Corporation Act? How might this law have upset former Parliamentarians?

The keystone of the Church Settlement passed by the Cavalier Parliament was the Uniformity Act of 1662 (14 Car. II, c. 4). Among its many provisions was:

that every parson, vicar, or other minister whatsoever..., within this realm of England..., shall...before the feast of St. Bartholomew...[1662], openly, publicly, and solemnly read the morning and evening prayer appointed to be read by and according to the said Book of Common Prayer at the times appointed, and after such reading thereof, shall openly and publicly...declare his unfeigned assent and consent to the use of all things in the said Book.[5]

Bishop and historian Gilbert Burnet (1643–1714) later recalled:

The Act passed by no great majority: and by it all who did not conform to the liturgy by August [24], St. Bartholomew's day...1662, were deprived of all ecclesiastical benefices, without leaving any discretional power with the king in the execution of it, and without making provision for the maintenance of those who should be so deprived: a severity neither practiced by Queen Elizabeth in the enacting her liturgy, nor by Cromwell in ejecting the Royalists, [in both which] a fifth part of the benefice was reserved for their subsistence. St. Bartholomew's day was pitched on, that, if they were then deprived, they should lose the profits of the whole year, since the tithes are commonly due at Michaelmas [September 29]....But the Presbyterians were now in great difficulties. They had many meetings, and much disputing about conformity. Reynolds accepted the bishopric of Norwich. But Calamy and Baxter refused the sees of Litchfield and Hereford.[6]

Did Burnet approve of the Act? Why was it so severe? Nearly one thousand clergymen, about one-tenth of the total in England and Wales, were removed by the Act. Altogether about 1,760 clergy were forced out of their livings between 1660 and 1663. In some dioceses the bishop and local magistrates oversaw a harsh purge; in others they allowed a degree of latitude in the wearing of the

---

[4] *SR,* 5: 322; compared with W. C. Costin and J. S. Watson, eds., *The Law and Working of the Constitution: Documents, 1660–1914,* vol. 1, *1660–1783,* 2nd ed. (1961), 15–17.
[5] *SR,* 5: 365; compared with Costin and Watson, *Law and Working of the Constitution,* 20–3.
[6] *Burnet's History of My Own Time,* ed. O. Airy (Oxford, 1897), 1: 327–8; compared with J. Wroughton, *Seventeenth-Century Britain* (1980), 84–5.

surplice, bowing at the name of Jesus, and other matters prescribed by the Prayer Book. Why was consent to the Book of Common Prayer such a touchstone of religious allegiance for both sides? One might compare and contrast the effects of the Uniformity Act with those of other religious changes stretching back to the mid-sixteenth century. In December 1662, Charles II tried to dampen Anglican zeal in persecuting opponents of the established Church by reminding them of his Declaration of Breda, but Parliament produced further legislation. The Conventicle Act of 1664 proscribed nonconformist meetings (conventicles), and the Five Mile Act of 1665 restricted the freedom of nonconformist preachers (document 8.2). To judge from its preamble, what problems had the Uniformity Act created?

In some dioceses, repeated skirmishes pitted some JPs and Anglican clergy on one side against nonconformist ministers and some sympathetic townspeople and gentry on the other. The religious war provoked seditious talk, such as that of one Hereford clothier, who "said that he would come to hear sermons but that he had as like hear a fart as the Book of Common Prayer."[7] At a more elevated level, the poet and MP Andrew Marvell (1621–78) attacked the Anglican clergy in *The Rehearsal Transpros'd* (1672), which suggested that the late Civil Wars could be blamed on the bad advice given to Charles I by Arminian clergy (see chapter 7).

For his late majesty...was...inclined to esteem and favor the clergy. And...they having gained this ascendent upon him..., and having made the whole business of state, their Arminian jangles, and the persecution for ceremonies, did for recompense assign him that imaginary absolute government, upon which rock we all ruined.[8]

How might Marvell's argument be applied to Restoration England? The archdeacon of Canterbury, Samuel Parker (1640–88), responded with *A Reproof to the Rehearsal Transpros'd* (1673), "showing that certain and inviolable confederacy that there has always been between Non-conformity and the *Good Old Cause.*"[9] The Good Old Cause, of course, referred to the aims of the Parliamentarian and Cromwellian armies during the 1640s. Was Parker correct? Did religious dissent and political radicalism go hand in hand?

The Conventicle Act lapsed in 1667, only to be replaced by the Conventicle Act of 1670. But in the latter year Charles II tried to solve his constitutional, religious, foreign policy and financial problems by signing the Treaty of Dover (see Bucholz and Key, chapter 9). Two years later, as part of this strategy, he tried to put his "liberty to tender consciences" into practice by a Declaration of Indulgence (March 15, 1672) that would be in effect until Parliament met again and could pass a law to make it permanent.

We...declare our will and pleasure to be that the execution of all and all manner of penal laws in matters ecclesiastical against whatsoever sort of Nonconformists or recusants be

---

[7] Hereford RO, Hereford City MSS., V, f. 61, July 7, 1670.
[8] [Marvell], *The Rehearsal Transpros'd*, ed. D. I. B. Smith (Oxford, 1971), 134; compared with R. Sharrock, ed., *The Pelican Book of English Prose: From the Beginnings to 1800* (Baltimore, 1970), 1: 603.
[9] [Parker], *A Reproof to the Rehearsal*, sig. A(4–5).

immediately suspended.... We do further declare that this our indulgence as to the allowance of public places of worship, and approbation of teachers, shall extend to all sorts of Nonconformists and recusants, except the recusants of the Roman Catholic religion; to whom we shall no ways allow in public places of worship, but only indulge them their share in the common exemption from the executing the penal laws and the exercise of their worship in their private houses only.[10]

Who might support such a Declaration? Who might fear it, especially the private practice of Catholicism? Why? When Parliament reassembled in February 1673, they petitioned the king pointedly that "we find ourselves bound in duty to inform your majesty that penal statutes in matters ecclesiastical cannot be suspended but by act of Parliament."[11] Is this a religious or a constitutional (sovereignty) issue? Ten days later, on February 24, Charles responded by noting

he never had thoughts of using it [the suspending power] otherwise than as it hath been entrusted in him, to the peace and establishment of the Church of England, and the ease of all his subjects in general.... But his only design in this was to take off the penalties the statutes inflict upon Dissenters.[12]

The Commons was nonplussed that Charles continued to claim "a power to suspend penal statutes." Even former Royalists, such as Sir Edward Dering, began to see the Indulgence as part of a broader conspiracy:

[After the Restoration] for twelve years more, we lived in peace, plenty, and happiness above all nations.... But this blessing was too great to be continued long to those who deserved it so ill as we, and then the nation began to think that the court inclined to favor Popery and France, grounding their suspicion upon:

1. The declaration coming out about this time for laying aside all the penal laws in matters of religion.

2. The second war made with the Dutch in conjunction with France, there being no sufficient visible cause to provoke us to it....

6. The employing of several known or suspected Papists in great places of trust....

7. Lastly to these, and much more than all these together, was the duke of York's being first suspected and afterwards universally believed to be a Papist, which gave no unreasonable foundation to fear that, the king having no children, when the duke should come to the crown the Protestant religion would be at least oppressed, if not extirpated.[13]

---

[10] *Cobbett's Parliamentary History of England* (1808), 4: 515–16; compared with C. Stephenson and F. G. Marcham, eds., *Sources of English Constitutional History: A Selection of Documents*, rev. ed. (New York, 1972), 2: 559–60.

[11] *CJ*, 9: 252; compared with Stephenson and Marcham, *Sources*, 2: 567.

[12] *CJ*, 9: 256; compared with J. P. Kenyon, *The Stuart Constitution: Documents and Commentary* (Cambridge, 1966), 409.

[13] *Diaries and Papers of Sir Edward Dering, Second Baronet*, ed. M. F. Bond (1976), 125–6; compared with Miller, *Restoration England*, 98–9.

What part of the Declaration of Indulgence probably bothered Dering most? Instead of a bill of Indulgence, the Commons moved to establish the Test Act (1673, document 8.3). How is the Test Act related to the Declaration of Breda? To the Indulgence? How would it change the make-up of the government? What are its implications for the issues of sovereignty and religion? Of foreign policy and finance?

The rest of the 1670s saw intermittent prosecution of Dissenters and Catholics. John Bunyan, a Calvinist Baptist, who had been imprisoned soon after the Restoration for preaching outdoors until freed by the Declaration of Indulgence, was imprisoned again for about six months after the Indulgence lapsed. Bunyan's *The Pilgrim's Progress* (1678, document 8.4) is an allegory of the protagonist Christian's journey in this life and his salvation. After considering the selection as an allegory of how a Calvinist believer relates to the secular world (what does Vanity Fair symbolize?), consider it again as a description of the relationship between nonconformists and local legal structures. What does it suggest was the basis for legal action against Dissenters? What was Bunyan's view of contemporary social status distinctions? While it may seem counterintuitive, can you defend the view of Judge Hategood and the crowd (that is, critique the actions of Christian and Faithful)?

Persecution of nonconformists continued, but many in the political nation, like Dering, became increasingly worried that Popery was in the ascendant. Parliamentary speeches through the 1670s echoed this fear (1674–8, document 8.5). After the abortive experiment with religious toleration under the Indulgence and the ruling Cabal (see Bucholz and Key, chapter 9), Charles II entrusted his government to the safely Anglican Thomas Osborne, earl of Danby. From this point, king and minister relied for political support upon those who strongly defended the Anglican Church and Divine Right, much like those who had supported Charles I. These became known as the Court faction, while their opponents were known as the Country faction. From the parliamentary speeches on religion (8.5), can you identify who might be a Court and who a Country supporter? Why, and in what ways, might both sides fear Popery?

In the late summer of 1678, allegations surfaced about a Popish Plot to murder Charles II, to massacre eminent Protestants, and to reestablish Catholicism in England through Jesuit manipulation of James, duke of York, as a figurehead ruler. The characters who revealed the Plot – the unpleasant Titus Oates and the conspiracy-monger Israel Tonge – were just as fantastic as their charges of a vast, violent Catholic network. One anonymous account gives a summary of how people believed such an unlikely Plot was to have been executed:

one Conyers, a Jesuit, with four Irish ruffians, undertook to murder the king at Windsor, 21 September last, and thereupon a great cry was to be made that the fanatics [that is, Dissenters] had murdered the king, an alarm presently thereupon to be given to the whole army, being then about 16,000, quartered in and near London, whereof two regiments of 4,000 men, consisting all of Irish, Scots, and French Papists, were about a month before brought out of France and quartered...[and] were immediately to march to London to assist the proclaiming the duke of York, and under that pretense to fall upon and massacre and slaughter the people, under the notion of fanatics who had murdered the king. . . . The duke of York was to take the crown by gift from the pope, and least any opposition should be made, the French were to be ready with an army and fleet to seize upon our fleet, burn and destroy such as opposed, and take the rest, and then the whole nation to be shared among this crew.[14]

While all this seems rather incredible, and none of it occurred, what *had* happened during the 1670s to render the English credulous towards such reports (see Bucholz and Key, chapter 9)? In fact, as John Dryden would later relate in his satirical masterpiece, *Absalom and Achitophel*, people fell hard for Oates's and Tongue's allegations:

> From hence began that Plot, the Nation's Curse,
> Bad in itself, but represented worse:
> Rais'd in extremes, and in extremes decry'd;
> With Oaths affirm'd, with dying Vows deny'd.
> Not weigh'd, or winnow'd by the Multitude;
> But swallow'd in the Mass, unchew'd and Crude.
> Some Truth there was, but dash'd and brew'd with Lyes;
> To please the Fools, and puzzle all the Wise.
> Succeeding times did equal folly call,
> Believing nothing, or believing all.[15]

Amid widespread anti-Catholic hysteria, the House of Commons unanimously resolved on October 31, 1678, "that this House is of opinion that there hath been and still is a damnable and hellish plot contrived and carried on by the popish recusants for the assassinating and murdering of the king, and for subverting the government, and rooting out and destroying the Protestant religion."[16] A Second Test Act was passed (1678, 30 Car. II. st. 2, c. 1, see debate in document 8.5) requiring both MPs and Lords to make an extra declaration in addition to the oaths of allegiance and supremacy and that against transubstantiation previously required of officers: "that the invocation or adoration of the Virgin Mary or any other saint and the sacrifice of the Mass as they are now used in the Church of Rome are superstitious and idolatrous."[17] It should be fairly obvious against which group this declaration aimed. A proviso excepting the duke of York from the Act's provisions passed by only two votes. When Charles dissolved Parliament (January 24, 1679), the age of party politics was about to begin.

---

[14] Oct. 31, 1678, HMC, *Fourteenth Report, Appendix IV, Kenyon, 1524–1837* (1894), 107; compared with A. Browning, ed., *English Historical Documents, 1660–1714* (New York, 1953), 111, 206.

[15] *The Works of John Dryden* (Berkeley, 1972), 2: 8–9; compared with H. Love, ed., *The Penguin Book of Restoration Verse* (Harmondsworth, Middlesex, 1968), 119.

[16] *CJ*, 9: 530; compared with A. Stroud, *Stuart England* (1999), 171.

[17] *SR*, 5: 894; compared with Stephenson and Marcham, *Sources*, 2: 557.

Whig and Tory Ideas and Actions

In fact, as we have seen in the discussion of the Court and Country factions, a fundamental division on the great questions of the age had been growing among the ruling elite all through the 1670s. In 1675, *A Letter from a Person of Quality, to His Friend in the Country* (also mentioned in document 8.6, discussed below), perhaps composed by Anthony Ashley Cooper, earl of Shaftesbury (1621–83), decried the rise of Danby's Court faction as a "State Masterpiece...first hatcht...to make a distinct party from the rest of the nation of the High Episcopal Man, and the Old Cavalier, who are to swallow the hopes of enjoying all the power and office of the Kingdom."[18] The Lords ordered *A Letter from a Person of Quality* burnt by the common hangman. The pamphlet's foremost crime was publishing parliamentary speeches and votes (which was illegal), but do the quote above and the description in the newsletters below (8.6) suggest other reasons for the Lords to single out the *Letter*? Judging from the short selections printed from the newsletters 1675–8, what issues divided the political nation even before the Popish Plot scare?

Partisan division in ideology and organization was first clearly displayed during three general elections and Parliaments between 1679 and 1681, which have come to be known as the Exclusion Crisis. In the first Exclusion Parliament (March 6 to May 27, 1679), the first Exclusion Bill, barring York from the succession (based on his Catholicism and his high-handed defense of royal prerogative), passed its second reading by a two-to-one margin in the Commons. To kill the bill, Charles again dissolved Parliament. Elections for the second Exclusion Parliament (fall 1679) strengthened the exclusionists (the nucleus of the first Whigs). To them, Charles's successive prorogations (delaying Parliament meeting until October 21, 1680) suggested arbitrary rule and a flouting of the will of the people (that is, the ruling elite). Shaftesbury and exclusionists organized mass petitions to urge Charles to summon Parliament. The petitioners of 1680 became the "Whigs," at first an epithet, after the Scottish Whigs or nonconformists or Covenanters, and only later adopted as a badge of honor by the English party. Those organizing addresses "abhorring" the petitions – the Abhorrers – became the first Tories, named after Irish cattle thieves. Since English Whigs and Tories were obviously neither Scottish Presbyterians nor Irish cattle thieves, why did the titles stick?

Soon after Parliament finally met, the Commons passed the second Exclusion Bill on November 15, 1680:

Whereas James duke of York is notoriously known to have been perverted from the Protestant to the popish religion, whereby not only great encouragement hath been given to the popish party to enter into and carry on most devilish and horrid plots and conspir-

---

[18] J. L. Malcolm, ed., *The Struggles for Sovereignty: Seventeenth-Century English Political Tracts* (Indianapolis, 1999), 2: 606.

acies for the destruction of his majesty's sacred person and government, and for the extirpation of the true Protestant religion, but also, if the said duke should succeed to the imperial Crown of this realm, nothing is more manifest than that a total change of religion within these kingdoms would ensue; For the prevention whereof, be it therefore enacted...that...James duke of York shall be and is by authority of this present Parliament excluded and made for ever incapable to inherit, possess, or enjoy the imperial Crown of this realm and of the kingdom of Ireland and the dominions...of them belonging.[19]

When the Lords rejected the bill, speech after speech in the Commons denounced arbitrary and popish rule. For example, on December 15, 1680, MP Paul Foley (ca. 1645–99) linked the religious issue to those of sovereignty and foreign policy:

I think we cannot but conclude that the duke's [of York's] interest, the French interest, and popish interest are all one....And will not the divisions they carry on amongst us, as to churchmen and fanatics, Plot or no Plot, be very useful to [the Papists]; but especially their arraignments of Parliaments, and all that speak against Popery, as [16]41 men, and enemies to the government, occasion a great weakness on our side?...Is it not strange [the Exclusion Bill] should be rejected in the house of Lords? I cannot believe that the Fathers of the Church [the bishops] should join in that, which must infallibly give opportunity for the tearing out the bowels of their mother, and destroying her forever.[20]

Why did the Whigs associate arbitrary or absolute rule with Popery? Who, besides the Catholics, did Foley fear? Charles II summoned a new Parliament quickly to meet at Oxford, distant from London Whig radicals. Despite a Tory challenge, mainly Whigs were returned. The third Exclusion Parliament, the Oxford Parliament, met on March 21, 1681 and again considered excluding the duke of York from the throne. Some called for Charles II's illegitimate but Protestant son, James, duke of Monmouth, to be named the legitimate successor. But Charles dissolved Parliament a week later.

Exclusion Crisis partisanship continued after the dissolution of 1681, reverberating beyond the walls of Parliament. One source for understanding Whig and Tory thought and activism is that of contemporary journalism: newsletters (1675–84, document 8.6) and newspapers (1679–86, document 8.7). When the Licensing Act of 1662 lapsed in 1679, a torrent of newspapers and pamphlets flooded England. In the summer of 1680, Charles tried to stanch or channel the flood by prosecuting journalists supporting Exclusion and petitioning on charges of seditious libel. Newspapers were again effectively censored. Those who could afford it subscribed to a newsletter service, handwritten pages of relatively uncensored news and mailed at regular intervals to subscribers. Can you distinguish between Whig and Tory activity as reported in the newsletters?

---

[19] HMC, *Eleventh Report, Appendix II House of Lords, 1678–1688* (1887), 195–6; compared with Costin and Watson, *Law and Working of the Constitution*, 183–4.
[20] *Cobbett's Parliamentary History*, 4: 1245–7.

As this implies, the ruling elite split into Whig and Tory. So did their culture. There were Whig plays such as Thomas Shadwell's violently anti-Catholic *The Lancashire Witches* (1681) and Tory plays such as Aphra Behn's *The Roundheads* (1681). The partisan affiliation of Thomas Durfey's *The Royalist* (1682), written shortly after Exclusion's collapse, should be obvious from its prologue:

> How! the House full! and at a Loyal Play?
> That's strange! I never hop'd to see this day.
> But sure this must some change of State fore-tell;
> And th' Pit (methinks) looks like a Commonweal;
> Where Monarch Wit's bast'd by ev'ry Drudge,
> And each pert Rayling Brummingham's
>   [Birmingham artisan, supporter of Exclusion] a Judge.
> But know, ye Criticks of unequal'd Pride,
> The Dice now give kind chances on our side;
> Tories are upmost, and the Whigs defy'd.
> Your Factious Juries and Associations
> Must never think to ruine twice, Three Nations;
> No, there's one above you has too long had Patience.[21]

There were Whig and Tory sermons, such as the contrasting ones by Thomas Sprat and Thomas Jekyll intended to be preached before dueling feasts April 20 and 21, 1682 (though the government banned the latter). Sprat's political affinity in *A Sermon Preached before the Artillery Company of London* should be evident, as he noted: "As to the main doctrine here delivered, there is not any one true son of the Church of England, but will consent to it." What does he imply about his enemies in the following passage? What is their background?

What can be a more noble, or more pious cause, wherein to employ your arms, than this of the king, and his family? A cause, in which you will scarce meet with an enemy, but he, or his relations have been already forgiven. And so they will carry about with them the black guilt, not only of rebellion, but of an ungrateful rebellion, after pardon receiv'd.[22]

Jekyll's sermon, *True Religion Makes the Best Loyalty, Discovered...in a Sermon Prepar'd for that Assembly which Intended to Meet at St. Michael's Cornhil, April 21. 1682* (1682), defined loyalty differently from Sprat. Jekyll compared the Whigs to the apostles Peter and Paul, arguing that they were loyal to "the government they were either born or liv'd under"; even though "there was a general clamor raised against them, and the rest of the apostles, as men of dangerous spirits and principles, enemies to all the civil governments in the World...; but we never find any such thing prov'd upon them." He found true hypocrisy among those who pledged

---

[21]   Durfey, *The Royalist* (1682), n.p.
[22]   Sprat, *A Sermon Preached before the Artillery Company of London at St. Mary Le Bow, April 20. 1682*, 2nd ed. (1682), ded., 29.

loyalty to the king, and our good affection to the Church... [solely through] drinking his health...; as if no conformity to the Church... could make a man so true a son of it, as drinking the confusion of all that dissent from it, and damming and hectoring everything that is not of the same furious and violent temper with ourselves.[23]

Who was Jekyll criticizing?

The Whig/Tory faultline penetrated down to the lower orders. Among examples of Whig and Tory songs, sayings, and healths drunk, is this Hereford record (June 1679):

upon Saturday...evening Humphrey Rodd..., glover came into the dwelling house of Anne Howells..., widow, and called for a flagon of cider...and afterwards called for another but...one John Crumpton accidentally coming through the room was desired to drink by...Rodd, and the king's health was begun by...Rodd and pledg'd by...Crumpton, whereupon Crumpton drunk the duke of Monmouth's health, which was refused by Rodd and did drink the duke of York's health. And...Crumpton then saying that he would not drink any Papist's health in England..., Rodd called...Crumpton several times rogue, which occasioned...Crumpton to throw the cider which was in a glass in Rodd's face.[24]

Even more political were words spoken by one Henry Steward:

to hinder...James Pytts in his election to serve in the last Parliament, [Steward] did utter these words the 14th of January 1681: "that...Pytts...was not fit to be a Parliament man; for he was popishly affected, and did hunt with the duke of York's hounds; and if the Devil himself came, he should not stand."[25]

There were even Whig and Tory school assignments, as one Welsh schoolmaster gave his pupils an essay to translate into Latin about 1680 entitled "a prince that seeks his brother's life to succeed him in his Kingdom, ought to be banished."[26] The schoolmaster's political preference should be obvious.

Whigs and Tories gathered at rival coffeehouses and feasts (see documents 8.6–8.7). Do newsletters and newspapers mention specific Whig and Tory feasts (compare and contrast those of April 1682)? Street demonstrations? Coffeehouses? How do they differ? What role did political anniversaries (Gunpowder Treason Day, November 5; Queen Elizabeth's Accession Day, November 17) play? Taverns and coffeehouses were often the arena for partisan organization: drawing up and subscribing names to petitions and addresses, organizing street pageants and demonstrations, planning for possible future elections. When London apprentices subscribed some 20,000 signatures to a loyal address to Charles II, Whig newspaperman Richard Janeway (see also 8.7) derided their effort, claiming they had "procured subscriptions by indirect means, drawing in

---

[23]   Jekyll, *True Religion Makes the Best Loyalty* (1682), 6, 36.
[24]   Hereford RO, Hereford City Records, Quarter Sessions, July 1679, information of David Jenkins.
[25]   PRO, ASSI 5/5, 33 Ch. II (1681), Herefordshire bundle.
[26]   PRO, SP29/419/120I, ca. June 29, 1682.

idle fellows by pots of ale." A Tory pamphlet defended the apprentices and, in so doing, explained workings of the partisan culture of the metropolis:

We never cross'd the water [the Thames] to the Hope on Bear-Garden days, to offer to get hands there; nor were ever concerned to create a bull-baiting, on purpose to draw the rabble in, to fill up our number, as some of the famous Essex-Patriots [Whigs] did to fill up their petition for a Parliament. We never went to any country-fairs, amongst the ballad-singers; nor in all humility addressed our selves to the little boys of a free-school to pleasure us with two or three hundred hands. We never hired any one to subscribe, nor ever told a refuser that we would put him in our black book, as Mr. S. H. [Samuel Harris] did those that would not sign his Good Old Cause petition. We never called a conventicle, to get well-wishers together: but honestly left our papers where we thought fit, though the republican rats had so little manners to gnaw them in pieces when they were full of hands.[27]

From this pamphlet and from newspaper and newsletter passages below, how would you describe Whig and Tory organizational activity in the early 1680s?

The Whigs' strongest suit was their success in parliamentary election campaigns. When Charles II ended his last Parliament in March 1681, the Whigs wilted. In April 1681, his *Declaration* explaining the dissolution claimed that some members of Parliament had planned to go beyond Exclusion and to return to their "old beloved Commonwealth principles." This evocation of the Civil War became a touchstone for loyal Tory addresses. The Rye House Plot of 1683, evidence of a radical Whig plan to kidnap and kill the royal brothers Charles and James, became the excuse to mop up remaining Whig organization. Tory ideology, which equated Whiggism with fanaticism, was vindicated (see plate 11). "Ever since the discovery of this fanatick conspiracy, the pulpits for the most part have been busied with nothing but discourses against the Dissenters, preaching up loyalty and passive obedience."[28] A plethora of Tory tracts and sermons on the evils of resistance reinforced Sir Robert Filmer's *Patriarcha* (pub. 1680, document 6.5) and its arguments for submission to the Crown. Even local juries attacked Whig and Dissenter "fanatics," as did that of Hereford in January 1683:

We of the grand jury do present . . . as our opinion that the best way to secure the monarchy to preserve the king's person in safety and his majesty's government in peace is the due execution of the laws. . . . We present that all persons who do not frequent the church according to law are recusants; it being not possible to know the hearts of men for what cause they refuse to come to church and that all connivance or indulgence in that case upon any person is a ready way to bring in Popery. We present that those persons who publish libelous matter, etc. against the Government or false news ought to be inquired after and

---

[27] *Vox Juvenilis: Or, the Loyal Apprentices Vindication of the Design and Promoters of their late Humble Address to his Majesty* (1681), 2–3.
[28] N. Luttrell, *A Brief Historical Relation of State Affairs from September 1678 to April 1714* (Oxford, 1867, 1969), 1: 278.

Plate 11 *A History of the New Plot* (August 17, 1683), detail. (*Source*: Bridgeman Art Library)

This print traces the history of the Rye House Plot, a radical Whig plan (there is little indication it was put into action) to seize Charles II and James, duke of York, on their way back from the races at Newmarket. It begins with a reference to the earl of Shaftesbury's list of Parliament men divided between "Worthy Men" and "Men Worthy" (to be hanged). In fact, Shaftesbury divided them between "W"orthy and "V"ile. Why might such a partisan list be viewed as the beginning of a "Damnable Plot"? Is this a Whig or Tory print? How do you know?

punished. We present as our opinion that Popery and fanatics are equally dangerous to the Government by law established.[29]

The Tories, who had opposed the Exclusion of James, duke of York, were in the ascendant and highly supportive of the monarchy. But, from the sources above, might there be any hint of danger to the Crown when James ascended to the throne?

James II, William of Orange, and the Revolution

The Tories who had successfully opposed Exclusion dominated local and national politics when, in February 1685, Charles II died and his brother, James, became king. The Tory Sir John Bramston (1611–1700), an anti-Dissenter once marked by the Whig leader Shaftesbury as "thrice vile," related in his autobiography (document 8.8) James II's first speech in Council, which was obviously designed to shore up this loyalist support. Does James simply attempt to reassure his supporters about his religion, or does he address other concerns? Do you think this speech was successful?

Within a few months James II faced rebellion when Charles II's illegitimate son, James, duke of Monmouth, landed with armed supporters in Southwest England. Monmouth claimed to be the real "James Rex," and he issued a proclamation which bears comparison to that of Perkin Warbeck, Richard III, or Henry VII (see chapter 2):

Whereas upon our first landing at Lyme in our county of Dorset on Thursday the 11th . . . of June, we did publish a declaration in the name of ourself, by the name of James, duke of Monmouth, and the noblemen, gentlemen, and others now in arms for defense and vindication of the Protestant religion, and of the laws, rights, and privileges of England, from the invasion made upon them and for delivering the kingdom from the usurpation and tyranny of James, duke of York: wherein . . . we did declare that out of the love we bear to the English nation . . . we would not at present insist upon our title, but leave the determination thereof to the authority of a Parliament legally chosen and acting with freedom. Since which it hath pleased Almighty God to succeed and prosper us hitherto in a very eminent manner, and also disposed the hearts of our loving subjects that from all parts of the country they flock in unanimously for the defense of our person and of the righteous cause we are engaged in; by which we have been enabled to march from Lyme . . . unto our good town of Taunton to the terror and amazement of all our enemies round about us . . . , as son and heir apparent to Charles the Second, king of England, our royal father lately deceased. We have therefore . . . [allowed] our being proclaimed king on . . . 20 . . . June at . . . Taunton.[30]

---

[29] Hereford RO, Hereford City Records, Quarter Sessions, Jan. 31, 1683.
[30] HMC, *Calendar of the Manuscripts of the Marquis of Bath* (Dublin, 1907), 2: 170–1; compared with Browning, *English Historical Documents*, 119–20.

Note how Bramston (8.8) characterized Monmouth's Declaration. Are any of Monmouth's claims convincing? Could you draw up an alternative claim to the throne that would have been convincing to contemporaries in 1685? Monmouth's rebellion was short-lived and brutally put down, and Monmouth himself was executed. For the moment, James II was not only securely on the throne, but he had the strong backing of most of the political nation.

By 1686, however, James made it clear that he intended to allow fellow Catholics to practice their religion and to serve in the military and government, first by granting dispensations for specific persons, and, later, by encouraging Parliament to repeal the penal laws and Test Acts (of 1673 and 1678). In a test case, one Sir Edward Hales appealed a ruling against him (and in favor of his coachman, Arthur Godden) for being commissioned a colonel without taking the declarations required by the Test Act. Hales held a dispensation from the king and he appealed to the King's Bench. On June 16, Lord Chief Justice Herbert gave judgment in Godden v. Hales:

Having the concurrence of eleven out of twelve, we think we may very well declare the opinion of the court to be that the king may dispense in this case; and the judges go upon these grounds:

1. That the kings of England are sovereign princes;

2. That the laws of England are the king's laws;

3. That therefore it is an inseparable prerogative in the kings of England to dispense with penal laws in particular cases and upon particular necessary reasons;

4. That of those reasons and those necessities, the king himself is sole judge . . . ;

5. . . . And therefore, such a dispensation appearing upon record to come time enough to save him from the forfeiture, judgment ought to be given for the defendant.[31]

What does this legal judgment suggest about the limits to royal power? What does it suggest about the future role of the Church of England in government? Certainly its future at court looked dim, as James moved to restore Catholic services there. The diarist John Evelyn (1620–1706), an Anglican Tory gentleman of letters and science, was both fascinated and repelled by mass at James II's Catholic Chapel, which he attended on December 29, 1686:

I was to hear the music of the Italians in the new chapel, now first of all opened at Whitehall publicly for the popish Service. . . . Here we saw the bishop in his miter and rich copes, with six or seven Jesuits and others in rich copes richly habited, often taking off and putting on the bishops miter, who sat in a chair with arms pontifically, was adored and censed by 3 Jesuits in their copes. Then he went to the altar and made diverse cringes there, censing the images and glorious tabernacle placed upon the altar, and now and then changing place; the crosier (which was of silver) put into his hand, with a world of

---

[31] T. B. Howell, comp., *A Complete Collection of State Trials* (1816), 11: 1198–9; compared with S. E. Prall, *The Bloodless Revolution: England, 1688* (Madison, 1985), 297–8.

mysterious ceremony the music playing and singing. And so I came away, not believing I should ever have lived to see such things in the king of England's palace, after it had pleased God to enlighten this nation.[32]

If this represented Tory reaction, what might Whigs think?

In April 1687, James II went one step further towards repealing penal laws and Test Acts, issuing his Declaration of Indulgence (document 8.9). Compare and contrast it with that of Charles II (1672, above). Did James seek unity of Church and State? What was the reaction? To secure a compliant Parliament in the next election, at the end of 1687, James asked the lords lieutenant to lobby gentry in their regions and sent out agents to lobby the boroughs, instructing them "to make acquaintance with the leading, active and interested men in the county, or in the towns and corporations, who are inclinable to abrogate the penal laws for religion, and the tests, and engage them to improve their interest for effecting it," as well as "to inform yourself (as privately as may be) whether the persons proposed to be chosen, by the list given you, be right-principled."[33] Who would be most inclinable to acquiesce in the king's wishes? Who least? What would the Anglican–Tory coalition which had served his brother make of this? What kind of alliance did James hope to forge to secure his wishes in the intended, next Parliament? What were the strengths and weaknesses of such an alliance? Would he be depending on former exclusionists or anti-exclusionists? Note Tory Herbert Aubrey's reaction (from June 1687) to the rising political fortunes of Dissenters under James's new campaign:

All England over as far as I have heard, those who were before thought the greatest fanatics and enemies to crowned heads were making interests to be elected, and began to value themselves upon their power and interest. I am afraid his majesty will never find those same ill-leavened men faithful to him or his interest, for those who could in the face of the Sun dare to attempt such a rebellion as they had formed, that would have murdered two princes at once, that would have excluded this king from the throne, that after his peaceful accession to it both openly and secretly supported the mock prince [Monmouth], the Perkin Warbeck of the age, for all their hypocritical addresses whenever there is an opportunity offered will act according to their avowed king-killing principles.[34]

In 1688 James reissued his Indulgence with the added instructions that all Anglican clergy read it from their pulpits. On May 18, 1688, William Sancroft, archbishop of Canterbury, and six other bishops petitioned the king that they not be required to order reading the Indulgence in their dioceses:

That the great averseness they find in themselves to the distributing and publishing in all their churches your majesty's late declaration for liberty of conscience proceedeth [not] from any want of duty and obedience to your majesty..., but among many other consider-

[32] *The Diary of John Evelyn*, ed. E. S. de Beer (Oxford, 1955), 4: 534–5.
[33] G. [F.] Duckett, *Penal Laws and Test Act: Questions Touching Their Repeal Propounded in 1687–8 by James II* (1883), 1: 198; compared with Kenyon, *Stuart Constitution*, 509–10.
[34] BL, Add. MS. 28,876, ff. 13–14, June 27, 1687.

ations from this especially, because that declaration is founded upon such a dispensing power as hath often been declared illegal in Parliament, and particularly in the years 1662, 1672 [1673], and in the beginning of your majesty's reign, and is a matter of so great moment and consequence to the whole nation..., that your petitioners cannot in prudence, honor, or conscience so far make themselves parties to it.[35]

James was furious and he had the bishops arrested. The trial of the seven bishops (document 8.10) was a *cause célèbre*. What are the key components of the Crown's argument? Of the bishops' defense? How are these issues related to other documents found in this chapter? To documents found in chapters 6 and 7? To issues of sovereignty as well as religion? Sir Edward Harley's son, Edward, sent him a detailed report, adding: "The Court was extremely crowded. I was there from four in the morning till seven at night. They are making bonfires tonight." A few days later, after the court acquitted the bishops, he added, "The great joy and bonfires expressed at the bishops' delivery, occasions great anger [at Court]. [Judges] Powell and Holloway will be removed" by the king.[36] What specifically do you think the London populace were celebrating with their bonfires?

Just a few weeks before the trial of the seven bishops, Evelyn had noted in his diary, "A young prince born," adding later, "which will cause dispute."[37] What did the birth of the young James portend for the problems of sovereignty and religion (see Bucholz and Key, chapter 9)? How might it relate to the bishops' trial? In any case, the same day as the verdict exonerating the bishops, seven other prominent politicians, including Whigs, Trimmers, Tories, and the bishop of London, wrote to William of Orange in the Netherlands.

The people are so generally dissatisfied with the present conduct of the government in relation to their religion, liberties, and properties (all which have been greatly invaded), and they are in such expectation of their prospects being daily worse, that your highness may be assured there are nineteen parts of twenty of the people throughout the kingdom who are desirous of a change and who, we believe, would willingly contribute to it, if they had such a protection to countenance their rising as would secure them from being destroyed before they could get to be in a posture to defend themselves. It is no less certain that much the greatest part of the nobility and gentry are as much dissatisfied...; and there is no doubt but that some of the most considerable of them would venture themselves with your highness at your first landing....And...we...believe that their [James II's] army then would be very much divided among themselves, many of the officers being so discontented that they continue in their service only for a subsistence..., and very many of the common soldiers do daily show such an aversion to the popish religion that there is the greatest probability imaginable of great numbers of deserters which could come from them should there be such an occasion; and amongst the seamen it is almost certain there is not one in ten who would do them any service in such a war.

[35] [J. Gutch, ed.,] *Collectanea Curiosa* (Oxford, 1781), 1: 336–7; compared with Prall, *Bloodless Revolution*, 312.

[36] HMC, *Fourteenth Report, Appendix II, Portland III* (1894), 414, June 30 and July 3.

[37] *Diary of John Evelyn*, 4: 586.

After promising "to attend your highness upon your landing," they did chastise the Dutch *stadholder* on one point: "we must presume to inform your highness that your compliment upon the birth of the child (which not one in a thousand here believes to be the queen's) hath done you some injury."[38] Compare this view of the birth of James's son with that of Evelyn and Bramston (8.8). What does Bramston mean when he states that this invitation was "perfect rebellion"? Is he correct? The rationale behind William's acceptance of the invitation is complex (see Bucholz and Key, chapter 9). But he realized that he needed to explain it to the English political nation, which was now used to debating such issues. Thus, he issued a Declaration of his intention on September 30:

We [William] cannot any longer forbear to declare that, to our great regret, we see that those counselors who have now the chief credit with the king [James II] have overturned the religion, laws, and liberties of those realms and subjected them in all things relating to their consciences, liberties, and properties to arbitrary government. . . .

Those evil counselors for the advancing and coloring this with some plausible pretexts did invent and set on foot the king's dispensing power, by virtue of which they pretend that, according to the law, he can suspend and dispense with the execution of the laws that have been enacted by the authority of the king and Parliament for the security and happiness of the subject and so have rendered those laws of no effect.[39]

How does William justify his invasion? Compare James's justification for fleeing England (reported by Bramston, document 8.8) with the prince's Declaration (above). Who is most convincing? Whom does Bramston favor? Why? We shall examine the beginnings of the Revolution Settlement with the Bill of Rights and the Toleration Act of 1689 in the next chapter. We might best conclude this vision of religion and partisanship between the Restoration and the Revolution by examining Bramston's view of the political lay of the land after James II fled the country (8.8). To what degree were the Whigs revolutionaries? The Tories? What was the disposition of the English constitution in Church and State at the end of 1688?

HISTORIOGRAPHY

Until recently, the Restoration was simply viewed as the long opening act to the Glorious Revolution or the closing act to the Civil Wars: a period of religious and political calm – the secularization of society – in conscious reaction to earlier disputes and divisions. Reaction against this supposed secularization, as well as against the Whiggish emphasis on constitutional politics, can be seen in the articles in T. Harris, P. Seaward, and M. Goldie, eds., *The Politics of Religion in Restoration England* (Oxford, 1990).

[38] Browning, *English Historical Documents*, 120–1; compared with Prall, *Bloodless Revolution*, 313–14, from J. Dalrymple, *Memoirs of Great Britain and Ireland* (1771), App. 1, 228–31.
[39] Prall, *Bloodless Revolution*, 315.

Religion is also emphasized in M. Goldie, "Restoration Political Thought," and J. Spurr, "Religion in Restoration England," in *The Reigns of Charles II and James VII & II, 1660–1689*, ed. L. K. J. Glassey (Basingstoke, 1997); B. Till, "The Worcester House Declaration and the Restoration of the Church of England," *HR* 70 (1997); M. Goldie, "Priestcraft and the Birth of Whiggism," in *Political Discourse in Early Modern Britain*, ed. N. Phillipson and Q. Skinner (Cambridge, 1993); G. S. De Krey, "Reformation in the Restoration Crisis, 1679–1682," in *Religion, Literature, and Politics in Post-Reformation England, 1540–1688*, ed. D. B. Hamilton and R. Strier (Cambridge, 1996); J. Champion, "Religion after the Restoration," *HJ* 36 (1993); P. Jenkins, "'The Old Leaven': The Welsh Roundheads after 1660," *HJ* 24 (1981); and M. Goldie and J. Spurr, "Politics and the Restoration Parish: Edward Fowler and the Struggle for St Giles Cripplegate," *EHR* 109 (1994).

T. Harris, *London Crowds in the Reign of Charles II: Propaganda and Politics from the Restoration until the Exclusion Crisis* (Cambridge, 1987) revitalized study of popular politics in the Restoration period by emphasizing the thoughts and actions of both a Whig and a Tory "mob." See also his "Perceptions of the Crowd in later Stuart London," in *Imagining Early London: Perceptions and Portrayals of the City from Stow to Strype, 1598–1720*, ed. J. F. Merritt (Cambridge, 2001), and "The Parties and the People: The Press, the Crowd and Politics 'Out-of-doors' in Restoration England," in Glassey. For political discourse, see G. S. De Krey, "Radicals, Reformers and Republicans: Academic Language and Political Discourse in Restoration London," in *A Nation Transformed: England after the Restoration*, ed. A. Houston and S. C. A. Pincus (Cambridge, 2001); B. Worden, "Republicanism and the Restoration, 1660–1683," in *Republicanism, Liberty, and Commercial Society, 1649–1776*, ed. D. Wootton (Stanford, 1994); and essays in H. Nenner, ed., *Politics and the Political Imagination in Later Stuart Britain: Essays Presented to Lois Green Schwoerer* (Rochester, 1998). There are several brief introductions to Restoration politics, one or more of which are recommended before tackling political, religious, intellectual, or even cultural questions: T. Harris, *Politics under the Later Stuarts: Party Conflict in a Divided Society, 1660–1715* (1993); P. Seaward, *The Restoration, 1660–1688* (1991); J. Miller, *The Restoration and the England of Charles II*, 2nd ed. (1997); and K. D. H. Haley, *Politics in the Reign of Charles II* (Oxford, 1985).

The "public sphere" coined by Jürgen Habermas of coffeehouses, newspapers, and commensality has become a growth industry for study of Restoration political culture. See B. Cowan, "What Was Masculine about the Public Sphere?: Gender and the Coffeehouse Milieu in Post-Restoration England," *History Workshop Journal* 51 (2001); L. E. Klein, "Coffeehouse Civility, 1660–1714: An Aspect of Post-Courtly Culture in England," *Huntington Library Quarterly* 59, 1 (1997); and S. C. A. Pincus, "'Coffee

Politicions Does Create': Coffeehouses and Restoration Political Culture,"
JMH 67 (1995). For the political culture of the theater and feasts, see
S. C. A. Pincus, "Shadwell's Dramatic Trimming," in Hamilton and Strier;
and N. E. Key, "The Political Culture and Political Rhetoric of County
Feasts and Feast Sermons, 1654–1714," *JBS* 33 (1994). Ultimately, the
new political culture was about elections, for which see J. H. Plumb, "The
Growth of the Electorate in England from 1600 to 1715," *P & P* 45 (1969);
and M. A. Kishlansky, *Parliamentary Selection: Social and Political Choice
in Early Modern England* (Cambridge, 1986).

Historians disagree about whether the first Whigs introduced partisan
organization into English politics. J. R. Jones, *The First Whigs: The Politics
of the Exclusion Crisis, 1678–1683* (1961) argues that Shaftesbury organized
a parliamentary party committed solely to Exclusion; whereas J. Scott,
Algernon Sidney and the Restoration Crisis, 1677–1683 (Cambridge, 1991)
claims that the first parties were ideological, not organizational. That is,
was the Exclusion Crisis really just about the attempt to exclude James,
duke of York, from the line to the throne, or was it about unsolved religious
and constitutional issues from the Restoration? Or part of a longer
crisis stretching from 1603? These are questions advanced by revisionist
historiography in recent years. See J. Scott, "England's Troubles,
1603–1702," in *The Stuart Court and Europe: Essays in Politics and Political
Culture*, ed. R. M. Smuts (Cambridge, 1996); R. Weil, "The Family in the
Exclusion Crisis: Locke Versus Filmer Revisited," in Houston and Pincus;
M. Knights's lengthy *Politics and Opinion in Crisis, 1678–1681*
(Cambridge, 1994), as well as his articles "London's 'Monster' Petition of
1680," *HJ* 36 (1993), "London Petitions and Parliamentary Politics in 1679,"
PH 12 (1993), and "Petitioning and the Political Theorists: John Locke,
Algernon Sidney and London's 'Monster' Petition of 1680," *P & P* 138
(1993); and G. S. De Krey, "The London Whigs and the Exclusion Crisis," in
*The First Modern Society: Essays in English History in Honour of Lawrence
Stone*, ed. A. L. Beier and others (Cambridge, 1989); and especially the issue of
Albion 25 (1993) on the "Restoration Crisis," with articles and responses by
R. Greaves, G. S. De Krey, T. Harris, J. Rosenheim, and J. Scott.

The bicentennial of the Glorious Revolution led to some rethinking on the
reign of James II and its end. Prominent collections include J. I. Israel, ed., *The
Anglo-Dutch Moment: Essays on the Glorious Revolution and its World
Impact* (Cambridge, 1991), especially essays by Israel, J. R. Jones, and
J. Morrill; D. E. Hoak and M. Feingold, eds., *The World of William and
Mary: Anglo-Dutch Perspectives on the Revolution of 1688–89* (Stanford,
1996); J. R. Jones, ed., *Liberty Secured?: Britain Before and After 1688*
(Stanford, 1992); R. Beddard, ed., *The Revolutions of 1688* (Oxford, 1991);
E. Cruickshanks, ed., *By Force or by Default? The Revolution of 1688–1689*
(Edinburgh, 1989), especially T. Harris's "London Crowds and the
Revolution of 1688"; and L. G. Schwoerer, ed., *The Revolution of*

1688–1689: Changing Perspectives (Cambridge, 1992). See also W. A. Speck, *Reluctant Revolutionaries: Englishmen and the Revolution of 1688* (Oxford, 1988); J. Miller, *The Glorious Revolution*, 2nd ed. (Harlow, 1997); and two earlier studies of the 1680s, J. R. Jones, *The Revolution of 1688 in England* (1972) and J. R. Western, *Monarchy and Revolution: The English State in the 1680s* (1972). Important articles that extend the context of 1688 include T. Harris, "Reluctant Revolutionaries?: The Scots and the Revolution of 1688–89," and M. Zook, "Violence, Martyrdom, and Radical Politics: Rethinking the Glorious Revolution," in Nenner; M. Knights, "'Meer Religion' and the 'Church-State' of Restoration England: The Impact and Ideology of James II's Declarations of Indulgence," in Houston and Pincus; and T. Claydon, "William III's 'Declaration of Reasons' and the Glorious Revolution," *HJ* 39 (1996).

DOCUMENTS

8.1   Charles II, Declaration of Breda (April 14, 1660)[40]

Charles, by the grace of God, king of England, Scotland, France [the old medieval claim] and Ireland, defender of the Faith, etc., to all our loving subjects, of what degree or quality soever, greeting. If the general distraction and confusion which is spread over the whole kingdom doth not awaken all men to a desire and longing that those wounds which have so many years together been kept bleeding may be bound up, all we can say will be to no purpose. However, after this long silence, we have thought it our duty to declare how much we desire to contribute thereunto; and that as we can never give over the hope, in good time, to obtain the possession of that right which God and nature hath made our due, so we do make it our daily suit to the Divine Providence, that He will, in compassion to us and our subjects, after so long misery and sufferings, remit and put us into a quiet and peaceable possession of that our right, with as little blood and damage to our people as is possible....

And to the end that the fear of punishment may not engage any, conscious to themselves of what is past, to a perseverance in guilt for the future, by opposing the quiet and happiness of their country, in the restoration of king, Peers, and people to their just, ancient, and fundamental rights, we do, by these presents, declare, that we do grant a free and general pardon, which we are ready, upon demand, to pass under our Great Seal of England, to all our subjects, of what degree or quality soever, who, within forty days after the publishing hereof, shall lay hold upon this our grace and favor, and shall, by any public act, declare their doing so, and that they return to the loyalty and obedience of good subjects (excepting only such persons as shall hereafter be excepted by Parliament)....

And because the passion and uncharitableness of the times have produced several opinions in religion, by which men are engaged in parties and animosities

---

[40]   *LJ*, 11: 7; compared with H. Gee and W. J. Hardy, eds., *Documents Illustrative of English Church History* (1896), 586–8 (April 4, new style, i.e., on the continent).

against each other..., we do declare a liberty to tender consciences, and that no man shall be disquieted or called in question for differences of opinion in matter of religion, which do not disturb the peace of the kingdom; and that we shall be ready to consent to such an Act of Parliament, as, upon mature deliberation, shall be offered to us, for the full granting that indulgence.

And because, in the continued distractions of so many years and so many and great revolutions, many grants and purchases of estates have been made to and by many officers, soldiers, and others, who are now possessed of the same and who may be liable to actions at law upon several titles, we are likewise willing that all such differences...shall be determined in Parliament, which can best provide for the just satisfaction of all men who are concerned.

8.2 The "Five Mile" Act for Restraining Nonconformists from Inhabiting in Corporations (17 Car. II, c. 2) (1665)[41]

I. Whereas diverse parsons, vicars, curates, lecturers, and other persons in holy orders, have not declared their unfeigned assent and consent to the use of all things contained in and prescribed in the Book of Common Prayer, and administration of the Sacraments, and other rites and ceremonies of the Church of England, or have not subscribed to the declaration or acknowledgment contained in... "An Act for the Uniformity of Public Prayers and Administration of Sacraments" [1662].... And whereas they... and diverse other... persons not ordained according to the form of the Church of England, and as have since the Act of Oblivion taken upon themselves to preach in unlawful assemblies, conventicles, or meetings, under color or pretense of exercise of religion..., [and] have settled themselves in diverse corporations in England, sometimes three or more of them in a place, thereby taking an opportunity to distill the poisonous principles of schism and rebellion into the hearts of his majesty's subjects....

Be it therefore enacted...that the said parsons, vicars, curates, lecturers, [etc., shall not be allowed to preach]..., who have not declared their unfeigned assent and consent, as aforesaid, and subscribed the declaration aforesaid, and shall not take and subscribe the oath following:

"I, A. B., do swear, that it is not lawful upon any pretense whatsoever, to take arms against the king; and that I do abhor that traitorous position of taking arms by his authority against his person, or against those that are commissioned by him, in pursuance of such commissions; and that I will not at any time endeavor any alteration of government, either in Church or State."

II. And all such person and persons as shall take upon them to preach in any unlawful assembly, conventicle, or meeting, under color or pretense of any exercise of religion, contrary to the laws and statutes of this kingdom, shall not at any time from and after March [24]...1665, unless only in passing upon the road, come or be within five miles of any city or town corporate, or borough that send burgesses to the Parliament, within his majesty's kingdom of England,

[41] *SR*, 5: 375; compared with Costin and Watson, *Law and Working of the Constitution*, 34–5.

principality of Wales, or of the town of Berwick-upon-Tweed, or within five miles of any parish, town, or place wherein he or they have, since the Act of Oblivion, been parson, vicar, curate, stipendiary, or lecturer, or taken upon them to preach in any unlawful assembly, conventicle, or meeting, under color or pretense of any exercise of religion, contrary to the laws and statutes of this kingdom; before he or they have taken and subscribed the oath aforesaid...in open court...upon forfeiture for every such offense the sum of forty pounds.

8.3   The First Test Act (25 Car. II, c. 2) (1673)[42]

For preventing dangers which may happen from popish recusants and quieting the minds of his majesty's good subjects, be it enacted...that all and every person or persons as well peers as commoners that shall bear any office or offices civil or military or shall receive any pay, salary, fee, or wages by reason of any patent or grant from his majesty..., shall personally appear...and...in public and open court...take the several oaths of supremacy and allegiance....

And the said respective officers...shall also receive the Sacrament of the Lord's Supper according to the usage of the Church of England at or before August [1, 1673] in some public Church upon some...Sunday immediately after Divine Service and sermon....

And be it further enacted...that at the same time when the persons concerned in this Act shall take the aforesaid oaths of supremacy and allegiance, they shall likewise make and subscribe this declaration following...:

"I, A. B., do declare that I do believe that there is not any Transubstantiation in the Sacrament of the Lord's Supper, or in the elements of bread and wine, at, or after the consecration thereof by any person whatsoever."

8.4   John Bunyan, The Trial of Christian and Faithful at Vanity Fair, from Pilgrim's Progress (1678)[43]

Then I saw in my dream, that...[Christian and Faithful] saw a town before them, and the name of that town is Vanity; and at the town there is a fair kept, called Vanity Fair: it is kept all the year long....

This fair is no new-erected business, but a thing of ancient standing....At this fair are all such merchandise sold, as houses, lands, trades, places, honors, preferments, titles, countries, kingdoms, lusts, pleasures, and delights of all sorts, as whores, bawds, wives, husbands, children, masters, servants, lives, blood, bodies, souls, silver, gold, pearls, precious stones, and what not....

As in other fairs, some one commodity is as the chief of all the fair, so the ware of Rome and her merchandise is greatly promoted in this fair; only our English nation, with some others, have taken a dislike thereat....

Now these pilgrims...must needs go through this fair. Well, so they did: but, behold, even as they entered into the fair, all the people in the fair were moved,

---

42   *SR*, 5: 782–4; compared with Costin and Watson, *Law and Working of the Constitution*, 39–42.
43   Bunyan, *Pilgrim's Progress*, ed. R. Sharrock (Harmondsworth, Middlesex, 1965), 124–34.

and the town itself as it were in a hubbub about them . . . insomuch that all order was confounded. Now was word presently brought to the great one of the fair, who quickly came down, and deputed some of his most trusty friends to take these men into examination, about whom the fair was almost overturned. So the men were brought to examination; and they that sat upon them, asked them whence they came, whither they went, and what they did there, in such an unusual garb? The men told them that they were pilgrims and strangers in the world, and that they were going to their own country, which was the heavenly Jerusalem. . . . But they that were appointed to examine them did not believe them to be any other than bedlams and mad, or else such as came to put all things into a confusion in the fair. Therefore they took them and beat them, and besmeared them with dirt, and then put them into the cage, that they might be made a spectacle to all the men of the fair. . . .

Then a convenient time being appointed, they brought them forth to their trial, in order to their condemnation. When the time was come, they were brought before their enemies and arraigned. The judge's name was Lord Hategood. Their indictment was one and the same in substance, though somewhat varying in form, the contents whereof were this:

"That they were enemies to and disturbers of their trade; that they had made commotions and divisions in the town, and had won a party to their own most dangerous opinions, in contempt of the law of their prince." . . .

Then proclamation was made, that they that had aught to say for their lord the king against the prisoner at the bar, should forthwith appear and give in their evidence. So there came in three witnesses, to wit, Envy, Superstition, and Pickthank. . . .

Then stood forth Envy, and said to this effect: "My lord, I have known this man [Faithful] a long time, and will attest upon my oath before this honorable bench that he is –"

Judge: "Hold! Give him his oath." So they sware him.

Then [Envy] said, "My lord, this man, notwithstanding his plausible name, is one of the vilest men in our country. He neither regardeth prince nor people, law nor custom, but doth all that he can to possess all men with certain of his disloyal notions, which he in the general calls principles of faith and holiness. And, in particular, I heard him once myself affirm that Christianity and the customs of our town of Vanity were diametrically opposite, and could not be reconciled. . . ."

Then was Pickthank sworn, and bid say what he knew, in behalf of their lord the king, against the prisoner at the bar.

Pickthank: "My lord, and you gentlemen all, This fellow I have known of a long time, and have heard him speak things that ought not to be spoke; for he hath railed on our noble Prince Beelzebub, and hath spoken contemptibly of his honorable friends, whose names are the Lord Old Man, the Lord Carnal Delight, the Lord Luxurious, the Lord Desire of Vain Glory, my old Lord Lechery, Sir Having Greedy, with all the rest of our nobility; and he hath said, moreover, that if all men were of his mind . . . , there is not one of these noblemen should have any longer a being in this town. Besides, he hath not been afraid to rail on you, my lord, who are now appointed to be his judge, calling you an ungodly villain, with many other such like vilifying terms, with which he hath bespattered most of the gentry of our town."

When this Pickthank had told his tale, the judge directed his speech to the prisoner at the bar, saying, "Thou runagate [apostate], heretic, and traitor, hast thou heard what these honest gentlemen have witnessed against thee?"

Faithful: "May I speak a few words in my own defense?"

Judge: "Sirrah, sirrah, thou deservest to live no longer, but to be slain immediately upon the place; yet, that all men may see our gentleness towards thee, let us hear what thou, vile runagate, hast to say."

Faithful: "1. I say, then, in answer to what Mr. Envy hath spoken, I never said aught but this, That what rule, or laws, or customs, or people, were flat against the Word of God, are diametrically opposite to Christianity....

"3. As to what Mr. Pickthank hath said..., the prince of this town, with all the rabblement, his attendants, by this gentleman named, are more fit for a being in Hell, than in this town and country: and so, the Lord have mercy upon me!"

Then the judge called to the jury...: "Gentlemen of the jury, you see this man about whom so great an uproar hath been made in this town. You have also heard what these worthy gentlemen have witnessed against him. Also you have heard his reply and confession. It lieth now in your breasts to hang him or save his life; but yet I think meet to instruct you into our law....

"For [the law] of Pharaoh, his law was made upon a supposition, to prevent mischief, no crime being yet apparent; but here is a crime apparent. For the second and third, you see he disputeth against our religion; and for the treason he hath confessed, he deserveth to die the death."

Then went the jury out..., and afterwards unanimously concluded to bring him in guilty before the judge. And first Mr. Blind-man, the foreman, said, "I see clearly that this man is a heretic." Then said Mr. No-good, "Away with such a fellow from the earth." "Ay," said Mr. Malice, "for I hate the very looks of him." Then said Mr. Love-lust, "I could never endure him." "Nor I," said Mr. Live-loose, "for he would always be condemning my way."... "Hanging is too good for him," said Mr. Cruelty.... Then said Mr. Implacable, "Might I have all the world given me, I could not be reconciled to him; therefore, let us forthwith bring him in guilty of death." And so they did; therefore he was presently condemned to be had from the place where he was, to the place from whence he came, and there to be put to the most cruel death that could be invented....

Thus came Faithful to his end.... But as for Christian, he had some respite, and was remanded back to prison.

8.5   Members of Parliament's Speeches on Religion (1674–8)[44]

12 January 1674. *Col. Birch*: "Whoever divides religion into any other rivulets than Papist and Protestant ruins all."

[44]   A. Grey, ed., *Debates of the House of Commons, From the Year 1667 to the Year 1694* (1763), 2: 228; 4: 284, 294, 296; 5: 250, 252; 6: 86–8.

20 March 1677. Debate on first reading of "Act for farther securing the Protestant religion, by educating the children of the royal family therein, and providing for the continuance of a Protestant clergy."

Sir Thomas Littleton: "He fears that in this business we shall rather promote than hinder Popery. We have had a sort of clergy, ever since Archbishop Laud's time too much addicted to Popery....And men of that leaven are still in the Church....If we establish this power in the bishops..., they may gratify their prince another way."

Col. Birch: "As this bill is now penned, he has not heard one man show any safety in it....He would have any man find five Presbyterian ministers that signed any engagement in the late usurpation [1650, see chapter 7], and he will show fifty, on the other side, that did....His opinion is, that when this bill is passed, the king is not safe. Nothing can stand against a popish design when ripe. All disorders are in this bill; it lays us asleep [against Popery] till exercised."

Sir John Ernle: "He would have Birch consider, when General Monck came up to London [1660], how many of them [Presbyterian ministers] signed for the government by a single person?"

16 March 1678. Debate on whether Quakers should be convicted as Popish Recusants.

Sir John Birkenhead: "The fifth Monarchy-men are under the notion of Quakers; they are for King Jesus, and not King Charles. The Quaker says, 'He is not for arms.' But one I saw preaching by Aldersgate [London] lately, upon St. John's making plain the paths, etc, was beaten by the people. But he, watching his opportunity, beat four of the people soundly, with a crab-tree cudgel. What need you be doubtful in distinguishing them, for the Jesuits do lead them?"

Col. Silius Titus: "I wonder that Birkenhead, who has always expressed so great a zeal against conventicles, should be present at them....I hate them as much as he, but the question is, whether they are justly or unjustly used in their punishment."

12 June 1678. Debate on second reading of Second Test Act.

Mr William Harbord: "I am sorry to hear any arguments for jealousies and apprehensions that this bill should not pass the Lords' House. Look upon our neighbors; see what they have done in France and Holland. In Queen Elizabeth's time, the Protestants were favored in France; their judges and *Parlement* were mixed with them.... But since ... they have made laws so severe against them, as to root them quite out; and surely it is as wise for us, as for that great monarch [Louis XIV], to be tender of our religion. Holland is full of sects, but they suffer [allow] no religion in the government but Calvinistical. If we cannot support our [Anglican] religion, it is a wonder we should be contrary to all the world."

Sir Charles Wheeler: "I desire our government may be preserved as we have found it. Let those that come after us struggle as well as we, without these extreme and violent ways. Cannot a Lord that is not a Protestant, give a vote whether leather shall be transported, as well as a Commoner? Saying 'it is in our power to make the bill pass,' is an innovation as well as all the rest. We may save ourselves from the growth of Popery, in punishing those that go off from us. The danger is, we know not what may be hereafter. I believe the Catholic religion is idolatry. Bread in substance, transformed and transmuted into the body of our Savior, etc., is intrinsic idolatry."

Mr. Powle: "I cannot be of Wheeler's opinion; 'to leave the kingdom as we found it.' That is, never to mend it. Had your predecessors been of that opinion, we had had Popery long since established. I think the bill is very well calculated for this time. It meddles with nothing but keeping Papists out of the Government. I wish that the Protestants, all the world over, had no more severe treatment than to be excluded out of the Government. They are men so obnoxious to the penalty of the law, that they have not freedom of votes; and I am against any man's sitting here, that has not that freedom."

8.6 Selections from Newsletters Sent to Richard Newdigate, Sir Leoline Jenkins, and Sir Richard Bulstrode (1675–84)[45]

March 4, 1675. "Several returns are made into the Exchequer of Roman Catholics, and the [nonconformist] conventicles are looked after, one being taken at Dr. Martin's house in Covent Garden Sunday last and prosecution made according to law. At Great Yarmouth where there has been a very great conventicle the bailiffs of the place sent for some of the chief of them and forewarned them from meeting anymore."

May 14, 1675 [B]. "The Lords sat very late about the Test [Danby's bill for no alteration in Church and State, not document 8.3] and got over a piece of the oath, *viz.* 'I, A. B., do swear that I will not endeavor to alter the Protestant religion as it is established by law'; but it was a long time before everybody would understand what the Protestant religion was."

November 9, 1675 [B]. "The Lords met this day were entertained with a little book called *A Letter to a Friend in the Country* which is a history of so much of the last sessions as concerned the Test [see May 14, 1675] in the house of Lords with sharp reflections and remarks upon several bishops, and some great ministers of state; the book was brought in by a bishop and ordered to be burnt by the common hangman."

August 21, 1676 [B]. "Were it not for Popery the post office would be undone, for who would write if he had no news?"

September 15, 1676 [B]. "The duke of Buckingham was last night in the great coffeehouse in the city...where he had a very full audience, before which he declared himself freely and aloud without...any secrecy that he was absolutely for a new Parliament."

May 15, 1677 [J]. "On Friday night was apprehended one Mr. Gosnold a person that had dispersed several scandalous and seditious lampoons against the Government, a collection of which was seized as it was binding in a bookseller's shop.

---

[45] Folger Shakespeare Library, L. C. 153–1616 (to Richard Newdigate, Esq.); Huntington Library, HM 30314–30315, Sir Leoline Jenkins's Newsletters, 1676–1680 [J]; University of Texas, Ransome Center, MS.103c, Newsletters addressed to Sir Richard Bulstrode and others, Oct. 25, 1667–June 3, 1689 [B].

Together with this Gosnold there have been taken one Evans (who went by the name of Clerk) and Acton, who was his copyist."

August 30, 1678 [J]. "Ten days or a fortnight since there was a great election for the knight of the shire in Berkshire, which was highly contested between the Court and Country party as they call them."

October 4, 1678 [J]. "People's heads and hearts are full of reflections upon the late discovery that hath been made of a detestable design against his majesty's person and the peace of the Kingdom, and though the Roman Catholics do still say, that all is but a contrivance to ruin them, yet I can assure your excellency that the lords of the Privy Council do all say, that it is as plain as the day, that there has been a most dangerous and pernicious design carrying on for several years past, and therefore the Privy Council hath thought it necessary to send down orders into all the counties for disarming all Roman Catholics and reputed Roman Catholics, and this day they have begun to execute these orders here in towns and in the suburbs."

November 2, 1678. "The corpse of Sir Edmund Berry Godfrey was interred in St. Martins-in-the-Fields, attended thither...with all due solemnity by about 100 of the clergy and many hundreds of gentry and citizens. The house of Commons ...have unanimously resolved that it appears to them that there has been 'A Most Horrid and Hellish Plot for the Destruction of the King's Person and Government, Religion, etc.'"

March _, 1681 [B]. "The justices of the peace for Middlesex have received orders to issue out their warrants for summoning all such people before them that print, publish or spread those pamphlets about town and to proceed against them as spreaders of false news."

July 2, 1681 [B]. "On Thursday last the [ap]prentices of this city presented their petition to his majesty signed by 12,000 hands to give him thanks for his late declaration [explaining the dissolution of the Oxford Parliament]; it met with a gracious acceptance and those that carried it up were introduced by the Lord Chamberlain and had the honor to kiss his majesty's hands."

July 30, 1681 [B]. "His majesty hath been graciously pleased to grant a warrant to the keeper of Hyde Park to deliver to the loyal apprentices that made the address two of the fattest bucks...without fee with which they will make a feast on Wednesday next, several persons of quality being already invited."

October 6, 1681. Nathaniel Powell a Muggletonian (a radical sect), indicted at Westminster "for saying damn the duke of York for he was the son of a whore, a pimp, and that he had occasioned all the troubles of this nation, that he wished to meet him on Salisbury Plain to try which was the best man, and that [if] he met him in the streets he should take the wall of him and he would give him a box on the ear."

October 29, 1681. "The Stationers' Company were this day divided the Whigs dining at the hall and the Tories at the 2 Tun tavern which was caused by Whig renter wardens (who made the feast) providing a pitiful dinner."

October 31, 1681 [B]. "The king was received and entertained in the city on Saturday with all the expressions of duty and affection imaginable; and the king on the other side was very gracious to the lord mayor and several of the aldermen but of others and of the two [Whig] sheriffs he took no manner of notice."

November 17, 1681. "[Nathaniel] Thomson the printer [and publisher of a Tory newspaper, see document 8.7] was this day assaulted by the rabble in Fleet Street and after being beaten got home."

"This night the pope was carried through the city attended with Jesuits, etc., then burnt in Smithfield."

November 19, 1681. "At the burning of the pope the people cried 'God bless the king, duke of Monmouth, earl of Shaftesbury, and Capt. [Henry] Wilkinson [an associate of Shaftesbury].'"

December 6, 1681. On Sunday night "the Lord Kingston, Lord Hunsdon, with Capt. Billingsley and about 12 more went from Wills Coffee House to Peters in Covent Garden to affront the Whigs, where they looked about the room and cried 'God Damn all Whigs for rogues and sons of whores,' but nobody speaking to them they took hold of one Peachy a tailor as he was going and asked him whither he was a Whig or a Tory and he crying a Whig they burnt his periwig and Billingsley kicked him downstairs, of which he threatens to complain to the Council.

"They came again last night about 5 and had they stayed long they had met a party of Whigs to encounter them."

January 26, 1682. "Yesterday the duke of York's picture [portrait] in Guildhall was cut through the shins."

March 27, 1682 [B]. "The addresses declaring their abhorrence of the late designed Association [by Whigs to arm Protestants in defense of the king] come from all the countries, and though there are a sort of people among us that would make light of them, yet I am assured those that are the best friends to my Lord Shaftesbury do not like to see the nation make these declarations against a paper that was sworn to be found in his custody."

April 21, 1682 [B]. "Yesterday the duke [of York] dined at the Artillery feast. His royal highness went thither attended with a great number of nobility and persons of quality, and was met at Merchant Tailors' Hall by the lord mayor, aldermen, etc. In sum all things passed extremely to his royal highness's satisfaction.

"The Whigs in opposition to this had designed a mock feast; and for that purpose had given out several hundred of tickets, upon receipt whereof the persons invited gave their guineas apiece, but his majesty being informed thereof, [forbade] . . . the said meeting as you will see by the order of Council which is printed in *The Gazette*."

August 10, 1682. Loyal apprentices' great feast at Merchant Tailors' yesterday "where most of the court lords in town were present and by reason the tickets were given *gratis* there was a great appearance about 1500 of all sorts they were mightily stored with provisions especially venison, there being 50 pasties and one nag brought roasted whole to the table. There was 16 old stewards who deposited £50 each and they chose the same number of new ones there was also invited the commissioners of the admiralty . . . and that a ship hung up in the hall with two lads therein who upon learning of healths fired the guns which pleased the boys extremely and loyal Nathaniel Thompson being present there was much notice taken of him. Afterwards the wine in some of their heads made them commit disorders in Amsterdam Coffee House but were carried before a magistrate and bound over."

November 7, 1682. "Last night being kept for the 5th of November many bonfires were enkindled but the rabble began their accustomed rudeness of crying 'No York, but A Monmouth, A Monmouth' and were so outrageous in the Stocks market [Exchange] that they began to burn and pull down a vintner's signs, etc., but the soldiers dissipated the most and seized several who were committed to the Compter and Bridewell [prisons]."

November 11, 1682. "Sunday last several justices of peace at Theobalds coming to disturb a conventicle found the people gone upon which they pulled down the pulpit and made a bonfire therewith being Gunpowder treason day [November 5]."

"Yesterday the lord mayor and aldermen attended his majesty in Council where they gave an account of the late riotous proceeding on Monday last.... Thereupon his majesty was pleased to order that on the 17th being the anniversary of Queen Elizabeth they ordered a strong guard of trained bands and suffer no bonfires to be made and neither pope nor other effigies to be burnt to prevent which that the city gates be kept shut in the evening and all assemblies dispersed."

August 16, 1683. "Loyalty is now grown so much in fashion that we have two addresses from one town."

September 17, 1683. "It is the general belief we shall have a Parliament this winter..., the discovery of the late damnable fanatick plot [the Rye House Plot] having in great measure broken the faction, and opened the eyes of all honest men.... Thus you see for want of news I trouble you with the reflections of the politicians."

January 18, 1684. Mr. Norrell, comptroller of Middle Temple, attended with officers and gentlemen of that society to Whitehall in great state "where they presented a loyal address wherein they promise to maintain the right of succession in the lineal course of descent and delivered their abhorrence of a fanatical and republican designs."

8.7 *Whig and Tory Newspapers (1679–84)*[46]

Whig Newspapers

The Protestant (Domestick) Intelligence: Or, News both from City and Country, by Benjamin Harris

December 26, 1679. "There have been several persons in and about this city industriously endeavoring to promote petitions for the sitting of the Parliament, of which some persons in the Strand taking notice, and designing to suppress a petition set on foot in their neighborhood, and to which many hands had been procured, sent to invite the managers thereof to a tavern to take their subscrip-

---

[46] *The Protestant (Domestick) Intelligence,* no. 50, Dec. 26, 1679; no. 89, Jan. 18, 1681; *Impartial Protestant Mercury,* no. 104, April 18–21, 1682; no. 105, April 21–5, 1682; *The Weekly Pacquet of Advice from Rome,* vol. 3, no. 46, April 22, 1681; vol. 4, no. 12, Mar. 10, 1682; vol. 4, no. 343, Aug. 11, 1682; *Loyal Protestant and True Domestick Intelligence,* no. 1, Mar. 9, 1681; no. 7, Mar. 29, 1681; no. 142, April 15, 1682; *The Observator, in Dialogue,* no. 79, Dec. 10, 1681; no. 99, Feb. 15, 1682; no. 109, Mar. 10, 1682; no. 140, Sept. 27, 1684.

tions to it, and having by that means got it into their hands; they committed it to the flames.

"We may also observe a further project of countermining the said petitions, in the following form of an association, which is published here, *viz.*

"The Loyal Protestants Association [that is, an anti-Whig association]. 'Whereas several printed forms of petitions have been lately dispersed up and down the Kingdom, to procure subscriptions: And whereas the proceedings thereupon have been adjudged..., to be contrary to law..., we whose names are hereunder subscribed, out of a sense of our duty both to Church and State, and to witness our detestation of all illegal, and undutiful practices, do hereby unanimously declare..., that we abhor the thought of any such confederacy.'"

January 18, 1681. Wapping, London. "Two fellows coming into a victualling house, and desiring a private room, were showed up one pair of stairs, where they continued drinking for the space of four or five hours, being often observed to whisper to each other, and to be very private in their discourse.... After they were gone, the boy coming to take away, smelt so strong a scent of brimstone, that mistrusting something more than ordinary, he called up his master, who searching the room, found it on fire behind the hangings, which, as it is supposed, was done by the dextrous application of Jesuitick fire-balls..., so that we must conclude they were some of the pope's imps, whom he had employed to make bonfires of the remaining part of our ancient structure."

Impartial Protestant Mercury, by Richard Janeway

April 18–21, 1682. "There was intended another considerable feast to have been tomorrow in the city. For which purpose Haberdashers Hall and Goldsmiths Hall were taken up, and twas believed there would near a thousand of the nobility, gentry, clergy of the Church of England as establisht by law, and eminent citizens have there appeared. The occasion and scope of which treat appears in the tickets of invitations; which being maliciously mis-recited by [Nathaniel] Thompson we therefore shall here add a true copy thereof.

"'It having pleased Almighty God by his wonderful providence to deliver and protect his majesty's person, the Protestant religion, and English liberties (hitherto) from the Hellish and frequent attempts of their enemies (the Papists): in testimony of thankfulness herein, and for the preserving and improving mutual love and charity among such as are sensible thereof. You are desired to meet many of the loyal Protestant nobility, gentry, clergy, and citizens, on Friday the 21...April, 1682, at ten..., at St. Michaels..., there to hear a sermon, and from thence to go to Haberdashers Hall to dinner....'

"But it seems the intent of this sociable meeting being...misrepresented..., it pleased his sacred majesty..., yesterday to prohibit the same."

April 21–5, 1682. "After the Artillery-Dinner yesterday [April 20] was over, the members of that society, according to custom, proceeded to choose eight stewards for the year ensuing..., [including] the duke of Albemarle, the earl of Oxford..., [etc.]. His royal highness [the duke of York] was highly caressed amongst them and returned to Whitehall before six.... Amongst the rest of their entertainment, one

Durfey a poet sang several Tory-songs and was very much applauded. Though his royal highness was not present at the sermon, yet having an account given him thereof, we are informed, that he has desired Dr. Sprat to print the same. In the evening some bonfires were kindled, especially one before the Wonder Tavern in Ludgate Street, and a parcel of blades [young gallants] being planted in the balcony, threw out money to the rabble bidding them cry out 'a York!' which they did as long as they got liquor; and some hectors that managed them were very rude and abusive to the coaches and passengers that went by. At last a company of young men came and threw abroad the fire, slinging part of the brands in at the tavern windows and cry'd out 'No Papist! no Papist!' and so went their ways."

The Weekly Pacquet of Advice from Rome: Or, The History of Popery, by Henry Care, by Langley Curtis

April 22, 1681. "Enter Papist, and Masquerade. Papist: Since folks are so set upon dialoguing, let you and I have a touch."

March 10, 1682. "Tory: Tell me..., what thinkest of the abhorrencies of the Association which hath made such a figure in modern *Gazettes*?

"Trueman: ... As to the paper call'd the Association, it may be a very ill paper; but [even] if it were found at my Lord Shaftesbury's..., yet since there is no offer or pretense of proof that it was of that lord's writing; that he ever saw it, or heard it read; that he or any body else ever promoted it, or attempted getting of hands to it, or that any mortal ever approv'd of, or sign'd it: how is that lord concerned?... Why were you not, gentlemen, as zealous, and ready with your abhorrencies of Coleman's letters...?"

August 11, 1682. "Trueman: But what is this glorious feast of yours, so much talkt of?

"Tory: Why, there should have been fifteen hundred of us, and 'twas not our fault there was not so many, for the tickets were at last given abroad [freely]....

"Trueman: I'le assure you, 'twas a brave opportunity for loyal journey-man tailors, this cucumber-time [season when gentry were in town].

"Tory: Yes, they indented with their bellies not to eat again this fortnight. And then to see the condescention and charity, as well as policy of the business; illustrissimo's and grandee's, and porters, and sons of whores, and [ap]prentices, so sweetly mixt, you'd wonder at it!...

"Trueman: That's great I'le promise you; especially their prudence too, being put in the same balance with their vast estates!... I have a just veneration for any person of honor that might divert themselves at this conventicle [the Tory apprentices' feast], but for the rest..., an haunch of venison is not much more valuable than a mess of pottage, and for a few little people (boys and journeymen, and I know not who) to single out themselves, and appropriate... the title of *the loyal* (which every good subject in England is proud of), is not this in effect to call all those many thousands that join not in the ridiculous frolic, *traitors and rebels*? and do not such practices most apparently tend to faction, distinguishing and setting up of parties, and sedition? Nor is it difficult to imagine what influence such meetings will have on wild unbridled youth, when in defiance to their indentures..., they shall dare be scaperloitering to a right honorable feast....- Their loyalty...is demonstrated in being obedient to the law, and their masters, not in drinking healths, swearing, roaring, and huzza-ing."

Tory Newspapers

Loyal Protestant and True Domestick Intelligence, by Nathaniel Thompson

March 9, 1681. "When a club of factious scribblers do inflame the people against the government, and under the mask of religion, endeavor to run down both Church and State...; then I think it high time for all loyal subjects to declare themselves against such pernicious proceedings.... I have thought fit to renew this my *Intelligence*... For it is publisht for no other end, but to undeceive his majesty's loyal subjects."

March 29, 1681. "The inhabitants of [Oxford] conceive no small joy at the favor his majesty has done them in calling his Parliament to sit here; so that whenever his majesty takes coach, or is publicly to be seen, many hundreds flock about him, and express their loyal duty by wishing him a long life, and happy reign; praying that they that seek his hurt, may be taken in their own snares....

"Whereas in the *Oxford Intelligence*..., it was inserted that the duke of Monmouth attended with a great retinue was received here...with many shouts and acclamations of the people; this is to ascertain you, that he came...with 30 in his attendance, as well servants as gentlemen, some of which company began to make faint essays of humming (or applause), thereby to provoke others to do the like, both in Cat Street...and at his alighting at his lodging; but they were not in the least seconded by any."

April 15, 1682. "The feast of the artillery company having been deferred for some time, that his royal highness might honor them with his company; it is now resolved upon, that it shall be kept the Thursday in Easter-week, and 'tis hoped his royal highness will be present. They intend first to hear a sermon at St. Lawrence Church. And we are informed, that some persons (sober ones no doubt) have designed a feast to be held the same day in Drapers Hall, and resolve to invite several persons like themselves, intending to hear a sermon before dinner at Bow Church."

The Observator, in Dialogue, by Roger L'Estrange

December 10, 1681. On the Association to arm Protestants found in Shaftesbury's study. "Tory: The subscribers write themselves (according the very style of Jesuits) 'of the society and association,' and bind themselves in the 'bond of one firm and loyal society, or association.'"

February 15, 1682. "Whig: But where's the counter-association?

"Tory: I am told that the loyal nobility, gentry, and commonalty of the nation are ent'ring upon a resolution to have no sort of dealing in money-matters...with any of the Whig-party; and not to buy so much as a dish of coffee, or a pot of ale of any man that is not well affected to the king and the Church.

"Whig: D'ye call this an association, or a malicious confederacy?

"Tory: I do look upon it as one of the fairest expedients I can think of."

March 10, 1682. "Whig: But is it now lawful to associate for the defense of religion?

"Tory: Yes. In all cases where religion allows you to associate. But subjects can no more justify ent'ring into associations, without...the...consent of the supreme magistrate, than they can justify levying of arms without commission."

September 27, 1684. "Observer [replaces Tory]: The faction does everything in clubs; from the noble Peers' association, to the New-Castle Christian Society!...- What are their protestations, leagues, vows, covenants, and engagements, but political clubs, toward the ruin of their prince and country?...What are all their private meetings, but so many clubs: and those clubs, but so many rolls of conspirators?

8.8   Sir John Bramston on the Reign of James II (ca. 1685–8)[47]

The same day that the King Charles II died his present majesty King James II was proclaimed...and the next day a Council being called the king spake thus:...

"My Lords..., Since it hath pleased almighty God to place me in this station, and I am now to succeed so good and gracious a king, as well as so very kind a brother, I think it fit to declare to you that I will endeavor to follow his example, and most especially in that of his great clemency and tenderness to his people. I have been reported to have been a man for arbitrary power; but that is not the only story has been made of me, and I shall make it my endeavor to preserve this Government, both in Church and State, as it is now by law established. I know the principles of the Church of England are for monarchy, and the members of it have showed themselves good and loyal subjects; therefore I shall always take care to defend and support it. I know, too, that the laws of England are sufficient to make the king as great a monarch as I can wish; and as I shall never depart from the just rights and prerogatives of the Crown so I shall never invade any man's property...."

The duke of Monmouth landed at Lyme in Dorsetshire 11 June 1685....They brought some arms, but not enough for his business. He set out a most malicious, false, and scandalous declaration, wherein he termed the King James "Duke of York," calling him traitor, and laying to his charge the murder of Sir Edmunberry Godfrey, the cutting the throat of the earl of Essex, the firing the city of London, and the poisoning his brother, King Charles II; saying he had taken arms, and would admit of no treaty of peace until he had brought him to condign punishment, etc....

June 15 [1688], the attorney-general moved the court of King's Bench for an *habeas corpus* return immediate for the seven bishops, which was granted, and the seven appeared.... Then...they pleaded not guilty, and the Court demanded and required them to enter into recognizance for their appearance and standing to trial and judgment of the court.... In Hall Court, Palace Yard, from the water stairs, were infinite numbers of people, lords, gentlemen, and common people. The people on their knees made a lane and begged the bishops' blessing as they

---

[47]   *The Autobiography of Sir John Bramston, K.B., of Skreens, in the Hundred of Chelmsford*, ed. Lord Braybrooke (Camden Society, old ser., 32, 1845), 165–6, 184, 275–6, 308–11, 340–3, 355–7.

passed. In their return, the people seeing them go to their own houses thought they were discharged, and gave great huzzas.

On the day, that is the 29th, they [the bishops] came to the bar, and a jury impaneled; they were tried on the information.... Two of the judges ... spoke largely upon the subject's right of petitioning the king; the other two judges differed in opinion with them, but said not much. The jury went from the bar about 5 of clock; there was a majority for not guilty, but four or five then were for guilty; but by 12 of clock all but Arnold, the brewer, were agreed; about 6 in the morning he also agreed with the rest.... They resolved to give their verdict in open court; and about ten of clock, when the judges were set, they came and gave their verdict, not guilty. At which some standing within hearing gave a huzza, which others took, and it passed through the hall extreme loud; so into the yards and to the water side, and along the river, as far as the bridge.... Upon the day that the bishops appeared I was in the hall, and being joined with some of the nobility ... and several gentlemen, I was asked if ever I had seen the hall so full. I said, Yea, and fuller, when the cry was, "No bishops, no magpies, no popish Lords" [that is, 1641]. But the noise was less now, as the cry was otherwise, save only, "No popish Lords." ...

The king being come to Whitehall [at his return to London, December 16, 1688], and the people huzzaing as he came, put hopes into his majesty that the anger was not at his person, but at his religion, and that the desertion of his army and people was on that account.... The Papists flock to him again, five Papists to one Protestant.... The Papists were as bold and confident as ever. The city, upon the first going away of the king after his return, had sent to invite the prince [of Orange] to London, and the king after his return had sent to invite the prince to St. James's, and had ordered that house to be prepared. The prince ... sent ... [three Lords to desire] that he [James] would remove out of town before twelve ... next morning.... The king was in bed and asleep. The Lords caused him to be awakened, and about one ... delivered their errand, and the same time the prince his men took possession of the guards and posts about ... all the avenues. The king ... went with a guard of Dutch to Rochester..., and in the night went away again privately, leaving in the chamber ... where he lay, a paper to the effect following, *viz.*:

"The world cannot wonder at my withdrawing myself now this second time. I might have expected somewhat better usage after what I wrote to the prince of Orange ...; but, instead of an answer such as I might have hoped for, what was I to expect after the usage I received? The sending his own guards at eleven at night, to take possession of the posts at Whitehall, without advertizing me in the least manner of it; the sending to me at one of clock after midnight, when I was in bed, a kind of an order by three lords, to be gone out of mine own palace before twelve that morning. After all this, how could I hope to be safe so long as I was in the power of one who had not only done this to me, and invaded my kingdoms, without any just occasion given him for it, but that did, by his first Declaration, lay the greatest aspersion upon me that malice could invent, in that clause of it which concerns my son? ... What had I, then, to expect from one who by all arts hath taken such pains to make me appear as black as Hell to my people, as well as to all the world besides? What effect that hath had at home all mankind hath seen, by so general a defection in my army, as well as in the nation, amongst all sorts of people.... Tho' I have ventured my life very frankly, on several occasions, for the good and honor of my country, and am free to do it again (and which I hope I shall yet do, as old as I am, to redeem it from the slavery it is like to fall under), yet I think it not convenient to expose myself to be secured, as not to be at liberty to effect it, and for that reason do withdraw, but so as to be within call whensoever the nation's eyes shall be opened; so as, to see how they have been abused and imposed upon by the specious pretenses of liberty and property. I hope it will please God to touch their hearts, out of His infinite mercy, and to make them sensible of the ill condition they are in, and bring them to such a temper that a legal Parliament may be called; and that . . . they will agree to liberty of conscience for all Protestant Dissenters and that those of my own persuasion may be so far considered . . . ; and I appeal to all men who are considering men, and have had experience, whether anything can make this nation so great and flourishing as liberty of conscience. Rochester, December 22, 1688." . . .

So soon as it was known that the king was gone, the Lords spiritual and temporal assembled at Guildhall, London, and required the lord mayor to take care of the city; and then and there also sent to the prince of Orange, and invited him to come to London; so also did the lord mayor, aldermen, and common council. The paper left by the king tells what made him go away, and the prince's message was demonstrative what he desired. The prince came to St. James. And tho' King James his reign was short, not full four years; yet was his design very apparent, the Roman religion he resolved to establish, maugre [in spite of] all the laws, and what averseness soever in the nobility, gentry, and the common people also. He closeted particular men, and, tried them by promises and threats. He garbled the corporations, and sent emissaries amongst them to influence them for choice of members for Parliament, such as would take away the penal laws and test; gave indulgences, and dispensed by his own authority with all the laws: but this furious hasty driving ruin'd him. . . .

I know it will be objected that King James was forced away; that some Lords spiritual and temporal, and some gentlemen had invited the prince of Orange into the kingdom, that he accordingly came with an army, and that the king's army refused to fight, nay, that some were gone over to the prince, so that the king must either fly, or be contented to be a prisoner. I can only say, as to those that invited the prince in, they must answer for themselves; but I hold it was in them perfect rebellion. As to the prince, I think much more may be said for him than for them, tho' they allege religion, property, and liberty were in a dangerous condition, as in truth they were; for, whoever considers well the short reign of King James, he will see what havoc he was making in the Church and universities, the nurseries of our religion, what haste he made to settle Popery, and the means and ways he took to make his power and rule absolute, and the laws dispensable at his will and pleasure, must think all these were in danger; but all were established by laws, and could not be destroyed but by the same power that made them, that is, by a law, and who they are that made our laws, must conclude, as I did, that tho' many particular persons might be destroyed by his power, yet the nation could not, people would not be so mad as to send to Parliament such representatives as would cut their own throats; wherefore I must leave those that called in the prince inexcusable. But as for him [William], if the case be stated (as I think it ought) that he being a free prince, and having a just right in succession in his princess, and after her and her sister, and her issue, in himself also, and that the king, out of fondness for Popery, and enmity to the established religion, and for that cause to his daughters and their issue, and to the prince also, did give way to a Jesuitical contrivance, to impose upon the nation a supposititious son, as born of the body of the queen, and thereby to disinherit the above-mentioned prince and princesses; this, I say, being his belief and opinion, and there being no way for one prince to sue another, nor way to determine their controversies, but the sword, I dare not condemn the prince absolutely for making war on that occasion, tho' against an uncle and father.

8.9 *James II's Declaration of Indulgence (April 4, 1687, reissued April 27, 1688)*[48]

We ... have thought fit by virtue of our royal prerogative to issue forth this our declaration of indulgence, making no doubt of the concurrence of our two Houses of Parliament when we shall think it convenient for them to meet.

In the first place we do declare that we will protect and maintain our arch-bishops, bishops, and clergy, and all other our subjects of the Church of England in the free exercise of their religion as by law established, and in the quiet and full enjoyment of all their possessions. ...

We do likewise declare ... that from henceforth the execution of all and all manner of penal laws in matters ecclesiastical, for not coming to Church, or not receiving the sacrament, or for any other nonconformity to the religion established, or for or by reason of the exercise of religion in any manner whatsoever, be immediately suspended; and the further execution of the said penal laws and every of them [*sic*] is hereby suspended. ...

We do hereby further declare ... that the oaths commonly called the oaths of supremacy and allegiance, and also the several tests and declarations mentioned in the Acts of Parliament made in the 25th [1673] and 30th years [1678] of the reign of our late royal brother King Charles II, shall not at any time hereafter be required to be taken, declared, or subscribed by any person or persons whatsoever, who is or shall be employed in any office or place of trust, either civil or military, under us or in our government.

8.10 *Trial of the Seven Bishops (June 29, 1688)*[49]

Serjeant Levinz (for the defense): Now, my lord, this is a petition setting forth a grievance, and praying his majesty to give relief. And what is this grievance? It is

[48] Howell, *State Trials*, 12: 234–6; compared with Costin and Watson, *Law and Working of the Constitution*, 343–5; and Prall, *Bloodless Revolution*, 299–300.

[49] Howell, *State Trials*, 12: 393–4, 397, 412, 416, 425–7; compared with Costin and Watson, *Law and Working of the Constitution*, 258–71.

that command of his, by that order made upon my lords the bishops, to distribute the declaration and cause it to be read in the churches. And pray, my lord, let us consider what the effects and consequences of that distribution and reading is: it is to tell the people, that they need not submit to the Act of Uniformity [1662], nor to any act of Parliament made about ecclesiastical matters, for they are suspended and dispensed with. This my lords the bishops must do, if they obey this order; but your lordship sees, if they do it, they lie under an anathema by the statute of 1 Eliz. [1559], for there they are under a curse if they do not look to the preservation and observation of that Act. But this command to distribute and read the declaration, whereby all these laws are dispensed with, is to let the people know they will not do what the Act requires of them. . . .

My lord, . . . I never did meet with anything of such a nature, as a grant or dispensation that pretended to dispense with any one whole Act of Parliament; I have not so much as heard of any such thing mentioned that dispenses with a great many laws at once, truly I cannot take upon me to tell how many, there may be forty of above, for aught I know. . . .

Mr. Somers: My lord, I dare appeal to Mr. Attorney General himself, whether, in the case of Godden and Hales [1686], which was lately in this court, to make good that dispensation, he did not use it as an argument then, that it could not be expounded into a suspension. He admitted it not to be in the king's power to suspend a law, but that he might give a dispensation to a particular person, was all that he took upon to justify him at that time. . . .

The Solicitor-General (for the Crown): I dare say it will not be denied me, that the king may, by his prerogative royal, issue forth his proclamation; it is as essential a prerogative as it is to give his assent to an Act of Parliament to make it a law. And it is another principle, which I think cannot be denied, that the king may make constitutions and orders in matters ecclesiastical; and that these he may make out of Parliament, and without the Parliament. If the king may do so, and these are his prerogatives, then suppose the king do issue forth his royal proclamation (and such in effect is this declaration under the great seal) in a matter ecclesiastical, by virtue of his prerogative royal; and this declaration is read in the council and published to the world, and then the bishops come and tell the king, Sir, you have issued out an illegal proclamation or declaration, being contrary to what has been declared in Parliament, when there is no declaration in Parliament; is not this a diminishing the king's power and prerogative in issuing forth his proclamation or declaration, and making constitutions in matters ecclesiastical? Is not this a questioning his prerogative? Do not my lords the bishops in this case raise a question between the king and the people? Do not they, as much as in them lies, stir up the people to sedition? For who shall be judge between the king and the bishops? . . .

Justice Holloway: Pray give me leave, Sir: then the king having made such a declaration of a general toleration and liberty of conscience, and afterwards he comes and requires the bishops to disperse this declaration; this, they say, out of a tenderness of conscience, they cannot do, because they apprehend it is contrary to law, and contrary to their function: What can they do, if they may not petition?

Solicitor-General: I'll tell you what they should have done, Sir. If they were commanded to do anything against their consciences, they should have acquiesced till the meeting of the Parliament. [At which some people in the court hissed.]...

Lord Chief Justice: Gentlemen, upon the point of the publication, I have summed up all the evidence to you; and if you believe that the petition which these lords presented to the king was this petition, truly, I think, that is a publication sufficient. If you do not believe it was this petition, then my lords the bishops are not guilty of what is laid to their charge in this information, and consequently there needs no inquiry whether they are guilty of a libel. But if you do believe that this was the petition they presented to the king, then we must come to inquire whether this be a libel.

Now, gentlemen, anything that shall disturb the government, or make mischief and a stir among the people, is certainly within the case of "*Libellis Famosis*"; and I must in short give you my opinion, I do take it to be a libel. Now, this being a point of law, if my brothers have anything to say to it, I suppose they will deliver their opinions.

Justice Holloway: Look you, gentlemen, it is not usual for any person to say anything after the Chief Justice has summed up the evidence...: but this is a case of an extraordinary nature.... The question is, whether this petition of my lords the bishops be a libel or no. Gentlemen, the end and intention of every action is to be considered; and likewise, in this case, we are to consider the nature of the offense that these noble persons are charged with; it is for delivering a petition, which, according as they have made their defense, was with all the humility and decency that could be. So that if there was no ill intent, and they were not (as it is not, nor can be pretended they were) men of evil lives, or the like, to deliver a petition cannot be a fault, it being the right of every subject to petition....

Lord Chief Justice: Look you, by the way, brother, I did not ask you to sum up the evidence (for that is not usual) but only to deliver your opinion, whether it be a libel or no.

Justice Powell: Truly I cannot see, for my part, anything of sedition or any other crime fixed upon these reverend fathers, my lords the bishops.

For, gentlemen, to make it a libel, it must be false, it must be malicious, and it must tend to sedition. As to the falsehood, I see nothing that is offered by the king's counsel, nor anything as to the malice. It was presented with all the humility and decency that became the king's subjects to approach their prince with....

Justice Allybone: ... Gentlemen, consider what this petition is: this is a petition relating to something that was done and ordered by the government.... The government here has published such a declaration as this that has been read, relating to matters of government; and shall, or ought anybody to come and impeach that as illegal, which the government has done? Truly, in my opinion, I do not think he should, or ought: for by this rule may every act of the government be shaken, when there is not a Parliament *de facto* sitting.

[Verdict of the jury: Not Guilty, June 30, 1688.]

CHAPTER NINE

Later Stuart Thought and Society

Revolution Settlements Debated

Royal Personality, War, Religion, and the Rage of Party

Landed Interest versus Monied Interest, and the Reformation
  of Ideas

DISCUSSION

England teetered between anarchy and settlement for nearly fifty years from
the Long Parliament, through the Civil Wars, regicide, Restoration,
Exclusion Crisis, and regime change in 1688. And then? It depends on
your viewpoint. Religious and political turmoil continued. But many
historians have seen this as the era that laid the foundations of a
pluralistic and stable society. Social groups were pitted against each other
economically and culturally. But the economy and cultural production saw
a vast and vibrant expansion. As you read the documents in this chapter,
you might ask:

- How does the turmoil compare with that of the previous period? Was
  this society growing more or less stable?
- What faultlines remained most divisive (and which least) in later Stuart
  society? Were there ideas and institutions which helped to form a
  common English – after the Union of 1707, a British – identity?

Revolution Settlements Debated

What had happened in 1688 seemed to be clear: the political nation had risen up to
remove a king who threatened their view of the Constitution in Church and State –
and their political and religious hegemony (see chapter 8, and Bucholz and Key,
chapter 9). What should happen in 1689 to repair that Constitution was much less

clear. A Convention Parliament (that is, one called into existence by itself, not by a king) was called for January. But when John Evelyn interviewed some of its clerical and aristocratic members on the 15th, he could find no consensus:

Some would have the princess [Mary] made queen without any more dispute, others were for a regency. There was a Tory part (as then called so) who were for inviting his majesty [James II] again upon conditions; and there were republicarians, who would make the prince of Orange [William] like a state-holder [*stadholder*].[1]

In the event, the Lords punted to the Commons. There, Hugh Boscawen urged fellow MPs to issue a declaration of rights to limit the powers of the next ruler. The tough part was deciding who that should be. The Commons opted for a convenient fiction about the old king and a Whig solution on the new one. On the 23rd Evelyn

went to London. The great Convention being assembled the day before, falling upon the great question about the government, resolved that King James II, having by the advice of Jesuits and other wicked persons, endeavored to subvert the laws of Church and State, and deserting the Kingdom [carrying away the seals, etc.] without taking any care for the management of the government, had by demise, abdicated himself, and wholly vacated his right. And they did therefore desire the Lords' concurrence to their vote, to place the Crown upon the next heirs: the prince of Orange for his life, then to the princess his wife, and if she died without issue to the princess of Denmark [Anne], and she failing to the heirs of the prince, excluding for ever all possibility of admitting any Roman Catholic.

But the Tories were stronger in the Lords, where some, still devoted to passive obedience and hereditary monarchy, proposed that James remain king, the kingdom to be administered by a regent. Again, Evelyn was an eyewitness on the 29th:

I got a station by the prince's lodgings at the door of the lobby to the House, to hear much of the debate which held very long; the Lord Danby being in the chair... after all had spoken, it coming to the question: it was carried out by 3 voices, against a regency, which [many] were for, alleging the danger of dethroning kings, and scrupling many passages and expressions of the Commons' votes.... Some were for sending to his majesty with conditions, others that the king could do no wrong, and that the maladministration was chargeable on his ministers. There were not above 8 or 9 bishops and but two against the regency [that is, two bishops voted against the regency, twelve for the motion]. The archbishop was absent and the clergy now began anew to change their note, both in pulpit and discourse, upon their old passive obedience, so as people began to talk of the bishops being cast out of the House. In short, things tended to dissatisfaction on both sides; add to this the morose temper of the prince of Orange, who showed so little countenance to the noblemen and others, expecting a more gracious and cheerful reception, when they made their court. The English army likewise not so in order and firm to his interest, nor so weakened, but that it might, give interruption. Ireland in a very ill posture, as well as Scotland; nothing yet towards any settlement. God of his infinite mercy, compose these [things], that we may at last be a nation and a church under some fixt and sober establishment:

---

[1] *The Diary of John Evelyn*, ed. E. S. De Beer (Oxford, 1955), 4: 614, 616, 619, 621–2, for this and following quotes.

Why might some want a regency with James still on the throne? What were the objections to just giving the crown to William? Why might Mary seem a reasonable compromise in some eyes? How do the positions taken in the Commons debate of February 5 (document 9.1) match those Evelyn notes for the Lords?

On February 6, ironically, the anniversary of James II's accession, representatives of the Lords and Commons met to hammer out the wording of the Declaration of Rights and the disposition of the Crown. Debate first hinged on the Commons' assertion that James had "abdicated" the throne, which was, therefore, "vacant." What were the Lords' objections to these statements (previously expressed in document 9.1)? What are the implications of abdication and vacancy? Which MPs agreed with the Lords and why? Who disagreed and why? Can you detect Whig and Tory ideas in these positions?

In the end, the Whigs in the Commons won. King James's accession was ordered not to be observed, and as Evelyn noted:

The Convention of Lords and Commons now declare the prince and princess of Orange queen and king of England, France, and Ireland (Scotland being an independent kingdom). The prince and princess to enjoy it jointly during their lives, but the executive authority to be vested in the prince during life, though all proceedings to run in both names... [and to their descendants and those of Princess Anne, and, otherwise,] to devolve to the Parliament to choose as they think fit [actually, no such parliamentary role was included in the Bill of Rights].... [In a conference of the Lords with the Commons] there was much contest about the king's abdication, and whether he had vacated the government. Earl of Nottingham and about 20 lords and many bishops entered their protests, etc., but the concurrence was greater against them.

The Declaration of Rights was presented to William and Mary (reigned, 1689–1702, Mary d. 1694) at their proclamation ceremony on February 13 and enacted as a statute (as the Bill of Rights) on December 16 (document 9.2). What does it accuse James of doing? Is it fair? Accurate? How does it limit the power of future monarchs? Is this a contract? Is this constitutional monarchy?

Like the Restoration Settlement (see chapter 8), the Revolution Settlement included a series of Acts which shaped the country's constitutional, religious, and fiscal arrangements for years to come. While the Bill of Rights was the lynchpin of the Settlement, Parliament enhanced its rights with the Mutiny Act (1689, 1 Will. & Mary, c. 5), which established martial law courts for one year only (meaning that military discipline would only be maintained if Parliament renewed the law each year, thus making annual sessions a permanent part of the constitution), and the Triennial Act (1694, 6 & 7 Will. & Mary, c. 2), by which "from henceforth a Parliament shall be holden once in three years at the least," and each for three years at most (ensuring regular elections).[2]

Parliament also passed what has become known as the Toleration Act (1689, document 9.3). What does the original title of the Toleration Act suggest about its

---

[2] *SR*, 6: 510; compared with G. Holmes and W. A. Speck, eds., *The Divided Society: Parties and Politics in England, 1694–1716* (New York, 1968), 11.

intent? Who and what did it tolerate? What did it not tolerate? Parliament followed this with an Act that the Solemn Affirmation and Declaration of the People called Quakers shall be Accepted instead of an Oath in the Usual Form (1696, 7 & 8 Will. III, c. 34). How close was the religious settlement in these Acts to James II's desire to remove the Penal Laws and Test Acts?

Finally, the Act of Settlement (1701, document 9.4) dealt with the very practical problem, evident at the end of William's reign, that neither he nor his successor, Princess Anne (reigned 1702–14), would produce any children who could inherit the throne. Worse, James II had just died and Louis XIV had recognized his son, "James III," as the rightful, English monarch. How did the Act "settle" the succession while avoiding James II's son and other Catholics in line for the throne (those "in Spain, in Savoy...and where I know not," of whom Col. Birch complained, document 9.1)? The Act of Settlement revisited the problems of sovereignty debated in 1689. What did the 1701 Act suggest about the constitutional role of Parliament? What were the reasons for clauses II and III? How were they a comment on William's reign so far?

Like the Revolution of the 1640s (see chapter 7), the Glorious Revolution had its counterpart in Scotland, Ireland, and even the colonies. The Scottish one of 1688–9 began on Christmas Day 1688 with violence against incumbent Anglican clergy led by covenanting Presbyterians in Southwest Scotland. (This was revenge for the fact that Scots Presbyterianism had been practically outlawed in favor of an Anglican-style Church of Scotland at the Restoration in 1660: see Bucholz and Key, chapter 10.) There followed a Scottish Convention Parliament which settled the Crown as had been done in England. According to the Jacobite Colin Lindsay, earl of Balcarres (1652–1723), writing to the exiled James II, those attending

were in difficulties as to the manner of declaring the crown vacant. Some were for abdication, as had been done in England; but that could not pass, as the most violent could not pretend you [James II] had abdicated Scotland. Others were for making use of an old obsolete word, "fore-letting," used for a bird's forsaking her nest; but Sir John Dalrymple ended the controversy by giving such reasons against both...[and] to have it declared that by doing acts contrary to law you had forfeited your right to the crown...that you of yourself had forfeited, which would render the whole clear, and likewise remove any right the prince of Wales might afterwards pretend to. Next day it was voted [nearly] unanimously.... After the crown was declared vacant they immediately proposed the filling it; and the duke of Hamilton...proposed to make an humble offer of the crown to the prince and princess of Orange, now king and queen of England. This last vote passed more unanimously than the other declaring the throne vacant.[3]

Why would the question of whether James had abdicated be different in Scotland than in England? Why might the Scottish response be more unanimous than that in England? After settling the Crown, the Scottish Convention turned to the religious settlement, reestablishing Presbyterianism in 1690:

[3] A. Browning, ed., *English Historical Documents, 1660–1714* (New York, 1953), 247, from *Memoirs Touching the Revolution in Scotland, Presented to King James* (1841), 35–6.

their majesties, with advice and consent of the said three estates, do hereby revive, ratify, and perpetually confirm all...Acts of Parliament made against Popery and Papists, and for the maintenance and preservation of the true reformed Protestant religion, and...ratify and confirm the Presbyterian Church government and discipline, that is to say, the government of the Church by kirk sessions, presbyteries, provincial synods, and general assemblies.[4]

Compare the Scottish and English revolutionary religious settlements. Which was more tolerant?

Following King James's return in the spring of 1689, Irish Protestants faced not only a Jacobite Parliament in Dublin in 1689, but also a Jacobite army. Protestants in Londonderry (1689, document 9.5) and Enniskillen held out against James II. Compare the violence and bitterness of their resistance to the relative bloodlessness of England's revolution in 1688 (see chapter 8). Why might Ulster Protestants, who styled themselves Orangemen, remember the siege and its relief by William (of Orange) for hundreds of years after 1689? What did these events mean to them? Why do they frame Irish history to this very day?

The colonies experienced a variety of Revolutions. To take one example, Bostonians had viewed their own position under the later Stuarts as virtual slavery after their charter had been canceled and replaced by the Dominion of New England under Charles II and James II (1689, document 9.6). On May 23, 1689 the Puritan clergyman Cotton Mather preached in praise of "the late Revolutions," when Bostonians "arose as one man, seized upon Sir E. Andros the late governor," and returned "our government, into the hands of our ancient magistrates."[5] When, in 1691, his father, Increase Mather, personally pleaded with the king for the renewal of the old charter, he, too, emphasized "ancient privileges":

May it please your majesty that they may be restored to their ancient privileges, and that their settlement may be expedited..., which will cause your subjects there to be your servants forever. And your name will then be great and famous in those ends of the earth unto all posterity.[6]

How ancient could the privileges, colonial charter, and magistrates of Massachusetts have been in 1689? Why does the Declaration refer to the Magna Carta of 1215? In 1692, Increase Mather returned to Boston with a "Magna Charta" for Massachusetts signed by William and Mary, which restored charter government. But under the new charter, the governor would be appointed by the Crown, not

---

[4] *The Acts of the Parliaments of Scotland* (1822), 9: 133–4; compared with Browning, *English Historical Documents*, 640.

[5] Mather, *The Way to Prosperity. A Sermon Preached to the Honourable Convention Of the Governour, Council, and Representatives of the Massachuset-Colony in New-England; on May 23. 1689* (Boston, 1690), [sig. A2v].

[6] M. G. Hall, ed., "The Autobiography of Increase Mather," *Proceedings of the American Antiquarian Society* 71 (1962): 335; compared with M. G. Hall, L. H. Leder, and M. G. Kammen, eds., *The Glorious Revolution in America: Documents on the Colonial Crisis of 1689* (Chapel Hill, 1964), 75.

elected as under the old charter. Why did William do this? What does this say about the attitude of the English Crown to its colonies?

The Revolution Settlements in Church and State provoked debate high and low. Take, for example, the following reports from 1689. In February, a contemporary noted "the inauguration [accession day] of James II was observed by the parson in several places," contrary to law.[7] Festival days often revealed political tensions. One John Pritchard of Hereford, a wheelwright, deposed:

that upon...[11] April [William and Mary's coronation day] he had been in the country...and...in the evening did overtake Mr. Herbert Herring with his wife behind him on horseback. This deponent did pass by him and...did tell...Herring he did hope we should have good times now, he seeing so many bonfires in several places of the country....Herring...called this deponent "Damn'd dog," and "Damned rogue" and said "What do the bonfires mean and what be they for?"...This deponent replied, "So I will; they are for their majesties' coronation, are they not?" "Coronation, a turd then," answered...Herring, saying "I will crown you, you dog."[8]

That summer a judge instructed a grand jury at Hereford "that kings are made by the people," of which a contemporary observed: "The judge's charge would have been high treason eighteen months ago."[9] On November 5, 1689, the anniversary of the Catholic Gunpowder Plot of 1605 and William's landing in 1688, Gilbert Burnet, bishop of Salisbury, preached before the Lords. First, he reminded his auditors of Catholic treachery dating back to 1588. Then he argued that James II had almost succeeded where the Armada and Guy Fawkes left off because of Protestant disunity:

At last a design was laid....And when they could conceal it no longer, but that the mask must fall off, they even then could so far work on our mutual animosities as to make us instruments for doing half their work: while some were so far deluded, as to be their tools in the destroying our civil liberties, and others, who complained of the former, had yet no sooner an opportunity offered them, then they struck in to overthrow all the security that we had for our religion, under the pretense of enjoying a toleration, when the price of it was the owning a dispensing power, that must needs have devoured all in a little time.[10]

Can you distinguish Whigs, Tories, and Jacobites among the various speakers in the selections in this paragraph?

One reason that emotions ran so high over the Revolution Settlement was that it precipitated the Nine Years' War with France. In 1692, in the midst of a French invasion scare, clergyman William Sherlock (1641?–1707) defended the Williamite Revolution, and speculated about what a French victory would mean, in his *Letter to a Friend Concerning a French Invasion to Restore the Late King James to his Throne*:

[7] HMC, *Fourteenth Report, Appendix, Part II, The Manuscripts of his Grace the Duke of Portland*, III (1894), 428, Feb. 7, 1689.
[8] Hereford RO, Hereford City MSS., V, f. 75.
[9] *Portland*, III, 439, July 27.
[10] Burnet, *A Sermon Preached before the House of Peers... On the 5th of November 1689* (1689), 16–20.

He [James] wanted nothing but power to make himself absolute, and to make us all Papists, or martyrs, or refugees; and that he will now have. For if a French power can conquer us, it will make him…, though not an absolute prince, yet an absolute viceroy and minister of France. He will administer an absolute power and government under the influence and direction of French councils: and then we know what will become of the liberties and religion of England.… And whatever some fancy, they will find it a very easy and natural thing, for the late king, if he return by force and power, to make himself absolute by law. Princes always gain new powers by the ineffectual opposition of subjects.[11]

In contrast, Sir William Parkins explained Jacobite loyalty at his execution for engaging in the Assassination Plot of 1696 against William:

I freely acknowledge, and think it for my honor to say, that I was entirely in the interest of the king [James II], being always firmly persuaded of the justice of his cause, and looked upon it as my duty, both as a subject and an English-man, to assist him in the recovery of his throne, which I believed him to be deprived of, contrary to all right and justice; taking the laws and constitutions of my country for my guide.[12]

Compare and contrast these two statements: which appeals to practicality? Which to duty? How can each assert loyalty to the law and Constitution of England? Who has the more compelling case? Where would you stand in the 1690s regarding the succession to the Crown and why?

Note the interconnections between religion and politics above. Examine the report of an attack on a Presbyterian meeting house in Ludlow in 1693 (document 9.7). Why did the mob attack not only a meeting house, but also tavern signs, particularly that of "The King's Arms"? Can you characterize the religious and political affiliation of those attacking the meeting house? Of the author of the report? Of the local authorities? What does their inaction say about the problem of local control? In what way might this attack be seen as a referendum on the recent religious settlement? On the constitutional settlement? Can mobs have ideological agendas?

Royal Personality, War, Religion, and the Rage of Party

Despite the limitations placed on royal power by the Bill of Rights and Act of Settlement, royal personality remained an important factor in politics in the 1690s and 1700s. Bishop Burnet penned the following portrait of his master, the future William III, a year or two before the descent upon England in 1688:

---

[11] [Sherlock], *A Letter to a Friend* (1692), 17; compared with B. P. Lenman and J. S. Gibson, eds., *The Jacobite Threat – England, Scotland, Ireland, France: A Source Book* (Edinburgh, 1990), 65–6.

[12] Lenman and Gibson, *Jacobite Threat*, 70, from *The Tryal and Condemnation of Sir William Parkyns, Kt. for the Horrid and Execrable Conspiracy to Assassinate His Sacred Majesty King William* (n.d.).

He has a true notion of government and liberty, and does not think that subjects were made to be slaves; but after the laws and foundations of government are overturned by those who ought to maintain them, he thinks the people may assert their freedom. He is a close manager of his affairs, and though he spends much in building yet he is not thought so free-hearted and generous as a great prince ought to be. His martial inclination will naturally carry him, when he comes to the crown of England, to bear down the greatness of France. And if he but hits the nature of the English nation right at first he will be able to give laws to all Europe.... But if the prince does not in many things change his way he will hardly gain the hearts of the nation. His coldness will look like contempt, and that the English cannot bear; and they are impatient to digest that slowness that is almost become natural to him in the most inconsiderable things, and his silent way will pass for superciliousness. But that which is more important, he will be both the king of England and *stadholder*. The Dutch will perhaps think a king of England too great to be their *stadholder*, and the English will hardly be brought to trust a prince that has an army of 30,000 men at his command so near them.[13]

What were William's strengths and weaknesses as a potential king of England? How do you suppose he "played" to his subjects? (Compare your speculation with Bucholz and Key, chapter 10.)

Upon William's death in 1702 he was succeeded by his sister-in-law and James II's last living daughter, Anne. Consider her speeches from the year of her accession (1702, document 9.8) at the beginning of the War of the Spanish Succession (1702–14, see Bucholz and Key, chapter 10). She delivered the March 11 speech, her first to Parliament, wearing a gown closely resembling one worn by Queen Elizabeth in a famous portrait. How was her speech calculated to emphasize the comparison to the glorious memory of Elizabeth? How might it have been calculated to contrast Anne with her predecessor? Which groups would have been most pleased by her May 25 speech? Which least? Did this speech contradict itself in any way? (Consider what Anglican zeal might entail.)

Like William, Anne wanted to rule with the support of both Whigs and Tories. She expected politicians to adhere to a higher loyalty when they served her, as she indicated in a letter of August 30, 1706, rejecting Lord Treasurer Godolphin's advice regarding an appointment to her cabinet:

I must own freely to you, I am of the opinion, that making a party man secretary of state, when there are so many of their friends in employment of all kinds already, is throwing myself into the hands of a party, which is a thing I have been desirous to avoid. Maybe some may think I would be willing to be in the hands of the Tories...; but...I am not inclined, nor [n]ever will be, to employ any of the violent persons, that have behaved themselves so ill towards me. All I desire is, my liberty in encouraging and employing all those that concur faithfully in my service, whether they are called Whigs or Tories, not to be tied to one nor the other. For if I should be so unfortunate as to fall into the hands of either, I shall not imagine myself, though I have the name of queen, to be in reality but their slave, which as it will be my personal ruin, so it will be the destroying all government; for

---

[13] H. C. Foxcroft, ed., *A Supplement to Burnet's History of My Own Time* (Oxford, 1902), 192–3; compared with Browning, *English Historical Documents*, 905.

instead of putting an end to faction, it will lay a lasting foundation for it. You press the bringing Lord Sunderland into business, that there may be one of that party in a place of trust, to help carry on the business this winter; and you think if this is not complied with, they will not be hearty in pursuing my service in Parliament. But is it not very hard that men of sense and honor will not promote the good of their country because everything in the world is not done that they desire!…Why, for God's sake, must I, who have no interest, no end, no thought, but for the good of my country, be made so miserable, as to be brought into the power of one set of men?[14]

Was Anne closer to being a Whig, a Tory, or neither? What was her great fear? What does her letter imply about the strength of party loyalties versus those to the sovereign?

Anne had her work cut out for her, for the politics of this period are usually referred to as "the Rage of Party." Still, it is important to remember that many MPs, even those nominally Whig or Tory, saw themselves as above partisanship and independent or uncommitted "Country members" (as opposed to a "Court" bloc that William and Mary sought to build). The following assessment of English politics was written for the elector of Brandenburg, December 17, 1700:

Though the English are nearly all divided into Whigs and Tories, there are many country members in Parliament who have never joined with these parties to the extent of closely espousing either. These men speak and vote in the House according to their lights, which rarely reach beyond the shores of their own island. The principles which govern their reasoning are their care for

1. the religion of this country

2. the liberty of the individual

3. the trade which enhances the value of their produce, and

4. the cultivation of their lands.

No matter which is the party in power, and no matter how eloquent its appeal may be, it will never win over these members unless it can convince them that one of these four points is under attack.[15]

As you consider the positions of Whigs and Tories, which would appeal to the independent Country members, and why?

The key to religion, individual liberty, the profitability of trade and land and, indeed, the succession itself, was war, specifically the War of the Spanish Succession and the taxes needed to finance it. For many years victory followed victory, from the duke of Marlborough's brilliant defeat of the French army at Blenheim (1704), Ramillies (1706), and Oudenarde (1708), to the capture of Gibraltar in

---

[14]   W. Coxe, *Memoirs of the Duke of Marlborough*, rev. ed. (1893), 2: 2–3; compared with W. C. Costin and J. S. Watson, eds., *The Law and Working of the Constitution: Documents, 1660–1914*, 2nd ed. (1961), 359–40.

[15]   Holmes and Speck, *Divided Society*, 19, from BL, Add. MSS. 30,000 D, f. 363, F. Bonet to Frederick III, elector of Brandenburg (trans.).

1704 and Port Mahon, Minorca, in 1708. Following the last, Lieutenant General James Stanhope wrote to Charles, earl of Sunderland, upon the strategic significance of this prize:

I hope the want [lack] of ports will no longer be an objection to wintering a squadron here, her majesty being now mistress of the two best ports in the Mediterranean, this and Fornelles in the same island, which though not so much known is by many seamen preferred to this.... This consideration makes me offer it as my humble opinion that England ought never to part with this island, which will give the law to the Mediterranean both in time of war and peace.[16]

What is Stanhope's vision of England's – since the 1707 Union with Scotland, Britain's – role in the world?

At first, the war barely affected the economy. But by 1711 polemicists like the Tory churchman Jonathan Swift (1667–1745) came to feel that it was enriching new men at the expense of the old landed families (document 9.9). Who were these new men? How might the war have a different impact on the uncommitted Country members and the landed interest than on the generals and monied interest? Between Whig and Tory? What, in Swift's view, was the role of the queen's favorites, the duke and duchess of Marlborough, and Sidney, Lord Godolphin? If Swift was right, how did their power compare to Wolsey's or Buckingham's? Why were favorites thought to be destructive to the Constitution? What made them so unpopular?

Popularity and public opinion mattered during this period as never before. Between 1690 and 1715, Whigs and Tories fought for the votes of a growing electorate, and over an increasing number of elections. More general elections occurred between 1690 and 1715 than ever before or since. And more individual seats were contested then than in any other period of British history until the first decades of the twentieth century. One way to influence those elections was for great aristocratic landowners to pressure their tenants and clients to vote as directed (for most constituencies, each voter had two votes). Thus, the Whig Sarah Churchill, duchess of Marlborough (1660–1744), tried to influence the 1705 election at St. Albans, her family seat (document 9.10). If aristocratic and party loyalties were so powerful, why was it important for her to claim to represent "the queen's interest and the good of the nation"? How convincing were those claims? What does this document tell us about the relationship between the ruling elite and those they ruled?

Another way to influence elections was through propaganda. After the lapse of the Licensing Act in 1695, newspapers were an important source for partisan comment – *The Post Boy* for Tories; *The Flying Post* and *The Post Man* for Whigs – and for creation of an audience through advertisements, as in the *Daily Courant*, the first daily from 1702 (1708 and 1710, document 9.11). Note the two advertisements regarding the 1708 elections for London. What do such advertisements tell us

[16] Sept. 30, *The Byng Papers* (1931), ed. B. Tunstall, 2: 301; compared with Browning, *English Historical Documents*, 586–7.

about politics in the period? About the electorate? What did it mean for the candidates to claim to be "well known to be zealously affected to her majesty's person and government both in Church and State, and to the Protestant succession as by law established"? The London poll of May 14, 1708 was as follows (the top four were returned as MPs):

Sir William Withers (T)	3,189 votes
Sir William Ashurst (W)	3,209
Sir Gilbert Heathcote (W)	3,216
John Ward (T)	3,353
Sir Samuel Stanier (W)	3,012
Sir John Buckworth (W)	2,284
Sir Richard Hoare (T)	2,245
Sir Francis Child (T)	2,026

Buckworth withdrew halfway through the polling and directed his supporters to Stanier.[17] Each London voter had four votes, though he didn't have to use them all. What do the engagements from the advertisements and the results tell you about voting patterns? From the election reports for 1710, what appears to have been the chief electoral issue? Can you document the political bias of *The Post Boy*?

Apart from elections, the greatest *cause célèbre* of Anne's final years was the impeachment of Dr. Henry Sacheverell (ca. 1674–1724) and his trial (1710, document 9.12). Sacheverell had preached a sermon, "The Perils of False Brethren, both in Church and State," on November 5, 1709. He took the opportunity of the anniversary both of the Gunpowder Plot of 1605 and William's landing in 1688 to assert that "the grand security of our government, and the very pillar upon which it stands, is founded upon the steady belief in the subject's obligation to an absolute and unconditional obedience to the supreme power." What does this say about the Revolution of 1688? If anyone missed the point, he portrayed the Marlborough–Godolphin ministry, Whigs, Low Church Anglicans, and occasionally conforming Dissenters as

sworn adversaries to passive obedience, and the royal family..., [in whom] the old leaven of their forefathers is still working in their present generation, and...this traditional poison still remains in this brood of vipers to sting us to death.... And what better could have been expected from miscreants, begot in rebellion, born in sedition, and nursed up in faction?[18]

How different was this message from that of Bishop Burnet's November 5 sermon, above? Can you see why the Whig ministry felt itself compelled to

---

[17] E. Cruickshanks, S. Handley, and D. W. Hayton, *The History of Parliament. The House of Commons, 1690–1715* (Cambridge, 2002), 2: 374.

[18] Sacheverell, *The Perils of False Brethren*, in T. B. Howell, comp., *A Complete Collection of State Trials* (1816), 15: 79, 84, 87–8.

impeach him as they did in December? The trial began in the House of Lords on February 27: how do the arguments for the prosecution and the defense differ? How different were their views of 1688? At the end of March 1710, the Lords found Sacheverell guilty by 69 to 52 votes. They suspended him from preaching for three years and ordered his sermons burnt by the common hangman. While this barely satiated Whig desires, it made him a martyr in the eyes of the populace (see plate 12). Indeed, by November, papers carried advertisements for "Music just published. The True Loyalist's Health to the Church, Queen, Dr. Sacheverell, and the new Loyal Members of Parliament; price 2d."[19] Note the case of Daniel Dammarree [Damarie], a royal waterman (bargeman), arrested for his part in the attack on meeting houses after the Sacheverell indictment was announced (1710, document 9.13). Why might he have thought that attacking a Presbyterian meeting house was not inconsistent with his status as a royal servant? That is, why might he have thought that Anne, too, was for "High Church and Sacheverell"? Why did he lose his job? What does this case say about popular politics in the age of Anne? Compare it with the attack on a Ludlow meeting house from 1693 (9.7). In light of these attacks, how convinced are you of the assertion, made by some historians, that the dawn of the eighteenth century saw a rise of secularism and a decline in religious politics? (Before answering that, you might want to read Locke's *Letter Concerning Toleration*, document 9.18, below.)

Landed Interest versus Monied Interest, and the Reformation of Ideas

As we shall see, late Stuart contemporaries were very concerned with the issue of wealth from cities and trade. But it is important to recall that at least 80 percent of the population continued to live in the countryside ca. 1700. And, at the apex of the rural social structure still stood the landed interest: the relatively few nobles and the more numerous landed gentry. The gentry's influence (see Bucholz and Key, Conclusion) could be seen in art, dress, the architecture of country estates, and, increasingly, in the culture of country towns and spas. Celia Fiennes (1662–1741) traveled throughout much of England from the 1680s to the early 1700s, and her journal was published in the nineteenth century. About 1697, she visited one of these resorts, Tunbridge Wells.

They have made the wells very commodious by the many good buildings all about it and 2 or 3 mile round, which are lodgings for the company that drink the waters, and they have increased their buildings so much that makes them very cheap; all people buy their own provision at the market which is just by the wells and furnished with great plenty of all sorts flesh, fowl, and fish, and in great plenty is brought from Rye and Deal, etc., this being the road to London, so all the season the water is drank they stop here which makes it very cheap, as also the country people come with all their back yard and barn door affords, to

---

[19]   *The Post Boy*, no. 2415, Nov. 2–4, 1710.

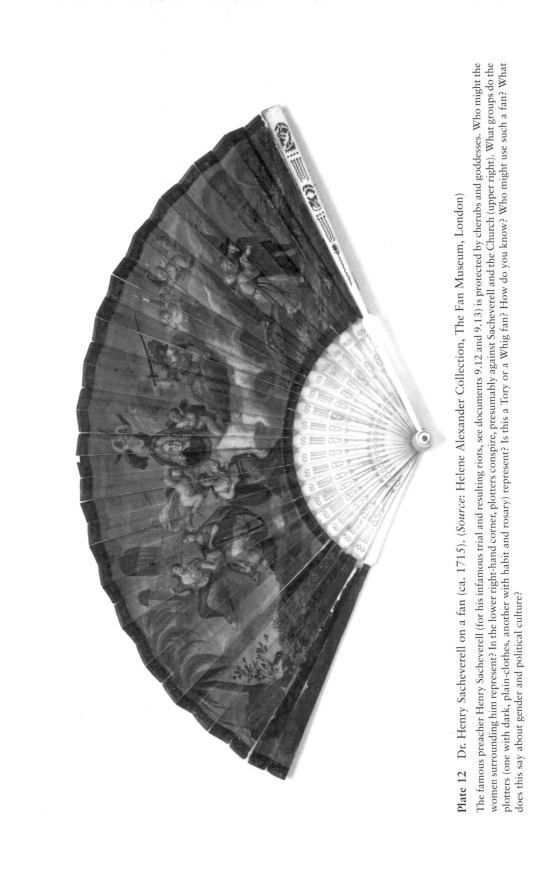

Plate 12 Dr. Henry Sacheverell on a fan (ca. 1715). (*Source:* Helene Alexander Collection, The Fan Museum, London)

The famous preacher Henry Sacheverell (for his infamous trial and resulting riots, see documents 9.12 and 9.13) is protected by cherubs and goddesses. Who might the women surrounding him represent? In the lower right-hand corner, plotters conspire, presumably against Sacheverell and the Church (upper right). What groups do the plotters (one with dark, plain-clothes, another with habit and rosary) represent? Is this a Tory or a Whig fan? How do you know? Who might use such a fan? What does this say about gender and political culture?

supply them with, and their gardens and orchards which makes the markets well stored and provision cheap, which the gentry takes as a diversion while drinking the waters to go and buy their dinners it being every day's market and runs the whole length of the walk, which is between high trees on the market side for shade and secured with a row of buildings on the right side which are shops full of all sorts of toys, silver, china, milliners, and all sorts of curious wooden ware, which this place is noted for the delicate neat and thin ware of wood both white and Lignum vitae wood [inlay work]. Besides which there are two large coffeehouses for tea, chocolate, etc., and two rooms for the lottery and hazard board [gambling game with dice]. These are all built with an arch or pent house beyond the shops some of which are supported by pillars like a peasa [piazza], which is paved with brick and stone for the dry walking of the company in rain.[20]

Why did the gentry visit Tunbridge Wells? Is this the beginning of a consumer economy? What was the relation between town and country?

The great estates in the countryside depended upon careful management of land and marriage, especially as rental values remained depressed for about a century after 1640. Land could be consolidated at marriage, especially as the gentry followed a fairly strict pattern of primogeniture. But that meant that younger sons had to be found alternate careers, which meant, in turn, that the division between landed and non-landed families was porous. These realities permeate the *Huntington Divertisement, or, an Enterlude For the Generall Entertainment at the County-Feast*, held in London in June 1678 (document 9.14). The masque-like *Divertisement* reflects the concerns of its audience, who celebrated their "country," Huntingdonshire, at an annual London feast. How does the author contrast the country and the city? How does he contrast the elder son, Ralph, with his younger brothers, Richard and Thomas? How do their fates differ? What opportunities were there for younger sons? What does "young brothers oft make the best gentlemen" mean? How, then, does the author define gentlemen or gentry? Daniel Defoe (1660?–1731) comments on the blurred boundary between gentlemen and others through the title character of his novel *Moll Flanders* (1721). Moll, who had hidden her own humble background, sought to marry a London draper who acted like a landed squire:

I was not averse to a tradesman, but then I would have a tradesman, forsooth, that was something of a gentleman too; that when my husband had a mind to carry me to the court, or to the play, he might become a sword, and look as like a gentleman as another man; and not be one that had the mark of his apron-strings upon his coat, or the mark of his hat upon his periwig; that should look as if he was set on to his sword, when his sword was put on to him, and that carried his trade in his countenance.

Well, at last I found this amphibious creature, this land-water thing called a gentleman-tradesman; and as a just plague upon my folly, I was catched in the very snare which, as I might say, I laid for myself.[21]

<hr/>

[20]   C. Morris, ed., *The Journeys of Celia Fiennes* (1949), 132–5; compared with R. C. Richardson and T. B. James, eds., *The Urban Experience, a Sourcebook: English, Scottish and Welsh Towns, 1450–1700* (Manchester, 1983), 29.

[21]   Defoe, *The Fortunes and Misfortunes of the Famous Moll Flanders* (New York, 1964), 56.

Why might marrying someone like the draper be "folly"? What problem does the "gentleman-tradesman" reveal? By this definition, who is of gentle status?

The distinction between the landed and the non-landed had a political component. As one pamphlet from the 1720s recalled, "It was not many years ago, since an unhappy distinction was set on foot, between the landed and the money'd interest."[22] In 1709, Henry St. John, Viscount Bolingbroke (1678–1751), developed the distinction at length, with a lament that many landed gentlemen would endorse during Anne's reign:

We have now been twenty years engaged in the two most expensive wars that Europe ever saw. The whole burden of this charge has lain upon landed interest during the whole time. The men of estates have, generally speaking, neither served in the fleets nor armies, nor meddled in the public funds and management of the treasure.

A new interest has been created out of their fortunes, and a sort of property which was not known twenty years ago is now increased to almost equal to the *terra firma* of our island. The consequence of all this is that the landed men are become poor and dispirited. They either abandon all thoughts of the public, turn arrant farmers and improve their estates they have left; or else they seek to repair their shattered fortunes by [en-]listing at Court, or under the head of parties. In the meanwhile those men are become their masters, who formerly with joy would have been their servants.[23]

What did the war have to do with the fate of the landed classes? The monied interest? How was the difference between them political? How was it social?

The English were fascinated with how the monied interest worked, whether they lauded or decried it. *The Spectator* often lauded it (1711, document 9.15, written by Joseph Addison). Why does Addison (1672–1719) take such satisfaction in the Royal Exchange? What is so good about trade? How did the Royal Exchange reinforce a hierarchical social order? How did it bring the order into question? The relation between landed interest and monied interest was repeated in microcosm in the relation between London and Westminster, between the East End and the West End, between City and Court. Note Defoe on this relationship, ca. 1726:

The City is the center of its commerce and wealth. The Court of its gallantry and splendor. The out-parts [suburbs] of its numbers and mechanics [manual workers]; and in all these, no city in the world can equal it. Between the Court and the City, there is a constant communication of business to that degree, that nothing in the world can come up to it.[24]

---

[22]   J. Hoppit, *A Land of Liberty?: England, 1689–1727* (Oxford, 2000), 365, from *Considerations on Publick Credit* (1724), 6.

[23]   G. Holmes, *British Politics in the Age of Anne* (1967, 1987), 177, from Bodleian Library, MS. Eng.misc.e.180, ff. 4–5.

[24]   Defoe, *A Tour Through the Whole Island of Great Britain* (1724–6), ed. P. N. Furbank and W. R. Owens (New Haven, 1991), 144; compared with A. N. Wilson, ed., *The Norton Book of London* (New York, 1993), 432–4.

Compare Defoe's description of London with that of Tom Brown (1663–1704) from 1700:

"While I behold this town of London," said our contemplative traveler, "I fancy I behold a prodigious animal. The streets are so many veins, wherein the people circulate. With what hurry and swiftness is the circulation of London performed?" "You behold," cried I to him, "the circulation that is made in the heart of London, but it moves more briskly in the blood of the citizens; they are always in motion and activity. Their actions succeed one another with so much rapidity that they begin a thousand things before they have finished one, and finish a thousand others before they may properly be said to have begun them."[25]

What types of "circulation" do the two commentators highlight? Can you see the influence of the scientific revolution in these descriptions?

Not every form of London commerce was respectable or beneficent, as Sir Richard Steele (1662–1729) noted in one issue of *The Spectator* (1712, document 9.16). The woman he meets was probably one of the 8,000 new immigrants who came to London every year. What has happened to her? Why do you suppose she has opted for this life? *The Spectator* was often viewed, even in its own time, as sexist (later, a *Female Spectator* arose in response). In this case, would you describe Steele's response as sexist or proto-feminist? Was he "wholly unconcerned" with the plight of the young girl? Is there a humanitarian ethos here, and, if so, what should be done? The connection between urban capitalism and urban vice was most memorably drawn by Bernard Mandeville (1670–1733), a Dutch writer who lived in London. He portrayed his adopted city as a corrupt yet prosperous beehive in his *Fable of the Bees* (1714).

> Luxury
> Employ'd a Million of the Poor,
> And odious Pride a Million more:
> Envy it self, and Vanity,
> Were Ministers of Industry;
> Their darling Folly, Fickleness,
> In Diet, Furniture and Dress,
> That strange ridic'lous Vice, was made
> The very Wheel that turn'd the Trade.
> Their Laws and Clothes were equally
> Objects of Mutability;
> For, what was well done for a time,
> In half a Year became a Crime....
> Thus Vice nurs'd Ingenuity,
> Which join'd with Time and Industry,
> Had carry'd Life's Conveniences,
> It's [sic] real Pleasures, Comforts, Ease,

---

[25] Brown, *Amusements Serious and Comical, and Other Works*, ed. A. L. Hayward (New York, 1927), 20–1; compared with R. Allen, *The Moving Pageant: A Literary Sourcebook on London Street-Life, 1700–1914* (1998), 31.

> To such a height, the very Poor
> Liv'd better than the Rich before.[26]

Is this a defense of capitalism? Does the author approve of London's vices? Does the fact that the subtitle of his "Fable" is "Private Vices, Public Benefits" change your answer? (It should be noted that Mandeville also wrote in favor of public stews, that is, regulated brothels, and against charity schools, as educating the poor would only render them unfit for the menial jobs for which they were destined.)

Private vice called out movements to promote public virtue. On January 21, 1692, William and Mary issued a proclamation against profaneness and immorality. A subsequent reissue inspired one London preacher in 1698 to urge his auditors to:

strike in with his majesty's late Proclamation against atheism, irreligion and profaneness: and let the World, to the eternal honor of our county, see we make it our study to execute aright his royal will, and gracious directions; and to lend him in this (as we have in every thing else) our utmost assistance in promoting the glory of God, and the public welfare of this nation.[27]

This humanitarian and reform ethos was echoed in the activities of the Societies for the Reformation of Manners (from 1690), the Society for Promoting Christian Knowledge (1699), the Society for the Propagation of the Gospel in Foreign Parts (1702), and SPCK charity schools (1704). The Societies for the Reformation of Manners encouraged members to inform on their neighbors to local authorities to help enforce laws against vice. Josiah Woodward (1660–1712), in his history of the societies published 1698, defended their actions, such as, among other attacks on swearing, drunkenness, and fornication, having been "instrumental to put down several music-houses which had degenerated into nurseries of lewdness and debauchery"; "God is preparing the way of a more general Reformation of Manners among us," he noted.[28] Woodward "acknowledge[d] the brotherly assistance which is given us by some of our dissenting brethren (especially those of the Presbyterian persuasion)," as well as Archbishop Tillotson's "opinion publicly...that these societies were a support to our Church." Why did Anglicans and Dissenters come together in these societies? Why might others object to their activities? How do those activities reconcile with older notions of neighborliness (see chapter 5, and Bucholz and Key, chapter 6)?

It is, of course, impossible to determine whether the English were more or less virtuous under the late Stuarts than under the early Tudors. Nor is it easy to pin down whether England was more or less disorderly in 1700 than in 1500

---

[26] Mandeville, *The Fable of the Bees: Or, Private Vices, Public Benefits*, ed. F. B. Kaye (Oxford, 1924, reprinted Indianapolis, 1988), 25–6.

[27] J. Petter, *A Sermon Preach'd before the Honourable Society of the Natives of the County of Kent* (1698), 21.

[28] Woodward, *Account of the Rise and Progress*, 2nd ed. (1698), 21, 63–4, 79, 85, 133.

(compare the documents in this chapter with those in chapters 1 and 5). But many contemporaries were in no doubt that England was richer and more populous. Take, for example, Sir William Petty (1690, document 9.17). What did Petty (1623–87) think was the basis for a nation's power and wealth? What appears to have been the effect of the Civil Wars and Glorious Revolution on that power and wealth? In explaining them, why does he describe Negroes as "men of great labor and little expense"? How had the "late tumults in Ireland" affected England's might? What was the human cost of such power and wealth?

Petty, one of the new theorists of "political arithmetick" and co-founder of the Royal Society for the Improvement of Natural Knowledge (chartered 1662, though its roots stretch back to the 1640s), is a prime exemplar of the use of reason and experiment to understand human nature and society in later Stuart England. Petty claimed that "instead of using only comparative and superlative words and intellectual arguments, I have taken the course . . . to express myself in terms of number, weight, or measure; to use only arguments of sense, and to consider only such causes, as have visible foundations in nature."[29] John Aubrey (1626–97), author of a number of idiosyncratic biographies collected later as *Brief Lives*, wrote about Petty, his contemporary and acquaintance. What does Aubrey find most significant about Petty in the selection below? How does this biographical information square with Petty's own words (above and document 9.17)?

[In] 1663 he made his double-bottomed vessel . . . , of which he gave a model to the Royal Society made with his own hands, and it is kept in the repository at Gresham College. It did do very good service, but *anno* 16__ happened to be lost in an extraordinary storm in the Irish sea. . . .

He is a person of an admirable inventive head, and practical parts. He hath told me that he hath read but little, that is to say not since twenty-five [years of age] and is of Mr. Hobbes' his mind, that had he read much, as some men have, he had not known so much as he does; nor should have made such discoveries and improvements. . . .

I remember one St. Andrew's day (which is the day of the general meeting of the Royal Society for annual elections) I said, methought 'twas not so well that we should pitch upon the patron of Scotland's day; we should rather have taken St. George, or St. Isidore (a philosopher canonized). "No," said Sir William, "I would rather have had it been on St. Thomas's day, for he would not believe till he had seen and put his fingers into the holes, according to the motto [of the Royal Society] *Nullius in Verba* [Trust no man's word]."[30]

More famous and more influential on the period than Petty was John Locke (1632–1704). Locke was physician and secretary to the earl of Shaftesbury, and it was, perhaps, the great Whig who inspired him to write his *Two Treatises on Government* in the early 1680s, which were modified slightly when published

[29]   C. H. Hull, ed., *The Economic Writings of Sir William Petty* (Cambridge, 1899), 1: 244; compared with R. Porter, *The Creation of the Modern World: The Untold Story of the British Enlightenment* (New York, 2000), 54.

[30]   Aubrey, *Brief Lives*, ed. A. Powell (1949), 271–2; compared with *Brief Lives*, ed. J. Buchanan-Brown (Harmondsworth, Middlesex, 2000), 401–2.

after the Glorious Revolution to justify the overthrow of James and setting up of William. But such a justification of the use of force by the people was too radical for widespread acceptance and Locke published it anonymously. Instead, his fame rested on his other works which fit the new spirit of rational, calm enquiry adopted by much of the intellectual elite. Newton's *Optiks* (1704), which delineated principles (and the particles) that light obeys, had its analog in thinking about man in Locke's *Essay Concerning Human Understanding* (1690), which used visual metaphor to explain the thought process.

Methinks the understanding is not much unlike a closet wholly shut from light, with only some little opening left, to let in external visible resemblances, or ideas of things without: would the pictures coming into a dark room but stay there, and lie so orderly as to be found upon occasion, it would very much resemble the understanding of a man.[31]

During this early Enlightenment, supporters such as Catherine Cockburn, with her *Defence of Mr. Locke's Essay on the Human Understanding* (1702), popularized Locke's views. How might such a view of the mind, shaped by external stimulus, affect views of government? Of education? Of religion?

Locke's *The Reasonableness of Christianity* (1695), embraced by Latitudinarian bishops and lay writers, downplayed religious fervor ("enthusiasm") in favor of reason and tolerance. Such an enterprise laid the foundations of the English Enlightenment. Even such a conservative upholder of the status quo as Thomas Sprat, in his *History of the Royal Society* (1667), noted "the universal disposition of this age is bent upon a rational religion."[32] How does Locke's *Letter Concerning Toleration* (1685, pub. 1689, document 9.18) reflect the use of scientific method in questions of religion? How might it have influenced the Revolution Settlement, particularly the Toleration Act (document 9.3)? What view of the government is shown in the *Letter*? Of course, promoting toleration and rational religion could easily lead to anticlericalism. As John Toland, author of *Christianity Not Mysterious* (1695), wrote in 1700:

> Religion's safe, with priestcraft is the war,
> All friends to priestcraft, foes of mankind are.[33]

One might consider what Sacheverell thought about Locke and Toland, and vice versa. Also, how is Locke both a conservative and a radical thinker?

Defoe was the great optimist of first England's and then Britain's (for he supported the Union with Scotland in 1707) progress through trade. While even he noted in 1724 how London's growth tended to starve other, lesser cities of

---

[31] Locke, *Essay Concerning Human Understanding*, book 2, ch. 11, para. 17, in *The Works of John Locke* (1823), 1: 152; compared with Porter, *Creation of the Modern World*, 63.

[32] Porter, *Creation of the Modern World*, 96, from Sprat, *History*, 334.

[33] M. Goldie, "Priestcraft and the Birth of Whiggism," in *Political Discourse in Early Modern Britain*, ed. N. Phillipson and Q. Skinner (Cambridge, 1993), 218; compared with Porter, *Creation of the Modern World*, 110.

trade and population, he argued that, in the end, the war, and the trading boom it spawned, produced plenty of wealth to go around:

But the neighborhood of London, which sucks the vitals of trade in this island to itself, is the chief reason of any decay of business in this place [East Anglia]; and I shall, in the course of these observations, hint at it, where many good seaports and large towns, though farther off than Ipswich, and as well fitted for commerce, are yet swallowed up by the immense in-draft of trade to the city of London; and more decayed beyond all comparison than Ipswich is supposed to be: as Southampton, Weymouth, Dartmouth, and several others which I shall speak to in their order. And if it be otherwise at this time, with some other towns, which are lately increased in trade and navigation, wealth, and people, while their neighbors decay, it is because they have some particular trade, or accident to trade, which is a kind of nostrum to them, inseparable to the place, and which fixes there by the nature of the thing; as the herring-fishery to Yarmouth; the coal trade to Newcastle; the Leeds clothing trade; the export of butter and lead, and the great corn trade for Holland, is to Hull; the Virginia and West India trade at Liverpool; the Irish trade at Bristol, and the like. Thus the war has brought a flux of business and people, and consequently of wealth, to several places, as well as to Portsmouth, Chatham, Plymouth, Falmouth, and others.[34]

Ultimately, for Defoe, as for most of the (propertied) inhabitants of early modern England, wealth was based on secure property. The political, religious, and social struggles of the preceding two centuries had in many ways been about precisely that: "Pray, what is a liberty – but a freedom to possess property, a liberty to enjoy it, and a right to defend it."[35] Which of the authors of the many sources you have read would agree or disagree with Defoe?

HISTORIOGRAPHY

Debate on the Revolution Settlements hinges – as it did at the time – on how one defines the Glorious Revolution. For the historiography of the Glorious Revolution, see works mentioned in chapter 8, especially R. Beddard, "The Unexpected Whig Revolution of 1688," and M. Goldie, "The Political Thought of the Anglican Revolution," in *The Revolutions of 1688*, ed. Beddard (Oxford, 1991); W. A. Speck, "William – and Mary?," in *The Revolution of 1688–1689: Changing Perspectives*, ed. L. G. Schwoerer (Cambridge, 1992); and Speck, "Some Consequences of the Glorious Revolution," in *The World of William and Mary: Anglo-Dutch Perspectives on the Revolution of 1688–89*, ed. D. E. Hoak and M. Feingold (Stanford, 1996). See also J. C. D. Clark, "1688: Glorious Revolution or Glorious Reaction?," in *Fabrics and Fabrications: The Myth and Making of William and Mary*, ed. C. C. Barfoot and P. Hoftijzer (Amsterdam, 1990);

---

[34] Defoe, *A Tour Through the Whole Island*, 17.
[35] *Review*, 5, no. 158, March 31, 1709; compared with P. Langford, *Public Life and the Propertied Englishman, 1689–1798* (Oxford, 1991), 4.

H. T. Dickinson, "The Debate on the 'Glorious Revolution,'" *History* 61 (1976); J. Childs, "1688," *History* 73 (1988); H. Horwitz, "1689 (And All That)," *PH* 6 (1987); J. R. Hertzler, "Who Dubbed it 'the Glorious Revolution'?," *Albion* 19 (1987); and G. Holmes, ed., *Britain after the Glorious Revolution, 1689–1714* (1969), which collection might be profitably compared with C. Jones, ed., *Britain in the First Age of Party* (1987).

Were the Tory and Whig parties under William and Anne responding to an aware and independent electorate? That party allegiance was strong and deep is the argument of G. S. Holmes, J. H. Plumb, and W. A. Speck, in classic, full-length studies, and in essays, such as Holmes, *The Electorate and the National Will in the First Age of Party* (Lancaster, 1976); his collected essays, *Politics, Religion and Society in England, 1672–1742* (1986); Holmes, "Revolution, War and Politics, 1689–1714," in *Stuart England*, ed. B. Worden (Oxford, 1986); Plumb, "The Growth of the Electorate in England from 1600 to 1715," *P & P* 45 (1969); and Speck, "The Electorate in the First Age of Party," in Jones, *Britain in the First Age of Party*. (Plumb's thesis of the growth of political stability between 1675 and 1725 is reconsidered in *Albion* 25, 1993, by C. Roberts, S. Baxter, and N. Landau.) But J. C. D. Clark has argued that party politics was played mainly at the higher levels, with little attention to popular reaction, and that, in any case, monarchy, a landed aristocracy, and a monolithic Anglican Church dominated politics. See his *English Society 1660–1832: Religion, Ideology and Politics During the Ancien Regime*, 2nd ed. (Cambridge, 1985, 2000), and "England's Ancien Régime as a Confessional State," *Albion* 21 (1989).

Party organization and ideology are discussed in P. Jenkins, "Party Conflict and Political Stability in Monmouthshire, 1690–1740," *HJ* 29 (1986); Jenkins, *The Making of a Ruling Class: Glamorgan Gentry, 1640–1790* (Cambridge, 1983); H. Horwitz, "The 1690s Revisited: Recent Work on Politics and Political Ideas in the Reign of William III," *PH* 15 (1996); D. Hayton, "The 'Country' Interest and the Party System, *c*.1689–1720," in *Party and Party Management in Parliament 1660–1784*, ed. C. Jones (Leicester, 1984); C. R. Roberts, "The Constitutional Significance of the Financial Settlement of 1690," *HJ* 20, 1 (1977); J. P. Kenyon, *Revolution Principles: The Politics of Party, 1689–1720* (Cambridge, 1977); and Kenyon, "The Revolution of 1688: Resistance and Contract," in *Historical Perspectives: Studies in English Thought and Society in Honour of J. H. Plumb*, ed. N. McKendrick (1974).

An important phenomenon, which tempers any tendency to view the period after the Glorious Revolution as a progressive, modernizing one, is that of Jacobitism; see J. C. D. Clark, "On Moving the Middle Ground: The Significance of Jacobitism in Historical Studies," in *The Jacobite Challenge*, ed. E. Cruickshanks and J. Black (Edinburgh, 1988); P. Monod, "Jacobitism and Country Principles in the Reign of William III," *HJ* 30 (1987); E. Cruickshanks and E. T. Corp, eds., *The Stuart Court in Exile and the Jacobites* (1995), especially Cruickshanks, "Attempts to Restore the Stuarts, 1689–96"; D. Szechi, "The Jacobite Revolution Settlement, 1689–1696," *EHR* 108 (1993); and E. Cruickshanks, ed., *Ideology and Conspiracy: Aspects of Jacobitism, 1689–1759* (Edinburgh, 1982), especially P. Hopkins, "Sham Plots and Real Plots in the 1690s." The revisionist alternatives to the Whig view of the Revolution Settlement, however, are in turn questioned in G. V. Bennett, "English Jacobitism, 1710–1715: Myth and Reality," *TRHS* 5th ser., 32 (1982); C. Jones, "Evidence, Interpretation and Definitions in Jacobite Historiography: A Reply to Eveline Cruickshanks," *EHR* 113 (1998); and E. Gregg, "Was Queen Anne a Jacobite?," *History* 57 (1972).

Mary has been better served recently by historians than William. See B. Bevan, *King William III: Prince of Orange, the First European* (1997); J. Van den Berg, "Religion and Politics in the Life of William and Mary," in Barfoot and Hoftijzer; and M. Zook, "History's Mary: The Propagation of Queen Mary II, 1689–1694," in *Women and Sovereignty*, ed. L. O. Fradenburg (Edinburgh, 1992). Anne's court politics are well analyzed in E. Gregg, *Queen Anne*, new ed. (New Haven, 2001); F. Harris, "'The Honourable Sisterhood': Queen Anne's Maids of Honor," *British Library Journal* 19 (1993); and R. O. Bucholz, "'Nothing but Ceremony': Queen Anne and the Limitations of Royal Ritual," *JBS* 30, 3 (1991).

For the relation of the Reformation of Manners to party politics, see D. Hayton, "Moral Reform and Country Politics in the Late Seventeenth-Century House of Commons," *P & P* 128 (1990); T. C. Curtis and W. A. Speck, "The Societies for the Reformation of Manners: A Case Study in the Theory and Practice of Moral Reform," *Literature and History* 3 (1976); and J. Spurr, "The Church, the Societies and the Moral Revolution of 1688," in *The Church of England, c.1689–c.1833: From Toleration to Tractarianism*, ed. J. Walsh, C. Haydon, and S. Taylor (Cambridge, 1993).

Was England in 1700 dominated by an established landed interest or an incipient monied interest? For aspects of this question, see J. M. Rosenheim, *The Emergence of a Ruling Order: English Landed Society, 1650–1750* (1998); J. Cannon, "The British Nobility, 1660–1800," in *The European Nobilities in the Seventeenth and Eighteenth Centuries*, vol. 1, ed. H. M. Scott (1995); N. Rogers, "Money, Marriage, Mobility: The Big Bourgeoisie of Hanoverian London," *Journal of Family History* 24, 1 (1999); and H. Horwitz, "'The Mess of the Middle Class' Revisited: The Case of the 'Big Bourgeoisie' of Augustan London," *Continuity and Change* 2, 2 (1987).

The historiography of the social world of scientists, intellectuals, London sociability, and Grub Street print culture towards the end of the Stuart era is legion. Two huge works on the subjects are J. Brewer, *The Pleasures of the*

Imagination: English Culture in the Eighteenth Century (1997); and R.
Porter, The Creation of the Modern World: The Untold Story of the
British Enlightenment (New York, 2000).

DOCUMENTS

9.1   Commons' Debates on the Lords' Amendments to the Declaration of Rights (February 5, 1689)[36]

Earl of Nottingham [who managed the Conference]: The Lords have desired this
conference with the House of Commons.... The House of Commons are a wise
body, etc.; and I hope they will agree with the Lords in this great conjuncture of
affairs.

Mr. Richard Hampden [summarizing the Lords' position] ...: The Lords agree
not to the word "abdicated"; they do not find it to be a word in our known law of
England; therefore they would use such words as are understood according to the
law, to avoid doubtful interpretation; the word "abdicate" being a civil law word,
instead of "violated," "deserted," etc., which does express the consequence of
withdrawing. To the second amendment, "and that the throne is thereby vacant":
though the Lords have declared that the king has deserted the government, yet with
no other inference, than that the exercise of government ceased; and the Lords would
secure the nation against King James's return, and no such abdication; though King
James II ceased to be king, yet there could be no vacancy in the throne, the monarchy
being hereditary, and not elective. No act of the king can destroy the succession of his
heirs, and such persons to whom of right the succession of the crown belongs.

Sir Thomas Clarges: These reasons of the Lords seem to me to be so cogent,
that they deserve to be seriously weighed. I take the crown to be hereditary, and
that King James has "abdicated" the crown, and the pretended prince of Wales
being in the power of the French king, and the throne vacant, the crown ought to
proceed to the next Protestant successor.

Serjeant John Maynard: ....'Tis a sad thing, that the whole welfare of the nation
must depend upon a word of a grammatical construction....

[Debate] on the first amendment, "deserted" for "abdicated," etc....

Sir Joseph Tredenham: ...I thank God, we have a Protestant heir to the crown.
Of the prince of Wales [James II's son] I shall say the less, because much has been
said by Clarges; and 'tis the opinion of the House, that there is a legal incapacity,
as well as a natural. In the princess of Orange [Mary] there is no incapacity; she is
a Protestant; and as for her being a woman, Queen Elizabeth was so, and reigned
gloriously. I would be grateful to the prince of Orange, for the great things he has
done for the nation; but is this the way, to erect a throne to the ruin of his
princess?...If the government [the strict order of succession] be subverted, the

---

[36]   A. Grey, ed., *Debates of the House of Commons, From the Year 1667 to the Year 1694* (1763),
9: 53–60, 63–5; compared with D. L. Jones, *A Parliamentary History of the Glorious Revolution*
(1988), 149–61 (facsimile of Grey).

whole mob may have some more right than we.... When you eradicate the succession, all the crowns in Christendom will concern themselves. It will make such an earthquake, that all the Protestants in the world will fare the worse for it.... There is no other way to have peace and quiet, but by recognizing the princess, who has no legal nor natural impediment....

Sir Robert Sawyer: ... We fight, but with words. If we mean no more by "the throne being vacant," than that the last king has renounced the government; if we mean that the succession is good, the Lords' reasons cannot be opposed. No man can question that the kingdom of England is successive. Soon after the [Norman] Conquest, the kingdom was unsteady.... But, in all times in history, you found the succession did prevail. In Henry VII's time, and Henry VIII's, the right of the crown was declared hereditary. Can the king alter that right? Can either or both the Houses, without the king, alter the fundamental constitution of the kingdom? It will be a great injury to the successor to give away the crown from her [Mary]; you'll sully all the prince of Orange's glory. He came not hither to break through all your constitutions....

Col. John Birch: ... I am glad gentlemen have spoken so plainly of the succession of this noble lady, and to have it there settled, though the consequence is endless; it first puts us by all our hopes, what God has put into our hands will be taken away all at once. [You] say, gentlemen, "This is a sacred succession, and must not be altered." I heard a question the other day, whether the Government was not *jure divino* [by divine right], and that was over-ruled.... But I hold, that, *jure divino*, the Lords and Commons cannot do an unjust thing. We have taken from one brother to give to another, and it has not been questioned to [until] this hour. The Lords have not agreed the throne to be vacant; and, if so, where is the government? Had you spoken plain English t'other day, that the disposal of the crown was in the Lords and Commons, there had been no room for this debate; and you, by that authority..., might have talked of the succession.... God has brought us from Popery and tyranny; and, at this rate, nothing will content us but to go into it again. You have heirs in Spain, in Savoy, and all up and down, and where more I know not; and poor England, for want of speaking one plain word, will be ruined, you and your posterity. Say but where your power is, and the debate is at an end. There may be claims to the crown, but their claims will signify nothing; for the Lords and Commons have other thoughts.... I will conclude, that the power of disposing of the crown is in the Lords and Commons; and by virtue of that power fill the vacancy. And I would not agree with the Lords in leaving out "The throne is vacant." ...

Mr. Henry Pollexfen: If this discourse had been made sooner, perhaps we had been much forwarder.... Letters, papers, and the pulpit, beat a pace confusion of your principal end, which the three kingdoms, the Protestant part of the World, are interested in. But lest what has been said should make impression, I shall answer, first, 'tis pretended that this vote does make ours an elective kingdom. All men love their monarchy, and if you make men believe that it is elective, you will catch [offend] a great many.... I have as much inclination to the princess of Orange as anybody, but you do not really mind the good of your country, and the Protestant religion. If she be now proclaimed queen, can anything be more desirable than that her husband be joined with her in the government? – Now, if you settle the crown on her, and we are to secure a title we cannot make, if any transient issue should arise, she is gone, and he [William] will be in war with her father [James] to defend her title – And does any think the prince of Orange will come in to be a subject to his own wife in England? This is not possible, nor ought to be in nature.…

Mr. William Williams: I take this question to be for the unity of the Lords and Commons in this great conjuncture. Let the power be where it will, I speak for all England. All agree, that the late King James II has departed from the throne, and that his reign over us ceases. If the Lords are of opinion that the reign of King James is ceased, we are all agreed. The Lords say, he shall never return again; they are not for his returning again to his government. I am not for the monarchy of a child; I am not for one to subvert the laws of the government. If this may be done by the Lords and the Commons, I would agree.

(The question being put, That this House do agree with the Lords in the second amendment, it passed in the negative [failed], 282 to 151. A free conference [with the Lords] was desired.)

9.2   The Bill of Rights (An Act for Declaring the Rights and Liberties of the Subject and Settling the Succession of the Crown, 1 Will. and Mary, sess. 2, c. 2) (presented to William and Mary, February 13, 1689; enacted as statute, December 16)[37]

Whereas the Lords spiritual and temporal and Commons assembled at Westminster, lawfully, fully, and freely representing all the estates of the people of this realm, did upon [13] February [1689] present unto their majesties, then called…William and Mary, prince and princess of Orange, being present in their proper persons, a certain declaration in writing made by the said Lords and Commons in the words following, *viz*.:

Whereas the late King James the Second, by the assistance of diverse evil counselors, judges, and ministers employed by him, did endeavor to subvert and extirpate the Protestant religion and the laws and liberties of this kingdom:

1. By assuming and exercising a power of dispensing with and suspending of laws and the execution of laws without consent of Parliament.
2. By committing and prosecuting diverse worthy prelates for humbly petitioning to be excused from concurring to the said assumed power [see chapter 8].
3. By issuing and causing to be executed a commission under the great seal for erecting a court called the Court of Commissioners for Ecclesiastical Causes.
4. By levying money for and to the use of the Crown by pretense of prerogative for other time and in other manner than the same was granted by Parliament.
5. By raising and keeping a standing army within this kingdom in time of peace without consent of Parliament, and quartering soldiers contrary to law.

---

[37]   *SR*, 6: 142–4; compared with E. N. Williams, ed., *A Documentary History of England* (Baltimore, 1965), 2: 107–15.

6. By causing several good subjects being Protestants to be disarmed at the same time when Papists were both armed and employed contrary to law.
7. By violating the freedom of election of members to serve in Parliament.
8. By prosecutions in the Court of King's Bench for matters and causes [re]cognizable only in Parliament, and by diverse other arbitrary and illegal courses.
9. And whereas of late years partial corrupt and unqualified persons have been returned and served on juries in trials, and particularly diverse jurors in trials for high treason which were not freeholders.
10. And excessive bail hath been required of persons committed in criminal cases to elude the benefit of the laws made for the liberty of the subjects.
11. And excessive fines have been imposed; and illegal and cruel punishments inflicted.
12. And several grants and promises made of fines and forfeitures before any conviction or judgment against the persons upon whom the same were to be levied.

All which are utterly and directly contrary to the known laws and statutes and freedom of this realm.

And whereas the said late King James the Second having abdicated the government and the throne being thereby vacant, his highness the prince of Orange (whom it hath pleased almighty God to make the glorious instrument of delivering this kingdom from Popery and arbitrary power) did (by the advice of the Lords spiritual and temporal and diverse principal persons of the Commons) cause letters to be written to the Lords spiritual and temporal being Protestants, and other letters to the several counties, cities, universities, boroughs, and cinque ports, for the choosing of such persons to represent them as were of right to be sent to Parliament, to meet and sit at Westminster upon [22] January [1689], in order to such an establishment as that their religion, laws, and liberties might not again be in danger of being subverted, upon which letters elections having been accordingly made.

And thereupon the said Lords spiritual and temporal and Commons, pursuant to their respective letters and elections, being now assembled in a full and free representative of this nation, taking into their most serious consideration the best means for attaining the ends aforesaid, do in the first place (as their ancestors in like case have usually done) for the vindicating and asserting their ancient rights and liberties declare:

1. That the pretended power of suspending the laws or the execution of laws by regal authority without consent of Parliament is illegal.
2. That the pretended power of dispensing with laws or the execution of laws by regal authority, as it hath been assumed and exercised of late, is illegal.
3. That the commission for erecting the late Court of Commissioners for Ecclesiastical Causes, and all other commissions and courts of like nature, are illegal and pernicious.
4. That levying money for or to the use of the Crown by pretense of prerogative, without grant of Parliament, for longer time, or in other manner than the same is or shall be granted, is illegal.

5. That it is the right of the subjects to petition the king, and all commitments and prosecutions for such petitioning are illegal.
6. That the raising or keeping a standing army within the kingdom in time of peace, unless it be with consent of Parliament, is against law.
7. That the subjects which are Protestants may have arms for their defense suitable to their conditions and as allowed by law.
8. That election of members of Parliament ought to be free.
9. That the freedom of speech and debates or proceedings in Parliament ought not to be impeached or questioned in any court or place out of Parliament.
10. That excessive bail ought not to be required, nor excessive fines imposed, nor cruel and unusual punishments inflicted.
11. That jurors ought to be duly impaneled and returned, and jurors which pass upon men in trials for high treason ought to be freeholders.
12. That all grants and promises of fines and forfeitures of particular persons before conviction are illegal and void.
13. And that for redress of all grievances, and for the amending, strengthening and preserving of the laws, Parliaments ought to be held frequently.

And they do claim, demand, and insist upon all and singular the premises as their undoubted rights and liberties . . . ; to which demand of their rights they are particularly encouraged by the declaration of his highness the prince of Orange [September 30, 1688, see chapter 8] as being the only means for obtaining a full redress and remedy therein. Having therefore an entire confidence that his said highness the prince of Orange will perfect the deliverance so far advanced by him, and will still preserve them from the violation of their rights which they have here asserted, and from all other attempts upon their religion, rights, and liberties.

II. The said Lords spiritual and temporal and Commons assembled at Westminster do resolve that William and Mary, prince and princess of Orange, be and be declared king and queen of England, France, and Ireland and the dominions thereunto belonging, to hold the crown and royal dignity of the said kingdoms and dominions to them, the said prince and princess, during their lives and the life of the survivor to them, and that the sole and full exercise of the regal power be only in and executed by the said prince of Orange in the names of the said prince and princess during their joint lives, and after their deceases the said crown and royal dignity of the same kingdoms and dominions to be to the heirs of the body of the said princess, and for default of such issue to the Princess Anne of Denmark and the heirs of her body, and for default of such issue to the heirs of the body of the said prince of Orange. And the Lords spiritual and temporal and Commons do pray the said prince and princess to accept the same accordingly.

III. And that the oaths hereafter mentioned be taken by all persons of whom the oaths of allegiance and supremacy might be required by law, instead of them; and that the said oaths of allegiance and supremacy be abrogated.

"I, A. B., do sincerely promise and swear that I will be faithful and bear true allegiance to their majesties King William and Queen Mary. So help me God."

"I, A. B., do swear that I do from my heart abhor, detest, and abjure as impious and heretical this damnable doctrine and position, that princes excommunicated or deprived by the pope . . . may be deposed or murdered by their subjects or any other whatsoever. And I do declare that no foreign prince, person, prelate, state, or potentate hath or ought to have any jurisdiction, power, superiority, pre-eminence or authority, ecclesiastical or spiritual, within this realm. So help me God."

IV. Upon which their said majesties did accept the crown and royal dignity of the kingdoms of England, France, and Ireland, and the dominions thereunto belonging, according to the resolution and desire of the said Lords and Commons contained in the said declaration. . . .

IX. And whereas it hath been found by experience that it is inconsistent with the safety and welfare of this Protestant kingdom to be governed by a popish prince, or by any king or queen marrying a Papist, the said Lords spiritual and temporal and Commons do further pray that it may be enacted, that all and every person and persons that is, are or shall be reconciled to or shall hold communion with the see or Church of Rome, or shall profess the popish religion, or shall marry a Papist, shall be excluded and be for ever incapable to inherit, possess or enjoy the crown and government of this realm and Ireland and the dominions thereunto belonging.

9.3 The Toleration Act (An Act for Exempting their Majesties' Protestant Subjects, Dissenting from the Church of England, from the Penalties of Certain Laws, 1 Will. & Mary, c. 18) (1689)[38]

I. Forasmuch as some ease to scrupulous consciences in the exercise of religion may be an effectual means to unite their majesties' Protestant subjects in interest and affection:

II. Be it enacted . . . that neither the statute . . . entitled, "An Act to Retain the Queen's Majesty's Subjects in Their Due Obedience" [1581, see document 4.8]; nor the statute . . . entitled, "An Act for the More Speedy and Due Execution of Certain Branches of the Statute" [1587] . . . *viz.*, the aforesaid act; nor that branch or clause of a statute . . . entitled, "An Act for the Uniformity of Common Prayer and Service in the Church" [1559] . . . , whereby all persons . . . , are required to resort to their parish church or chapel, or some usual place where the common prayer shall be used . . . , upon pain that every person so offending shall forfeit for every such offense twelve pence; nor . . . any other law or statute of this realm, made against Papists or popish recusants, except the statute . . . entitled, "An Act for Preventing Dangers Which May Happen from Popish Recusants" [1673]; and except also the statute . . . entitled, "An Act for the More Effectual Preserving the King's Person and Government by Disabling Papists from Sitting in Either House of Parliament" [1661]; shall be construed to extend to any person or persons

---

[38] *SR*, 6: 74–6; compared with Costin and Watson, *Law and Working of the Constitution*, 163–7.

dissenting from the Church of England, that shall take the oaths mentioned in a statute made this present Parliament, entitled "An Act for Removing and Preventing All Questions and Disputes concerning the Assembling and Sitting of this Present Parliament" [1 Will. & Mary, c. 1], and [that] shall make and subscribe the declaration mentioned in a statute made in [30] King Charles II [1678, Test Act, see chapter 8]..., which oaths and declaration the justices of peace at the general sessions of the peace...are hereby required to tender and administer to such persons as shall offer themselves to take....

IV. Provided always...that if any assembly of persons dissenting from the Church of England shall be had in any place for religious worship with the doors locked, barred, or bolted during any time of such meeting together, all and every person or persons, that shall come to and be at such meeting, shall not receive any benefit from this law, but be liable to all the pains and penalties of all the aforesaid laws recited....

Provided always, that nothing herein contained shall...exempt any of the persons aforesaid from paying of tithes or other parochial duties....

X. And whereas there are certain other persons, dissenters from the Church of England, who scruple the taking of any oath, be it enacted...that every such person shall make and subscribe the aforesaid declaration, and also this declaration of fidelity following, *viz.*:

"I, A. B., do sincerely promise and solemnly declare before God and the world, that I will be true and faithful to King William and Queen Mary; and I do solemnly profess and declare, that I do from my heart abhor, detest, and renounce, as impious and heretical, that damnable doctrine and position, 'that princes excommunicated or deprived by the pope..., may be deposed or murdered by their subjects, [etc.]'...[as that contained in the Bill of Rights, see document 9.2]."...

XIII. Provided always, and it is the true intent and meaning of this Act, that all the laws made and provided for the frequenting of divine service on the Lord's day, commonly called Sunday, shall be still in force....

XIV. Provided always...that neither this Act, nor any clause, article, or thing herein contained, shall extend...to give any ease, benefit, or advantage to any Papist..., or any person that shall deny, in his preaching or writing, the doctrine of the blessed Trinity.

9.4   *Act of Settlement (12 & 13 Will., c. 2) (1701)*[39]

It having...pleased Almighty God to take away our...sovereign lady [Mary], and also the most hopeful Prince William, duke of Gloucester (the only surviving issue of her royal highness the Princess Anne of Denmark) to the unspeakable grief and sorrow of your majesty and your said good subjects...; and it being

[39]   *SR*, 7: 636–7; compared with S. E. Prall, *The Bloodless Revolution: England, 1688* (Madison, 1985), 321–5.

absolutely necessary for the safety, peace, and quiet of this realm, to obviate all doubts and contentions in the [succession] . . . : therefore for a further provision of the succession of the Crown in the Protestant line, we your majesty's most dutiful and loyal subjects, the Lords spiritual and temporal and Commons in this present Parliament assembled, do beseech your majesty that it may be enacted and declared, and be it enacted and declared . . . , that the most excellent Princess Sophia, electress and duchess dowager of Hanover, daughter of the most excellent Princess Elizabeth, late queen of Bohemia, daughter of our late sovereign lord King James the First of happy memory, be and is hereby declared to be the next in succession in the Protestant line to the imperial Crown and dignity of the said realms of England, France, and Ireland, with the dominions and territories thereunto belonging, after his majesty, and the Princess Anne of Denmark, and in default of issue of the said Princess Anne, and of his majesty respectively. . . .

II. Provided always, and be it hereby enacted, that all and every person and persons, who shall or may take or inherit the said Crown, by virtue of the limitation of this present Act, and is, are or shall be reconciled to, or shall hold communion with, the See or Church of Rome, or shall profess the popish religion, or shall marry a Papist, shall be subject to such incapacities, as in such case or cases are by the said recited Act provided, enacted, and established. . . .

III. And whereas it is requisite and necessary that some further provision be made for securing our religion, laws, and liberties . . . ; that whosoever shall hereafter come to the possession of this Crown, shall join in communion with the Church of England, as by law established;

That in case the Crown and imperial dignity of this realm shall hereafter come to any person, not being a native of this kingdom of England, this nation be not obliged to engage in any war for the defense of any dominions or territories which do not belong to the Crown of England, without the consent of Parliament;

That no person who shall hereafter come to the possession of this Crown, shall go out of the dominions of England, Scotland, or Ireland, without the consent of Parliament. . . .

That . . . no person born out of the kingdoms of England, Scotland, or Ireland or the dominions thereunto belonging (although he be naturalized or made a denizen, except such as are born of English parents), shall be capable to be of the Privy Council, or a member of either house of Parliament, or to enjoy any office or place of trust either civil or military, or to have any grant of lands, tenements, or hereditaments from the Crown. . . .

That no person who has an office or place of profit under the king, or receives a pension from the crown, shall be capable of serving as a member of the House of Commons. . . .

That no pardon under the great seal of England be pleadable to an impeachment by the Commons in Parliament.

9.5 George Holmes at Strabane to William Fleming on the Siege of Londonderry (November 16, 1689)[40]

I was one of the first (that did wear a red coat [that is, that served in the army]) that revolted from King James and helped to set up a flag of defiance against him and Popery in the city of Londonderry, that now lies in a ruinous condition, yet defies all the king and queen's enemies.

After some little routs in the country, on [12] April last the Irish army appeared before our city, but at that distance that one of our cannons had enough to do to reach them; but in short time they approached nearer to our walls. In the first place we burned all our suburbs and hewed down all our brave orchards, making all about us as plain as a bowling-green. About the 18th of April King James came within a mile of our walls, but had no better entertainment than bullets of 14, 16, and 22 pounds weight. He sent us a letter under his own hand, sealed with his own seal, to desire us to surrender, and we should have our own conditions. . . . In short, we would not yield.

Then we proceeded and chose captains and completed regiments, made two governors. We had 116 companies in the city. All our officers fled away, so we made officers of those that did deserve to be officers. I was made captain. And then we began to sally out, and the first sally that we made we slew their French general and several of their men, with the loss of nine or ten of our men, which was the greatest loss that ever we lost in the field. Every day afterward we sallied out and daily killed our enemies, which put us in great heart. But it being so soon of the year, and we having no forage for our horses, we was forced to let them out, and the enemy got many. The rest of them died for hunger. . . .

But at last our provision grew scant and our allowance small. One pound of oatmeal and one pound of tallow served a man a week; sometimes salt hides. . . . I saw 2s. a quarter given for a little dog, horse blood at 4d. per pint; all the starch was eaten, the graves of tallow, horse flesh was a rarity, and still we resolved to hold out.

Four days before we got relief from England we saw a great drove of cows very near us, and we were very weak, but we resolved to sally out, and in order thereto we played our great guns off the walls and sallied out on our enemy. I led the forlorn hope, which was about 100 men of the best we had, with which I ran full tilt into their trenches; and before our body came up we had slain 80 men, put many to the rout. We got arms enough and some beef, but durst not stay long, not above half an hour. This vexed our enemies much; they said we took them asleep. . . .

After the ships came in with provision to us our enemies thought it was in vain to stay any longer, so on Lammas day [August 1] they left us the wide fields to walk in. In the siege we had not above 60 men killed, except with the bombs

---

[40] HMC, *Twelfth Report, Appendix VII, The Manuscripts of S. H. Le Fleming, Esq., of Rydal Hall* (1890), 264–5; compared with Browning, *English Historical Documents*, 753–4.

killed. But I believe there died 15,000 men, women, and children, many of which died for meat [solid food]. But we had a great fever amongst us, and all the children died, almost whole families not one left alive.

9.6   The Declaration of the Gentlemen, Merchants, and Inhabitants of Boston (April 18, 1689)[41]

II. To get us within the reach of the desolation desired for us, ... and the hedge which kept us from the wild beasts of the field, effectually broken down ... Our charter was with a most injurious pretense (and scarce that) of law, condemned before it was possible for us to appear at Westminster in the legal defense of it; and without a fair leave to answer for ourselves, concerning the crimes falsely laid to our charge, we were put under a president and council, without any liberty for an assembly, which the other American plantations have, by a commission from his majesty [James II]. ...

IV. In a little more than half a year we saw this commission superseded by another, yet more absolute and arbitrary, with which Sir Edmund Andros arrived as our governor: who besides his power, with the advice and consent of his council, to make laws and raise taxes as he pleased; had also authority by himself to muster and employ all persons residing in the territory ... ; and to transfer such forces to any English plantation in America. ... And several companies of soldiers were now brought from Europe, to support what was to be imposed upon us. ...

VI. It was now plainly affirmed, both by some in open council, and by the same in private converse, that the people in New England were all slaves, and the only difference between them and slaves is their not being bought and sold; and it was a maxim delivered in open court unto us by one of the council, that we must not think the privileges of English men would follow us to the end of the world. Accordingly we have been treated with multiplied contradictions to Magna Carta, the rights of which we laid claim unto.

9.7   Attacks on a Ludlow Dissenter Meeting House (November 1693)[42]

The house in Ludlow ..., [Shropshire] commonly known by the sign of the Bull was certified [by] Dr. Gilbert Ironside, bishop of Hereford, as a place intended for religious worship. ...

On Saturday ... [11] November the said license ... was ... shown and delivered to the bailiff of Ludlow ... ; and at same time acquainted them [the bailiffs] that according to the liberty granted to their majesties' Protestant subjects by an Act of Parliament entitled An Act for Exempting Their Majesties' Protestant Subjects,

---

[41]   Lenman and Gibson, *Jacobite Threat*, 33–4, from N. Byfield, *An Account of the Late Revolution in New England Together with the Declaration of the Gentlemen, Merchants, and Inhabitants of Boston and the Country Adjacent* (1689).

[42]   Nottingham RO, DD4P 72/115.

Dissenting from the Church of England, from the Penalty of Certain Laws [1689, document 9.3], there would be a meeting for religious worship.... They were desired... that effectual care might be taken for preserving the peace, suppressing any tumult, or insurrection, that might happen.... The high bailiff promised fair but the low bailiff did not.... On the Lords' day... a meeting for religious worship was held... by persons of the Presbyterian persuasion; and... the place was well filled. But then some disturbance arose by breaking of the glass window on the South part from the... garden of a person of account in the town.... [S]oon after a solemn signal is made... by ringing the bells of the parish church backward and crying out "Fire, fire!," which caused a very great uproar in the town. All were directed to The Bull... by which means vast numbers of idle and ill-affected people were gathered together, whereupon a fierce assault began in showers of stones, bats, etc., for breaking the windows...: The rioters headed... by... John Vere an exciseman..., [who] for the greater encouragement...- making use of the power of his office and their Majesties' name for the cloaking his rebellion.... By th[e] time they had satiated their zeal by breaking and destroying all they could come at, the minister had finished.... One of those zealots came into the meeting and cast a stone... at the minister, but the Lord suffered not his arm to perform his design. The person being suspected and searched was found to have another in his hand for the same purpose which he was persuaded to part with, and so with shame departed.

The meeting being over, the people peaceably repairing home were... assaulted in the streets.... A gentleman of the neighborhood who hath eminently evidenced his zeal for, and firm adherence to, the present government as well by his early hazardous and chargeable appearance on their majesties' behalf [that is, in 1688]... had his coach standing at the door assaulted [with] dirt, etc., thrown at it and into it, and... his servants and attendants that followed the coach for its preservation were struck, beaten, and abused.... In the beginning of the tumult inquiry was made for the bailiffs but they were found to have withdrawn themselves out of town... to a small alehouse to pass the Sabbath in....

It was thought fit on Saturday the 18th November that some persons should attend the bailiffs to let them know the meeting was designed to be continued the next day and how that through their absence from the town the last Lords' day a great insurrection had happened.... Accordingly a meeting was had with the high bailiff..., but after the low bailiff his son-in-law came in..., he seemed to retract or qualify his former promise; and the low one... burst forth in a warm, threatening way wishing it ended not in blood, and that what happened to them [the Presbyterians] was their own fault, unhandsomely inveighing against them as the causes of the riot and insurrection, and they might thank themselves if any further mischief befell them.... And it being somewhat warmly urged by a tradesman of the town present that it was his right and liberty confirmed by Parliament..., he [the under-bailiff] could not bridle himself from saying with a great deal of concern, "Mr. J__s, that doctrine won't down in this town," meaning... Ludlow and that liberty for religious worship allowed by Act of Parliament...; that he was not bound to attend and would not be instructed in his duty...; and all that could be got from them was they intended not to be out of town, whereby those present readily judged the issue would not be peaceable, however having the protection of the laws it was resolved to continue the meeting next day.

Accordingly the place being prepared and beginning to fill with persons drawing thither to hear the Gospel of peace; the minister no sooner got thither but immediately a solemn signal was given by the market bell, and then the alarm was sounded from the parish church as before..., and the storm began...led on by the servant of the parson of the parish who appeared as captain general for that day. And the sons of violence and blood gathering together from all parts of the town...(flushed with drink and money for the work of the day by one who should by virtue of his profession [have] been a promoter of peace and not of tumults, insurrections and villains) flocked apace....It was concluded to adjourn the meeting till there should appear some real authority in the town....

Finding they had missed their prey they became like the ravening wolves of the evening and detaching themselves into several parties ravaged through the whole town where any prey might be found wreaking themselves on any they met, that seemed strangers or supposed to have come to, or had kindness for, the meeting, not sparing women and maidens....[One Presbyterian] being alone and peaceably repairing homewards was fiercely set upon by one of the detachments of about a hundred or more and endeavoring to outgo them was followed so closely and furiously, and received so many blows with stones, bats, staves, and clubs and coming so thick on him that he was not likely to support himself anytime resolving rather to die with his face towards them turned upon them and advancing in some rage with an oaken plank in his hand...that gave him opportunity of withdrawing and securing himself, by which it's seen as the persecuting rabble of Ludlow are cruel so also very cowardly.

After all persons were gone the rage and violence of these dragooners ceased not, but...broke every window in the house towards the street (the rest being broke before)..., damaging the rooms and goods therein by the largeness of the stones, bats, etc....Having fully perfected that work they fell to further fury the pulling down the house and proceeded to...breaking down the doors..., and after that, to the destroying the sign post; and it's remarkable it was the grave advice of one among the hottest of those to repair down with that first....The sign post being down the signs were broken to pieces every one scrambling for a part...and happy he that could get some of the painting there being two signs one "The Bull" belonging to the house the other "The King's Arms" at which the people formerly lived, and against which some it's thought had the greatest spite. They yielded many pieces, which were carried away..., as a trophy of their achievements....

Though the bailiffs were...present this [day] in the town, yet it was observed that the rage and impudence of the dragooning rabble was far greater, and threatened much more bloody work this day than before....

The parson of the parish having been absent the former Sabbath day was present this, who always declared himself a most bitter cruel enemy to...all good people as well as against the present government. 'Tis the same person that upon the _ [presumably ca. 6] February 1689 told his congregations from the pulpit he was not come to celebrate the remembrance of an abdicated king, but of King James their rightful legal undeposable prince, and the next day when he should have given thanks for our deliverance from Popery, slavery, and tyranny he appeared not, and forbear to take the oath, till the fear of loss of his place which is the king's gift or the hopes of doing more good to the Jacobite interest thereby obliged him, and it was a longer season ere he prayed for their majesties, and he doth it seldom not and but faintly and for which he was presented by the grand jury at sessions. It's the same person that said he had rather a plague should come to town than a [Dissenter] meeting, nor was he wanting this day to signalize his zeal against the interest of Christ and laws of the land to advance the work he made a sorry sermon on purpose, as all people judge that heard it thereby sounding a trumpet from the pulpit from him and by his directions the alarm was given by ringing the bells by his encouragement. His servant furiously acted as captain general for the great red Dragon [the mob].

9.8 Queen Anne Tells Parliament her Beliefs (March 11 and May 25, 1702)[43]

[Speech to both Houses, March 11:] My lords and gentlemen,

I cannot too much lament my own unhappiness in succeeding to the Crown so immediately after the loss of a king who was the great support not only of these kingdoms but of all Europe: and I am extremely sensible of the weight and difficulty it brings upon me:

But the true concern I have for our religion, for the laws and liberties of England, for the maintaining the succession to the Crown in the Protestant line, and the government in Church and State as by law established, encourages me in this great undertaking; which I promise myself will be successful, by the blessing of God and the continuance of that fidelity and affection of which you have given me so full assurance.

The present conjuncture of affairs requires the greatest application and dispatch; and I am very glad to find in your several addresses so unanimous a concurrence in the same opinion with me, that too much cannot be done for the encouragement of our allies, to reduce the exorbitant power of France. . . .

It shall be my constant endeavor to make you the best return for that duty and affection you have expressed to me by a careful and diligent administration for the good of all my subjects; and as I know my own heart to be entirely English, I can very sincerely assure you there is not anything you can expect or desire from me which I shall not be ready to do for the happiness and prosperity of England. . . .

[Speech to both Houses, May 25:] My lords and gentlemen,

---

[43] [A. Boyer,] *The History of the Reign of Queen Anne Digested into Annals. Year the First* (1703), 6–7, 41–2; compared with Holmes and Speck, *Divided Society*, 25–6.

I cannot conclude this session without repeating my hearty thanks to you all for your great care of the public and the many marks you have given of your duty and affection to me. And I must thank you, gentlemen of the House of Commons, in particular, both for the supplies you have given to support me in this necessary war, and the provisions you have made for the debts contracted in the former....

I shall always wish that no difference of opinion among those that are equally affected to my service may be the occasion of heats and animosities among themselves. I shall be very careful to preserve and maintain the Act of Toleration [document 9.3], and to set the minds of all my people at quiet. My own principles must always keep me entirely firm to the interests and religion of the Church of England, and will incline me to countenance those who have the truest zeal to support it.

9.9 *Jonathan Swift,* The Conduct of the Allies *(1711)*[44]

If in laying open the real causes of our present misery, I am forced to speak with some freedom, I think it will require no apology.... But as it will be some satisfaction to the people, to know by whom they have been so long abused; so it may be of great use to us and our posterity, not to trust the safety of their country in the hands of those, who act by such principles, and from such motives.

I have already observed, that when the counsels of this war were debated in the late king's [William's] time, a certain Great Man [Lord Godolphin] was then so averse from entering into it, that he rather chose to give up his employment, and tell the king he could serve him no longer. Upon that prince's death, although the grounds of our quarrel with France had received no manner of addition, yet this lord thought fit to alter his sentiments; for the scene was quite changed. His lordship, and the family [the Churchills, soon to be duke and duchess of Marlborough] with whom he was engaged by so complicated an alliance, were in the highest credit possible with the Q_n [Anne]. The treasurer's staff was ready for his lordship, the duke [of Marlborough] was to command the army, and the duchess by her employments, and the favor she was possessed of, to be always nearest her majesty's person; by which the whole power, at home and abroad, would be devolved upon that family. This was a prospect so very inviting, that...it could not be easily withstood by any who have so keen an appetite for wealth or ambition. By an agreement subsequent to the Grand Alliance, we were to assist the Dutch with forty thousand men, all to be commanded by the D. of M. [duke of Marlborough]. So that whether this war were prudently begun or not, it is plain that the true spring or motive of it was the aggrandizing a particular family, and in short, a war of the general and the ministry, and not of the prince or people; since those very persons were against it when they knew the power, and consequently the profit, would be in other hands.

With these measures fell in all that set of people, who are called the monied men; such as had raised vast sums by trading with stocks and funds, and lending

[44] Swift, *The Conduct of the Allies* (1711, 1712), 58–60; compared with R. Sharrock, ed., *The Pelican Book of English Prose: From the Beginnings to 1800* (Baltimore, 1970), 1: 630–2.

upon great interest and premiums; whose perpetual harvest is war, and whose beneficial way of traffick must very much decline by a peace.

9.10 The Duchess of Marlborough's Electioneering at St. Albans (1705)[45]

Upon the petition of Henry Killigrew, Esq., complaining of an undue election and return of John Gape, Esq., to serve for the borough of St. Albans. . . .

The sitting member's counsel . . . insisted on several irregular practices on behalf of the petitioner; and as to that they called several witnesses:

Charles Turner said he was sent for by the duchess of Marlborough; and he went to her, and she desired his vote for both admirals [Killigrew and Churchill, the latter being the duchess's brother-in-law]: that he answered, he was engaged for Mr. Gape; to which the duchess replied, she had no prejudice to Mr. Gape, but it was the queen's desire that no such men should be chose[n], for such men would unhinge the government, and the Papists' horses stood saddled day and night, whipping and spurring.

John Miller said that he was asked by one to go to my Lady Marlborough's; and when he came the duchess asked him who he was for, and he answered, for Colonel [*sic*] Churchill and Mr. Gape. Thereupon the duchess asked him if he would be for such men as were against the queen's interest and the good of the nation? That she asked him to oblige her with one vote; and he said, he thought he did by giving her brother [Admiral Churchill] one. . . .

Sam Beech said he was sent for the duchess. . . . He told her, he had promised Mr. Gape . . .; and thereupon the duchess told him, [if] he would not be willing, his goods should be taken out of his shop and tor[n].

9.11 Newspapers and Party Politics (1708 and 1710)[46]

Election Advertisements from the Daily Courant *(May 4, 1708)*
"At a meeting of many hundred of the most eminent citizens . . . it was agreed to nominate and promote the election of these four citizens to represent this city [London] in the ensuing Parliament, *viz.* Sir William Ashurst, Sir Gilbert Heathcote, Sir Samuel Stanier, Kts. and aldermen; and Sir John Buckworth, Kt., Bart., and Turkey merchant. Being all gentlemen well known to be zealously affected to her majesty's person and government both in Church and State, and to the Protestant succession as by law established. The said four gentlemen have mutually engaged to promote each other's interest accordingly."

"Whereas diverse tickets, differing from those agreed on at the general meeting of the citizens on the 21st of April last have been industriously dispersed; These are to certify that the said tickets were printed and dispersed without the privity,

---

[45] *CJ*, 15: 37–8; compared with Holmes and Speck, *Divided Society*, 85–6.
[46] *Daily Courant*, no. 1938, May 4, 1708; and *The Post Boy*, no. 2411, October 24–6, 1710; compared with Holmes and Speck, *Divided Society*, 70–1 (for 1710).

consent, or knowledge of the right honorable Sir William Withers, lord mayor, Sir Francis Child, Sir Richard Hoare, Kts. and aldermen, and John Ward, Esq. Who have unanimously agreed to promote each other's interest in the ensuing election."

Newspaper Election Reports from The Post Boy *(October 24–6, 1710)*
"On Friday...came on the election for the borough of Pembroke. Sir Arthur Owen and Lewis Wogan, Esq., were candidates. Sir Arthur Owen had 283 voices and Lewis Wogan, Esq., 335. But the mayor, being a Dissenter and the son of a Presbyterian preacher, does declare that he will return Sir Arthur Owen."

"Haverfordwest, October 17. The election for the county of Pembroke came on this day. The candidates were Sir Arthur Owen, Bart. [one could run in multiple constituencies] and John Barlow, Esq. Sir Arthur polled his votes, in all 190. Mr. Barlow polled till night came on, and then, being unwilling to detain the gentlemen, dismissed them, well satisfied with the defeat he had given the enemy, without the help of the body of reserve, polling only 493. In this election the diligence of the clergy was remarkable, 50 of them polling for Mr. Barlow. But there was a Judas among the apostles; 7 of them polled for Sir Arthur, amongst those, one...Solomon Henden...polled twice."

"Coventry, October 20....Robert Craven...and Thomas Gery, Esqs., were upon a vast majority...declared duly elected by two sheriffs chosen on purpose to serve the Whig interest....The issue [outcome] of this election is the more remarkable because the government of this corporation is in the hands of professed Dissenters, who have of late been notorious for electing per_ns [persons] of known disaffection to, and activity against, the Ch__ch [Church]....It's further observable that Sir William Boughton, Sir Richard Newdigate, William Bromley, Esq., and a great number of persons of distinction, and clergymen, appeared in favor of the Church candidates; whereas the other party was made up of mean tradesmen and the scum of the rabble. The night ended with ringing of bells, illuminations, bonfires, and all other demonstrations of a public satisfaction."

9.12   *The Trial of Dr. Henry Sacheverell (February 27 and March 3, 1710)*[47]

Articles of Impeachment (January 9, 1710)
I. Henry Sacheverell, in his said sermon preached at St. Paul's, doth suggest and maintain that the necessary means used to bring about the said happy Revolution were odious and unjustifiable, that his late majesty, in his Declaration, disclaimed the least imputation of resistance; and that to impute resistance to the said Revolution is to cast black and odious colors upon his late majesty and the said Revolution.

---

[47]   *CJ*, 16: 258 (for the articles); and Howell, *State Trials*, 15: 55–6, 202, 205–6; compared with Costin and Watson, *Law and Working of the Constitution*, 197–207; and Browning, *English Historical Documents*, 206–7.

II. He...doth suggest and maintain that the aforesaid Toleration granted by law is unreasonable and the allowance of it unwarrantable; and asserts that he is a false brother, with relation to God, religion, or the Church, who defends Toleration and liberty of conscience....

III. He...doth falsely and seditiously suggest and assert that the Church of England is in a condition of great peril and adversity under her majesty's administration; and...doth suggest the Church to be in danger: and, as a parallel, mentions...that the person of King Charles [I] was voted to be out of danger at the same time that his murderers were conspiring his death....

IV. He...doth falsely and maliciously suggest that her majesty's administration, both in ecclesiastical and civil affairs, tends to the destruction of the constitution. And that there are men of characters and stations in Church and State who are false brethren, and do themselves weaken, undermine, and betray, and do encourage, and put it in the power of others, who are professed enemies, to overturn and destroy the constitution and establishment....

27 February. *Attorney General Sir John Montague*: To show his [Sacheverell's] little liking of the great work which was begun...by the arrival of his late majesty, the chief turn of his discourse is to cry up non-resistance and passive obedience.

And to make it most evident that what he said of non-resistance was to cast black and odious colors upon the Revolution; he lays down a general position, "That it is not lawful, upon any pretense whatsoever, to make resistance to the supreme power"; which supreme power, by other passages, he explains to be the regal power.

If what the doctor very frequently asserts in this sermon be true, that all are false sons of the Church, who assisted in bringing about the Revolution, or that joined in the opposition that was made to the encroachments which were begun by evil ministers in the reign of King James II, against our religion and liberties; let the doctor a little consider, how far his character of a false brother may be carried!

Everybody knows, that lived in those days, that the body of the clergy of the Church of England made a noble stand against the encroachments which were then making, and appeared as active as any of the laity.

And was it not by their writings, preaching, and example, that the nobility and gentry were animated to maintain and defend their rights, religion, and liberties?...

3 March. *Sir Simon Harcourt* (for the defense):...I shall endeavor to satisfy your lordships, first, that the doctor's assertion of the illegality of resistance to the supreme power on any pretense whatsoever, in general terms, without expressing any exception, or that any exception is to be made, is warranted by the authority of the Church of England. And secondly, that his manner of expression is agreeable to the law of England....

My lords, is this doctrine of non-resistance taught in the homilies in general terms, in the same manner as Doctor Sacheverell has asserted it, without expressing any exception? Do the articles of our religion declare the doctrine taught in the homilies to be a godly and wholesome doctrine? And will your lordships permit this gentleman to suffer for preaching it? Is it criminal in any man to preach that doctrine, which it is his duty to read?...

That your lordships may not think this doctrine died at the Revolution, I shall humbly lay before your lordships the opinions of three archbishops, and eleven bishops, made since the Revolution, which will fully show the doctrine of non-resistance is still the doctrine of our Church.... I am sure it is impossible to enter into the heart of man to conceive, that what these reverend prelates have asserted, that any general position they have laid down concerning non-resistance, is an affirmance that necessary means used to bring about the Revolution were odious and unjustifiable. Why then is Doctor Sacheverell, by having taught the same doctrine, in the same manner as they did, to be charged for having suggested or maintained any such thing?

9.13   The Trial of Daniel Dammarree for his Role in the Sacheverell Riots (April 1710)[48]

Daniel Dammarree..., waterman [bargeman on River Thames] to Queen Anne..., on the 18th of April 1710 was indicted for being concerned with a multitude of men, to the number of five hundred, armed with swords..., clubs, [etc.], to levy war against the queen.

A gentleman deposed, that, going through the Temple, he saw some thousands of people, who had attended Dr. Sacheverell from Westminster Hall; that some of them said they would pull down Dr. Burgess's [Presbyterian] meeting-house that night; others differed as to the time of doing it; but all agreed on the act, and the meeting-house was demolished on the following night. Here it should be observed that Dr. Burgess and Mr. Bradbury were two dissenting ministers, who had made themselves conspicuous by preaching in opposition to Sacheverell's doctrine.

Captain Orril swore, that, on the 1st of March, hearing that the mob had pulled down Dr. Burgess's meeting-house, he resolved to go among them, to do what service he could to government by making discoveries. This witness, going to Mr. Bradbury's meeting, found the people plundering it, who obliged him to pull off his hat. After this he went to Lincoln's Inn Fields, where he saw a bonfire made of some of the materials of Dr. Burgess's meeting-house, and saw the prisoner [Dammarree], who twirled his hat, and said "Damn it, I will lead you on; we will have all the meetinghouses down. High Church and Sacheverell, huzza!"

It was proved by another evidence, that the prisoner having headed part of the mob, some of them proposed to go to the meeting-house in Wild Street; but this was objected to by others, who recommended going to Drury Lane, saying "that meetinghouse was worth ten of that in Wild Street."

Joseph Collier swore that he saw the prisoner carry a brass sconce from Dr. Burgess's meeting-house, and throw it into the fire in Lincoln's Inn Fields, huzzaing and crying, "High Church and Sacheverell."

---

[48]   A. Knapp and W. Baldwin, eds., *The Newgate Calendar* (1824), 1: 59–60. Compare this description of the event and trial with Howell, *State Trials*, 15: 522–614.

[Dammarree was found guilty and sentenced to be hung, drawn, and quartered for high treason. The queen reprieved and subsequently pardoned him and restored him as a royal waterman. He was, however, terminated from this position at Anne's death in 1714.]

9.14   W. M., "An Enterlude For the Generall Entertainment at the County-Feast, Held at Merchant-Taylors Hall," London (June 29, 1678)[49]

Enter Sir Jeofry Doe-Right with Horace's Odes in his hand.

Sir Jeofry: "What unknown Blisse, what singular content
   Attends this happy Rural Banishment?
   Whilst Courts and Cities finde their Joy and Glory
   (At best) but weak, short liv'd, and transitory....
   Till wearyed by such interchange of weather
   In Court and Citty, I at length confin'd
   All my Ambition to the Golden Mean...."
Generous Goodman: "Nor would I change my Country freedom t'gain
   A petty Kingdome."

Theo. Meanwell's Sonnet on The Country Life:

   "Happy's the pesant [sic], whose indulgent fate
   Hath fixt him in a Rural state...,
   He studies th' nature of the flowers and trees,
   Th' politick Government of th' Bees...,
   Nor doth's bloud-thirsty sword or hand delight,
   To murder, plunder, rob, or t'fight,
   Except for th' Countreys Good;
   But for the Welfare of the Common-weal,
   His heart's inflam'd with pious zeal,
   T' spend's Money, Goods, or Bloud....
   This is the only Man that can defy
   The frowns of human destiny
   The Cheats of th' Court and City...."

Enter Richard and Thomas, younger sons to Sir Jeofry in gentleman and young scholar habits.

Thomas: "A pox on this hard fate of younger brothers; where the eldest...must run away with the estate...."
Richard: "In troth, I wonder our ancestors should take so little care for younger brothers; who being born gentlemen, are bred up little better than plough-boys; if a little school-learning would raise us a portion; or an off-cast preferment at Court, or perhaps some

[49]   *Huntington Divertisement, or, an Enterlude For the Generall Entertainment at the County-Feast, Held at Merchant-Taylors Hall, June 29. 1678* (1678), 1–5, 8–13, 15.

small office about the law might help us to a livelihood, endeavors of friends might be used; otherwise small prospect of comfort....

"Introth, he aims to breed us up scholars fit for fellowships in the university or some despicable parsonage; or some subservient offices at the Inns of Court, for none of which we care a rush...."

Thomas: "My father indeed threatens to bind me to the plough tail, if I will not be a scholar; But... I'll ramble to the East or West-Indies first."

Thomas reads a mock Sonnet on the Country Life

"Unhappy's th' Pesant whom malicious fate,
Hath damn'd unto this Rustick state,
Emplung'd in anxious Care;
Whose heart's still rackt with jealousies and fears....
He dares not trust Gods providence on th' Seas,
Where ships as sheep seem, men as fleas...
He never covets more....
He dreads to touch a sword, or fire a gun,
Th' sight of a Soldier makes him run,
And for the publick Good;
Though squeez'd or rackt with Taxes unto th' Death,
By King or Rebels; So he breathe
Free, he'll ne're venture's bloud....
This is th' unhappy Man whose fortunes lie
Subject t'all th' frowns of Destiny,
A fool to th' Court and City...."

Sir Jeofry: "Idle and vain! only the froth of Wit....
That neither th' Camp, or Court, or City can
Yield any species of a true content
Parallel to this Rural state...."

Ralph, eldest son to Sir Jeofry in hunting habit: "My head is so muddy at the last night's club, that I have not yet recovered my right senses; if the fresh air will not help me, I must turn in, and take a small nap at the next town.... These old gentlemen forget the frolics of their own youth, and think that we at 20 years must be as reserved as themselves at 60 years....

"He hath something to brag on that can boast of a clap [i.e., venereal disease], or the Covent Garden gout; that is one of the best evidences, that we have seen London, and learnt the fashions...."

Richard: "Fare him well!... The sense of his indiscretion makes me the better contented with my own fortune; perhaps if I had been the eldest son, nature would have allowed me as little wit as he now hath.... Young brothers oft make the best gentlemen."

9.15 *Joseph Addison on the Royal Exchange (May 19, 1711)*[50]

There is no place in the town which I so much love to frequent as the Royal Exchange. It gives me a secret satisfaction, and in some measure gratifies my

[50] *The Spectator*, ed. D. F. Bond (Oxford, 1965), 1: 292–6; compared with Wilson, *Norton Book of London*, 262–4.

vanity, as I am an Englishman, to see so rich an assembly of countrymen and foreigners consulting together upon the private business of mankind, and making this metropolis a kind of *emporium* for the whole earth. I must confess I look upon high-change [time of greatest activity at the Exchange] to be a great council, in which all considerable nations have their representatives. Factors in the trading world are what ambassadors are in the politic world; they negotiate affairs, conclude treaties, and maintain a good correspondence between those wealthy societies of men that are divided from one another by seas and oceans, or live on the different extremities of a continent. I have often been pleased to hear disputes adjusted between an inhabitant of Japan and an alderman of London; or to see a subject of the Great Mogul entering into a league with one of the Czar of Muscovy. I am infinitely delighted in mixing with these several ministers of commerce, as they are distinguished by their different walks and different languages. Sometimes I am jostled among a body of Armenians; sometimes I am lost in a crowd of Jews; and sometimes make one in a group of Dutchmen....

If we consider our own country in its natural prospect, without any of the benefits and advantages of commerce, what a barren, uncomfortable spot of earth falls to our share! Natural historians tell us, that no fruit grows originally among us, besides hips and haws, acorns and pig-nuts, with other delicacies of the like nature....Nor has traffic more enriched our vegetable world, than it has improved the whole face of nature among us. Our ships are laden with the harvest of every climate. Our tables are stored with spices, and oils, and wines. Our rooms are filled with pyramids of China, and adorned with the workmanship of Japan. Our morning's draught [drink] comes to us from the remotest corners of the earth. We repair our bodies by the drugs of America, and repose ourselves under Indian canopies. My friend, Sir Andrew, calls the vineyards of France our gardens; the spice-islands our hot-beds; the Persians our silk-weavers, and the Chinese our potters. Nature, indeed, furnishes us with the bare necessaries of life, but traffic gives us a great variety of what is useful, and at the same time supplies us with every thing that is convenient and ornamental. Nor is it the least part of this our happiness, that whilst we enjoy the remotest products of the north and south, we are free from those extremities of weather which give them birth; that our eyes are refreshed with the green fields of Britain, at the same time that our palates are feasted with fruits that rise between the tropics.

For these reasons there are not more useful members in a commonwealth than merchants. They knit mankind together in a mutual intercourse of good offices, distribute the gifts of nature, find work for the poor, add wealth to the rich, and magnificence to the great. Our English merchant converts the tin of his own country into gold, and exchanges its wool for rubies. The Mahometans are clothed in our British manufacture, and the inhabitants of the frozen zone warmed with the fleeces of our sheep....

Trade, without enlarging the British territories, has given us a kind of additional empire. It has multiplied the number of the rich, made our landed estates infinitely more valuable than they were formerly, and added to them an accession of other estates as valuable as the lands themselves.

9.16   Richard Steele's "Discourse upon Wenches" (January 4, 1712)[51]

No vice or wickedness, which people fall into from indulgence to desires which are natural to all, ought to place them below the compassion of the virtuous part of the world; which indeed often makes me a little apt to suspect the sincerity of their virtue, who are too warmly provoked at other people's personal sins. The unlawful commerce of the sexes is of all other the hardest to avoid; and yet there is no one which you shall hear the rigider part of womankind speak of with so little mercy....

The other evening, passing along near Covent Garden, I was jogged on the elbow as I turned into the Piazza, on the right hand coming out of James Street, by a slim young girl of about seventeen, who with a pert air asked me if I was for a pint of wine. I do not know but I should have indulged my curiosity in having some chat with her, but that I am informed the man of the Bumper [Tavern] knows me; and it would have made a story for him not very agreeable to some part of my writings, though I have in others so frequently said that I am wholly unconcerned in any scene I am in, but merely as a spectator. This impediment being in my way, we stood under one of the arches by twilight; and there I could observe as exact features as I had ever seen, the most agreeable shape, the finest neck and bosom, in a word the whole person of a woman exquisitely beautiful. She affected to allure me with a forced wantonness in her look and air, but I saw it checked with hunger and cold; her eyes were wan and eager, her dress thin and tawdry, her mien genteel and childish. This strange figure gave me much anguish of heart, and to avoid being seen with her I went away, but could not forbear giving her a crown [5s.]. The poor thing sighed, curtsied, and with a blessing expressed with the utmost vehemence, turned from me. This creature is what they call "newly come upon the town," but who, I suppose, falling into cruel hands, was left in the first month from her dishonor and exposed to pass through the hands and discipline of one of those hags of hell whom we call bawds....

It must not be thought a digression from my intended speculation to talk of bawds in a discourse upon wenches, for a woman of the town is not thoroughly and properly such without having gone through the education of one of these houses.

9.17   Sir William Petty, "That the Power and Wealth of England Hath Increased this Last Forty Years" (1690)[52]

It is not much to be doubted but that the territories under the king's dominion have increased: forasmuch as New England, Virginia, Barbados, and Jamaica, Tangier, and Bombay, have, since that time, been either added to his majesty's

---

[51] *The Spectator*, ed. G. A. Aitken (1898), 4: 73–4, 76; compared with Allen, *Moving Pageant*, 31.

[52] Petty, *Political Arithmetick* (1691), 16–18; compared with G. A. Aitken, ed., *An English Garner: Later Stuart Tracts* (New York, [1903]), 56–7.

territories, or improved from a desert condition, to abound with people, buildings, shipping, and the production of many useful commodities. And as for the land of England, Scotland, and Ireland, as it is not less in quantity than it was forty years since [ago], so it is manifest that, by reason of the draining of the fens, watering of dry grounds, improving of forests and commons, making of heathy and barren grounds to bear sainfoin and clover grass, [a]meliorating and multiplying several sorts of fruits and garden-stuff, making some rivers navigable, etc.; I say, it is manifest that the land in its present condition is able to bear more provisions and commodities than it was forty years ago.

Secondly, although the people of England, Scotland, and Ireland, which have extraordinarily perished by the plague and sword, within these last forty years, do amount to about 300,000 above what [would] have died in the ordinary way: yet the ordinary increase by generation of 10,000,000 which doubles in 200 years, as hath been shown by the observators upon the bills of mortality, may, in forty years, which is a fifth part of the same time, have increased one-fifth part of the whole number, or 2,000,000. Where note by the way, that the accession of Negroes to the American plantations, being all men of great labor and little expense, is not inconsiderable. Besides, it is hoped that New England (where few or no women are barren, and most have many children; and where people live long and healthfully) hath produced an increase of as many people as were destroyed in the late tumults in Ireland.

9.18 *John Locke*, A Letter Concerning Toleration (1685, pub. 1689)[53]

I esteem that toleration to be the chief characteristic mark of the true Church....If the Gospel and the apostles may be credited, no man can be a Christian without charity, and without that faith which works, not by force, but by love. Now, I appeal to the consciences of those that persecute, torment, destroy, and kill other men upon pretense of religion, whether they do it out of friendship and kindness towards them or no? And I shall then indeed, and not until then, believe they do so, when I shall see those fiery zealots correcting, in the same manner, their friends and familiar acquaintance for the manifest sins they commit against the precepts of the Gospel....

I esteem it above all things necessary to distinguish exactly the business of civil government from that of religion, and to settle the just bounds that lie between the one and the other. If this be not done, there can be no end put to the controversies that will be always arising between those that have, or at least pretend to have, on the one side, a concernment for the interest of men's souls, and, on the other side, a care of the commonwealth.

The commonwealth seems to me to be a society of men constituted only for the procuring, preserving, and advancing of their own civil interests.

[53] Locke, *A Letter Concerning Toleration*, in *The Works of John Locke*, 6: 5–6, 9–11; compared with M. L. Kekewich, ed., *Princes and Peoples: France and the British Isles, 1620–1714* (Manchester, 1994), 97–9.

Civil interests I call life, liberty, health, and indolency [freedom from pain] of body; and the possession of outward things, such as money, lands, houses, furniture, and the like.

It is the duty of the civil magistrate, by the impartial execution of equal laws, to secure unto all the people in general, and to every one of his subjects in particular, the just possession of these things belonging to this life. . . .

Now that the whole jurisdiction of the magistrate reaches only to these civil concernments, and that all civil power, right, and dominion, is bounded and confined to the only care of promoting these things; and that it neither can nor ought in any manner to be extended to the salvation of souls, these following considerations seem unto me abundantly to demonstrate.

First. Because the care of souls is not committed to the civil magistrate, any more than to other men. It is not committed unto him, I say, by God; because it appears not that God has ever given any such authority to one man over another, as to compel any one to his religion. Nor can any such power be vested in the magistrate by the consent of the people, because no man can so far abandon the care of his own salvation as blindly to leave to the choice of any other, whether prince or subject, to prescribe to him what faith or worship he shall embrace. For no man can, if he would, conform his faith to the dictates of another. All the life and power of true religion consist in the inward and full persuasion of the mind; and faith is not faith without believing. . . .

In the second place. The care of souls cannot belong to the civil magistrate, because his power consists only in outward force; but true and saving religion consists in the inward persuasion of the mind, without which nothing can be acceptable to God. And such is the nature of the understanding, that it cannot be compelled to the belief of anything by outward force.

Bibliography, including Online Documents

In the "Historiography" section to each chapter we list relevant secondary works, focusing on articles and shorter works, as we have indicated in the Preface. For additional works by historians, we recommend consulting *Historical Abstracts* online and the *Royal Historical Society Bibliography: The History of Britain, Ireland, and the British Overseas* (printed annually; on CD-ROM, 1998; and online, <http://www.rhs.ac.uk/bibl/>). Robert Bucholz and Newton Key, *Early Modern England, 1485–1714: A Narrative History* (Oxford: Blackwell, 2004) includes a bibliography organized by categories.

The notes for each chapter list accessible source collections as well as more obscure sources, and, as we have often included a recent collection along with the original source citation with which it was compared, we highly recommend consulting those collections for additional sources. Rather than repeating the notes here, we list some of the major document and text sources available online (check <http://www.blackwellpublishing.com/earlymodernengland/>, for a selection of additional documents and discussion related to this book):

The American Colonist's Library, <http://personal.pitnet.net/primarysources/#16>. Includes "Fifteenth- and Sixteenth-Century Sources Profoundly Impacting the History of America" and "Seventeenth-Century Sources Relating to American History," most of which are English in origin.

The Diary of John Evelyn, <http://www.astext.com/history/ed_main.html>. Full text with search engine. Site includes *The Correspondence of Samuel Pepys and John Evelyn*; *Tyrannus Or, the Mode* (1661); and *Fumifugium: Or the Inconveniencie of the Aer and Smoak of London Dissipated* (1661).

Early English Books Online, <http://wwwlib.umi.com/eebo>. Massive collection that aims to make all sources in English printed before 1700 available. Available to universities and libraries by subscription.

Early Modern Literary Studies: Electronic Texts, <http://www.shu.ac.uk/emls/emlsetxt.html>. Linking to mainly literary texts (but including works by Elizabeth, Henry VIII, etc.) online.

Fire and Ice: Puritan and Reformed Writings, <http://www.puritansermons.com/toc.htm>. Sermons by Richard Baxter and many others.

Gardiner, S. R., ed., *The Constitutional Documents of the Puritan Revolution. 1625–1660*, 3rd ed. (Oxford, 1906), <http://www.constitution.org/eng/conpur.htm>.

Internet Modern History Sourcebook, Reformation Europe, <http://www.fordham.edu/halsall/mod/modsbook02.html>. Includes numerous documents relating to the English Reformation.

The Jacobite Heritage: Documents Illustrating Jacobite History, <http://members.rogers.com/jacobites/documents/index.htm>. Impressive collection of materials, 1680–1715, and beyond.

James VI and I, *Dæmonologie* (1597) and *Newes from Scotland* (1591), <http://www.sacred-texts.com/pag/kjd/>.

Luminarium, <http://www.luminarium.org/lumina.htm>. Includes sections on Renaissance and seventeenth century. Mainly literary, but includes works of monarchs, John Foxe, etc.

Montpellier Early Modern English Documents. <http://alor.univ-montp3.fr/MEMED/>. Collection of electronic texts prepared by the Centre d'Études et de Recherches sur la Renaissance Anglaise in Montpellier.

Renascence Editions, <http://darkwing.uoregon.edu/rbear/ren.htm>. An online repository of works printed in English between the years 1477 and 1799 (largely literary, includes T. Hobbes, *Leviathan*).

Richard III Society Online Library, <http://www.r3.org/bookcase/index.html>. Numerous chronicles and documents relating to late fifteenth-century England.

Seventeenth-Century Resources, <http://www.swan.ac.uk/history/teaching/teaching resources/Revolutionary England/resources.htm>. Includes Declaration of Breda, Declaration of Indulgence, etc.

Stephenson, C. and Marcham, F. G., *Sources of English Constitutional History: A Selection of Documents from A.D. 600 to the Present* (New York, 1937), <http://www.constitution.org/sech/sech_.htm>.

Index

Note: Peers are listed under the title by which they are most frequently identified in the text. Where other titles are referred to in the text, a cross-reference is provided. Page references in *italic* are to illustrations.

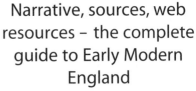